1986

Israel and
the Soviet Union

Westview Special Studies

The concept of Westview Special Studies is a response to the continuing crisis in academic and informational publishing. Library budgets for books have been severely curtailed. Ever larger portions of general library budgets are being diverted from the purchase of books and used for data banks, computers, micromedia, and other methods of information retrieval. Interlibrary loan structures further reduce the edition sizes required to satisfy the needs of the scholarly community. Economic pressures on the university presses and the few private scholarly publishing companies have severely limited the capacity of the industry to properly serve the academic and research communities. As a result, many manuscripts dealing with important subjects, often representing the highest level of scholarship, are no longer economically viable publishing projects--or, if accepted for publication, are typically subject to lead times ranging from one to three years.

Westview Special Studies are our practical solution to the problem. We accept a manuscript in camera-ready form, typed according to our specifications, and move it immediately into the production process. As always, the selection criteria include the importance of the subject, the work's contribution to scholarship, and its insight, originality of thought, and excellence of exposition. The responsibility for editing and proofreading lies with the author or sponsoring institution. We prepare chapter headings and display pages, file for copyright, and obtain Library of Congress Cataloging in Publication Data. A detailed manual contains simple instructions for preparing the final typescript, and our editorial staff is always available to answer questions.

The result is a book printed on acid-free paper and bound in sturdy library-quality soft covers. We manufacture these books ourselves using equipment that does not require a lengthy make-ready process and that allows us to publish first editions of 300 to 1000 copies and to reprint even smaller quantities as needed. Thus, we can produce Special Studies quickly and can keep even very specialized books in print as long as there is a demand for them.

About the Book and Authors

In June 1967, the Soviet Union severed official diplomatic relations with Israel to protest Israel's actions during the Six-Day War. Extensive Soviet-Israeli contacts continue despite strong Soviet support for the PLO and radical Arab states, Israel's close ties to the United States, and controversy over the issue of Soviet Jewry. This study is the first to reveal the intricacies of Soviet-Israeli secret diplomacy since 1967, with reference to a wealth of documentary material gathered from Israeli archives and insights gained in interviews with Israeli officials, journalists, and academicians.

Professor Klinghoffer explains why the Soviet Union opposes Arab destruction of Israel, why Israel has worked against Soviet-U.S. détente, why the United States did not favor an Arab-Israeli peace settlement during the early seventies, and why Soviet officials who are the most moderate toward Israel are also the strongest supporters of the PLO. In addition to providing a detailed examination of the interaction between Moscow and Jerusalem, this book thoroughly explores the issue of Soviet Jewry, the activities of the Israeli communists, the Soviet role in Middle East peace negotiations, and the question of whether Soviet-Israeli diplomatic relations can possibly be restored.

Arthur Jay Klinghoffer is a professor of political science and chairman of the department at Rutgers University, Camden, New Jersey. His publications include Soviet Perspectives on African Socialism, The Soviet Union and International Oil Politics, and The Angolan War: A Study in Soviet Policy in the Third World (Westview, 1980), and he coauthored The Global Politics of Gold. Judith Apter did graduate work in history at Hebrew University in Jerusalem and has spent more than twenty years in Israel. Fluent in Hebrew, she gathered and translated the Hebrew materials used in the research for this book and contributed significantly to the outlining of the chapters and the interpretive development of this study.

Israel and
the Soviet Union

Alienation or Reconciliation?

Arthur Jay Klinghoffer,
with Judith Apter

Westview Press / Boulder and London

To Joella,

who patiently endured

the preoccupation of her parents

Westview Special Studies on the Middle East

Copyright © 1985 by Westview Press, Inc.

Published in 1985 in the United States of America by Westview Press, Inc., 5500 Central Avenue, Boulder, Colorado 80301; Frederick A. Praeger, Publisher

Library of Congress Catalog Card Number: 85-50335
ISBN: 0-8133-7029-9

Printed and bound in the United States of America

10 9 8 7 6 5 4 3 2 1

Contents

Acknowledgments ix

1 THROUGH THE LOOKING GLASS 1

2 THE LOOSE KNOT 11

3 ALIENATION OF AFFECTIONS 27

4 OUT IN THE COLD 59

5 COMING TO BLOWS 77

6 UNREWARDED FLIRTATIONS 95

7 THE BREAKING POINT 117

8 SHUNTED ASIDE 133

9 SOME STEPS TOWARD RECONCILIATION 153

10 SEPARATE PATHS 173

11 COOL EMBRACE 185

12 DISTANT PARTNERS 209

13 ALIENATION OR RECONCILIATION? 233

Notes 247

Index 291

Acknowledgments

Research for this book was conducted in the Philadelphia area and in Israel. The Fulbright Program deserves special thanks for enabling me to spend a year at Hebrew University in Jerusalem, where I was able to delve into primary sources and interact with Israeli scholars. Dan Krauskopf, who administered the Fulbright Program in Israel through the United States-Israel Educational Foundation, was extremely helpful in arranging the details for a pleasant year in Jerusalem and he contributed greatly to an environment conducive to scholarly endeavor. In addition, the Rutgers Research Council provided significant funding to cover typing, duplicating, telephone and other expenses.

Many Israeli academics and diplomats made substantial contributions, including Simcha Dinitz, Mordechai Gazit, Yosef Govrin, Aryeh Yodfat, Galia Golan, Yaacov Ro'i, Israel Meh Ameeh, Shlomo Avineri, Pinhas Eliav, Eli Avrahami, Mikhail Agursky, Edith Frankel and Jonathan Frankel. Ron Finkel provided valuable information on Israeli tourism arrangements with East European states and graduate assistant Zach Levey was most adept at ferreting out obscure sources and in combing the minutes of Knesset sessions. In the United States, I have benefited from the sage comments of Robert Freedman and I am particularly grateful to former president Jimmy Carter for providing the time to discuss Middle East diplomacy during the period when he was in office.

Judith Apter must be congratulated for her diligence in researching Hebrew sources and for her extensive contributions to the analysis presented in this volume. Rosemarie Kenerley is responsible for the expert typing of the original manuscript and the final grid sheets. Please note that the sources used during my research used many different systems of transliterating Soviet, Israeli and Arab names. In the text, I used a consistent system of transliteration except in the rare instances when some other form has become the standard. In the notes, names are usually spelled as they appear in the sources cited.

The views expressed in this study are those of Judith Apter and myself and we bear the ultimate responsibility for any inaccuracies or omissions.

Arthur Jay Klinghoffer
Rutgers University

1
Through the Looking Glass

It was a sunny May day in 1979. Three military
officers stepped forward and were awarded ribbons for
meritorious service. An Israeli army representative
joined in the ceremony. Who was being honored and where
was this event taking place? Amazingly, the recipients
were Soviet United Nations' observers who served in
Syria! The location was Tiberias, Israel, on the shores
of the Sea of Galilee. It would seem to be a rather
unlikely scenario but, in fact, it was repeated in
October 1983.

As one delves into the Soviet-Israeli relationship,
things certainly do get curiouser and curiouser. In
June 1971, a Soviet journalist and political courier
paid a visit to the Western Wall. It is in contested
East Jerusalem and is the most sacred Jewish site. In
March 1978, there was a demonstration in Moscow against
the Palestinians who carried out an attack along
Israel's coastal highway! How about the incongruous
effort in July 1970 by the mayor of Netanya, Israel. He
tried to offer a blessing for Defense Minister Moshe
Dayan in a Leningrad synagogue! In September 1976, the
body of a Jewish Soviet colonel who died in Minsk a year
earlier was sent to Israel for burial on the Mount of
Olives. Also unusual is the fact that in 1978, an
Israeli kibbutz built a textile plant that uses Soviet
equipment. Or ponder the strange case of Igor Beliaev,
a commentator on Middle Eastern affairs for Soviet
newspapers. In April 1983, he was appointed Deputy
Chairman of the Anti-Zionist Committee; in May, he was
in Israel to celebrate the anniversary of the defeat of
Nazi Germany.

How can we explain this apparently anomalous
behavior? Aren't the Soviet Union and Israel sworn
enemies who severed diplomatic relations in 1967? Isn't
the Soviet Union a patron of the Palestine Liberation
Organization (PLO) and arms merchant to the Arabs in
their wars against Israel? Only qualified yesses to
these questions will suffice, as a simplistic approach

to the issues will be of limited analytical value.
Few remember that the Soviet Union voted at the United
Nations in favor of the partition of Palestine, and
was the first state to extend de jure recognition to
Israel. The Soviets assisted Israel in its war of
independence in 1948 by encouraging arrangements for
the transport of arms from Czechoslovakia and oil from
Rumania. Diplomatic relations were surely broken in
1967, as they had been once previously in 1953, but
extensive contacts have been maintained and active
secret diplomacy has been conducted. In fact, Soviet
emissaries were even received by Prime Minister Yitzhak
Rabin during their covert April 1975 mission.

Soviet-Israeli contacts range from high level
diplomacy to mere curiosity items. For example,
Israeli beekeepers visited the Soviet Union in August
1971, and an Israeli delegation attended a Moscow
conference early in 1983 on interference by birds with
air traffic. In order to understand the foundations
of this rather odd relationship, we must provide
explanations for some striking paradoxes: The Soviet
Union, despite its opposition to Zionism, supported
the creation of a Jewish state in Palestine. Once
relations with Israel soured, the Soviets continued to
insist on Israel's right to exist. A Soviet diplomat
said to Nahum Goldmann, former president of the World
Zionist Organization, that if Israel didn't exist, the
Soviet Union would have had to create her.[1] While rejecting Zionism, the Soviets insist that all Jewish
emigrants get visas for Israel, and many non-Jews also
leave the Soviet Union in the same manner. Foreign
Minister Andrei Gromyko expressed anger that Soviet
Jews were often going to the United States rather than
Israel; in October 1981, the chief rabbi of Moscow
phoned the chief Ashkenazi rabbi of Israel to say that
emigration would be stopped if too many Soviet Jews
went to countries other than Israel.[2]

Why are those Soviets who are most supportive of
a political solution to the Arab-Israeli conflict also
the strongest proponents of the PLO? How can the provision of advanced weaponry to Arab states act as a
military constraint on their behavior? Why does Israel
benefit from Soviet influence in the Middle East? Why
do the most extreme rightist elements in the Israeli
government favor an improvement of relations with the
Soviet Union? Why does the rate of Soviet Jewish
emigration tend to have virtually no correlation with
the state of Soviet-Israeli ties? To begin to unravel
these enigmas, we must first deal with the issue of
mutual perceptions.

Perceptions

The late King Feisal of Saudi Arabia, an opponent

of both communism and Zionism, had a conspiratorial
view of history which linked these two ideologies. He
correctly pointed out that the Bolshevik movement in
Russia included many Jews, some of whom became
prominent in the Soviet government. Similarly, the
Marxist foundations of nineteenth century Zionism were
noted and the Soviet Union indeed supported the establishment of the state of Israel. Weren't there
kibbutzim in Israel which were applying Marxist col-
lectivist principles? Feisal argued that Jews established the Soviet Union and then Israel, and he even
viewed the emigration of Soviet Jews to Israel as part
of a plot to create a communist base in the Middle
East.[3] Feisal's interpretation evolved into the
fantasy that the Soviet Union and Israel were engaged
in a joint endeavor to undermine the Islamic Arab
world. This belief is surely delusional but it has
been derived from the valid principle that communism
and Zionism have for long shared a symbiotic relationship.

Both ideologies explosively emerged from East-
Central Europe in the late nineteenth century. They
were conditioned by the same social circumstances, and
they were revolutionary in their approach to change.
The major distinction was that the communists emphasized class identity, whereas the Zionists favored national identity. They struggled for the soul of European
Jewry, both movements succeeding. The Soviet Union and
Israel emerged as their creations but their conflict
goes on, centered on the loyalty of Soviet Jewry. Prior
to 1948, the Soviets believed that the battle was
already over, but they were then amazed at the emotional response of their Jews to the creation of a Jewish
state. The upsurge of Jewish nationalism, long latent,
revealed significant fissures in the entire edifice of
Soviet nationality policies and the Soviet system is
now beset with problems on many ethnic fronts. Furthermore, the emigration of Soviet Jews has cut an ideological swath through communist doctrine as many Jews have
opted for a Jewish state rather than a workers' state.
On the other hand, Zionism itself has been threatened
as a majority of the emigrants now choose the United
States over the Jewish homeland.

Communism and Zionism wage a particularly fierce
struggle because they are estranged relatives reared
with similar traditions. Familiarity indeed breeds
contempt and this is more easily understandable if we
look at the backgrounds of the Israeli political elite.
Every Israeli prime minister but one was born in what
is now the Soviet Union or Poland. The exception was
Yitzhak Rabin, a native Sabra, but his parents both
came from Russia. The leading Israeli political
personality who never became prime minister, Moshe
Dayan, also had two Russian-born parents. The four

most prominent Jews in the Israeli communist movement
were all born in the Soviet Union or Poland, namely
Meir Wilner, Moshe Sneh, Shmuel Mikunis and Esther
Wilenska. Israelis feel that they know the Soviet
Union, and this raises their adrenalin when it is being
discussed. Some Israeli prime ministers are strongly
conditioned by negative memories. Menachem Begin
will surely not forget his September 1940 arrest by
the Soviet secret police in Lithuania and his subsequent terms in prison and Siberian labor camps. He
stayed incarcerated only until the following summer,
but such an experience must have been psychologically
searing. Golda Meir left as a child, but with bitter
recollections. She writes about her paternal grandfather, who was drafted into the Russian army when he
was twelve and not permitted to follow his religious
rituals. After completing his service, he slept on a
wooden bench with a stone for a pillow. This was his
method of atoning for infidelities of piety.[4] Levi
Eshkol had a more positive image of his childhood, and
this seemed to be reflected in his political attitudes
while prime minister.

Israelis are extremely sensitive to the Soviet
Union, as is reflected in a public opinion poll of 1200
respondents in late 1981. When asked which threat to
Israel was greater, the Arab or Soviet, 42.5% said the
Arab, 25.9% the Soviet, 25.5% said they were equal, and
6% had no opinion.[5] The fact that more than half the
respondents believed the Soviet threat to be greater or
equal is rather illuminating as Israel had repeatedly
confronted the Arabs in war but had never faced the
Soviet Union. Also interesting was the Israeli reaction to a Soviet peace plan proposed in December 1968.
It was rejected in January, with Foreign Minister Abba
Eban commenting that "Israel regards and will regard
with severe suspicion any Soviet plan, by virtue of it
being Soviet."[6] Rather interesting from the man who
three years earlier had sought Soviet participation in
the Middle East peace process.

The Soviet attitude toward Israel is no less
charged. The Soviet media constantly revile Zionism
and prominent Soviet Jews are often included in
orchestrated campaigns against an ideology deemed
perfidious. Zionism is equated with racism and fascism,
and Israel was alleged to have been involved in a plot
in 1952-53 to kill Soviet officials through improper
medical care. Cyrus Sulzberger has summarized the views
expressed to him by Henry Kissinger as follows: "The
Russians, however, are not entirely rational on Israel.
There is a hysterical edge. They are basically anti-
Semitic and hate being licked by Jews. When Kissinger
was in Moscow in 1968 he found he could talk to the
Russians rationally on all subjects, even including
Vietnam--except for Israel."[7]

A Roaring Mouse?

For the Soviets, Israel's importance greatly transcends its size and influence. It receives media attention far exceeding its newsworthiness and has been the target of a break in diplomatic relations on two occasions, 1953 and 1967. No other country has come close in arousing Soviet passions, as the only other Soviet severance of relations was with Chile in 1973 after the military overthrew Salvador Allende. Why is Israel accorded this special attention? Why are Soviet-Israeli relations much more crucial and explosive than those between the Soviet Union and other small states of similar power? As the first step in arriving at an adequate response, one must turn again to the issue of anti-Semitism.

Russian anti-Semitism predates the 1917 revolution but was developed into an art by Stalin as he struggled against Leon Trotskii, a Jew. Gradually, almost all Jews were removed from positions of authority but they remained useful scapegoats for systemic inadequacies or examples of alien influence attempting to undermine the Russian culture. Jews were accused of "cosmopolitanism" during the late forties, were implicated in a "doctors' plot" against Kremlin leaders in 1952-53, and represented the majority of those executed for "economic crimes" during the early sixties. Jews have been portrayed as dissidents and anti-government activists in both the Soviet Union and East European states. In the latter, Jews were prominent among the defendants in show trials during the early fifties, and an alleged Zionist conspiracy was a common prosecutorial theme.

It is not considered appropriate for Marxists to denounce Jews, so the Soviets attack Judaism and Zionism. In the twenties and thirties, Jews were tarnished with the brush of Trotskyism. By the late forties, Zionism had become the main epithet, a catchword for disloyalty and subversive influence. Israel, in a symbolic sense, became an integral component of Soviet domestic politics and this inevitably was translated into foreign policy realities. In a way, the Soviet Jewish factor led to a negative approach toward Israel; in the United States, the impact of the Jewish factor turned out exactly the opposite.[8]

Many Soviet political analysts view Israel as part of an international Jewish conspiracy linked to imperialism, banking interests and high finance. Jews are depicted as capitalist businessmen bent on world domination, an amazing reversal of the equally posterous Feisal theory. Allegations about Jews and Israel serve some vital functional needs of the Soviet system, and are not proffered as idle diatribes. The need for a scapegoat and the allegorization of internal power struggles thus coalesce around the Jew and Zionism.

Such a process has been particularly evident in Poland and Czechoslovakia, but it still exists in the Soviet Union despite the almost total absence of Jews from high political positions.[9] Of course, Israel is not the real issue but competing factions use Zionism as a code word which helps classify one's political affiliation and identify which groups may include Jews. John Armstrong, a political scientist specializing in Soviet affairs, has astutely observed: "If the USSR and its satellites did not have large Jewish minorities, the prospect of their adopting a more flexible policy toward Israel would be brighter. If, on the other hand, Israel did not exist it is possible that some of the anti-Semitic tendencies within the Soviet block would be moderated."[10]

The Soviets attach importance to Israel as they see it as a lodestone attracting the sympathies of the world's Jews. Soviet backing of Israel in the late forties was aimed, in part, at securing greater support for the Soviet Union from Western Jews, particularly left-leaning intellectuals and socialists. Later, the Soviet Union made periodic overtures to Israel in order to influence Jewish opinion in the United States. The intent was to secure support for detente, and American extension of economic benefits to the Soviet Union, from Jewish public figures and pro-Israeli members of Congress. The Soviet Union has even moderated its position toward Israel to silence the protests of Jewish communists, particularly those in West European parties.

Soviet permission for Jews to emigrate during the seventies was based on recognition of its impact on world Jewish opinion, but internal suppression of Zionist tendencies produced a countervailing effect. Harsh treatment of those who applied to emigrate, the sad cases of refuseniks who were denied the right to leave, and the arrest for treason of Jewish activist Anatolii Shcharanskii all blackened the Soviet image and served only to raise the level of condemnation. Somewhat illogically, the Soviets were giving with one hand but taking back with the other.

From the Israeli perspective, Israel is seen as the homeland of world Jewry, the bastion of Zionist ideology, and the crucible for preserving the Jewish culture and religion from assimilationist tendencies. The fate of the Jewish people is a major foreign policy concern and Michael Brecher, a prominent analyst of Israeli foreign affairs, has described "a special link" between Israel and Jews in the Diaspora. He averred: "It may indeed be argued that world Jewry is the most important component of the global system for Israel."[11] Israel's first foreign minister, Moshe Sharett, even stipulated in June 1949 that states desiring good relations with the Jewish state must support Zionism.

He was alluding to the Soviet Union and had Jewish
emigration in mind.[12] Prime Minister David Ben Gurion
declared: "In our policy towards Russia the position
of Russian Jews is the main concern." He believed that
one-third of them desired to move to Israel.[13]

Israel strives to protect Jews in states like Iran,
Ethiopia, South Africa and Argentina so the welfare of
world Jewry acts as a constraint on its foreign policy.
This is true to a limited degree in regard to
Jerusalem's relations with Moscow, but the main concern
there is the right of emigration for the second largest
overseas Jewish community. On May 17, 1971, the Knesset
went so far as to pass a bill extending Israeli citizenship to Soviet Jews who had been denied the right to
emigrate. On July 10, 1978, Yigal Allon reacted to
Shcharanskii's treason trial by declaring in the
Knesset that Shcharanskii was not disloyal to his
homeland, Israel. Israeli relations with the Soviet
Union as a superpower are inextricably entwined with
the issue of Soviet Jewry, just as relations with the
United States are also related to the fact that more
Jews live there than anywhere else, including Israel.

Israel is a major religious center, with
Jerusalem sacred to Christians, Moslems and Jews. Its
strong spiritual appeal runs counter to the Marxist
emphasis on materialism and atheism, and presents other
problems for the Soviets as well. The Russian Orthodox
Church maintains properties in Israel and continues to
sponsor pilgrimages of church officials to Jerusalem.
Such activities are carried out with the approval of
the Soviet government, but they surely indicate some
inherent doctrinal inconsistencies. The Soviets are
also confronted with the fact that strong American
support for Israel derives in part from the Christian
image of Israel as the Holy Land. In recent years,
fundamentalist Protestant denominations have been
especially energetic in backing the Jewish state. On
the other side of the ledger, the Soviet Union benefits
from Islamic hostility to a state which has incorporated East Jerusalem and its holy sites (although permitting Moslem and Christian administration of their
respective properties).

Patterns and Peculiarities

As we examine Soviet-Israeli relations, it becomes
apparent that a methodology emphasizing bilateral
interaction is insufficient. For example, Soviet
gestures toward Israel are often made to send signals
to the United States or Arab countries; no intent to
improve ties to Israel is even contemplated. Consequently, Israel feels itself used by the Soviets and it
registers an apparent rebuff to Soviet overtures. This
scenario was acted out in 1975 when Israeli Ambassador

to the United States Simcha Dinitz broke off talks with
his Soviet counterpart Anatolii Dobrynin. The Soviets
also try to use contacts with Israel to try to learn as
much as possible about developments in the Arab world.
In this manner, they seek clues about anticipated Arab
policies toward the Soviet Union.

Policy fluctuations in the Soviet-Israeli relationship are often related as much to personalities as to
the course of international diplomacy. The Soviet
attitude toward Israel moderated when Georgii Malenkov
succeeded the deceased Stalin in 1953, and a similar
trend was evident from the Israeli side when Levi
Eshkol replaced the retired Ben Gurion in 1963. Personality may also have been decisive during the 1982
Lebanon war, when the Soviet Union failed to support
the beleaguered Palestinians and reacted rather mildly to
frequent Israeli shellings of its embassy in Beirut.
Perhaps Soviet inaction was related to its "aged
leadership" in the last months of the Brezhnev regime?[14]
Projecting into the near future, it could be argued
that the Soviet Union may be in a position to alter its
stance toward Israel as Chernenko and his colleagues
may be replaced by younger leaders who are not tied to
current policies. The foreign policy establishment
should also be radically transformed as the youngest of
the top fifteen foreign policy specialists was born in
1918.[15] Changes in the Israeli hierarchy will not have
the same potential for altering policy as there is a
feeling among most Israeli political figures that
Israel can do little to effect a change in Soviet
positions. For them, the first step is up to the
Soviet Union.

The policies of Israel and the Soviet Union are
not monolithic. Israeli cabinets are coalitions of
disparate parties, and communists and Arabs are represented in the legislature. Also, as a result of a
democratic electoral process, governments dominated by
the Labor Alignment and the LIKUD have both held
office. Disagreements within the Soviet system are
not as readily apparent due to rigid censorship and a
one-party political structure, but they exist nevertheless. Institutional differences affected policies
toward the Middle East in the months preceding the 1967
war, and Soviet newspapers do reveal the advocacy of
alternative policies if one applies a trained Kremlin-
ological eye. Dina Spechler and Ilana Dimant-Kass
have carried out comparative studies of the treatment
of Arab-Israeli issues in the Soviet press and have
found considerable policy differentiation. The communist party organ _Pravda_, for example, tends to be
the most moderate in its castigation of Israel, the
firmest advocate of a peaceful solution, and the
strongest supporter of Palestinian Arab rights while
the military paper _Krasnaia Zvezda_ is least favorable

toward a political solution and Palestinian rights and most concerned about Soviet access to strategic facilities and the Suez Canal.[16] In analyzing the nuances of both Israeli and Soviet expressed policy disagreements, one must bear in mind that they are sometimes meant for internal consumption and are indicative of bureaucratic infighting regarding budgets, channels of command, and assignment of responsibilities. When this is the case, they do not affect the actual conduct of foreign policy.

What statements and acts of these two states have official sanction? In a sense, all Soviet media comments have been approved by censors and seem to have the state's imprimatur, but this is misleading as policy differences do emerge. In Israel, censorship is applied only to matters of military security and the secrecy of certain government deliberations. Political commentary is not affected. However, it is often difficult to ascertain an official position due to major differences of opinion within the Cabinet and to the common practice of leaking positions as trial balloons, rather than having a minister express them directly and publicly.

Since there have been no diplomatic relations since June 1967, all contacts between the Soviet Union and Israel are in a sense unofficial. Visits by emissaries are treated as such in regard to protocol. However, there is a definite twilight zone. Foreign ministers of the two states have met on several occasions, but never in the Soviet Union or Israel. Groups traveling to the opposite state frequently receive government briefings before their departure, but remarks of participants are not considered as officially representative of their government's position. When members of the Israeli Knesset are invited to the Soviet Union, it is always done through individual invitations. The Soviets never ask the Knesset to send a delegation, even though individual Knesset members are usually invited to come in groups. Determining who represents a government is a complicated matter. Soviet journalist Victor Louis has visited Israel frequently, and he still writes occasional articles for an Israeli newspaper, but one can never be quite sure if his views and apparent signals are reflective of an official Soviet position.

In order to understand fluctuations in the Soviet-Israeli relationship, it is necessary to look for clues which indicate that some new trend is in the offing. This is especially true when secret diplomacy is under inquiry, but the analyst must try to avoid red herrings when he is actually looking for caviar. Sometimes, an action may appear significant but turn out to be incongruous rather than prognostic. In April 1970, the Soviet press attache in Amman, Jordan called for the overthrow of the Israeli government. Certainly a

radical departure but it was an anomalous declaration
that was immediately repudiated by the Soviet embassy
there.[17] In June 1971, the captain of a Soviet vessel
near the Bab el-Mandeb Strait asked an Israeli freighter to identify itself. This was the first such request
in those waters and it was ignored by the Israeli
crew.[18] Again an isolated act as it was not repeated.
On September 12, 1973, the Soviet Union stopped jamming
Israeli radio broadcasts to its citizens but, nine days
later, the policy was renewed with even stronger interference.[19]

Some Soviet and Israeli actions may be attributable
to good will rather than a warming of the political
environment. In August 1968, a Soviet ship sailing
near Turkey picked up five Israelis whose ship had
capsized. They were taken to Limassol, Cyprus and
received jointly by representatives of both the Soviet
and Israeli embassies.[20] Then in January 1969, a
Soviet ship near Mexico provided medical assistance for
an injured crewman on an Israeli vessel.[21] In June
1971, Israeli Foreign Minister Abba Eban sent condolences upon the deaths of three Soviet cosmonauts and,
in April 1975, a Soviet civilian airliner was driven
off course in a thunderstorm while on its way to Cairo.
It passed over the Israeli-occupied Sinai peninsula,
but was not fired upon. The Israelis probably didn't
know at the time that one of the passengers was the
Soviet ambassador to Egypt, Vladimir Poliakov.[22]

Occasionally, actions appear to be important but
emerge as unnecessary footnotes to history. In June
1968, the chief rabbi of Moscow Yehuda Leib Levin was
permitted to make his first tour to Western states.
While in New York, he had a meeting with Israeli
general Ariel (Arik) Sharon.[23] Nothing of consequence
resulted. In August 1973, a crewman on a Soviet fish-
ing trawler near Japan jumped overboard and was rescued
by the Japanese. He requested political asylum in
Israel and it was granted.[24] No Soviet protest was
heard.

As one begins to examine the complex Soviet-
Israeli relationship, numerous strands of evidence must
be woven together into an harmonious fabric and
numerous hypotheses must be evaluated in regard to
their validity. Is it true that Israel has consistently
worked against Soviet-American detente? Does the
Soviet Union care more about the process of an Arab-
Israeli peace settlement than it does about the actual
terms? Is Israel a military asset for the United
States, but a political liability? Is it a political
asset for the Soviet Union, but a military liability?
In order to arrive at meaningful responses, it is first
necessary to delve into the early period of Soviet-
Israeli kinship, which turned into a honeymoon gone
sour.

2
The Loose Knot

Soviet analysts consistently opposed Zionism as a bourgeois nationalist ideology which was contrary to the interests of the Jewish working class. Stalin, the party specialist on nationality matters, did not believe that Jews constituted a nation, but he eventually extended cynical recognition of Jewish national rights by establishing a homeland in the frigid expanse of Eastern Siberia. No Jews inhabited this remote area, but Stalin created a Jewish autonomous region in Birobidjan in 1928. Very few Jews moved there and Jewish nationalist aspirations continued to pose a problem for the Soviet leadership. The struggle between Zionism and Marxism was not over, and became even more pronounced as Jews in Palestine intensified their struggle to establish their own state. This brought into focus the allegiance of Soviet Jews but, surprisingly, the Soviet Union decided to come to terms with the Zionists and to support the creation of Israel! What prompted this dramatic turnabout? Why did the evolving Soviet-Israeli relationship soon deteriorate? Why were diplomatic relations broken, and later restored, in 1953? To what degree was the course of Soviet-Israeli relations affected by the development of Soviet-Arab relations? These are issues that must be carefully examined in order to understand the forces that produced such stormy interaction by the late sixties.

Laying the Groundwork

After the Soviet Union was invaded by Germany in 1941, it became aligned with the United States and Britain and relied heavily upon them for military and economic assistance. Stalin therefore decided that Soviet Jews could play a useful role in trying to retain this Western support, so he established a Jewish Anti-Fascist Committee in April 1942. Members of the committee tried to rally Western Jews to the Soviet cause, and delegations were sent to the U.S. and

11

Britain in 1943. The committee maintained contact with
the Zionist movement and sent birthday greetings in
December 1944 to Chaim Weizmann, President of the Jewish
Agency for Palestine.[1]

Ivan Maiskii, Vice Commissar for Foreign Affairs
and former Ambassador to Britain, served as a liaison
with Zionists, and he visited Palestine in October 1943
to evaluate the situation. He met with Ben Gurion,
made inquiries about Palestine's capacity to absorb
more Jews, and returned to the Soviet Union with a very
favorable report on the Jewish nationalist movement.
In January 1944, Jewish produce from Palestine was displayed in Moscow and, in November, the journal of the
Jewish Anti-Fascist Committee asserted that "the Jewish
people has a right to political independence in
Palestine." In February 1945, the Soviet representatives at a London trade union conference supported a
resolution that "the Jewish people must be enabled to
continue the rebuilding of Palestine as their National
Home."[2]

Once the war ended, and Western Jewish opinion was
less vital, it was likely that the Soviet Union would
revert to its traditional anti-Zionist position and
oppose the creation of a Jewish state in Palestine. It
was therefore somewhat of a surprise when the Soviets,
at the United Nations in 1947, again expressed sympathy
for Jewish nationalist aspirations. Semyon Tsarapkin,
a member of the Soviet delegation, presaged the Soviet
stance when he held a publicized meeting with the
president of the Zionist Organization of America.[3]
Then Andrei Gromyko dropped the diplomatic bombshell
before the General Assembly on May 14, declaring that
the Soviet Union favored a binational state in
Palestine but would accept a partition into Jewish and
Arab states. On October 13, Tsarapkin indicated Soviet
support for partition, as Jews and Arabs could not work
together to establish a binational state. During this
period, Soviet envoys had frequent contacts with left-
wing Palestinian Zionists, and a delegation of communists and socialists attended celebrations in Moscow
on November 7 marking the thirtieth anniversary of the
Bolshevik revolution.[4] On November 29, the Soviet
Union voted with the General Assembly majority to
partition Palestine.

By voting to establish a Jewish state, the Soviet
Union antagonized the Arabs and placed Arab communists
in a most precarious position. Their allegiance to
Moscow led them to back the Soviet stance, but this
weakened their local standing and produced the ransack-
ing by violent mobs of communist offices in Damascus
and Aleppo, Syria.[5] At midnight on May 14-15, 1948,
Israel became independent and neighboring Arab states
immediately declared war and attacked. The Egyptian
parliament obviously saw a significant connection

between the Soviet Union and Israel as it voted to go
to war "in defense of Arab rights and against Communist
atheism and nihilism."[6] The Soviet Union extended de
jure recognition (the first country to do so) to Israel
on May 18 and, in collaboration with Czechoslovakia and
Rumania, it contributed substantially to Israel's war
effort by providing arms, military training, and fuel.
For its part, Israel appointed its first foreign envoys
to Czechoslovakia and the Soviet Union.

Why did the Soviet Union vote for the partition of
Palestine and come to the aid of the fledgling Jewish
state? The answer seems to lie within the context of
evolving superpower relations in the aftermath of the
Second World War. The Soviet Union emerged from the
war as one of the victorious Allies and as a permanent
member of the United Nations' Security Council. Its
influence was on the upsurge and it was surpassing
Britain and France to become the second strongest world
power, after the United States. In such a situation,
the Soviets hoped to gain the maximum spoils of victory;
this policy was evident in Eastern Europe and the Far
East. In the Mediterranean and Middle East regions, the
Soviets continued to emphasize strategic naval egress
from the Black Sea and the acquisition of warm water
ports but their policy became highly aggressive, leading to territorial claims on Turkey. The main thrust,
however, was directed against the British as the Soviets
hoped to supplant a state whose regional power was in
decline.

During the years 1945-47, the British tried to
buttress their fortunes by organizing and arming a
League of Arab States (Arab League). The Soviets therefore viewed most Arab governments as British puppets
(Britain had indeed established artificial monarchies
ruled by outsiders in both Jordan and Iraq after the
First World War), and they fostered the growth of communist parties to challenge British suzerainty. They
also cultivated Kurdish forces in Iraq, which were
operating against the Hashemite monarchy. Soviet reluctance to withdraw from northern Iran, which was
occupied during the war as an anti-Nazi measure , may
also be seen as a component of the regional rivalry
with Britain. The British had ended their occupation
of southern Iran but still retained close ties to the
Shah and remained dominant in the Iranian oil industry.
In Greece, the Soviets (with their Yugoslav allies)
supported domestic communist efforts to seize power in
a country that had close ties to Britain. In fact, the
Soviet-British "percentage deal" of October 1944 had
given Britain ninety percent of the influence in
Greece. In Libya, the Soviets competed with the British
to secure a trusteeship over the former Italian colony.
Consequently, Soviet support for the Jews of Palestine
was part of a broader anti-British strategy. The Jews

were effectively combating the British, while Arab
nationalism was weak and often subservient to British
interests.
Britain turned the Palestine problem over to the
United Nations, where the Soviet Union was able to play
a significant role in its resolution. Despite growing
Soviet differences with the United States, the two
superpowers eventually agreed on partition and this
collaboration was crucial in establishing Israel. In a
way, the Soviets were using the opportunity to exacerbate British-American tensions over the Palestine issue,
while at the same time catering the good will of Jews,
liberals and Jewish communists in Western states.
Another motivating factor was that several communist-
ruled states in Eastern Europe were enthusiastic about
the creation of a Jewish state as they saw it as a
means of resolving the serious post-war refugee problem
with which they were confronted.[7]
Sympathy for the Jews resulting from the Holocaust
probably had little impact on Soviet policy, nor did
any belief that the establishment of Israel provided a
solution to the Soviet Union's internal Jewish problem.
Suppression of the Jews would have sufficed for Stalin,
and it is clear that no granting of permission to
emigrate to Israel was linked to the Soviet decision on
partition. Did the Soviet Union expect Israel to
develop as a socialist state opposed to Western
interests? Did it believe that the Marxist aspect of
Zionism would become dominant through the efforts of
socialist parties and Israeli communists? Apparently
not, as Soviet leaders had a much firmer grasp on
reality. Nahum Goldmann, a prominent American Zionist,
relates what Soviet diplomats told him prior to the
November 1947 Security Council vote. They anticipated
an Israeli turn toward the West because the large
Jewish communities living there would provide financial
support for the new state.[8] This view paralleled that
later expressed by Iakov Malik in a discussion with
Israeli diplomat Abba Eban. Malik said that the Soviet
Union knew that Israel would be pro-Western but supported its establishment in order to create good will among
Americans for the Soviet Union. He also maintained
that pro-Western Arab governments were expected to look
weak compared to Israel, giving the Soviet Union greater
political entree into the Arab world.[9]
As the Soviet Union warmed toward the Zionist
state, it did not change its negative evaluation of
Zionism. Israel was viewed as the fruition of Jewish
nationalist efforts, but Zionism (especially in regard
to its ingathering of the exiles philosophy) was rejected as an appropriate ideological foundation for the
Jewish state. Instead, the Soviets continued to advocate Marxism-Leninism, which was based on class rather
than ethnic considerations and which could accomodate

both Jewish and Arab aspirations.

Tying the Knot

On June 27, 1948, the Soviet Union and Israel agreed to exchange representatives at the level of minister. Pavel Ershov arrived in Tel Aviv on August 10 to open the Soviet legation and Golda Meir, who had been detained in New York by a foot injury, reached Moscow on September 3. Relations proceeded rather smoothly, and Ershov appeared at the Knesset for its initial session in February 1949. The Soviets even permitted the exchange of mail in both directions, and Soviet Jews were able to receive a Russian-language Israeli magazine.[10] Israel, for its part, was favorably disposed toward Soviet church interests in the Holy Land. Many properties belonged to the Russian Orthodox Church, but a schism had developed after the Bolshevik revolution between a "Red" church headquartered in Moscow and a "White" church based in New York. The "Red" church did not fare well under the British mandate and the Soviet government discontinued funding for the upkeep of church properties. Once Palestine was partitioned, Israel was sympathetic to Soviet claims and the Knesset recognized "Red" authority over the church in August 1949. Jordan, which occupied the West Bank and East Jerusalem, recognized "White" authority in its territory.

Israel also legalized the communist party, which had been outlawed by the British, and the Soviets were pleased with the merger of Jewish and Arab factions in October 1948. The communists participated in the election to the first Knesset in January, 1949 and received 3.5 percent of the total vote. More significantly, they garnered 22.2 percent of the Arab vote, despite the fact that the party supported the establishment of a Jewish state. The communists won 4 of the 120 Knesset seats, while the pro-Soviet MAPAM secured 19. MAPAM thus became the second largest party in the Knesset, after David Ben Gurion's MAPAI which had 46 seats.[11]

Soviet-Israeli relations were proceeding harmoniously, but a new factor emerged that began to cause complications. Unexpectedly for the Soviets, an upsurge of Jewish national identity was taking place as many Soviet Jews became enamored with Israel. Such an eventuality had not been given serious consideration in deliberations on foreign policy toward the Middle East. For the Israelis, contacts with Soviet Jews were to be fostered and emigration encouraged but, for the Soviets, such acts were anathema and doubt was cast on the loyalty of Jewish citizens. Although the Soviet Union backed Israel in the war against the Arabs, Soviet Jews were not permitted to fight for Israel. Three men who tried to leave for the front by crossing into Turkey were arrested by Soviet authorities.[12]

The xenophobia prevalent in 1947-48 during the Zhdanovshchina (a period when Andrei Zhdanov was second in prominence to Stalin) had some anti-Semitic overtones and a leading Jewish actor and director, Solomon (Shlomo) Mikhoels, was mysteriously killed in January 1948. There does not appear to be any connection between these events and the development of Soviet policy toward the Middle East; internal political considerations and the evolution of a Cold War with the West were the salient variables. However, the Soviet Jewry issue became linked to that of Israel once diplomatic relations were established and Golda Meir became the Israeli minister in Moscow.

Meir and her legation staff tried to be liaisons to the Soviet Jewish community. They distributed literature about Israel, discussed emigration and attended synagogue services on Saturdays and Jewish holidays. They were often mobbed by enthusiastic Soviet Jews when they appeared at the Moscow synagogue, and Soviet authorities became concerned. On September 21, 1948, Jewish author Ilia Ehrenburg published a warning to Soviet Jews, drawing sharp distinctions between Jews and Zionism.[13] Many Jewish cultural institutions were soon closed down and the Jewish Anti-Fascist Committee was disbanded. On February 7, 1949, Meir was summoned to the Soviet foreign ministry to hear a protest about her relations with Soviet Jews. She was accused of advocating emigration and sending newsletters to Jewish organizations.[14] Large numbers of Jews were applying for Israeli visas, but the Soviets rigidly controlled the pace of emigration. From May 1948 to the end of 1951, only four old women and a disabled veteran were given permission to relocate in Israel.[15]

Soviet measures against Jews were not applied in conjunction with any change of policy toward Israel, but they became more severe once Israeli diplomats irritated the Soviets by their Zionist activities. Israel then took umbrage as it was concerned about the fate of Soviet Jews and was unwilling to restrain its Zionist zeal in order to assure proper relations with the Soviet Union. For example, radio broadcasts directed at Soviet Jews were initiated late in 1948. The Soviets saw no inconsistency in their own behavior, believing that they could maintain cordial relations with Israel while combating Zionism. Golda Meir departed from the Soviet Union on April 20, 1949 to become a member of the Israeli Cabinet. Her brief stint as minister in Moscow ended at a time when relations were correct, although somewhat strained.

The Path to Estrangement

Israel had difficulty in gaining membership in the United Nations but managed to do so with Soviet support. It was first voted down by the eleven member Security Council as Syria voted "no" and five countries abstained; the Soviets voted affirmatively. Later, it was approved by nine states, with one abstention and a negative vote from Egypt. Again the Soviets voted "yes" and Israel was admitted to the United Nations on May 11, 1949. Once a member, Israel joined the Soviet Union and other states to oppose successfully the establishment of a British trusteeship in Libya. On January 9, 1950, Israel recognized the new communist government of China and, in September, supported its vain effort to be seated in the United Nations.

Relations remained proper as Israel did not become an ally of the Western camp. Ben Gurion was clearly pro-Western in his sympathies, but he also felt that any intentional antagonizing of the Soviet Union would harm the welfare of Jews in the Soviet Union and East European states. Foreign Minister Moshe Sharett had a more neutralist perspective and he was the architect of a foreign policy of "non-identification." Even the vital issue of Soviet Jewish emigration was kept on the back burner; Ben Gurion did not publicize it until 1950 and it was not raised with the Soviets on an official basis until later that year.[16] Israel was receiving more immigrants than it could handle from Arab states and Rumania so the emigration of Soviet Jews was not a major concern at the time. Despite this cautious approach, MAPAI leaders did verbally attack the Soviet Union. However, this should be viewed primarily as an aspect of internal politics reflecting competition with the pro-Soviet MAPAM party.[17]

Diplomatic correctness was the norm, but changing strategic assessments had a negative impact on the cordiality of ties. For the Soviets, the main goal of removing the British from Palestine had been achieved and the utility of Israel in this process was made obsolescent. Trying to undermine British influence in Arab states became the next concern, and this could not easily be accomplished if the Soviet Union was perceived by Arabs to be pro-Israeli. Consequently, the Soviets moved toward a position of neutrality in regard to the Arab-Israeli conflict and they started to point out fissures in the Arab League, no longer claiming that its members were British puppets. In May 1950, the United States, Britain and France issued the Tripartite Declaration, ostensibly an effort to control the flow of arms to the Middle East. To the Soviets, it was Western assertion of a sphere of influence in the region and it was directed against them. They pointed out that arms would still be delivered for purposes of defense and maintaining internal order, and it does appear that Israel expected to receive Western arms within its framework.[18]

For Israel, ties to the West became stronger than those to the East. There was a need for economic assistance, donations from Western Jews, and a guarantee of her security. Israel's democratic electoral system also was more compatible with Western political values. Western ability to aid Israel was made apparent in January 1949 when the United States provided a $100 million loan. An October request for a Soviet loan did not bear fruit. Contributions from Western Jews poured in to help develop the new state, while none came from Soviet Jews, who were not permitted to send such funds.

Israel began to flirt with the idea of joining NATO but the key event in crystallizing Israel's identification with the West was the Korean War, which began in June 1950. Israel refused to provide token forces for the South Korean side (which was fighting under a United Nations' command umbrella), but it furnished food and medical aid and diplomatically supported the UN cause. The United States applied great pressure on Israel to do so, whereas the Soviets were not active in pressuring Israel in the opposite direction. In a related matter, Israel deferred to U.S. entreaties and decided not to export goods to China.[19]

Soviet disenchantment with Israel had set in prior to the Korean War, but Israel's turn to the West and practical abandonment of "non-identification" made the Soviets even more disquieted. In January 1951, they refused to accept Zalman Shazar as the new Israeli minister appointed to replace Mordechai Namir, in part because he had been engaged in Zionist activities when living in the Soviet Union. That same month, Foreign Minister Sharett told the Knesset that Israel should be pro-Western because it was dependent on aid from Western Jews.[20] In the fall, Israel was kept informed about American proposals to establish a Middle East Command. It was interested in participating, but was not invited as this would have prevented any Arab role. The plan proved stillborn but represented a steppingstone to the anti-Soviet Baghdad Pact.

The "doctors' plot" emerged out of internal Soviet rivalries and probably represented the first step in a major purge of high officials. Nevertheless, it came to involve Israel as most of the accused doctors were Jewish and they were charged with participation in a conspiracy that included Israel. Consternation was aroused in the Jewish state, and some militants set off a bomb at the Soviet legation in Tel Aviv, injuring minister Ershov's wife and two others. Israel apologized the next day and offered to pay compensation, but the Soviet Union broke diplomatic relations on February 11 to register its protest. The Netherlands then represented Israeli interests in the Soviet Union, and Bulgaria did likewise for the Soviets in Israel. East European states maintained their diplomatic links.

It is possible that internal conflicts in the Soviet Union and East European states played a role in producing the break with Israel, but the evidence is highly speculative and fragmentary.[21] Andrei Zhdanov exercised great power in the Kremlin in 1947-48 when relations with Israel were being established, so perhaps he was largely responsible for the favorable Soviet attitude. He died on August 31, 1948 under extremely mysterious circumstances (he was probably killed) and his funeral on September 3 symbolicly coincided with Golda Meir's arrival in Moscow. Campaigns against Zionism, and accusations that Soviet Jews were "cosmopolitans," were initiated after his death and may therefore be attributed to Georgii Malenkov, who rose to be second in command to Stalin.

Another critical factor is Zhdanov's link to Tito and many East European Jewish communists. Zhdanov coordinated Soviet relations with European communist parties, and he had particularly close connections to Tito (who had spent many years in Moscow during the late thirties) and Jewish communist exiles who managed to evade the Nazis and come to the Soviet capital during the war years. When the Soviet Union and Yugoslavia split in the spring of 1948, Zhdanov may have become a Soviet scapegoat and his "death" soon thereafter may be viewed in this context. At the same time, a struggle was being waged in many East European communist parties between those who had been partisan activists against the Nazis and those who had been exiled in Moscow. As the partisans began to gain the upper hand, charges of "Titoism" and "Zionism" were leveled against their opponents and this campaign peaked at the trial in 1952 of Rudolf Slansky, General Secretary of the Czechoslovak communist party. Eleven of the fourteen defendants were Jewish, and the initiation of the "doctors' plot" in the Soviet Union immediately afterward seemed to be part of a similar process.

If such an interpretation is valid, it appears that there was reciprocal interaction between the issue of Israel and that of internal power rivalry. The worsening of Soviet-Israeli relations may have taken place, in part, as a result of Zhdanov's demise and the purge of East European Jewish communists may have been abetted by the Soviet anti-Zionist campaign. Unfortunately, there are some discrepancies in this scenario. If Malenkov was responsible for a change in policy detrimental to Israel, why did he try to improve relations with the Jewish state once he became prime minister after Stalin's death in 1953? Also, was

Malenkov a mastermind of the anti-Semitic and anti-Zionist "doctors' plot" or was he one of its intended victims? This line of analysis does indeed have its shortcomings, but some significant connection between Zhdanov, Tito and Zionism probably existed and deserves fuller investigation and elaboration.

Reconciliation and Retrogression

Despite the break in relations, Israel sent condolences to the Soviet leaders in March 1953 upon the death of Stalin, and an Israeli delegation joined the mourners that month at the funeral of Czechoslovak party leader Klement Gottwald. In the Soviet Union, Stalin's successors ended the "doctors' plot" purge process and announced the release and rehabilitation of the doctors. These steps augured well for a more congenial political atmosphere and helped lead to Soviet-Israeli negotiations in Sofia, Bulgaria.

At a celebration of Hungarian independence day, Israeli charge d'affaires Ben-Tsion Razin was approached by Soviet ambassador Bodrov, who told him that he was proud that the new Kremlin leaders had released the doctors. Razin queried about improving bilateral relations but Bodrov didn't respond directly. Nevertheless, Bodrov's initial comment was deemed important and Razin notified his superiors in Jerusalem. After the Israeli foreign ministry had announced that the freeing of the doctors could help foster a reconciliation, Razin wrote to Bodrov and cited this pronouncement. Again no response. However, Razin was encouraged by indirect signals from other East European states which had not severed relations with Israel. The Czechoslovak ambassador in Sofia said that he hoped for better Soviet-Israeli relations, and the Polish ambassador came to the Israeli mission to suggest that Israel should secretly offer a renewal of relations with the Soviets. Israeli Prime Minister Ben Gurion authorized such an effort and the Israeli charge in Hungary was brought into the negotiations. On May 28, the two Israeli charges presented their proposal to Bodrov at the Soviet embassy. He was interested but made two demands: Israel must not join any alliance against the Soviet Union and it must put on trial the perpetrators of the bombing at the Soviet legation in Tel Aviv. The Israelis agreed to consider these demands.[22]

On June 8, the Israeli foreign ministry sent a favorable response to Bodrov and some disagreements then developed over the wording of statements and over Israel being asked to make public announcements. These were soon overcome and foreign ministers Sharett and Molotov signed the final statement on the resumption of relations. On July 21, relations were officially restored. Israel had agreed not to join any anti-

Soviet alliance and the Soviets had signified a desire
for "friendly" relations after the Israelis objected
to the word "normal."[23] In August, Israel attacked
across the Jordanian border in response to Palestinian
assaults that had been launched from there. All
members of the UN Security Council condemned Israel's
action except the Soviet Union, which abstained.[24]

On December 2, designated Soviet minister
Aleksandr Abramov took the unusual step of presenting
his credentials in Israel's capital city of Jerusalem.
He was the first foreign emissary to do so but the
Soviet Union did not change its position of refusing
to recognize Jerusalem as the capital. That same
month, the Israeli minister in Moscow, Shmuel
Eliashiv, met with First Deputy Foreign Minister
Andrei Gromyko to request the right of emigration for
Soviet Jews. Gromyko turned him down but said that
exit visas for the purpose of family reunification
would possibly be granted.[25] They were, and small
numbers of Jews began to leave the Soviet Union for
Israel.

As early as August 1953, Israel had asked the
Soviets to raise the level of diplomatic representation from ministers to ambassadors and to convert
legations into embassies. Israel repeated this request
several times and the Soviets finally acquiesced. In
June 1954, an agreement was reached on upgrading representation. It should be added that the Egyptian legation in Moscow was also elevated to embassy status.

On the economic front, the Soviet Union and Israel
developed an extensive oil trade. Deliveries of fuel
oil early in 1954 were followed by large supplies of
crude oil, and the total annual volume amounted to
almost 400,000 tons over the next few years. This
represented a substantial export commitment for the
Soviets as total oil exports in 1954 were only 6.5
million tons. Israel paid the Soviets less for oil
than it paid any supplier but, more importantly, the
payments were made with citrus fruit rather than hard
currency. In July 1956, a two-year contract called
for annual shipments of 700,000 tons, with the possibility that they could rise to one million tons in
1957-58.[26]

Why did the Soviet Union effect a rapprochement
with Israel in 1953 and then sustain it for several
years? Stalin's death was the critical event as his
successors implemented a more pragmatic and moderate
approach to foreign policy. Concerned with domestic
affairs and the internal power struggle, they attempted to mend fences in many parts of the world. Israel
fit into this pattern, while other noteworthy acts
were support for negotiations to end the Korean and
Vietnamese wars, movement toward ending four-power
military occupation of Austria, withdrawal of terri-

torial claims against Turkey and reconciliation with Yugoslavia. Israel was anxious to improve relations with the Soviet Union due to its concern for Soviet Jews and the desire to balance strong ties to Western states.

It was not until the mid-fifties that the Arab factor became an important component of the Soviet-Israeli equation. From 1949 through 1953, the Soviet Union cautiously abstained at the United Nations whenever an Arab-Israeli issue was voted upon, but a change in policy started to become evident in 1954. On January 22, the Soviets sided with the Syrians in a controversy over Israel's development of the demilitarized zone and, in March, they supported Egypt in denying Israel's right to use the Suez Canal. By 1955 they had adopted a completely pro-Arab position, which was in line with the new Third World approach of the politically ascendant Nikita Khrushchev. Khrushchev recognized the anti-Western essence of much Afro-Asian nationalism and he made a determined effort to solidify relations with leaders such as Nasser, Nehru and Sukarno. In the Middle East, this was translated into a pro-Arab policy which was clearly detrimental to Israel.

During the years 1954-55, the United States and Britain were organizing the Baghdad Pact as part of their strategy of surrounding the Soviet Union with pro-Western military alliances. The Soviets obviously opposed this development, and Israel was also apprehensive as Iraq was to receive more Western arms. A coincidence of Soviet and Israeli interests was conceivable, but events did not turn out that way. Egypt became the center of Arab forces opposed to the Baghdad Pact, and it was also sponsoring Palestinian raids against Israel. Israeli retaliation in the Egyptian-occupied Gaza Strip was therefore seen by the Soviets as collusion with the Baghdad Pact states against Egypt. More significantly, the Egyptian-Czechoslovak arms deal of September 1955 alarmed Israel, despite Soviet claims that these arms were not directed against her. The Soviet Union clearly sponsored the arms arrangement, but it probably did so in the context of countering Britain (which still had some control over the Suez Canal) and the British-aligned Baghdad Pact. In a way, motivation was similar to that evident in 1948 when Czechoslovakia armed Israel. Israeli minister to Moscow Eliashiv had presciently written in March 1954: "The elimination of British influence in the area is the principal goal, and to reach this aim, the Soviet Union will support Egypt in everything, just as it supported us, for the same reason, in 1947."[27] Israel had started to receive French arms in 1954 (France was embroiled at the time with Arab nationalism in Algeria, Tunisia and Morocco)

but its initial reaction to the Czechoslovak deal was
not to turn only to the West for more assistance.
Sharett (who was prime minister from January 1954 until
being replaced by Ben Gurion in November 1955) said
that Israel wanted arms from "all suppliers," which
was an oblique solicitation of Soviet arms as well.
None were forthcoming and Israel extended its military
dependence on the West.

By April 1956, tension was developing between
Egypt and Britain over ownership of the Suez Canal,
and Palestinian fedayeen were intensifying their
activities against Israel from Egyptian soil. The
Soviet Union took this opportunity to try to assert
itself as a legitimate superpower in the region so it
offered to serve as a mediator. The Soviet proposal
was balanced in its attitudes toward Israel and the
Arab states, and it seems to have been motivated to a
large extent by consideration of the British factor.
It opposed the introduction of foreign troops (ostensibly British) and was released the day before
Khrushchev left for a visit to Britain.[28] The Soviet
Union apparently believed that its strong position in
Egypt would serve to enhance its regional diplomatic
role. Especially interesting is the fact that exiled
Egyptian communist leader Yusuf Hilmi wrote three
articles during this period which called for an international conference on the Arab-Israeli conflict
(including Soviet participation) and direct negotiations under its framework between Egypt and Israel.[29]
Israel, Britain and the United States all opposed a
negotiating role for the Soviets so their proposal
became moribund. In July, Israel invited Soviet
Foreign Minister Dmitrii Shepilov to visit, but no
response was received.[30] Israel and the Soviet Union
were displaying mutual mistrust, and the Middle East
situation deteriorated into war as Egypt nationalized
the Suez Canal.

At the beginning of November, Britain and France
seized major installations in the Canal zone, and
Israel advanced rapidly through Sinai. The Soviet
Union lent strong verbal support to the Egyptians,
and even suggested joint intervention with the United
States to restore order. Once Israel and Egypt had
agreed to a cease-fire (although hostilities continued)
the Soviets threatened to send "volunteers" to support
the Egyptians. Prime Minister Bulganin sent ominous
warnings to Britain and France that rockets would be
unleased against London and Paris, and his note to
Ben Gurion charged that Israeli behavior "will place
a question upon the very existence of Israel as a
State."[31] The United States pressured Israel to end
the conflict and evacuate all occupied territory, so
the two superpowers were acting in a parallel manner
on this issue. Israel acquiesced, but the American

stance was probably more instrumental than the Soviet
threat. Nevertheless, many Arabs believed that the
Soviet threat had turned the tide so the prestige of the
U.S.S.R. rose in Arab states.

To protest Israel's role in the war, the Soviet
Union withdrew its ambassador, Aleksandr Abramov, and
abrogated all oil agreements by invoking the principle
of "force majeure." The Soviet oil trading organization Soiuznefteeksport claimed that it could not fulfill
its contracts because the Soviet government would not
permit it to do so. Israel later brought suit in a
Soviet court but, not surprisingly, lost the case.
After Israel completed its evacuation of Egyptian territory, Abramov returned to Israel to reassume his post.
Diplomatic relations had not been broken but the
ambassador registered his country's displeasure by
spending five months in the Soviet Union. Official
relations continued but they were formal and stiff. A
point of no return had been reached as Israel had col-
luded militarily with Britain and France, while the
Soviet Union had clearly backed the Egyptian position
against Israel. The Soviet Union had originally
applied an anti-colonial and anti-British tactic when
supporting the establishment of Israel; now Israel was
aligned with Britain and France in defense of their
remaining colonial interests in the Suez Canal.

In the Doldrums

The period from 1956 to 1963 was mainly one of
benign neglect from the standpoint of the Soviets.
They curried favor with the Arabs, generally disregarded Israel but did not act decisively against its
interests. In July 1958, Ben Gurion tried to convince
Soviet Ambassador Mikhail Bodrov that Israel's receipt
of Western arms did not signify that it was serving
Western interests. He requested Soviet arms to prove
his point, but the Soviets did not provide any. In
1960, Ben Gurion was turned down by Khrushchev when he
requested a meeting.[32]

To the Soviets, Israel was aligned with the West.
The Eisenhower Doctrine, approved by Congress in March
1957, seemed to include Israel under its security
umbrella. Furthermore, Ben Gurion told the Knesset in
November 1957: "In the U.S. a Jew may assist the State
of Israel, in the Soviet Union this is forbidden--and
the prohibition existed even before the rise of the
State. Should the State of Israel declare that it is
'neutral' in regard to these two attitudes?"[33] Ben
Gurion opted for political affiliation with the United
States. He also had been developing closer relations
with West Germany since the reparations agreement of
September 1952 and later, in July 1958, he granted
permission for British aircraft to fly over Israel on
their way to Jordan. Britain was sending troops there

to bolster Hussein's government in the wake of the overthrow of his fellow Hashemite monarchy in Iraq that
same month. In fact, this assistance to the British
was rendered the day before his discussion with Bodrov!

Some of the usual recriminations marked the Soviet-
Israeli relationship during this period. In 1957,
Soviet Jews mingled with Israelis at the International
Youth Festival in Moscow. This led to the arrest of
many of the former and, for some, the loss of jobs. In
1961, Foreign Minister Meir charged that Soviet Jews
were being put on trial as a result of their contacts
with Israeli diplomats and, in 1962, the Soviets
accused Israeli diplomats of spying. The following
year, Israel arrested an alleged Soviet agent, and the
Soviet cultural attache (and suspected KGB station
chief) hurriedly departed for Moscow.[34]

Although relations were far from cordial, the
small flow of Soviet Jewish emigrants that began in
1954 continued. The total for the years 1954-63 was
approximately 1500 and there were emigrants every year,
despite the temporary cut-off produced by the 1956 Suez
War. The number given permission to leave the Soviet
Union for family reunification was extremely small. On
the other hand, about 14,000 additional Jews left the
Soviet Union for Poland under the auspices of a March
1957 repatriation agreement. Many of them then found
their way to Israel.

It is rather paradoxical that this limited Jewish
emigration was permitted when diplomatic relations with
Israel were poor, while virtually no emigration was
allowed at the high point of the relationship in 1948.
It therefore becomes apparent that emigration is not a
function of bilateral relations. During the period in
question, the major factor seems to have been foreign
opinion. Israel, operating behind the scenes, organized
a world campaign in the mid-fifties on the Soviet Jewry
issue, featuring the establishment of committees and
research centers. In 1959, Israeli diplomats went
public and emissaries were dispatched to orchestrate an
international effort regarding maltreatment of Soviet
Jews and their right to emigrate. The subject was
raised at international conferences and in UN committees, leading even the British communist party to publish a report accusing the Soviet Union of discrimin-
ating against Jews. In 1959, Soviet Deputy Prime
Minister Mikoian met in New York with leaders of the
American Jewish Committee to discuss the subject.[35]

The Soviet Union and Israel entered 1963 with their
relations in a state of phlegmatic disanimation, but
greater passions were soon aroused. Increased ardor and
acrimonious disputes both became evident, as the dol-
drums gave way to stormier seas.

3
Alienation of Affections

An examination of the relations between Israel and
the Soviet Union during the years 1963-67 is essential
if one is to understand the deep antagonism that developed between these two states in the aftermath of
the 1967 Arab-Israeli war. The beginning of this period
was marked by a mutual reevaluation of relations and a
clear attempt by Israel to improve them. The Soviet
Union responded cautiously, but positively. Both sides
made an effort to mend fences, but each ended up deeply
disappointed and alienated as this test case of reconciliation resulted in failure. The critical questions
to be posed are: Why was Israel interested in a
rapprochement with the Soviet Union? Why did the
Soviets respond favorably? Why were the results so
devastating to both parties?

In June 1963, an intra-party feud led to the resignation of David Ben Gurion as Prime Minister of
Israel and he was replaced by a MAPAI colleague, Levi
Eshkol. Eshkol was a man of moderate temperament, a non-
flamboyant bureaucrat who contrasted with his passionate, cosmopolitan and charismatic predecessor. There
was a popular humoristic jibe that when asked if he
wanted coffee or tea, Eshkol replied "half and half."
In a far more serious vein, there was widespread public
doubt that he was capable of providing the strong
leadership needed as Israel anticipated its participation in another war in June 1967. It was with great
relief that most Israelis greeted the June 2 entry into
the Cabinet of Moshe Dayan as Minister of Defense.

These public perceptions of Eshkol were truly a
disservice to the man as he was not, in fact, weak or
indecisive. He was, however, a gentle and non-abrasive
political personality who wanted to tone down the rhetoric of the Cold War and improve relations with the
Soviet Union. From the Soviet standpoint, he was less
objectionable than Ben Gurion and the communist rulers
were somewhat amenable to his overtures. This was
especially true after the removal of Nikita Khrushchev

in October 1964, as a fresh start could be made in patching up a frayed relationship. Khrushchev had been vitriolic while the new Soviet leadership, headed by Leonid Brezhnev and Aleksei Kosygin, was more pragmatic and diplomatic. However, these leaders did not act decisively in regard to Israel and sent out confusing and contradictory signals. Israeli communists were so perplexed that they constantly tuned into Radio Moscow for the latest policy interpretation, before committing themselves to any position.

The temperament of authority had shifted in both countries so prospects augured well for an attempt at reconciliation. Indeed, Soviet-Israeli ties improved briefly but then, in 1967, the Middle East situation deteriorated into another state of war. The Soviet Union, partially as a gesture toward the Arab states, severed diplomatic relations with Israel and they have not been renewed to this day. What led to this fallout and legal separation? The key lay in Syria but it is necessary to look as far afield as China, Vietnam, Greece and Yemen to help fill in the pieces of this puzzle. Divisions within the Soviet hierarchy were also pertinent, as was the issue of Soviet Jewry. Serious repercussions are still evident as both the Soviet Union and Israel have been scarred by this experience and are reluctant to take any meaningful steps toward another reconciliation.

The Arena of Contact

Levi Eshkol was usually conciliatory in his approach toward the Soviet Union. Shortly after assuming office, he tried to reassure the Soviets of Israel's intentions by reiterating the 1953 commitment not to join any anti-Soviet alliance. He met frequently with Soviet ambassador Dmitrii Chuvakhin, conversing in Russian and calling for warmer bilateral relations. He condemned the "Cold War," said Israel would play no part in it and indicated that he did not accept the concept of a struggle between the "free world" and "communist" states. He declared that Israel belonged to neither East nor West and he often portrayed Soviet intentions in a favorable light, such as when he revealed a Soviet message indicating that force should not be used to change state boundaries.[1] Eshkol's effort at rapprochement was given added impetus in January 1966 when urbane Abba Eban replaced the more provocative Golda Meir as foreign minister, Eban constantly called for an improvement in relations, advocated Soviet participation in any Arab-Israeli peace process and tried to encourage the Soviets by claiming that their relations with the Arabs would not suffer.[2]

The Soviet media viewed Eshkol as less extremist than Ben Gurion in his policy toward the Arabs, and

Israeli ambassador to the U.S.S.R. Katriel Katz
maintained that Eshkol did not offend the Soviets as
much as Ben Gurion had.[3] Esther Wilenska, a prominent
Israeli communist, wrote that Ben Gurion's resignation
"created more favorable conditions for developing the
struggle for democracy." She averred that the communists were increasing their cooperation with
"democratic forces" to redirect Israeli policy but that
"ultras" were pressuring Eshkol to forego his predilec-
tion for such change. Wilenska praised Eshkol, in
comparison to Ben Gurion, as he was less inclined to use
force against Syria and more sensitive to the "Arab
refugee problem."[4] Some Israeli communists were less
sympathetic, with Meir Wilner maintaining that Eshkol
at first sounded as if he was going to institute new
policies, but he then carried out old ones.[5]

There was very little Soviet-Israeli trade after
1956, but limited tourist exchanges began in 1963 and
there were other indications of an improved diplomatic
atmosphere. Extensive cultural exchanges took place
during the period 1964-66 and, in October 1964, a deal
was worked out regarding the dispensation of "Red"
church properties in Jerusalem. Some buildings which
had been vacant and not used for ecclesiastical purposes had been taken over by the Israeli government and
Israel therefore agreed to compensate the Soviet Union
by paying $1.5 million in hard currency and $3 million
in goods. The Soviet Union benefited from the financial settlement but, more importantly, it received
acknowledgment of its ownership of "Red" church properties, rather than mere authority over them.

Israel took the initiative in seeking improved relations as it hoped to arrange for the emigration of
greater numbers of Soviet Jews. It also lacked any
powerful Western sponsorship at the time as Britain and
France were in the process of withdrawing their support
and the United States had not yet replaced these states
on a meaningful scale. Israel therefore sought security through the preemptive diplomatic neutralization of
any potential Soviet threat. The Soviet Union responded to Israeli overtures but it did so hesitantly and
cautiously as it was constrained by an anticipated Arab
backlash. The Soviets hoped to drive a wedge between
Israel and the Western camp, particularly on the issues
of Vietnam and West German nuclearization, but they
also seem to have had a contradictory tactic in mind as
well. The Soviet Union increasingly came to view Israel
as a U.S. proxy and it appears that more cordial
relations with Israel were thought to have a salient
effect on the course of Soviet-American relations. The
Soviet Union was engaged in bitter dispute with China
and it was moving closer to the U.S., as evidenced by
the hot line agreement of 1963 and the text ban treaty
of 1964.

Soviet-Israeli relations hit their second highest point in 1965 and early 1966, the apogee having been achieved briefly in 1948. The campaign against Jews as economic criminals was muted and a rabbi sentenced to death for "speculation" had his sentence commuted to a prison term.[6] Synagogues were no longer closed down by the authorities and Pravda for the first time referred to the role of Jews who fought with the Red Army against the Nazis. Pravda also condemned anti-Semitism.[7] On September 2, 1965, Katriel Katz presented his credentials as the new Israeli ambassador and he received extensive press coverage. New Times (Novoe Vremia) displayed his photo and biography and Sovetskaia Rossiia interviewed him, the first such interview with an Israeli emissary since 1948.[8] The positive tone was so pronounced that an Israeli specialist on this period has been able to cite ten instances from August 1965 to March 1966 when statements including negative references to Israel were altered or abridged by the media to exclude the offending remarks.[9]

An especially curious episode took place in November 1965 when New Times devoted an entire article to the views of an Israeli communist journalist who was generally supportive of Israeli positions! The letter from Mordechai Kaspi was not reprinted in full but was extensively paraphrased and, in parts, quoted. New Times indicated: "We publish these comments of an Israeli Communist journalist in the belief that they will give our readers a more rounded and objective picture of Arab-Israeli relations."[10] In March 1966, New Times publicized the February 28 solo flight to Port Said, Egypt by Israeli peace activist Abie Nathan. It sympathized with his act and called for the peaceful settlement of disputes.[11]

Soviet behavior during the winter of 1965-66 was related to the possibility that the Soviets would sponsor Arab-Israeli peace negotiations by convening another "Tashkent" (this will be discussed below).[12] As part of this process, Soviet diplomats in Tel Aviv began to provide information to Israeli journalists and ambassador Chuvakhin even addressed the Israeli branch of the World Jewish Congress. However, retrogression became evident during the spring as the Soviet Union came to assess positively the February revolution carried out by the left wing of the Baathist movement in Syria. In May, only low level Soviet officials came to the embassy in Moscow to celebrate Israeli independence day and a planned exchange of orchestras was postponed to November, possibly as a result of the April visit to Moscow of the Syrian prime minister. In September, the Israeli foreign ministry was informed that the exchange visits of the Moscow State Orchestra and the Israeli Philharmonic Orchestra were cancelled. Nevertheless,

some degree of interaction was maintained. In January
1967, Soviet church and fisheries delegations visited
Israel and, in March, Israelis attended the Soviet
tribute to the Year of the Woman.

Throughout the course of Soviet-Israeli relations
from 1948 to June 1967, no Israeli ambassador to the
Soviet Union was ever received by the communist party
first (or general) secretary or the Soviet prime
minister. Furthermore, no Politburo member ever
visited Israel and no Israeli cabinet member ever
traveled to the Soviet Union until the journey of
Minister of Labor Yigal Allon just before the outbreak
of the 1967 war. Contact was frequently maintained at
the level of foreign minister, witness the Eban-Gromyko
meeting in September 1966, but always at a neutral site.
On occasion, Israeli ambassadors to the Soviet Union
were received by the Soviet foreign minister.

A major obstacle to improved relations was the
issue of Soviet Jewry. In fact, Soviet diplomats
constantly made two demands upon Israel: stop clamoring
for the rights of Soviet Jews and start disengaging
politically from the West.[13] Ambassador Chuvakhin
admonished an Israeli foreign ministry official in
April 1965: "You know well what stands in the way of
an improvement of our relations with you. It is the
problem of Soviet Jews and of your activities on this
subject, especially in international forums. If you
change your policy on this point and if you stop provoking us, an improvement in relations will follow."[14]

Israel was unwilling to reduce pressure on the
Soviet Jewry issue, even at the expense of cordial ties
to the U.S.S.R., as Director General of the Foreign
Ministry Aryeh Levavi (1964-67) indicated that Israel
could not relent despite the consequences. The issue
was becoming a cause celebre in Israel due to the
pseudonymous publication in 1965 of veteran diplomat
Arie Eliav's Between Hammer & Sickle and the serializa-
tion in Yediot Achronot of Eli Wiesel's The Jews of
Silence, which soon appeared in 1966 in book form. Eban
brought up the subject with Gromyko and Israel raised
the issue at the United Nations in late 1966, by which
time relations had already started to deteriorate. The
Soviet Union was particularly upset by Israel's staging
of a "Soviet Jewry Week" in late February 1967.[15]

Soviet Jewish emigration increased during the
Eshkol period. There is some minor disagreement over
the exact statistics, but the exodus was approximately
184 in 1962; 305 in 1963; 537 in 1964; 891 in 1965;
2047 in 1966; and 1406 prior to the June war of 1967.[16]
The number of Jews permitted to leave the Soviet Union
since the Second World War paled in comparison with the
number of Germans, Poles, Armenians and Spaniards but
an upsurge was clearly evident in the mid-sixties. One
may logically assume that emigration is a function of

bilateral Soviet-Israeli relations, but logic can
occasionally pervert one's clarity of judgment.
Actually, emigration picked up after the Soviet Union
had hardened its attitude toward Israel in other areas.
On December 3, 1966, Prime Minister Kosygin released a
statement in Paris which declared: "We, on our side,
shall do all possible for us if some families want to
meet or even if some among them would like to leave us,
to open for them the road, and this does not raise here,
naturally, any problem of principles and will not raise
any."[17] Kosygin restricted his comments to family reunification, but they were still a long awaited clarion
for hopeful Jewish emigrants. Significantly, Kosygin's
statement was printed on the front page of the state
newspaper Izvestiia on December 5 and Jewish emigration
during the first five months of 1967 proceeded at the
highest rate ever.

Perhaps the Soviet Union was catering to world
opinion, or it was expecting the demand for emigration
to decline after the departure of leading activists.
However, other explanations appear to be pertinent.
Often overlooked is the embarrassing fact that many
communists in the United States, Britain, France, Italy,
Australia and Canada were condemning Soviet treatment
of the Jews.[18] Also, the Soviets infiltrated agents
among the emigrants and this would have served their
espionage interests in Israel. Another possible consideration was that the flow of emigrants could be
used as a lever to pressure Israel diplomatically in
regard to the Arab-Israeli conflict; the threat to
reduce or curtail the flow could then be used to modify
Israeli behavior.[19]

In 1948, close relations with Israel led to Soviet
efforts to limit social contact between Israelis and
Soviet Jews, and the same scenario unfolded in 1965-66
during the period of warm cultural interaction.
Particularly alarming was the enthusiastic response to
the concerts of Israeli singer Geula Gil in July 1966,
as she was mobbed by Jewish admirers. Soviet motivations became even stronger as emigration increased as
there was fear that Israeli diplomats in the U.S.S.R.
would contribute to the snowballing of the emigration
movement. Consequently, the Soviet media accused
Israelis of various nefarious deeds, many of them deemed criminal. From the Israeli perspective, disseminat-
ing information about Israel and Judaism and advising
Jews on emigration were legitimate activities, even
within the rigid confines of Soviet law.

The Soviets claimed that Israeli diplomats were
distributing Zionist propaganda, collecting evidence
to accuse the U.S.S.R. of mistreating Jews, spreading
anti-Soviet slander, fostering emigration, spying and
discouraging Soviet Jews from assimilating.[20] Soviet
attacks on Zionism seemed to be counterproductive at

this time as Jewish identity was increasing, along with the demand for emigration. Mohammed Heikal, Egyptian journalist and key political adviser to Nasser, provides an interesting perspective. He believes that the Soviets were trying to place the blame for the Jewish upsurge on Egypt by claiming that the Soviet anti-Zionist stance was aimed at serving Arab interests.[21] The implication of Heikal's remark is that the anti-Zionist campaign produced the Jewish upsurge, but it is more likely that it was actually a response. The Soviets used it to balance their improved relations with Israel, thereby attempting to appease the Arabs and dampen the Zionist ardor which had become more pronounced among Soviet Jews.

In May 1965, the Soviets accused Israeli first secretary David Bar-Tov of subversion among Georgian Jews. He was said to have visited synagogues along with ambassador Yosef Tekoah and to have encouraged emigration.[22] In October, the Soviets for the first time equated Zionism and racism before a UN committee. Then in August 1966, just after the Geula Gil concerts, second secretary David Gavish was expelled for alleged espionage. In early September, third secretary Ephraim Paz, his wife, and an Israeli tourist were accused of spreading Zionist propaganda through the dissemination of postcards, stamps and calendars during a Black Sea vacation. It was also claimed that they propagandized at a synagogue and distributed prayer books.[23] In February 1967, a Soviet citizen was brought to trial for spying on behalf of former second secretary David Gavish. He was charged with distributing Zionist and anti-Soviet materials, and with preparing tables on military topography.[24] Israeli tourists to the U.S.S.R. were often accused of Zionist propaganda offenses and it was alleged that some of them were intelligence agents. Several were expelled when they came to Moscow in May 1966 as part of the delegation to the International Modern Farm Machinery and Equipment Exhibition.[25]

By April 1967, Soviet-Israeli ties were already fraying. Israel felt that Eshkol's overtures had been largely rebuffed and concluded that it really didn't matter what constituted Israel's policy toward the Soviet Union, the latter would remain implacably hostile. This attitude strongly conditioned subsequent Israeli foreign policy deliberations, producing a reluctance to try the same tack again. The Soviet Union was upset that it had been unable to separate the Soviet Jewry issue from its bilateral relationship with Israel. It felt that Israel had taken advantage of an improved political atmosphere by interfering in Soviet domestic affairs.

Israeli Communists: the Wagging Tail?

The Israeli communist party was rent by dissension and it gradually split into two parties, MAKI and RAKAH.26 MAKI, led by Moshe Sneh, Shmuel Mikunis and Esther Wilenska, had the support of a majority of Jewish members while most Arab communists backed RAKAH, which was led by Meir Wilner (a Jew) and Tewfiq Toubi. MAKI retained control of the party's organ Kol Ha'am and it called upon the Soviets to treat Israel and the Arab states with equal favor. In a sense, MAKI was moving closer to the Zionist parties in terms of patriotic sentiments, while RAKAH espoused a strongly anti-Zionist position.

Curiously, the Israeli communist factions tried to influence Soviet foreign policy in the Middle East. On December 31, 1963, Nikita Khrushchev addressed a letter to world leaders (including Eshkol) which called for the peaceful settlement of disputes. MAKI lobbied to have this principle applied specifically to the Arab-Israeli situation, while RAKAH opposed such an interpretation. The Soviet Union wavered as it was improving relations with Israel and simultaneously courting Egypt and other Arab states. As it eventually moved away from Israel, this decision ran parallel to its increasing support for RAKAH at the expense of MAKI.

The MAKI-RAKAH split began in 1963 and slowly became more acrimonious. In September 1964, Ahmed Ben Bella of Algeria received a Lenin Peace Prize and called for the elimination of Israel. Mikunis of MAKI was angered that Ben Bella would express such views in Moscow and he attacked him in the September 20 edition of Kol Ha'am.27 In May 1965, the Soviets dispatched to Israel Iurii Ivanov, editor of the Novosti news agency. He attended the celebration of the twentieth anniversay of the defeat of Nazism, but also attempted to mediate between the communist factions. His effort was to no avail as, on May 19, Kol Ha'am published the positions of the competing groups. The next month, a Soviet delegation arrived to arrange a postponement of the Israeli communist party congress. It hoped to reconcile the factions prior to a rescheduled congress, but was successful only in the matter of postponement. The continual mediation of Chuvakhin had no effect and separate conferences of the two factions took place in August. On August 26, the RAKAH faction launched its own journal, Zo Haderech.

Foreign communist delegates did not attend the August conferences but the MAKI group appears to have received more messages from East European and West European communist parties.28 The Soviet Union sent identically worded greetings to the conferences but leaned slightly toward MAKI. Pravda on August 10 printed MAKI's criticism of the "divisive activities" of those (obviously RAKAH) "who have abandoned the principles of internationalism and gone over to subversive, factional activity."[29] Then, in November, New Times carried the comments of Kaspi, MAKI's Moscow correspondent. Nevertheless, another mediation effort took place in Moscow in November, led by Mikhail Suslov and Boris Ponomarev. The former was a Politburo member and chief Soviet ideologist, and the latter was the principal Central Committee liaison with foreign communist parties. At the time, each of the Israeli communist factions believed that it was acting in accordance with Moscow's wishes; the problem was that the Soviet position toward Israel was filled with ambiguities.

Moshe Sneh was probably correct in stating that Soviet preference for RAKAH began to emerge as a result of the Syrian revolution of February 1966.[30] The fact that RAKAH received 2.3% of the vote in the November 1965 Knesset elections, while MAKI garnered only 1.1%, may also have influenced the Soviet attitude. Both factions attended the Twenty-third Congress of the Soviet communist party in March 1966 but the handwriting was soon on the wall as Izvestiia (on May 6) for the first time since the split referred to RAKAH leader Meir Wilner as "a communist member of the Knesset." As Israeli-Syrian border conflicts escalated, RAKAH's pro-Syrian position coincided with that of the Soviet Union, while MAKI was more evenhanded. In September, Kaspi was expelled from the Soviet Union after the successful application of pressure by RAKAH, which did not have its own Moscow correspondent. In November, an article by Wilner appeared in New Times.

In February 1967, the Soviets failed to send greetings to MAKI's Kol Ha'am on the occasion of its twentieth anniversary and in April, Zo Haderech but not Kol Ha'am had its greeting printed in Izvestiia to mark its fortieth anniversary.[31] Also in April, another Wilner article was published. This time, his views appeared in World Marxist Review, the official organ of the world's communist parties aligned with the Soviet Union.

MAKI was clearly displeased as the Soviets swung behind RAKAH. Mikunis sent a letter to the Central Committee, protesting the expulsion of Kaspi, and Sneh had numerous discussions with Chuvakhin in which he criticized the Soviet position on the Syrian border conflict. Sneh even offered to accompany Chuvakhin to the area of confrontation, but the Soviet ambassador refused.[32] It should be noted that MAKI still enjoyed some support within the communist world, especially among Jews. It also had considerable backing from Italian and

Yugoslav communists and from a segment of the
Czechoslovak communist party.[33]
     In June 1967, RAKAH and the Soviet Union had
similar anti-Israeli analyses of the war. MAKI accused
the Arabs of initiating the conflict and called for the
defense of Israel. In July, the Soviets recognized
RAKAH as the sole legitimate Israeli communist party.

The Middle East Dimension

     British withdrawal from the Middle East, which
had been taking place gradually ever since the Second
World War, continued during the mid-sixties. Kuwait,
Bahrein and Qatar were granted independence in 1961 and
the Persian Gulf emirates were proceeding in that
direction. Insurgency against the British raged in
Aden (South Yemen), a key area logistically as it controlled southern access to the Suez Canal. More importantly for Israel, it controlled the sea route to its
port of Eilat so the potential for interference with
oil imports and trade with Afro-Asian states could not
be discounted. Across the Bab el-Mandeb Strait in the
Territory of Afars and Issas (now Djibouti), the French
were contemplating the granting of independence so
Israeli military strategists (as exemplified by numerous articles in _Maarchot_ and _Skira Chodshit_) were
extremely apprehensive.
     France, a military supplier and ally of Israel,
was moving in a more pro-Arab direction. France had
incurred the wrath of the Arabs as a result of the
Suez conflict of 1956 and the Algerian war but the
achievement of independence by Algeria in 1962 changed
France's strategic priorities. In need of oil, it
courted Arab friendship and developed harmonious relations with states that had just recently supported
the Algerian FLN against her. Israel expected France
to weaken its commitment, especially after Ben Gurion
and Shimon Peres were no longer in the Cabinet. They
had been the leading advocates of friendship with
France.
     Israel saw a partial vacuum developing in the
region, with the Soviet Union and United States having
reciprocal fears of the other stepping into it. A
foreign ministry evaluation in the summer of 1966
anticipated Soviet advances in the area and concluded
that Israel was an obstacle to Soviet regional designs.
American assistance was sought to counter the Soviet
threat, but Secretary of State Dean Rusk reportedly
said that extensive involvement in Vietnam prevented
the U.S. from acting more decisively in the Middle
East. Back in May 1963, the United States had turned
down Ben Gurion's request for a security pact so it is
not too difficult to see why Israel sought political
accommodation with the Soviet Union during this period.[34]

     The Soviet Union was concerned primarily with pro-
tecting its southern flank by neutralizing Western
strategic assets, and it also wanted to assert its role
as a legitimate regional power. Considerable effort
was devoted to improving relations with Turkey (a member of both NATO and CENTO) and Iran (a member of CENTO)
as ideological considerations were subordinated to
geopolitical realities. Such a course became increasingly consistent with Soviet policies elsewhere in the
Third World as the Soviets had been stung by the re-
volutions which had overthrown their ideological allies
Ben Bella of Algeria and Sukarno of Indonesia in 1965
and Nkrumah of Ghana in January 1966. Pragmatism and
Realpolitik became the keynotes as dependence on
charismatic leftists was discarded as a policy priority.
Iran was clearly a Western-aligned, feudo-capitalistic
monarchy and yet chief of state Brezhnev journeyed there
in November 1963 and the Shah repaid the visit in the
summer of 1965. A major agreement on Iranian natural
gas development and export to the U.S.S.R. was signed
in January 1966, and Soviet arms sales to Iran were
arranged in July 1966 and announced the following
January.
     Soviet relations with Egypt had been the corner-
stone of Middle East policy since the mid-fifties, but
they were not always harmonious. By 1963, they had
deteriorated to such an extent that World Marxist Review published an amazing appeal from jailed Egyptian
communists who complained about living conditions, food,
medical care and torture.[35] The situation improved in
July as most communists were released, and a high point
in relations was registered in March 1966 when the Soviet Union received logistic rights at Egyptian ports
and airfields. Nevertheless, General Secretary
Brezhnev's planned visit in January 1967 was cancelled,
allegedly (and perhaps legitimately) on the ground of
ill health. It was never rescheduled.
     Baathist governments came to power in Iraq in
February 1963 and in Syria in March of that year.
While they were socialistic and generally anti-Western,
both regimes persecuted domestic communists and did not
initially develop cordial ties to the Soviet Union. As
will be discussed below, the Soviet attitude toward the
Syrian Baathists was by degrees transformed in a positive direction and relations improved. A major Soviet
concern was to forge Arab unity by reconciling Egypt
and Syria, which had been rivals since the dissolution
of their United Arab Republic in September 1961.
Soviet efforts accelerated after a more leftist
Baathist faction seized control of Syria in February
1966, and an Egyptian-Syrian trade agreement was concluded that June. A mutual defense treaty on November 4
then highlighted the rapprochement. It should be
noted that the Soviet Union often seeks to improve its

relationship with Israel whenever the radical Arab camp
is divided. This acts as pressure on the Arabs to
unify their ranks, and may help explain Soviet behavior
during the period 1964-1966.[36] Once Egypt and Syria
began to overcome their differences, the Soviet Union
hardened its position toward Israel.

Soviet analysts did not view the Middle East in
terms of Soviet-American superpower competition but
rather saw a struggle between imperialist forces and
progressive, socialist Arab regimes. The former, led
by the United States, were collaborating with reactionary Arab monarchies to undermine the national
liberation movement and protect their access to oil.
An internecine struggle was thus being waged between
conservative and leftist Arab forces and the Soviets
viewed with alarm the effort of King Feisal of Saudi
Arabia (initiated in December 1965) to organize an
Islamic Pact which would use religion to unify the
conservatives. A joint Soviet-Syrian statement of
April 25, 1966 charged that the projected pact really
had nothing to do with religion, and only served oil
monopolies and reaction.[37]

France was disengaging from its role as chief
military supplier of Israel and the United States was
slowly stepping in as a replacement. An agreement on
Hawk missiles was reached in 1962 and another on Patton
tanks in February 1966, but the key event was the
February 1966 Syrian revolution which dramatically
increased Syrian tensions with both Israel and conservative Arab monarchies. On May 20, the U.S. announced
the sale of Skyhawk bombers to Israel, and arms began
flowing to Jordan and Saudi Arabia as well. Jordan
received Starfighter jets and deliveries were speeded
up in December due to fears of imminent Syrian attack. Soviet Deputy Foreign Minister Vladimir Semenov
had the special responsibility of rallying radical Arab
forces against the American-monarchist entente and he
spent much of the winter of 1966-67 shuttling between
Egypt, Iraq and Syria.

Evidence indicates that during the period prior to
April 1967, the Soviet Union was not advocating nor
preparing for an Arab assault on Israel. In fact, the
Soviets considered playing the role of peacemaker but
were obstructed by Nasser. Khrushchev's letter to
world leaders in December 1963 was pointedly sent to
Eshkol as well, and a positive Israeli response was
given to Gromyko by Israeli ambassador Tekoah. The
Israelis wanted the principle of peaceful resolution
of conflicts to be applied to the Arab-Israeli stalemate, but Nasser maintained that it could not. On
March 26, 1964, Eshkol wrote to Khrushchev objecting to
Nasser's stance, but his letter was not answered.[38]
Nasser prevented the Soviets from pursuing the matter,
although Gromyko assured Eban that the Soviet proposal

was indeed applicable to Israel.

Then came the "Tashkent" affair. In January 1966, Kosygin successfully negotiated a peace settlement between India and Pakistan, following their most recent war. Newly appointed Israeli Foreign Minister Abba Eban publicly suggested similar mediation in the Middle East and Eshkol wrote to Kosygin to solicit his participation. Kosygin raised the issue with Nasser, who rejected the proposal as it would have meant direct Egyptian talks with Israel. When Kosygin visited Paris in December, he declared that a Middle East "Tashkent" was not possible as the concerned parties had not agreed to participate. Curiously, the Israelis were prepared to accept Soviet mediation even though this would have irritated the United States. The Egyptians were unwilling and appeared to favor U.S. mediation.[39]

The Soviet Union armed Egypt but discouraged any inclination to go to war with Israel. In May 1964, Khrushchev offered more weapons to Egypt but adopted a nonbelligerent stance: "It is better to have first-class weapons, and the enemy must know that, so that we are not forced to use them."[40] Kosygin tried to tone down Nasser's hostility toward Israel when he visited Egypt in May 1966. This occurred shortly after RAKAH had advocated a Soviet-American agreement on limiting arms deliveries to the Middle East.[41] Particularly revealing is Heikal's commentary on the visit to the Soviet Union of the Commander in Chief, Field Marshal Abdul Hakim Amer: "...In November 1966, Amer was in Moscow, and Kosygin raised with him the Arab-Israeli question. It seemed that for the first time, the Soviet Union had begun to try to think seriously about possible solutions for the problem. Might there not, asked Kosygin, be some means of diminishing the level of arms in the area? This was the sort of question Eqypt was more accustomed to hear from the Americans than from the Russians."[42]

Soviet weapons deliveries to Egypt and other Arab states were related to superpower rivalry, not an intention to encourage an Arab assault on Israel. Soviet weapons balanced those supplied to Saudi Arabia, Iran and Jordan by the West and the Soviets apparently hoped that Arab arms dependence could serve as a lever to secure naval and aircraft facilities. The Soviet aim was global, but Arab perceptions of their growing military strength were surely regional and directed against Israel. The Soviet Union was willing to negotiate an agreement on the reduction of arms deliveries to the Middle East, and Israel approved of such an endeavor. However, the Soviets insisted on an accompanying agreement to turn the region into a nuclear-free zone; Israel rejected this approach as it was the only state in the region with atomic potential.

The Soviet Union sponsored the Syrian-Egyptian

defense pact of November 1966 but it was not related to
any practical military coordination against Israel.
The real target was Jordan, as was foreshadowed by the
comment in the Soviet New Times in October: "Many
observers suggest that the design is as follows: Israel
is to provoke war with Syria; on the pretext of defending Syria, Jordanian troops are to be marched in; and
they are to install a new government in Damascus."43
At the time, Jordan was giving refuge to opponents of
the Syrian government who had unsuccessfully attempted
a coup in September. By December, Syria was calling
for the overthrow of Hussein and the U.S. was rushing
new armaments to Jordan.

Also contributing to the evidence that the Syrian-
Egyptian pact was not directed against Israel are the
contents of a secret protocol. When Syrian leaders
went to Cairo at the beginning of November, the Soviet
ambassador and the Egyptians asked them to sign a
document that would be attached to the defense treaty.
It stated that Syria could not attack Israel nor
intentially provoke an Israeli attack without first
securing Egyptian approval. If Syria failed to abide
by this provision, Egypt would no longer be committed
to the defense of Syria.44 This was surely an effort
by both the Soviets and Egyptians to restrain the
Syrians. In January 1967, Nasser was again concerned
about Syrian militancy and he threatened the cancellation of the treaty if Syria did not refrain from
attacking Israel without prior consultation.45 In fact
the Syrians were creating tension with Turkey as well.
They charged that there was a Turkish plot to overthrow
their government and this led to the seizure of Turkish
property and the expulsion of Turkish nationals. Syria
also renewed its claim to Turkey's Iskenderun region.46

Meanwhile, Deputy Foreign Minister Semenov met in
Baghdad with Soviet ambassadors to Middle East states
and the main topic of discussion was how to curb
Syria.47 It is difficult to prove any causality, but
it is certainly an extremely interesting fact that
Syria temporarily moderated its position. On January
25, 1967, the Syrians attended a meeting with the
Israelis of the mixed armistice commission, which was
an arm of the United Nations Truce Supervision Organization. This was Syria's first appearance since
March 1959 and Syrian representatives then attended
two more sessions into early February. They then refused to participate further. The Syrian position
clearly hardened after a Baathist delegation returned
from the Soviet Union and Bulgaria. Elements of the
Soviet military and the KGB (the intelligence network)
may have been responsible, indicating policy differences between these organizations and the Soviet
foreign ministry.

The Radical Flank

The Sino-Soviet dispute emerged from closed communist forums and exploded with extreme public vitriol
in 1963. The Soviet open letter to the Chinese
initiated a series of sharp mutual recriminations, and
the Chinese Cultural Revolution of 1966 later accentuated the huge ideological gap between the communist
powers. Competition raged in the Third World, with the
Chinese condemning the Soviets as non-revolutionary
"revisionists" while advocating radicalization through
guerrilla warfare. The Soviet Union was clearly
worried about the Chinese challenge from the left, even
believing that the Chinese might be able to undermine
Soviet relations with Egypt. Kosygin expressed Soviet
concern during his visit to Nasser in May 1966 and even
told him that the danger from China exceeded that from
Israel.[48]

The Soviets were particularly alarmed by growing
Chinese support for the Palestinians. An Arab summit
conference in Cairo in January 1964 called for the
creation of a new Palestinian movement and the
Palestine Liberation Organization (PLO) was formed in
May. Headed by Ahmed Shukairy, it was based in Egypt
and was in competition with Yasir Arafat's al-Fatah,
which soon began operating out of Syria. In fact. the
division between the PLO and al-Fatah mirrored the
division in the Arab world between Egypt and Syria.

China backed both Palestinian movements and was
therefore stressing armed struggle at a time when the
Soviet Union was enjoying rather correct relations
with Israel. In March 1964, Arafat attended a pro-
Palestinian demonstration in Peking; a PLO delegation
headed by Shukairy arrived there in May 1965. Mao received the PLO representatives and staged a celebration of "Palestine Day" on May 15. A PLO office, with
the diplomatic status of an embassy, was opened and
Chinese military support was promised.[49] The Chinese
then trained members of the PLO and al-Fatah, and
delivered arms to both movements.

Meanwhile, the Soviet Union was acting coolly
toward the PLO as it preferred to work through governments rather than liberation movements; it also
believed the PLO to be of little practical military
value against Israel. Shukairy was consistently refused assistance, and was not even permitted to visit the
Soviet Union. However, contact was maintained due to
the insistence of Nasser, and Khrushchev met Shukairy
in Cairo in May 1964 and Kosygin did likewise in May
1966. By the spring of 1966, the Soviet attitude had
softened somewhat and a meeting of Arab communist
parties in April called the founding of the PLO "an

important achievement."50   Perhaps the more favorable
Soviet assessment of the PLO was part of a trade-off
with Egypt in order to encourage the latter to reconcile with Syria. It may additionally have been aimed
at tempering Chinese influence.

The Soviet Union did not come to terms with al-
Fatah. It was much more active militarily than the
PLO and was applying guerrilla tactics along Israel's
frontiers with Lebanon, Syria and Jordan. The Soviets
feared Israeli retaliation against Syria, al-Fatah's
home base, so they accused Arafat's men of terrorism.
They also deemed them agents of Western intelligence
and it appears (as will be discussed below) that al-
Fatah did receive some support from the British during
this period.

The Soviet Union feared that the most influential
communist party leader in the Middle East, Syria's
Khaled Bakdash, would turn toward China so his advocacy
of a pro-Soviet position in December 1965 was welcome
news. Bakdash had been living in exile for eight years
and the Soviets then tried to arrange for his return to
help foster closer Soviet-Syrian ties. With Soviet
backing, Bakdash approached some leftist member of the
Baathist government with an offer of Soviet arms and
financial aid in exchange for his right to come back
to Syria.51 Before any agreement had been consummated,
the left wing of the Baath seized power and announced
(on April 13) that Bakdash could return; he did so that
same month and communists were added to the cabinet.

The Soviets were still concerned about the Chinese
role in Syria. A Chinese delegation visited in April
1966 and Chinese officers were training the Syrian army.
They probably worked, as well, with the Hittin Brigade
of the Palestine Liberation Army, which was based in
Syria.52 Ahmed Sweidani, newly appointed chief of
staff who had served as a military attache in Peking,
was an admirer of Mao's guerrilla theories and had
close ties to al-Fatah.53 Furthermore, an internal
Baath newsletter indicated in June that the Soviet
stance toward the Palestinians was political, while
that of the Chinese was principled.54 The Sino-Soviet
context must certainly be kept in mind as we now turn
our attention to the Soviet-Syrian-Israeli triangle.

The Syrian Connection

The Soviet Union and Syrian communists reacted
negatively to the Baathists who seized control of Syria
in March 1963 as they repressed local communists and
were hostile to Egypt. An account in World Marxist
Review referred to "the right-wing Baath" and claimed
that its advent to power was an imperialist conspiracy.
It was condemned for its application of terror. A
manifesto of the Syrian communist pary referred to the

the Palestinian movement. In April, an unsuccessful
effort was made to have al-Fatah replace Arafat and, on
May 6, Damascus Radio began a two month refusal to
transmit al-Fatah broadcasts.58 The height of indignity to Arafat was registered that month when he was
imprisoned for conducting an unauthorized attack
across the Israeli border at Almagor.
    The Syrian-Israeli frontier was heating up.
Israeli ambassador Katriel Katz was summoned to the
Soviet foreign ministry, where he was read a warning
by the chief specialist on Middle Eastern affairs.
Israel was accused of concentrating troops along the
Syrian front and the statement declared: "The Soviet
Union, for its part, needless to say, cannot and will
not remain indifferent to attempts at disturbing the
peace in a region situated in immediate proximity to
the borders of the Soviet Union."59 Eshkol rejected
the charges but called for an improvement in relations
with the Soviet Union. On June 28, Chuvakhin met with
former ambassador to the Soviet Union Tekoah and said
that the Soviets would try to further the prospects
for peace on the Syrian border, but hostilities continued. On July 14, Israel carried out an air attack
on Syrian territory and dogfights ensued. A Syrian
MiG was downed on July 14 and another the next day. On
August 16, Israel displayed the wing of a Syrian MiG-17,
as well as an intact MiG-21 which had been flown to
Israel by an Iraqi pilot. He had been recruited by
Israeli intelligence and he capped his daring escapade
with a press conference. The Soviets must surely have
been rankled by these embarrassing episodes.
    Syrian hostility toward Israel was based on Arab
radicalism, ties to the Palestinians, and the desire
to establish influence over the region of "southern
Syria" which existed prior to the establishment of the
Palestine mandate in 1919. However, even more germane
during the sixties was the issue of water. Israel and
Syria had never come to an agreement on the allocation
of water resources and Syria was adamant that Israel
should not appropriate water for its needs. Israel,
on the other hand, felt entitled to a fair share of the
water resources in the absence of Syrian willingness
to come to terms so it began to implement unilaterally
an American plan which had been rejected by Syria.
Israel therefore used water from the Sea of Galilee
and Jordan River for irrigation, and Syrian attacks
were often prompted by such actions. For their part,
the Syrians obstructed the flow of water from tributar-
ies of the Jordan in order to reduce the quantity
going to Israel; this precipitated Israeli assaults
on Syrian water projects in the Banias area. An added
complication was Israel's cultivating of land in the
neutral zone established under the 1949 armistice
agreement. This land was on the Israeli side of the

armistice line, but working it was forbidden.

Syria was rocked by an attempted coup in early September as supporters of the previous regime tried to return to power. The communists helped in the successful defense of the left-wing Baathist government as many of the plotters fled to Jordan. A few days later, Chief of Staff Yitzhak Rabin implied that Israel might attack Syria in an effort to topple its rulers. He said that the trouble with Syria was its regime and that the situation reminded him of 1955-56 in Egypt.[60] Of course, Israel had attacked Egypt in the Suez war during the fall of 1956. Eshkol immediately repudiated Rabin's remarks but it is possible that Israeli threats were aimed at drawing Syrian forces to the border, thereby facilitating any internal efforts to overthrow the government.

Border hostilities erupted again. Four Israeli border policemen were killed by a mine on October 9 and the Soviets sent a note to Eshkol accusing Israel of planning an invasion to overthrow the Syrian government. Chuvakhin met twice with Eshkol and turned down the latter's invitation to visit the Syrian front. Eshkol had hoped to show that the Soviet charges were groundless. Anticipating that the Soviets were not going to play a constructive role, Eshkol charged that they were encouraging the Syrians. Israel's brief against Syria was brought to the UN Security Council and the Knesset passed a resolution that called for awaiting UN action before resorting to "other methods."[61] No UN action was forthcoming so Israel lengthened its period of required military service. On November 9, the Soviets presented a note to ambassador Katz which denied Syrian support for al-Fatah. It claimed that this organization was aided in its provocations by Western intelligence services and oil companies.[62] The Soviet note acknowledged attacks on Israel from Syrian territory, and one may infer that the Israelis had some justification in retaliating. At the same time, the Syrians were made to appear blameless. Perhaps this was an oblique Soviet attempt to defuse the situation. On November 13, Israeli forces attacked Samu in northern Jordan. Al-Fatah units had often passed through Jordan in order to gain access to the Israeli border; therefore, the Israeli blow was somewhat logical. However, Israel intentionally avoided an attack on Syria, al-Fatah's home base, so its move may also have been a discrete signal to the Soviets to restrain the Syrians. Many Israelis accused Eshkol of timidity, leading him to deny any fear of challenging the Syrians. He declared that Israel would act, if necessary.[63]

The Israeli-Syrian confrontation in late 1966 and early 1967 took place at the same time as an acrimonious dispute between Syria and the British-owned Iraq Petrolleum Company. The IPC pipeline from Iraq had a Mediterranean terminal at Banias, Syria and it also passed through Syrian territory to another terminal at Tripoli, Lebanon. Syria insisted on higher transit fees and IPC refused to meet the Syrian demand. Soviet charges regarding Western intelligence services and oil companies were not as far-fetched as they may at first appear, and clandestine British undermining of the Syrian government may actually have been attempted. If the British helped finance al-Fatah, one motivation must surely have been to provoke Israel into attacking Syria. Israel was certainly not in cahoots with either the British or IPC but its avowed hostility toward the Syrian government, at least in Soviet eyes, placed it on the side of "imperialism" against the forces of "national liberation" and "socialism."

Pieces of the International Puzzle

The issues of Vietnam, a resurgent West Germany, the Mediterranean power balance, and Israeli activities in the Third World all had an impact on Soviet-Israeli relations. The U.S. sharply escalated its military involvement in Vietnam in 1965 and the Soviets viewed this as part of a new aggressive strategy that was also applied in the Dominican Republic and other Third World locations. One Soviet analyst queried: "Why was the year 1965 chosen by the leaders of the imperialist world for another attempt to launch an offensive which has now embraced almost the whole world, including the 'peripheral areas'?" He provided his own response, alleging that the "imperialists" wanted to destroy the world socialist system (communist bloc) by first attacking weaker "peripheral areas."[64] Another Soviet observer directly related Vietnam to the Middle East, maintaining that the U.S. was applying a strategy of local wars against national liberation movements, a strategy developed during the early sixties.[65]

Vietnam was portrayed as the prime target and it was claimed that the "imperialists" fomented trouble in the Middle East as a distraction. Also, the U.S. was accused by the Israeli communists of raising the issue of Soviet anti-Semitism as a smokescreen for its own activities in Vietnam.[66] The Soviet Union was particularly concerned about possible Israeli participation in the Vietnam war. At his February 1966 Honolulu conference with South Vietnamese Premier Nguyen Cao Ky, Johnson indicated that he wanted Israel to provide military advisers, and Chief of Staff Rabin journeyed to Thailand, the Philippines and South Korea that April. He did not go to Vietnam but he managed to visit the

chief regional allies of the United States, who were all
contributing to the war effort. In July, former Chief of
Staff Moshe Dayan appeared in Vietnam, ostensibly to
cover the war as a journalist. In fact, Israel did not
come to the assistance of the U.S. and Foreign Minister
Eban announced in April 1966 that Israel would not
establish diplomatic relations with South Vietnam. In
1967, an American request to supply token forces was
rejected.67

In February 1966, the Soviet embassy asked Israel
to denounce American policy in Vietnam. Israel refused
to do so and another setback to Soviet interests took
place in the spring, following the American decision to
sell Skyhawks to Israel. Johnson began a concerted
campaign to rally Jewish support for the war effort,
arguing that Jews were indebted to him because of his
backing of Israel. In 1967, allegedly with secret
government backing, Meir Kahane (later the head of the
Jewish Defense League) and his colleagues published a
book explaining why Jews should champion the American
cause in Vietnam.68 Over the ensuing years, the role
of American Jews was to be an important component of the
Soviet-Israeli relationship, with the Soviet Union
making entreaties to Israel in order to effect changes
in American policy. Perhaps the Soviets already had
such a tactic in mind in February 1966, as Israeli
denunciation of the U.S. role in Vietnam would have
influenced some American Jews to speak out against the
war.

As the 1967 Arab-Israeli war approached, Vietnam
continued to be a major bone of contention. In late
May, Kosygin told British Foreign Secretary George Brown
that the Soviet Union would not participate in Big Four
Talks to resolve the Middle East crisis due to American
involvement in Vietnam.69

Based upon Jewish suffering at the hands of the
Nazis, the Soviet Union called upon Israel to act as a
moral force opposed to West German diplomatic rehabilitation. In particular, it expected Israel to denounce
West German rearmament and the plan to station American
nuclear weapons on German soil. Most Israelis had
similar anti-German sentiments, but their government had
decided in the early fifties that reconciliation with
West Germany was in the national interest. German willingness to pay extensive reparations to Israel and to
individual Jews could not be turned down by a country in
such serious financial straits. Furthermore, it was
felt that nothing could help the dead; it was the
survivors who needed assistance. Gradually, West
Germany began to aid Israel militarily as well. This
was encouraged by the United States, which avoided
direct military relations with Israel until 1962.

To the Soviet Union, Israel was identifying itself
with Western interests in a divided Europe. How could

Israel turn toward West Germany, when it was the Red
Army that rescued so many Jews from the Nazis in the
latter stages of the Second World War? The Soviets
expressed righteous outrage at Israeli behavior but, by
1970, they were effecting their own rapprochement with
the West Germans.

Diplomatic relations between Israel and West
Germany were established on May 12, 1965 and former
Chancellor Konrad Adenauer visited Israel for nine days
in May 1966. In conjunction with these developments,
Israel also made some significant gestures to appease
the Soviets on the German issue. It recognized Poland's
retention of the Oder-Neisse provinces, which had been
detached from Germany at the end of the Second World
War. They were claimed by West Germany (in the hope of
German reunification), although they actually bordered
East Germany. This move was in accord with Soviet
interests but Israel had another motivation as well:
the precedent of maintaining existing borders. Israel
wanted this principle applied to its own 1949 armistice
lines.

Israel also took the unusual step of scheduling a
meeting in Warsaw of its diplomats stationed in Eastern
Europe. Foreign Minister Abba Eban attended the May
1966 gathering (which served as a balance to Adenauer's
visit) of diplomats from the embassies in the Soviet
Union and Poland, and legations in other states. There
was no Israeli diplomatic representation in East Germany.
Eban met twice with Polish Foreign Minister Adam Rapacki
and Israel expected a positive Soviet reaction, which
was not forthcoming. It appears that the Soviet Union
viewed the affair as part of a Polish effort to exercise
greater policy independence.70

The Soviet Union viewed the Mediterranean power
balance as integrally related to Western actions in
Israel and Syria. In the early sixties, perhaps as a
reaction to their naval weakness displayed during the
Cuban missile crisis, the Soviets began to increase
their naval presence and to seek port facilities. However they claimed that this was a defensive measure
based on the nuclear threat posed by American Polaris
submarines. The Soviet buildup was accelerated in
January 1967 and yet Brezhnev called for the removal
of the U.S. Sixth Fleet on the ground that it threatened the independence of coastal states.71 At the same
time, the Soviet Union was opposing U.S. plans to
integrate NATO navies in the Eastern Mediterranean
under American command.

Soviet analyses portrayed the Sixth Fleet as an
arm of U.S. policy aimed at buttressing Israel and
undermining Syria, but there were broader regional
implications. The seizure of power by the Greek military in April 1967 was seen as part of an American
offensive and it was claimed that the new Greek

government would subvert the independence of Cyprus and force its amalgamation with Greece. It is in this context of Soviet apprehension that one must view the visit to Bulgaria of Leonid Brezhnev. On May 12, 1967, he signed a friendship treaty with the Bulgarians, even though the previous twenty-year treaty was not due to expire until March 1968.

Another arena of Soviet-Israeli contention was the Third World. The Soviets were trying to spread their influence and were assisted by Tito, Castro and Nasser in radicalizing the non-aligned movement and steering it in a more pro-Soviet direction. Israel served as a counter to Soviet interests as, in collaboration with Western states, it developed ties to the Third World. Aid was provided (often subsidized secretly by the U. S.); technical knowledge dispensed; connections to trade unions developed, and diplomatic contacts catered. Israel sought support at the United Nations, sympathy toward its positions on Arab-Israeli issues; sources of raw materials and markets for its manufactured goods, and normalization of its international relations through participation in the Asian athletic games and similar activities. This policy was generally successful and cordial ties were established with Burma, Ethiopia, Kenya and even Marxist Ghana. Israel, as a small Asian country, had much better entree than the distrusted former colonial powers and the superpower United States, and its interests usually coincided with those of the West. It had its own goals and was clearly not a direct agent, but the Soviets nevertheless depicted Israel as a Western Trojan horse.

DESCENT INTO THE MAELSTROM

Syrian-Israeli border tension continued as the spring of 1967 began, but there were no signs that a full-scale war was imminent. Israeli troops may have been mobilized in March; however, they were apparently called back after Israel downed six MiGs in an air battle with the Syrians on April 7.[72] The Soviets acted cautiously under the circumstances, not formally protesting the April 7 Israeli actions until April 21. Deputy Foreign Minister Iacov Malik summoned ambassador Katz to register Soviet disapproval, pointing out the region's proximity to Soviet borders. He also asserted that Israel was permitting itself to be used as "a puppet of foreign enemy forces," which was against its own interests.[73] It should be noted that these charges were presented the same day as the Greek coup, as this event may have triggered increased Soviet concern about the Syrian front as a component of the Eastern Mediterranean power balance.

The border heated up, leading Eshkol to warn on

April 30 that Israel would attack Syria if its settlements were shelled. On May 11, he said that Israel
would possibly have to act against Syria more compre-
hensively than on April 7. On May 14, Dayan asked
Syria to clamp down on the Palestinians, and Rabin implied that the Syrian government should be overthrown.[74]
On May 7, Syria had accused Jordan and Syrian exiles of
planning to topple its government, and there were
serious disturbances after an anti-religious article
appeared in an army publication.

Meanwhile, Soviet-Israeli contacts proceeded
normally. Gideon Rafael, newly appointed Israeli UN
delegate, traveled to Moscow in late April to meet with
Deputy Foreign Minister Semenov. He was told that oil
companies were trying to undermine the Syrian government, and that Israel was an unwitting accomplice.
Rafael's meeting took place less than a week after Malik
had spoken with Katz and it is interesting to note how
the Soviets refrained from blaming Israel directly for
its role against Syria. Rafael also discussed the
emigration issue with Soviet officials, and was informed that two thousand or more Jews would possibly be
permitted to leave on the basis of family reunification.
On the other hand, the Soviets claimed that they did
not want to endanger too many Jews by permitting them
to emigrate to the militarily dangerous Middle East.[75]
Rafael then went to New York, where he met with Soviet
UN delegate Nikolai Fedorenko on May 9. However,
Fedorenko failed to attend Israeli independence day
celebrations on May 12. On May 15, Minister of Labor
Yigal Allon arrived in the Soviet Union to attend a
conference of the International Social Insurance Federation. He had more than pensions on his mind as he also
met with Semenov at an Israeli independence day reception.[76] However, Allon's trip had been arranged earlier
and was unrelated to the diplomacy which led to war.

The Soviet Union was concerned about the internal
security situation in Syria and also feared an Israeli
strike against that state.[77] Israel was indeed contemplating such action, more as a consequence of water
needs than of al-Fatah incursions. In order to lesson
the pressure on Syria, the Soviet Union encouraged Egypt
to direct Israeli military attention southward. This
was accomplished, in part, by feeding the Egyptians
false information about alleged Israeli troop mobiliza-
tions along the Syrian frontier. This took place on
May 12 and Nasser moved into action. He did not want
a repetition of the Arab criticism directed at him for
failing to respond to Israel's earlier attack on Samu.
Egyptian troops entered the Sinai (May 14) and the
United Nations Emergency Force was asked to leave all
areas except Sharm el-Sheikh and the Gaza Strip (May 16).
Then Nasser demanded a complete UNEF departure (May 18)
and it was soon effected. He also announced (May 22) a

blockade of Israeli shipping in the Straits of Tiran,
the vital sea route controlling access to Israel's
only southern port, Eilat. That same day, Eshkol declared that the Soviet Union was responsible for restraining both Egypt and Syria.

To what degree should the Soviet Union be held
accountable for Egypt's actions? The Soviets leaked
accounts indicating that the decisions regarding UNEF
and Tiran were made by Egypt, but they surely deserve
some censure for the removal of UNEF.[78] False charges
against the Israelis helped precipitate Egypt's move,
and Chuvakhin did nothing to calm the situation when
he met with Eban on May 19. Eban called upon the
Soviet Union to encourage Egypt to withdraw from the
Sinai; Israel would then demobilize along the Egyptian
frontier. Chuvakhin turned down this offer and Eban
concluded that the Soviets did not want to reduce
tensions. Furthermore, George Brown was unable to
secure any commitment from the Soviets regarding a
proposed return of UNEF forces.[79]

Tiran was another matter altogether. There was
the possibility of an American effort to break the
blockade and the Soviet Union was uncomfortable with
the precedent of closing straits, considering its own
dependence on the Bosphorus and Dardanelles. A prominent Israeli specialist on intelligence affairs has
concluded that the Soviet Union was not responsible
for the Tiran closure. He points out that in their
press releases, notes to Israel, and statements to
Israeli officials, the Soviets never tried to justify
Egypt's action. He also claims that Gromyko was
furious at Soviet ambassador to Egypt Dmitrii
Pozhidaev for not knowing about Nasser's plan regarding Tiran.[80] It is certainly true that moves were
initiated at that time to replace Pozhidaev.

On May 23, a day after the Tiran blockade was announced, the Soviet Union issued a mixed warning to
Israel. It asserted that it would take "resolute
counteractions" if there was aggression against Arab
states, and it again pointed out the proximity of the
region to the Soviet Union. However, it did not
directly refer to Tiran and placed the blame for tensions on the "imperialists," oil companies and extremist elements in Israel. The Israeli people were not
held responsible and the statement asserted that "the
peoples have no interest in kindling a military conflict in the Middle East."[81] Under the circumstances,
it would appear that the Soviet Union was trying to
display its solidarity with the Arabs, but defuse a
potential military conflict.

The Soviet exercise in brinksmanship included the
Egyptian request for UNEF's withdrawal, but events
then got out of hand. U Thant and the UN acted more
quickly than anticipated, and Egypt then took the

provocative step of announcing a blockade of Tiran. As
will be explained below, the Soviet Union did not expect a war and did not plan to participate in one. In
fact, Israeli diplomats in Moscow at the time reached
the same conclusion, contending that the Soviet Union
wanted to protect its strategic interest in Syria but
did not desire war. The Soviets saw the Israeli attack
on Samu, Jordan in November 1966 as an ominous signal
for it reminded them of an assault on Kalkilia, Jordan
prior to Israel's participation in the 1956 Suez War.[82]
    As the crisis developed, it expanded beyond the
confines of regional instability and more deeply involved the superpowers.   Lyndon Johnson urged moderation in his messages to Nasser on May 26 and Eshkol on
May 28, as he asked each not to strike first. During
the night of May 26-27, Nasser was awakened to receive
a note from Kosygin advocating restraint and Eshkol too
was pulled from bed by an insistent Chuvakhin. The
Soviet ambassador delivered a letter from Kosygin which
warned against going to war. It was mild in tone,
calling for a peaceful solution, but Chuvakhin irritated Eshkol by pressing for an Israeli commitment not to
fire first. The Israeli prime minister refused to
answer definitively and asserted that Egypt's actions
were tantamount to having already fired first. Eshkol
accused Chuvakhin of not trying to improve Soviet-
Israeli relations, and he found his demeanor too
hostile. Eshkol may even have indicated a preference
for having Chuvakhin replaced. Chuvakhin was singularly unsuccessful in easing tensions, and the Soviet
Union failed to act on Eshkol's offer to go to Moscow
for further discussions.[83]
    Eshkol didn't answer Kosygin's letter until June 1,
when he emphasized the Tiran blockade as the major
impediment to peace. The next day, Gromyko delivered
the Soviet response to Katz: the Soviet Union hoped
that war could be avoided but Israel "will have to pay
the consequences in full" if it initiates conflict.
Israel was asked not to break the blockade by force.
Israel was thus faced with an untenable situation. It
had mobilized its reserves to counter Egypt's actions
and no peaceful resolution was in sight. Its economy
was suffering as a result of the reserve call-up and
the United States had not moved decisively to challenge
the Egyptian blockade. Israel had already informed
Johnson that Jordan and Lebanon would not be attacked
should it take offensive action.[84] It now prepared for
war with Egypt. A grand coalition was created, including Ben Gurion proteges Moshe Dayan and Shimon Peres
as well as opposition leader Menachem Begin. Begin
even wanted his arch-enemy Ben Gurion to return as
prime minister in this emergency situation, but Ben
Gurion refused and Eshkol remained in office. Israel
was buoyed by world public opinion, which was

generally sympathetic due to the perception that its existence was being threatened. Chief of military intelligence Meir Amit was sent to Washington to seek American approval for a first strike. Eban had already reported U.S. encouragement, but members of the Cabinet remained skeptical. Amit confirmed that a green light had been received.[85]

Egypt began to moderate its stance but it was too late. Nasser offered to send Vice-President Zakaria Mohieddin to the U.S. and he extended an invitation to Hubert Humphrey in return. He also permitted non-Israeli ships to pass through Tiran on their way to Eilat, provided that they did not bear strategic cargo. However, the die had been cast. Egypt's steps against Israel had galvanized Arab opinion, and turning back from the brink would have been extremely difficult. Israel was also preparing countermeasures.

The Soviet Union seemed to have been caught by surprise. Brezhnev and Kosygin inspected the northern fleet from May 31 through June 2 and chief of state Podgornyi was away on a diplomatic mission in Afghanistan. Chuvakhin allegedly informed Moscow two days before hostilities broke out that war would not take place for at least fifteen days.[86]

Conflict and Consequences

The war began on June 5. Chuvakhin met with former Israeli Ambassador to the Soviet Union Tekoah and gave him a note from Kosygin to Eshkol. It asked Israel to stop fighting and to leave conquered territories. An Eshkol message to Kosygin was given to Chuvakhin. It charged Egypt with aggression and requested Soviet assistance in achieving a peaceful resolution of the conflict.[87] The next day, Kosygin used the hot line for the first time, calling Johnson to demand a cease-fire and American pressure on Israel for a withdrawal. It was apparent that the Soviet Union considered the U.S. responsible for Israel's actions. Kosygin threatened to come to the assistance of Egypt if his terms were not met. Johnson agreed only to seek a cease-fire and he moved units of the Sixth Fleet closer to Israel.[88] About midnight, the UN Security Council voted for a cease-fire in place. The Soviet Union voted affirmatively.

On June 7, the Soviet Union threatened to sever diplomatic relations if Israel failed to comply with the Security Council's demand for a cease-fire. Its statement warned that the U.S.S.R. "will consider and implement other necessary measures" as well.[89] The next day, Egypt and Jordan agreed to the cease-fire and Israel had to consider a continuation of the war against Syria. On June 9, Israel advanced into Syria and the latter accepted the cease-fire. Israel fought on for one more day and hostilities ended on June 10.

Israel took the Soviet military factor into account, but then minimized it. The government consensus was in accord with the views of Yigal Allon, who discounted intervention on the grounds that there was Soviet unwillingness to risk confrontation with the U.S., a history of non-intervention, a weakness in combating Israel in its own region, and difficulty in intervening in an anticipated short conflict.[90] On the minority side of the issue was Defense Minister Dayan, who indicated prior to the war that the Soviet Union would not permit Israel to advance as far as the Suez Canal. It was too strategic in terms of aiding North Vietnam and republican forces in Yemen. He also believed that Nasser would not agree to a cease-fire if Israeli troops seized the east bank of the Canal, and that the Canal could not serve as an effective front line for Israeli occupation forces. Consequently, Dayan advised against an advance to Suez but military commanders carried it out nonetheless. Dayan's fears about Soviet intervention and Egyptian intransigency proved unfounded. Dayan also anticipated Soviet intervention if Israel took hold of Syrian territory. He advocated only the capture of some Syrian artillery positions, but the Israeli government decided to advance more deeply into Syria after receiving a green light from the United States. The American warning not to take Damascus was really unnecessary as Israel had no plan to do so.[91] As Israeli troops moved into the Golan Heights, the Syrians unexpectedly abandoned the town of Qeneitra and more territory was occupied than originally anticipated. Again, the Soviet Union failed to act.

The Soviet Union had no intention of intervening in the war unless the United States did so. It used the hot line to seek collaboration with the U.S. on a cease-fire and it did not resupply Arab armies which were on their way to calamitous defeat. Egypt tried to draw the Soviet Union into the war by falsely claiming that U.S. aircraft were fighting on the Israeli side, but the Soviets did not bite.[92] The issue that concerned the Soviets most was the protection of the Syrian government. On June 10, in a move aimed at saving the Syrian regime, Kosygin used the hot line for a second time. He threatened "necessary actions, including military" if Israel did not agree to a cease-fire. Fedorenko had already declared at the United Nations that relations with Israel would be broken if it continued to fight on the Syrian front; Israel then seized the town of Qeneitra and the Soviets lived up to their word.[93] All East European states except Rumania followed suit.

The Soviet embassy in Israel requested extra police protection on June 9 and the break in diplomatic relations was announced the following day, just hours before the war ended. Chuvakhin presented a note to Eban, and First Deputy Prime Minister Vassilii Kuznetsov gave the same message to ambassador Katz in Moscow. In addition to severing relations, the Soviets threatened "sanctions" if Israel did not stop its military action against Syria.[94]

The Soviet Union had boxed itself into a corner from which it was hard to back out gracefully. It lent no more than verbal support to the Arab cause and felt that it had to compensate with bellicose statements. Extreme language is often a substitute for effective Soviet action, and the public threats to break relations with Israel must be viewed in this context. The Soviets then had to follow through on these threats, as they had already been stated publicly. Egypt, Syria and many other Arab States has severed relations with the United States so the Soviet Union had to act in equivalent fashion.

Another factor for the Soviets to consider was the strong reaction among East European governments. Excluding Albania, a summit conference was held with the Soviet Union while the war was in progress and there was strong criticism of Moscow for not doing more to aid the Arabs. Tito, a close friend of Nasser, was particularly distressed as he accused the Soviets of selling out the interests of Third World leaders. Other participants agreed that the Soviets should have provided air support for Egypt (the Israeli advance into Syria had not yet started) and should not have counted on the United States to restrain Israel.[95] The final summit communique of June 9, which Rumania refused to sign, was strongly pro-Arab but it did not call for the breaking of relations with Israel. However, the Soviet Union may have felt that such action was advisable to soothe many of its communist allies, especially after Israel moved into Syrian territory.

The announcement of the break was accompanied by demonstrations outside the Israeli embassy in Moscow and anti-Israeli rallies at factories in the Soviet capital.[96] On June 11, Finland agreed to represent Soviet diplomatic interests in Israel; on June 12, the Netherlands ageed to do likewise for Israel in the U.S.S.R.. On June 15, a Soviet vessel arrived at Haifa to evacuate Soviet diplomats and their families. Ironically, this was the first Soviet passenger ship to ever dock at an Israeli port. On June 18, Chuvakhin departed from Israel, his diplomatic career in shambles.

Reflections

The Soviet Union claimed victory in the war as the governments of Egypt and Syria were not overthrown.

Brezhnev, in a speech to military academy graduates,
said that the "imperialists" had been unsuccessful in
undermining the "progressive" regimes, which were taking the "non-capitalist path."[97] It could also be
argued that the Arab states became more unified against
the West, an outcome which the Soviets were trying to
achieve through encouragement of Egypt's Sinai mobilization. Arab oil-producing states implemented an oil
embargo against the supporters of Israel, and a conservative Islamic grouping headed by Saudi Arabia did not
gather strength as the Arabs banded together against
Israel. In fact, moderate Arab states were pleased to
see the development of a war with Israel as it deflected Nasser and other Arab radicals from subverting
their governments.[98]

On the other side of the ledger, the Soviet
Union was put on the defensive in the Arab world due
to its lack of support, and suspicion grew that peaceful coexistence with the United States had inhibited
Soviet behavior in the Middle East. Also, Arab clients
using Soviet weapons had been defeated by a Western-
armed Israel, and the Soviets experienced some differences with their allies. Nicolae Ceausescu refused to
sign the statement of communsit leaders and Rumania
would not sever its diplomatic relations with Israel
despite Soviet pressure. Cuba too maintained its ties.
As will be discussed later in regard to Czechoslovakia
and Poland, use of the Israel issue became an important
tactic in internal communist politics.

There are conflicting interpretations of Soviet
motivations in regard to the war. Perhaps the Soviets
wanted to take advantage of U.S. involvement in Vietnam
by attempting to increase their influence in the Middle
East. According to one account, Brezhnev told Polish
and East German communist leaders Gomulka and Ulbricht
in April that he was trying to weaken the American
position in the Middle East and would soon be able to
deal a decisive blow.[99] After all, Chuvakhin was
reporting that Israel was not in the mood to fight and,
if it did, it could not be expected to do well.[100]
While the Soviets did prod the Egyptians into action,
it is unlikely that the aim was to bring about an
Israeli victory that would unify the Arabs against the
United States. Also improbable is the theory that the
Soviets desired war in order to make Egypt more
militarily dependent; the Soviet Union could then more
easily acquire bases there.[101] This may have been an
outcome of the war, but it is hard to believe the
Soviets would have favored an Egyptian defeat in order
to secure this advantage. From the opposite perspective, Soviet encouragement of Egypt's mobilization in
the Sinai should not be viewed as a step to prevent
war. According to this scenario, the Soviets expected
an Israeli attack on Syria but the available evidence

indicates that Israeli troops were not massing on the
Syrian border and some Soviet officials were aware of
this.[102]

The Soviets believed that Israel's leadership and
economy were weak so they assumed considerable risk and
created a crisis.[103] However, they expected to pressure Israel militarily and diplomatically, not precipitate a full-scale war. In fact, they had acted similarly after border incidents between Syria and Israel from
January 9 through February 4, 1960. They told Egypt
that Israel was concentrating forces on the Syrian
front and Egypt mobilized some troops into the Sinai.
In this case, Egypt demobilized two weeks later and
tensions died down.[104] In 1967, the Soviets were probably surprised by Israel's preemptive strike as they
expected the U.S. to restrain Israel rather than
encourage her. After all, didn't the U.S. apply strong
pressure in 1956, which turned an apparent Israeli
military victory into nought? Also, Israel did not
seem to be seriously threatened by the Egyptian troops
in the Sinai. Rather interesting are the comments of
former general Mati Peled and former air force commander
Ezer Weizman, who argue that Israel was not endangered
(it enjoyed a decisive manpower advantage on the Sinai
front) but acted to counter a Soviet effort to expand
influence at the expense of the United States.[105]
Israel attacked, not out of fear, but because it perceived Egyptian weakness at a time when crack units of
the Egyptian army were in Yemen.

The Soviet system was beset with internal divisions
and unreliable reporting from the field. Chuvakhin
failed to anticipate Israel's military action and
Pozhidaev in Egypt could not restrain the Egyptians in
regard to the Tiran blockade. When war broke out,
Pozhidaev made claims that the Arabs had achieved great
victories.[106] After he left Israel, Chuvakhin did not
receive any significant diplomatic assignment and the
removal of Pozhidaev was announced even before the war
began. On May 29, Sergei Vinogradov (former Ambassador
to France) was named to replace Pozhidaev, but Pozhidaev
remained on duty until August 28. Vinogradov finally
assumed his position in Egypt on September 17.

The details of Soviet infighting remain somewhat
obscure, even though Abraham Ben Tsur has written an
entire book on behind-the-scenes machinations related
to Syria.[107] Former Israeli diplomat (and current
president) Chaim Herzog maintains that the KGB and
military were supporting a more aggressive strategy
than the foreign ministry and that they even sought
assistance from Syrian Baathists in influencing the
Soviet hierarchy. According to this version, Chuvakhin
was aligned with the crisis fomenters as he was reporting Israeli plans to attack Syria and he never informed
Moscow that Eshkol had earlier asked him to visit the

Syrian front.108 Other than informed conjecture, there
is some hard evidence regarding personnel changes which
must have had an impact on policy toward the Middle East.
Unfortunately, the nature of that impact remains con-
cealed in the Kremlin. In April, Minister of Defense
Rodion Malinovskii died and was succeeded by Andrei
Grechko, the man who in 1973 agreed to provide the
advanced weaponry necessary for the Egyptian war effort
against Israel. The same month, Ambassador to Japan
Vladimir Vinogradov (who later replaced Sergei Vinogradov in Cairo) was appointed a deputy to Foreign Minister
Gromyko. On May 19, Iurii Andropov supplanted Vladimir
Semichastnyi as KGB chief. Could it be that Semichast-
nyi was held responsible for the fake reports that
Israel would attack Syria on May 17?

Not to be overlooked in the Middle East cauldron
is the crucial British ingredient. The confrontation
between IPC and the Syrians (and the related role of
al-Fatah) have already been discussed, but the conflict
in the Yemens is also vital. Britain controlled Aden
(South Yemen), which commanded the sea route from the
Suez Canal to the Indian Ocean, but it was faced with a
leftist insurgency aimed at securing independence. At
the same time, a civil war was raging in Yemen between
royalist forces aligned with Saudi Arabia and republic-
ans assisted by Egypt. Egypt committed 35,000 of its
best troops to the battle and Britain feared that a
republican victory would bolster the radical Arab camp
and further threaten its position in Aden. The Soviet
perspective was indeed similar. New Times maintained
that Britain wanted to preserve "medievalism" in Yemen
so that its revolution would not spread elsewhere in
the Arabian peninsula and it charged: "The main
objective of the intrigues woven by the imperialists
and the local reactionary forces in this region is the
republican Yemen."109 Britain wanted Egyptian troops to
be withdrawn from Yemen, and it may have favored increased tension between Israel and its neighbors so that
Egypt would be encouraged to act accordingly. British
policy on the Syrian front may therefore have been part
of a broader Middle Eastern strategy. In any case,
Egypt went to war against Israel in the absence of its
troops in Yemen and this sapped its combat ability. At
the Khartoum summit in August, an Egyptian-Saudi deal
led to the withdrawal of the troops and Britain then
granted independence to Aden on November 30.

The break between the Soviet Union and Israel is a
legal separation, but not a divorce. Alienation of
affections was caused by Soviet wooing of Syria, which
became a rather temperamental mistress. Israel was
shunted aside, but extensive contacts with the Jewish
state have been maintained. It is to this secret relationship since June 1967 that we now turn our attention.

4
Out in the Cold

The period from June 1967 to December 1969 was one
of military and political stalemate. Israel's power in
the area was preponderant and Arab states had almost no
ability to alter the unfavorable status quo. The United
States and Soviet Union became active in regional diplomacy but the clear advantage belonged to the Americans,
who were buoyed by the victory secured by Israel with
their weapons. Egypt and Syria had gone down to defeat
with their Soviet arsenals so the Soviet Union had to
adopt a strategy based on a recognition of the weakness
of her clients. Israel did not withdraw from any occupied territory, but the Soviets could do little to
alter the situation on behalf of the Arabs. A freeze
therefore set in, despite Soviet efforts to generate
some thawing effect.

Among the questions that need to be considered are:
Why did the Soviet Union emphasize Israel's right to exist,
while at the same time provide extensive military as-
istance to Egypt and Syria? Why was there a more favorable Soviet attitude toward the PLO? Why did the
Soviet Union have a greater interest in a political
solution than either the United States or Israel? Why
did Israel escalate its campaign for Soviet Jewry, and
why did the Soviet Union accelerate the pace of emigration? The search for appropriate answers must begin
with the aftermath of the Six-Day War, a time when
Israeli euphoria stood in stark contrast to Soviet
solemnity.

The Hegemony of Victory

The break in diplomatic relations had been implemented unilaterally from the Soviet side, but Israel
reacted calmly and moderately. It expressed regret
and hoped that the Soviet attitude would change in the
future.[1] Perhaps the desire to protect Soviet Jews
mitigated against any anti-Soviet polemics on this
issue (although the Soviets were roundly criticized for

precipitating the war), but the magnanimity of the
triumphant was probably the most significant factor.
For the Soviets, the catastrophic loss by their Arab
clients represented a monumental defeat so they expressed the magnified outrage of the vanquished by comparing
Israel's policies to those of the Nazis, condemning the
methods used in the occupied territories, and orchestrating a new anti-Zionist campaign in the Soviet Union.
Particularly rankling was Israel's incorporation into
its army of captured Soviet tanks and weapons. Later,
some weapons were even sold to communist-ruled Rumania.[2]

The Israeli victory enhanced American power in the
region at the expense of Soviet power and also made
Israel more attractive as an American strategic asset
against the Soviet Union. Israeli military strength
could help balance the increased Soviet naval presence
in the Eastern Mediterranean, and Israeli intelligence
could serve as a vital source of information on Soviet
activities. Israel was prepared to permit the examination of captured Soviet weapons and to advise the U.S.
on modifications needed for battle-tested American
weapons. Both services could surely be of great value
when applied to the American combat role in Vietnam.[3]
Additionally, Israeli occupation of the east bank of
the Suez Canal could ensure its continued closure. It
had become obstructed during the war by scuttled and
trapped vessels and Israel was not anxious to have it
reopened as this would enhance Soviet naval power.[4]
The Canal was a major trade route for Soviet vessels
sailing from Black Sea ports to Asian and African
states, and it could be transited by ships in the
Mediterranean squadron en route to the Indian Ocean.
It also served as the major route for arms deliveries
to North Vietnam. The Soviets obviously sought its reopening, but American and Israeli interests coincided
in keeping it closed. It therefore represented an
important bargaining chip for the Israelis, and a sore
point for the Soviets.

To overcome their weak position, the Soviets adopted a strategy of fortifying Egypt and Syria militarily,
cautioning against a renewal of combat due to Israel's
acknowledged predominance, and using enhanced Arab
strength as a lever to effect a favorable political
resolution of the Arab-Israeli conflict. Chief of state
Podgornyi rushed to Egypt on June 20, 1967 to assure it
of extensive Soviet rearmament. The Soviet Union had
to rebuild its prestige after failing to resupply Egypt
during the war, or coming to its assistance. However,
it certainly didn't want Egypt to renew hostilities as
Arab forces were militarily inferior and Israel could
possibly cross the Canal or advance toward Damascus;
the Soviets would then have to consider their own intervention to prevent another Arab defeat.[5] Egypt, recognizing its enfeebled condition, tried to internation-

alize the situation by entering into a defense pact
with the Soviet Union, but its request was rejected.[6]
    The Soviet Union constantly urged the Arabs to ac-
comodate themselves to Israel's military preeminence
and stressed the theme of Israel's right to exist. On
June 19, little more than a week after the war, Prime
Minister Kosygin assured the General Assembly of Soviet
recognition of Israel's existence. The Soviets expressed the same position to the Egyptians, Syrians and
Jordanians and accused the Arabs of maintaining an "in-
flexible policy."[7] Paradoxically, championing of
Israel's right to exist coincided with the anti-Zionist
campaign and the absence of Soviet-Israeli diplomatic
relations.
    The Soviets did not, however, advocate direct
negotiations with Israel, pointing out that agreements
could be reached under UN auspices. This procedure
would enhance the Soviet role and negate Israel's negotiating advantage over the Arabs while territories were
being occupied. The Soviets also called for Israeli
evacuation of the territories and made this a precondition for any regional arms limitation agreement. This
stance helped reestablish Soviet credibility in the Arab
world after the failure to supply arms during the war.
    Soviet pragmatism was evident in July 1967 when
Brezhnev commented to the leaders of Algeria and Iraq:
"You feel yourselves unable to recognize Israel, even
indirectly, but we all want to see the Israeli forces
withdraw. Is there not possibly a contradiction here?"
Brezhnev then compared the situation to Brest-Litovsk
in 1918, when Lenin agreed to the loss of extensive
territory in return for peace with Germany. This anal-
ogy was repeated often to Nasser, who came to understand
the Soviet emphasis on long-term evaluation at the expense of immediacy. Compromising with Israel on a
territorial settlement would be a temporary measure.
After all, Lenin did recover the ceded lands once
Germany was defeated less than a year later.[8] Soviet
advocacy of territorial concessions did not apply to
the land occupied by Israel in the Six-Day War, as
Israel was expected to withdraw from all occupied territories as part of a peace settlement. Significantly,
however, the Arabs were being asked to accept (for the
time being) the 1949 armistice lines as Israel's
legitimate borders and to forego their intention to
eliminate Israel and force it to return to the 1947
partition boundaries. Through the Brest-Litovsk anal-
ogy, the Soviets appeared to be signaling their eventual support for an Arab effort to truncate further the
Zionist state, although they may have overstated their
position to appease Arab militants. For the short term,
Israel's military power and atomic potential inspired
trepidation and cautious tactics.[9]
    On the diplomatic front, the Soviets actively

sought a political solution despite strong Arab rhetoric
(especially at the Khartoum summit in August 1967)
against one. The Middle East was dealt with only per-
functorily at the Glassboro summit between Kosygin and
Johnson in late June but Soviet Foreign Minister
Gromyko soon met U.S. Ambassador to the UN Arthur
Goldberg to iron out an agreement. On July 19, they
jointly advocated a complete Israeli withdrawal in
return for Arab non-belligerency and recognition of
Israel's right to exist. Arab UN delegations unanimous-
ly rejected this plan on July 21, and Israel too was
opposed. It probably was willing to give up all occupied territory except Jerusalem, but it had strong
reservations about any superpower plan which would be
substituted for direct negotiations with Arab states.

On November 22, the Soviet Union joined in the
passage of Security Council Resolution 242, which indicated "respect for and acknowledgment of the
sovereignty, territorial integrity and political independence of every state in the area and their right
to live in peace within secure and recognized boundaries free from threats or acts of force." It also
called for Israeli withdrawal "from territories occupied in the recent conflict" but the Soviet Union
always interpreted this passage to mean "all territories." Furthermore, the UN Secretary General was asked
to appoint a special representative to act as mediator.
U Thant appointed Swedish Ambassador to the Soviet
Union Gunnar Jarring, and his efforts received strong
Soviet backing. The Soviets, due to their seat on the
Security Council, favored a UN initiative and this was
consistent with Arab interests as direct negotiations
with Israel were to be avoided. Israel preferred direct talks, but they were not mentioned in SC 242. The
United States was not enthusiastic about UN mediation
as the Soviet Union would be able to compensate for its
disadvantage in the Middle East by playing a role at
the UN equal to that of the U.S.

On January 25, 1968, the Soviet Union presented
its own peace plan which was consistent with SC 242.
It discussed freedom of navigation, demilitarized zones,
a resolution of the refugee problem, recognition of
frontiers, and ending the state of war. A few new
wrinkles were added, however. Israel was to start its
withdrawal before documents on the other issues were
deposited with the United Nations and the UN was called
upon to reestablish the peacekeeping force that had been
withdrawn in May 1967. The Soviets suggested a Security
Council or Big Four guarantee of Israel's borders and,
in a gesture to the Israelis, proposed a two-stage withdrawal over a period of two months.10 Some points were
obviously not acceptable to Israel, such as the re-
linquishment of East Jerusalem and the initiation of

withdrawal prior to the filing of documents. Nevertheless, the Soviets were seeking a peaceful resolution of
the conflict and were encouraging the Arabs likewise.
One analyst maintains that the Soviet Union sought a
"formal peace" (signed agreements and the resolution
of all problems) from June 1967 to January 1969, while
the U.S. favored only a "minimal peace" (non-belligerency.).[11] This appears to have been true as the U.S.
marked time as long as the power relationship in the
Middle East remained favorable. In fact the U.S. moved
to strengthen Israel through the provision of jet
fighters. In January 1968, it began to deliver 48 A-4s
that had been promised prior to the war and it agreed
to supply an additional twenty aircraft.

Limited Motion

During 1968, little changed in the Middle East as
Israel continued to hold on to the occupied territories, the Soviets shored up Egypt and Syria militarily
in preparation for negotiations, and Israel (due to
deeper Soviet involvement in the region) hardened its
position. Movement was therefore full-circle rather
than forward.

Israel retained all occupied territories as an
obvious bargaining tactic, but it also felt that a
freezing of the situation would shorten the longevity
of the Egyptian and Syrian governments. Concessions
were to be avoided as they would have the opposite
effect. Of course, Hussein's rule in Jordan was also
on the line but Israel was prepared to assist the
monarchy if a crisis developed.[12] The Soviet Union,
meanwhile, was rebuilding the Egyptian and Syrian
armies in order to bolster the disabled Arab regimes.
It additionally was beginning to play a more direct
military role, acquiring port rights at Port Said and
Mersa Matruh, Egypt and airfield facilities for the
operation of surveillance flights. In May, a Soviet
surveillance aircraft passed over Israeli-occupied territory in the Sinai.[13]

The Soviets realized that Arab armies were still
weak so they discouraged any military operations against
Israel. An article in World Marxist Review asserted,
somewhat hopefully, that Egypt and Syria "appreciate
the correlation of strength in the region and the
dangerous consequences of provoking the enemy. Therefore, they object to actions in the immediate proximity
of the cease-fire line."[14] Nevertheless, Syria had not
accepted SC 242 and was obstructive in regard to a
political solution. Egypt was therefore praised for
its "sensible policy" and not giving in to "adventurist
appeals, which would only have played into the hands of
the enemy."[15] Egypt had approved SC 242 and thus was

prepared to recognize Israel's existence and right to
use the Suez Canal. The Soviets lauded this action and
indicated that opposition to such a policy would only
cause greater Israeli obduracy on withdrawal.[16] Even
Israeli Minister of Defense Dayan recognized the Soviet
Union's moderate intentions, saying that "she will support the Arabs to the hilt, politically, while warning
them against war."[17]

In September 1968, the Soviet Union presented
another peace plan. It did not contain any new proposals and was rejected by Israel. The U.S. too was non-
receptive, which was rather predictable considering the
international atmosphere less than a month after Soviet
troops intervened in Czechoslovakia. The Soviets were
using the occasion to recoup some of their prestige
and dramatized their support for a Middle East peace
process by organizing a foreign ministry press conference and by having Gromyko emphasize the issue in the
UN General Assembly.[18] It was basically a display of
theatrics as the new peace plan had no new components
and was unlikely to be acted upon by the United States
or Israel just prior to the American presidential election. In fact, the Soviets expected Israel to take a
hard line as U.S. politicians were reluctant to criticize the Jewish state at election time.[19]

The Soviet Union sparred with the U.S. in the
Eastern Mediterranean, calling for the removal of the
Sixth Fleet and justifying its own buildup of naval
forces. It charged that the U.S. navy threatened Middle Eastern states and was positioning nuclear weapons
against the Soviet Union. The proximity of the region
to Soviet borders was stressed, thereby portraying
Soviet naval actions as both defensive in nature and
supportive of Arab interests.[20] However, Israel was
becoming more apprehensive and it appears at this time
to have reversed its decision to relinquish all of
Sinai as part of a comprehensive peace settlement.
Yigal Allon discussed the Soviet military role in the
Knesset, indicating that some Israelis were seriously
concerned. He, however, denied a need to worry about
any direct Soviet assault on Israel because the U.S.
Sixth Fleet would provide protection. Implying a pledge
from the U.S., he averred that Israel would "not be
alone."[21]

The Israeli government realized that the Soviet
Union had no intention of attacking, nor of supporting
an Arab offensive. Nevertheless, an enhanced Soviet
military position in the region would in the long run
undermine Israel's strategic preponderance over the
Arabs. Israel therefore leaned more toward the United
States as a balance to the Soviets, especially since
French military assistance was ending in December 1968.
Thus superpower rivalry in the area became increasingly

significant as an ecstatic Israel recieved a new
American commitment to sell fifty Phantom aircraft.

Prime Minister Eshkol expressed uneasiness about
Soviet arms deliveries to the Arabs, but he also pointed
out that the Soviets were cautioning against militancy.
He called for greater Soviet encouragement of the peace
process and an improvement in relations with Israel. He
somewhat sarcastically observed: "If Russia is more
concerned about Socialism, then there is more Socialism
in one kibbutz such as Degania than there is in the
whole of Egypt."[22]

Richard Nixon was elected President of the United
States and, before being inaugurated, he dispatched
William Scranton to the Middle East to assess the situation. At the same time, Gunnar Jarring was ending his
mediation with no results. The Soviet Union therefore
decided to keep the peace initiative alive and to seek
cooperation with the United States. A new peace plan
was announced on December 22 and it was presented to
the U.S. eight days later with the statement: "Moscow
is convinced that a Middle East settlement is not a
matter solely for the countries of the region. The
Great Powers too are undoubtedly interested in such a
settlement."[23] For Israel, which was not even consulted, such an approach smacked of an attempted solution
imposed by the superpowers so it rejected the Soviet
plan. Syria did likewise as it opposed a political
settlement altogether. As for the plan itself, it did
not include any new departures except for some curious
omissions. Israel's right to use the Suez Canal was
not mentioned, nor was any specific reference to
Israeli withdrawal from East Jerusalem. Perhaps the
Soviets were proposing a trade-off on these issues.[24]

Jogging in Place

A hectic round of diplomacy was set in motion
when Richard Nixon assumed office in January 1969. The
new president tended to view world events in a superpower context and believed that the United States had a
role to play in Middle Eastern regional affairs. The
Soviet Union too was anxious for superpower diplomacy
as it was engaged in increasing hostilities with China
and sought some degree of collaboration with the United
States. In March, there were major clashes along the
Sino-Soviet frontier so the Soviets found it opportune
to play their American card. As the United States and
Soviet Union became more vigorous diplomatically,
Gunnar Jarring decided (in February) to resume his
mediation efforts. The year 1969 thus emerged as one
of frantic activity, but little accomplishment.

France proposed Big Four negotiations, but the
United States insisted that they must be preceded by
Big Two (U.S.-Soviet) talks. Sessions between Assistant Secretary of State Joseph Sisco and Soviet Ambassador Anatolii Dobrynin began on March 18 and nine

meetings were held through April 22. Dobrynin, also
in late March, met with Secretary of State William
Rogers. In addition, Big Four talks at the United
Nations started on April 3 and fifteen sessions took
place through July 1. Bilateral Soviet-American sessions were then renewed as Sisco went to Moscow in July
and Ambassador to the U.S.S.R. Jacob Beam met five
times in August with Deputy Foreign Minister Semenov.
In September in New York, Sisco met Dobrynin and
Rogers had three sessions with Foreign Minister Gromyko.
Big Four talks then resumed on December 2 and there were
six meetings that month.

Syria continued to oppose the peace process, but
Egypt and Jordan favored Big Four talks. They could
thus avoid direct negotiations with Israel and compensate for their weak regional position by international-
izing the framework of negotiations. Israel strenuous-
ly objected, feeling that the Soviet Union and France
were biased parties. Golda Meir's government (Eshkol
had died in February) insisted on direct negotiations
to press its regional advantage and to secure Arab recognition of Israel's legitimacy. On May 15, UN representative Tekoah submitted to the Security Council a
strong protest about proposed Big Four talks. Israel,
Egypt and Jordan were all wary of Big Two talks, anticipating an imposed solution without appropriate consul-
tation.

In the initial Soviet-American negotiations,
Dobrynin showed some flexibility on the issue of
Israel's borders and agreed to "minor adjustments" in
the pre-1967 frontiers. It seemed as if East Jerusalem
and the Golan Heights were the most negotiable territories.[25] At his March 3 meeting with National Security
adviser Henry Kissinger, he softened the usual Soviet
position by agreeing to the concept of a package deal
rather than demanding the beginning of Israel's withdrawal as the first step.[26] Actually, the Soviets had
to play a tricky double game, moderating their stance
in discussions with the Americans in order to achieve
some diplomatic momentum, but hardening their public
position to reassure the Arabs that their interests
were not being sold out. For example, Soviet publications maintained that the issue of Israel's use of
waterways should not be discussed until after other
provisions of SC 242 had been implemented and they called for an Israeli withdrawal as a precondition to the
termination of the state of war. They also called for
the normalization of relations rather than the conclusion of a formal peace treaty, asserting that conditions
for the latter did not yet exist.[27] At the time, Egypt
was anxious to renew hostilities with Israel, and Syria
was undergoing domestic turmol as Hafez al-Assad was
gaining the upper hand over Salah Jadid as the dominant
figure in the Baathist regime. Assad had criticized

Jadid for his connections to the Soviet Union and his
assumption of de facto control led to the dispatching
to Peking in May of Chief of Staff Mustapha Tlas. Again
the Soviets had to be concerned about their radical
flank

On March 31, Egypt broke the cease-fire along the
Canal. Nasser's initial actions represented a compromise with the Soviets, who approved of limited military
pressure on Israel but were wary of any broad plan of
action. Consequently, the Soviets asked the Egyptians
to operate only on the northern front, expecting that
the Soviet naval presence in the area would deter major
Israeli counterattacks. However, Israel struck back
more strongly than expected. This led the Soviets in
May to ask the Egyptians to cease hostilities, but Nasser
wouldn't comply and he announced a War of Attrition in
June. The Soviets became concerned about their own
ships and personnel so, during the summer, they sent a
warning to Israel via the Finnish embassy.28 In September, Soviet-Egyptian friction was evident over the mysterious Ali Sabry affair, and it is possible that the
Soviet Union had links to an anti-Nasser conspiracy.29

In the spring of 1969, the Soviets were hoping for
a political solution. At the June meeting in Moscow of
communist parties, their moderate positions on the
Middle East were rejected by Arab communists. The
Jordanian communist leader claimed that the Soviets were
too conscious of their own Jewish problem. Khaled
Bakdash, trying to place developments in a light more
favorable to the Soviets said: "We have to admit that
there is quite a bit of Jewish influence in European
communist parties, and that if it had not been for
Soviet influence the resolution on the Middle East at
the Moscow conference would have been weaker."30 A
hardening of attitude was soon apparent as Gromyko returned from Egypt with word that Nasser would not go
along with Soviet proposals. Nasser was furious that
the Soviets were willing to consider alterations in
Israel's pre-1967 borders and he feared a Soviet-
American deal at his expense.31 Without the ability to
carry Nasser along, the Soviets had to refrain from
meaningful suggestions about a peaceful settlement and
this was immediately apparent to the Israelis. Foreign
Minister Eban castigated the Soviets for their retrench-
ment and presented a detailed peace formula that went
far beyond SC 242, calling for direct negotiations, a
prohibition on terrorism, and a virtual Israeli veto
over any resolution of the Palestinian refugee problem.
More importantly, he seemed to be referring to Egyptian
and Syrian intransigence and greater Jordanian moderation when he mentioned the obligation and privilege of
each state to make peace with Israel without being subjected to conditions set by other states.32

Israel was concerned about the emergence of de-

tente, fearing that collaboration would produce an
imposed superpower solution in the Middle East. Eban
had said immediately after the 1967 war that Israel's
main aim was to prevent a common Soviet-American front
in the region, as had been formed in 1956, and Meir
expressed her apprehensions about detente to Nixon when
she visited the U.S. in September 1969.[33] In particular, the Israelis feared some deal on Vietnam and the
Middle East in which the U.S. would make concessions
affecting Israel in return for advantages in the Southeast Asian theater. Eshkol had commented on this possibility immediately after Nixon's election, and
Kissinger's memoirs have lent credence to the Israeli
anxiety. Kissinger writes that Nixon sought Soviet
cooperation on Vietnam in return for U.S. willingness
to negotiate about the Middle East. The U.S. had the
advantage in the Middle East so linkage would provide
some leverage against the Soviets on the Vietnam issue.
Kissinger cites a request by Dobrynin to work out a
common position on the Middle East and his response was
that it would be "difficult" as the Soviets were not
helpful regarding Vietnam. He also writes that the U.S.
stalled on issues of concern to the Soviets such as the
Middle East, bilateral economic ties and SALT because
of Soviet inaction on Vietnam. The apparent inference
to be derived from his remarks is that a more forthcoming Soviet approach on Vietnam would produce some
modifications in the American position on the Middle
East.[34] Meir recognized this linkage principle and
felt, that for self-protection, Israel should not
criticize the American role in Vietnam. Jewish organizations in the United States and the Israeli embassy
in Washington both advised this course of action.[35]

Perhaps the United States did envision a grand
scenario featuring solutions for Vietnam and the Middle
East but, in regard to the Middle East itself, it was
engaged in a dilatory game and was not seeking a
political settlement. Talks with the Soviet Union were
aimed at furthering detente, not a solution for the
Middle East, and Big Four sessions were held to pacify
the Western allies. Kissinger avers that he did not
desire progress in the Big Four negotiations and that
he did not want to include the Soviet Union in a Middle
East settlement. He preferred an agreement with Jordan
over one with Egypt, a Soviet ally. Furthermore, he
believed that "if the Soviet position in Egypt was bound
to deteriorate the longer a settlement was delayed, we
had no incentive whatever to accept the first Soviet or
Egyptian offer."[36]

Hesitant Steps

On June 12, 1967, just two days after the Soviet
Union broke relations, Eshkol called for their resumption and told the Knesset that he hoped the Soviets

would now work for peace. The Soviets were unreceptive
to such overtures, and only minimal contact was maintained over the next few years. The percentage of
Israel's trade directed toward East European states
remained at about 2 percent, with Hungary and Rumania
serving as the major commercial partners. The Soviet
percentage of total Israeli trade with Eastern Europe
dropped from 7.4 percent in 1966 to 1.2 percent in 1967
and 1.4 percent in 1968.[37] On the religious front, the
Israeli occupation of East Jerusalem and the West Bank
brought numerous "White" church properties under its
control. The Soviets asked Israel if the "Red" church
could take over their administration, but were rebuffed.[38] Therefore, no problem emerged regarding Soviet
cooperation with the Israelis in occupied territories.
The "Red" church continued to administer properties in
Israel.

In December 1968, the first high level Soviet-
Israeli contact since the break in relations took place
in New York. Deputy Foreign Minister Semenov met with
Israeli UN delegate Tekoah and apparently said that
Israel must withdraw from most occupied territories. He
wanted the withdrawal to begin before a final settlement
was arranged, but, of course, Israel wanted the proce-
dures reversed. This session was requested by the
Soviet side, probably in conjunction with the peace
plan released that month. Canada and France encouraged
the Soviets to ask for this meeting, while Israel refrained from initiating such unofficial contacts. The
Israeli position was that relations should be restored
and then negotiations could proceed. Israel didn't
want to permit the Soviets to carry on diplomatic business as usual, seeing this as a back-door approach which
avoided the resumption of formal ties. In this case,
however, Israel acceded to the Soviet request as it was
perceived as a step in the Israeli direction. The
Soviets had broken relations so they were appropriately
carrying the burden of seeking to renew diplomatic contact.[39]

Before the diplomatic ice was broken, only Israeli
communists were invited to the Soviet Union and no
Soviet citizens were invited to Israel. In the summer
of 1968, ten Israeli children went to camp in the Soviet
Union, and a delegation from RAKAH attended a youth
festival.[40] After the Semenov-Tekoah meeting, some
glacial improvement was evident as non-communist
Israelis participated in a dairy conference and a
chemist attended a conference in Armenia and afterward
visited Moscow. A machine he invented was displayed in
a Moscow exhibition.[41] On the other hand, Soviet diplomat Iacov Malik refused to meet with Israeli journalist
and non-Zionist gadfly Uri Avnery, possibly because he
was a member of the Knesset.[42] There was also the

strange affair of chief Sephardic rabbi Yitzhak
Nissim. Soviet Jews invited him to celebrations for the
seventy-fifth birthday of the chief rabbi of Moscow
Yehuda Leib Levin. At first, Nissim said that he was
unable to go. Then he changed his mind and requested a
visa through the Finnish embassy. There was no response
and an appeal was made to the Soviet foreign ministry to
speed up the process. No visa was received and he did
not go to Moscow. Similarly, Israel had not granted a
visa to the editor of Komsomol'skaia Pravda, who was
invited to Israel by a RAKAH youth organization.[43]

RAKAH leaders were more cordially accepted by
Moscow after the 1967 war as MAKI was completely written
of by the Soviets. Wilner and Toubi were received by
Suslov and Ponomarev in August 1967 and Wilner had his
first meeting with Brezhnev in June 1969, when he was
attending the communist party conference. The first
Soviet delegation to visit Israel since the break in
relations was composed of two Central Committee members,
who participated in RAKAH's sixteenth congress on
January 30-February 1, 1969. It is possible that some
contact was made with Israeli officials, but evidence is
sketchy. Eban first denied that any contact took place,
but then changed course and refused to comment on the
issue.[44]

RAKAH was a legal political party in Israel. It
operated freely in electoral campaigns, was represented
in the Knesset and published journals in Hebrew and
Arabic. However, its ties to the Soviet Union and
efforts to influence Arabs in the West Bank rendered
it suspect to the Israeli authorities. Restrictions
were placed on the movement of RAKAH members, particularly in the West Bank, and they drew stormy protests
from both the RAKAH and Soviet media.[45] Also controversial was the case of RAKAH Central Committee member
Emile Habibi. He was accused of making statements
during the 1967 war which were favorable to Nasser and
supportive of terrorism and hostility against Israel.
Dayan raised the issue in the Knesset, but Habibi was
cleared after an investigation.[46] Even more serious
was the wounding of Wilner by a knife-wielding assail-
ant in October 1967. The Soviets did not directly blame
the Israeli government, but cited the "chauvinistic and
militaristic atmosphere."[47] A few weeks later, Toubi
headed the RAKAH delegation to Moscow for the fiftieth
Bolshevik anniversary celebrations and he was pointedly
met at the airport by senior figures Suslov and
Ponomarev.

The Soviet Jewish issue attracted greater attention
after the 1967 war. The large emigration of the early
part of the year was terminated, and even those with
exit visas were not permitted to leave. The freeze on
Jewish emigration lasted until September 1968 and the
resulting thaw may have been related to the peace plan

issued that month and an attempt to improve the Soviet
image after the intervention in Czechoslovakia. About
225 Jews emigrated in late 1968, but the number rose to
approximately 3000 in 1969. The first stirrings of detente may have been responsible as the Soviets were embroiled in conflict with China and sought an improvement in relations with the United States.

Although Soviet Jews had been coming to Israel
sporadically for almost twenty years, Israel did not
publicly acknowledge such a phenomenon until November
1967 when Eshkol referred to the curtailment of emigration. He apparently felt that going public was pre-
ferable to quiet diplomacy, as mechanisms for the latter
were not immediately available in the absence of formal
ties. Strong Soviet Jewish emotional attachment to
Israel was evident after the war, and the virulent anti-
Zionist campaign unleased by the Soviets probably influenced Eshkol as well. By mid-1969, the internal
Soviet Jewish movement was being transformed from concern for human, religious and cultural rights into a
concerted and politicized campaign for emigration.[48] In
the United States, Jewish organizations joined the
bandwagon with the extra motivation of sullying the
Soviet image to counter the poor publicity received by
the U.S. over Vietnam. Israel became more outspoken on
the emigration theme, as was apparent by its treatment
of the letter from eighteen Georgian Jews who sought
emigration. Meir read it on Israeli television on November 10, and Tekoah brought it to the UN Commission on
Human Rights. Meir also declared that the Soviet Union
was as great an enemy as Egypt.[49] The Soviets retaliated with increased anti-Zionist polemics, trying both to
warn and influence Jews at a time when public pressure
for emigration was mounting.

The Palestinian Factor

The Soviet Union paid greater attention to the
Palestinian movements after the 1967 war as they were
a useful irritant to Israeli authorities in the
occupied territories at a time when weakened Arab states
were not in a position to act. The Palestinian problem,
which the Soviets had viewed primarily in terms of
refugees, was transformed into a territorial issue as
Israel was occupying the Palestinian lands of the West
Bank and Gaza. The movements could therefore play a
role in liberating occupied Palestinian territory,
though the Soviets opposed any operations within the
pre-1967 borders of Israel. In effect, the Soviets
were advocating an Israeli withdrawal from territories
seized in 1967 and not challenging Israel's hold on
territory gained in the first Arab-Israeli war of 1948-
49. While seeking an agreement on Israeli withdrawal,
the Soviets insisted on a comprehensive approach and
opposed any separate Jordanian-Israeli deal that would
not resolve the territorial claims of Egypt and Syria.

Yasir Arafat's al-Fatah began to operate in the West Bank in July 1967 and a headquarters was established in Jordan early in 1968. The Soviets approved of al-Fatah activities in Jordan as Israeli retaliation would be directed against a Western ally, not Egypt or Syria.[50] The Soviets were covering all bases, however, as Hussein was needed as a vital component of a peace process. He therefore paid his first visit to the Soviet Union in October 1967, and al-Fatah was advised to tone down its guerrilla operations. In December, Ahmed Shukairy was removed as leader of the PLO. The Soviets had no regrets as he had been considered ineffectual, extremist in his rhetoric and affiliated with China. Al-Fatah, which had reconciled with Egypt, began to merge with the PLO and Arafat became the "official spokesman" of the umbrella organization in April 1968.

In July 1968, Arafat made his initial visit to the Soviet Union as part of an Egyptian delegation headed by Nasser. He met Brezhnev, Kosygin and Podgornyi, but did not have formal talks with them. However, he was received by First Deputy Prime Minister Kiril Mazurov and the provision of Soviet arms was discussed. A few weeks later, Nasser received word that arms would be supplied indirectly (probably through Egypt as the notification went to Nasser).[51]

Nevertheless, the Soviets and Arab communists downplayed the PLO's military role. They asserted that guerrilla warfare would not lead to the recovery of territory, that Palestinian military operations were ineffective and that bases were lacking in the occupied areas because the PLO fedayeen were strangers there. They were probably concerned as well that Palestinian attacks would trigger Israeli retaliation against neighboring Arab states, possibly leading to the collapse of governments already weakened by the 1967 military debacle. Palestinians were asked to take "objective conditions" into account and to assess properly the power relationships in the wake of a major Arab defeat. They were also told that their struggle was part of a broader Arab national liberation movement, thereby necessitating Arab unity against imperialist interests. Political tactics were to be preferred to military ones and direct negotiations with Israel were advocated (although Arab states were not pressed to act likewise).[52] The Jordanian communists were the most vehement of all. They strongly opposed al-Fatah's efforts launched from their country and accused that organization of being "reckless," "unrealistic " and "extremist." Communists who joined al-Fatah units were required to leave the party.[53]

Soviet urging of Palestinian moderation during the last four months of 1968 was linked to the peace proposals announced in September and December, but a change of direction became evident early in 1969. The

Soviets obviously experienced considerable confusion
as Arafat, in February, became the PLO chairman and
tension between the U.S.S.R. and China mounted. The
policy adopted seems to have been one of outradicalizing
the Chinese rhetorically on the Palestinian issue, but
discouraging guerrilla activities in the field that
could challenge Israel within her pre-1967 boundaries.
　　The Soviets charged the PLO with a tendency toward
signing a separate peace treaty with Israel over the
fate of the West Bank and hinted at some linkage to the
CIA. Guerrilla operations in the occupied territories
came to be viewed more favorably, particularly those of
George Habash's militant Popular Front for the Liberation of Palestine, and acts of terrorism were no longer
condemned. For the first time, a specifically Palestinian national liberation struggle was recognized, but
Soviet comments implied criticism of Arafat's al-Fatah
for being too moderate. Just a few months earlier, the
complaint was extremism! Podgornyi refused to meet with
Arafat when he visited Algeria at the end of March 1969,
and al-Fatah's radio attacked the negativistic Soviet
stance, while favoring a reversal of Moscow's policy.[54]
　　Radicalism was advocated for the occupied territories, but accommodation with Israel was also stressed.
In an approach wrought with contradictions, the Soviets
realized Israel's military advantage and claimed that
al-Fatah was applying Trotskii's discredited "no war,
no peace" policy. The implication was that peace with
Israel was required. Al-Fatah was also criticized for
desiring a joint Jewish-Arab Palestine, which could
only be created by liquidating Israel. The Soviet
Union endorsed the continued existence of the Jewish
state. The Israeli and Jordanian communist parties
joined in the denunciation of al-Fatah on this issue.[55]
By September, the Soviets were praising al-Fatah and
labeling the PFLP "an extremist organization which pursued mass terror tactics."[56] Their motivation is hard
to fathom, but a belief in the possibility of a superpower solution may have been a factor.

Zionism and Eastern Europe
　　All communist-ruled states except Rumania and Cuba
joined the Soviet Union in breaking relations with
Israel in 1967, but this could not hide the dissension
engendered by the Soviet action. Opinions sympathetic
toward Israel were expressed within the communist
parties of France, Italy, Austria, the United States
and the Netherlands (within MAKI in Israel as well), but
the most serious challenges to the Soviet position came
from communists in Poland and Czechoslovakia.[57] The
commander of the Polish air force and two other top
officers were removed for not adhering to an anti-
Israeli line, and an extensive anti-Zionist campaign
seemed to be an instrument used by Minister of the

Interior Mieczslaw Moczar against First Secretary
Wladyslaw Gomulka (whose wife was Jewish).[58] This was
a continuation of an old feud between Partisan and
Muscovite factions but it took on anti-Israeli and anti-
Semitic overtones in 1967, forcing out many liberal
Jewish party leaders.

In March 1968, Poland was rocked by anti-government disturbances and the media tried to portray many
of the protesters as Jews, agents of Israel, or as
allies of discredited Jewish politicians. Distinctions
between Jews and Zionists were usually blurred. The
Soviets responded likewise, charging that the organizers
had "Zionist sentiments" and were adherents of a "dual
citizenship" theory.[59] Gomulka, trying to protect his
position, joined in the accusations. He claimed that
Jewish students participated in the disturbances, that
many Polish Jews were loyal to Israel rather than
Poland, and that Zionists were trying to equate Zionists and Jews in order to encourage the emigration of
non-Zionists. At the same time, Gomulka said that Jews
who considered Israel their fatherland could leave.[60]
More than 10,000 took up the offer, their visas being
handled by the Dutch embassy.

In Czechoslovakia, many Jewish political figures
and the Jewish Community Council objected to the break
in relations with Israel, and they were joined by non-
Jews who wanted to use the issue to attack the Novotny
regime at a time when its Soviet patron appeared weak
due to the Arab defeat. According to one observer,
comments sympathetic to Israel were really veiled
criticisms not only of the Soviet Union's Middle East
policy but of its domination of Eastern Europe. In
this situation, Novotny was representative of Soviet
interests in Czechoslovakia and he went along with
the anti-Zionist line. Anti-Zionism was therefore used
by the Soviets and their East European allies to
tarnish liberal forces with the Zionist label.[61]

After the 1967 war, Novotny's anti-Zionist stance
had anti-Semitic overtones as he cancelled celebrations
marking a thousand years of Jewish settlement in
Prague and those scheduled for the seven hundredth
anniversary of the Alt-Neu synagogue. However, several
non-Jewish intellectuals (including delegates at the
writers' congress in July) were challenging the official
position and registering their support for Israel and
the Jewish people. Ladislav Mnacko, a Slovak author
who had commented on remnants of Stalinism in his 1964
work Delayed Reports, pointedly went to Israel to work
on a kibbutz. He had been a reporter there in 1948
and returned to protest his government's policy. On
August 16, his Czechoslovak citizenship was revoked.[62]

Mounting criticism led to the removal of Novotny
as communist party leader and his replacement in
January 1968 by Alexander Dubcek. The liberal reform-

ist wing of the party was in ascendancy, and official attitudes toward Israel and Jews quickly changed. Pro-Israeli opinions were expressed in the media, some Czechoslovaks publicly called for the resumption of relations with Israel, military aid to Arab states was terminated, the celebration of Jewish settlement in Prague was rescheduled, an exhibition on the Jewish contribution to Czechoslovak culture took place at the Jewish museum in Prague, another exhibition of Jewish life appeared at the Slovak National Museum in Bratislava, emigration restrictions were relaxed, Mnacko regained his citizenship, a petition calling for a restoration of ties to Israel was signed by 13,000 people and presented to the foreign ministry by students at Charles University, an Israeli diplomat was interviewed in a Prague magazine, and Czechoslovak Jews for the first time served as observers at a meeting of the World Jewish Congress in Geneva.[63] Furthermore, there was an effort to rehabilitate Slansky and his wife's memoirs were published.

The Prague spring challenged the Soviet Union in many ways, but few realize that the course of events was closely connected to the issue of Israel. Soviet policy in the Middle East was being opposed vigorously by another communist-ruled state, and the 1967 Arab-Israeli war had provided a crucial spark to the Czechoslovak liberalization campaign. Soviet intervention in August quashed the Dubcek government, and Czechoslovakia again fell in line with Soviet policy. However, some interesting linkages to Israel still deserve mention. Many Czechoslovaks were in Israel at the time of the Soviet invasion of their homeland and some joined a protest rally at Tel Aviv University and sang their national anthem. Israel announced that those who desired could stay there, and at least thirty took up the offer. A former MAPAM political secretary from kibbutz Kfar Masaryk even declared (surely on the basis of emotion rather than logic) that Israel could serve as a base for those who wanted to liberate Czechoslovakia![64]

Israel condemned Soviet intervention in Czechoslovakia, with a government statement asserting: "The participation of German troops in the invasion and occupation, this time as part of the forces of the Warsaw Pact, arouses in us particularly terrible memories."[65] Egyptian journalist Mohammed Heikal had a mixed reaction to what the Soviets had done, but he was critical of Czechoslovakia for not supporting the negativistic Soviet policy toward Israel. He wrote: "On the strength of this point alone, I cannot imagine that any Arab, from a purely moral point of view, could condemn intervention in Czechoslovakia."[66] Syrian communist leader Khaled Bakdash said that "anti-socialist elements" in Czechoslovakia had supported Zionist

expansionism, and the Soviets charged that some
Czechoslovak reformists had wanted to restore relations
with Israel. They also claimed that an international
Zionist plot lay behind the "counterrevolutionary
uprising" and attempt to gain control of the
Czechoslovak media. Among Israeli communists, RAKAH
endorsed the Soviet intervention(although it did not
begin to criticize the Dubcek government until July)
and MAKI opposed it.67

. . . .

Soviet-Israeli relations were distant and cool
during the years 1967-69 but the two countries were
soon to become directly embroiled in explosive combat.
Nineteen seventy promised to be a very warm year
along the Suez front.

5
Coming to Blows

December 1969 brought an American proposal to resolve the Arab-Israeli stalemate, but it led to an escalation of hostilities and direct Soviet military involvement on the Egyptian front. Then a new round of negotiations defused the situation as another American plan produced a cease-fire between Israel and Egypt. Just when an atmosphere of calm was about to envelope the area, Black September burst upon the scene in Jordan as monarchist and Palestinian forces collided. The Soviet Union was not responsible for actions taken by the Palestinians, but it emerged as a loser in the regional power game. The United States, acting in collaboration with Israel, outmaneuvered the Soviet Union's Palestinian and Syrian allies and developed an even closer military relationship with the Jewish state.

Among the questions to consider are: Why did the United States sponsor a Middle East peace plan? Why did Israel reject this plan and then conduct deep penetration bombing raids against Egypt? Did Israel anticipate Soviet counteraction? Why did negotiations for a cease-fire then succeed? What policies did the Soviet Union and Israel adopt toward the conflict in Jordan? On the whole, it was a year featuring wild swings of the pendulum, including discussions about peace and the possibility of direct superpower clashes in both Egypt and Jordan.

Deceptive Diplomacy

Soviet-American negotiations in New York in September 1969 prompted the U.S. government to formulate a peace plan as the War of Attrition showed no signs of abating. A draft of the American proposals was given to Soviet ambassador Dobrynin on October 28 and then released publicly on December 9 as the "Rogers Plan." The Secretary of State did not present a detailed proposal, but rather a broad guideline which linked almost complete Israeli withdrawal to an Arab agreement on peace. Jerusalem was to remain a "united city" in which both Israel and Jordan were to have roles in "civic, economic and religious life." This wording could be interpreted to mean continued Israeli sovereignty over the entire city. Israel and Jordan were called upon to negotiate directly over the Jerusalem issue, and Israel's other Arab neighbors were encouraged to do likewise. The major powers were expected to facilitate the negotiating process. On December 18, an accompanying "Yost Plan" (named after the U.S. delegate to the UN) was presented to a meeting of the Big Four. It dealt more specifically with issues at stake between Israel and Jordan.

The Soviet Union rejected the American proposals on December 23, after Israel and Egypt had already signified their opposition. It had been consulted but still objected to the procedure of having the United States take the lead in the peace process. The substance was not a major problem, except for the advocacy of direct talks, as it was consistent with SC 242. Egypt was still carrying out a War of Attrition and was not amenable to a peaceful solution until its military situation improved. In fact, Sadat was in Moscow when the "Rogers Plan" was announced, seeking more advanced Soviet arms.

Israel objected to any territorial plan suggested by an outside power. It wanted the Arabs to ask for peace, not have the United States serve as a broker. After the 1967 war, Israel expected strong American pressure to return the occupied territories. It was surprised by American nonchalance, considering the adamant stance displayed after the 1956 conflict. This produced a hardening in the Israeli position regarding disposition of the territories and, by December 1969, Israel had "created facts" both militarily and in terms of settlement plans for its citizens. It was therefore unwilling to give up territory for peace on a grand scale, as it had been two years earlier, as it wanted to retain East Jerusalem, part of the Golan Heights, and perhaps a strip of land separating Gaza from Egypt. Israel also wanted adjustments in the West Bank's border near Latrun and Netanya and some security arrangement in the Jordan Valley. Since the United States did not accompany the "Rogers Plan" with any threat to reduce arms deliveries if Israel did not respond favorably (Kissinger wrote that Nixon had "no stomach" for imposing the plan on Israel), Israeli leaders believed that American actions were more significant than the message in the plan itself.[1] In fact, the Israelis were even told that they would receive more weapons if the plan failed! Israel therefore torpedoed the "Rogers Plan," thus improving the American image among Arab moderates in accordance with the dictum that anything opposed by

Israel must contain something of value to the Arabs.

One aim of the "Rogers Plan" was to display American evenhandedness toward the Arabs, but dividing the Arabs over its proposals was also beneficial as it would prevent a unified Arab position aligned with that of the Soviet Union. It is probably not coincidental that American peace initiatives prior to 1973 were released on the eve of Arab summit meetings, with the intent to undercut Arab efforts at cohesion in their struggle against Israel.[2] On this occasion, the "Rogers Plan" preceded an Islamic summit conference scheduled to convene in Rabat, Morocco on December 21. Saudi Arabia and Kuwait, perhaps influenced by the American initiative, refused to provide additional war funds to the front-line states. This prompted Nasser to storm out of the meeting, and no final communique was ever issued. Disunity was so prevalent in the Arab world that the chiefs of state of Syria, Iraq and Tunisia did not even attend the summit.

American motivations behind the "Rogers Plan" were fragmented and tied to bureaucratic infighting. Rogers and the State Department believed that the stalemate over the occupied territories favored the Soviet Union by increasing Arab dependence on Soviet arms. A peace initiative could therefore spur the negotiating process, weaken the Soviet position, and improve American relations with Arab states. National Security adviser Kissinger diasagreed, maintaining that the status quo favored the United States at the expense of the Soviet Union. He argued that the Arabs were coming to the realization that the Soviet Union could not help them regain territories and that they would have to turn to the United States, which was in a position to seek concessions from Israel. Freezing the situation somewhat longer would be in the American interest so Kissinger opposed the "Rogers Plan." He was particularly irked that the plan was announced the day before a scheduled session of the National Security Council, at which he expected debate over its merits. The meeting took place, but Kissingers's arguments could only be presented ex post facto.[3]

Nixon seemed to waver between Rogers and Kissinger. He permitted Rogers to present his proposal but, by late December, he apparently agreed with Kissinger that it was not the appropriate time for a peace settlement. Kissinger continued to argue that a comprehensive approach to the peace process would only permit Arab radicals (who were Soviet clients) to regain territory and that Soviet influence over them would not be reduced. In early February, he told Nixon that the Arabs would eventually have to turn toward the U.S. to get back territory but Nixon disagreed and maintained that the Soviets were benefiting from the situation created

by the 1967 war.4 If one is to rely on Kissinger's
version of events, it appears that Nixon had again
shifted toward the Rogers' position. In fact, Rogers
temporarily retained control over Middle East diplomacy
and Kissinger's advice was not heeded.

Escalation

During the War of Attrition, Israel consistently
suffered casualties but its military superiority was
never seriously challenged. It carried out a bold
attack in December 1969 in which an entire Soviet radar
system was carted off from Egypt and it even began to
use Soviet tanks captured in the 1967 war. Also in
December, Israel bombed a Soviet ship in the northern
Canal zone, the area where the Soviets expected Israel
to be cautious due to their own naval presence. Then,
after rejecting the "Rogers Plan," Israel had a top-
level policy reevaluation which led to the January 7
initiation of deep penetration bombing raids against
Egypt. Previously, military activity had been confined
to the area near the Canal but Israel now wanted to
show Egypt that constant harassing of its positions
would now produce massive retaliation.
Ambassador to the United States Yitzhak Rabin
argued that the American government approved of the
bombing missions. It had supplied Israel with Phantoms
in September, making such raids possible, and it
tacitly encouraged them once initiated in order to
undermine Nasser's hold over Egypt. Rabin was a strong
proponent of an American-oriented policy for Israel and
he enjoyed particularly warm relations with Kissinger.
Most likely, his interpretation of American motivations
was based on clues gathered from Kissinger rather than
the State Department, and Kissinger had his own reasons
to work against the "Rogers Plan."
The bombings had an anti-Soviet rationale that
appealed to both the Israelis and Kissinger. It was
hoped that the overthrow of Nasser would be effected,
or that he would be forced to seek accomodation with
the United States. The Soviets would lose in both
instances. Israel obviously viewed Nasser as a dangerous enemy, but the U.S. too wanted to secure his removal
as a warning to the radical Arab camp. In 1969, there
had been an attempted putsch against the Saudi monarchy
and King Idris of Libya had been turned out by Qaddafi.
The Israeli bombing campaign was intentionally
directed against military targets as there was fear that
destruction of factories and infrastructure components
would possibly bring about deeper Soviet involvement.
Rabin discounted this anxiety and advocated strikes
against these latter targets as the most efficient
means of weakening Nasser's government. However, the
Israeli Cabinet opposed such action. The February 12

bombing of a factory in Abu Zaabal, which resulted in the death of seventy civilians, was apparently acciden- tal and represents an isolated episode.

Israel acted cautiously during the War of Attri- tion in order to forestall more direct Soviet involve- ment in Egypt, but it gradually assumed a greater risk and upped the ante. The decision to conduct deep penetration raids was based upon careful consideration of the Soviet response, with a majority led by Allon minimizing the anticipated Soviet reaction. Allon maintained that the Soviet Union only intervenes in contiguous communist-ruled states and that it lacked the technology needed to assist Egypt. Dayan and Eban were in the minority in not wanting to provoke the Soviets, although the foreign ministry's report on the matter did not anticipate a direct Soviet military role in Egypt unless Israeli infantry crossed the Canal.5

The Israeli bombing raids did make Nasser somewhat frantic, but his government did not fall. To buttress his shaky position, Nasser undertook a secret mission to Moscow on January 22 in order to secure additional Soviet military support. The Soviets agreed to provide SAM-3 missiles but said that it would take six months to train Egyptian crews (which already were competent to operate (SAM-2's). Nasser then asked for Soviet crews and Brezhnev hesitated, explaining that air cover would also be needed. Nasser complained that the Soviets did not support Egypt as much as the U)S. aided Israel, and Brezhnev then agreed to consider Nasser's request. The Politburo went along with the proposal, leading eventually to Soviet missile crews being stationed in the interior and Soviet pilots contribut- ing to the air defense system. Maintaining the Egyptian government in power was the prime considera- tion, just as protecting the Syrian regime had been paramount in 1966-67. Brezhnev declared: "Comrade Nasser, the Soviet Union has today taken a decision fraught with grave consequences. It is a decision un- like any we have ever taken before. It will need your help in carrying out, and it will call for restraint on your part."6 The deep penetration raids therefore helped forge closer Soviet-Egyptian military relations and did not drive Nasser toward the United States. Of course, Israel did not know about the secret Soviet commitments to Egypt but it came to recognize the changed situation in March and April as Soviet military personnel began to play a direct role in Egypt's defense.

After deciding to strengthen Egypt, the Soviets felt that the Arabs would be in a better position to negotiate a settlement. Their military capability had improved considerably since the outbreak of the 1967 war, with Israeli Minister of Defense Dayan citing increases in armor of 170 percent in Egypt, 180 percent

in Syria and 120 percent in Iraq and corresponding increases in the number of aircraft of 170 percent, 220
percent and 140 percent. The quality of the weaponry
had also improved considerably.7 Taking cognizance of
this development, the Soviets on January 27 presented a
peace plan which referred to Israeli withdrawal to the
pre-June 1967 "boundaries." As explained in New Times,
these 1949 cease-fire lines would be Israel's permanent
and recognized borders. The Soviets also called for the
return of UN peacekeeping forces and the establishment
of demilitarized zones on both sides of the frontier.
A de facto end of the state of war would go into effect
as soon as a joint Israeli-Arab document was deposited
at the United Nations, but, most significantly, Israeli
withdrawal would not begin until after this deposit was
effected. Freedom of navigation for all states in the
Suez Canal, Gulf of Aqaba and Straits of Tiran was affirmed, but the interpretation in New Times did not give
absolute assurance of Israel's rights in the latter two
waterways.8

While some provisions may have been acceptable to
Israel, others were clearly not. Therefore, the plan
did not really get off the ground. The Soviets rejected direct negotiations, insisting on mediation by
Jarring. They also called for the repatriation of
Palestinian Arab refugees and financial compensation for
those who chose not to return. The settlement was to be
guaranteed by the Security Council or Big Four, a condition unacceptable to Israel. It wanted secure borders
and did not trust superpower guarantees due to its bad
experience with the United Nations and United States in
May 1967. It certainly didn't approve of the Soviet
Union as a guarantor.

The United States may have seen some hope in the
Soviet plan for, on January 30, it announced a thirty-
day freeze on the delivery of Phantom aircraft to Isra
This produced some confusion among Israeli diplomats,
with Rabin maintaining that the green light for deep
penetration raids had not been turned off, while Eban
was discerning a change in the American attitude. Both
were probably correct as U.S. policy was bifurcated at
the time. Rabin was getting his signals from
Kissinger; Eban was receiving his from Rogers and other
State Department officials.

On January 31, Soviet Prime Minister Kosygin sent
a message to Nixon, urging an American effort to secure
Israel's cessation of deep penetration bombing. He
warned that failure to restrain Israel would lead to
increased provision of arms for Egypt. This was a
clever maneuver as the decision had already been made to
establish a direct Soviet military presence in Egypt.
Therefore, American inability to pressure Israel successfully would place the onus on the U.S. for this
Soviet escalation. At the same time, American success

could have led the Soviets to withdraw their commitment
to Nasser. The American response was to call for a
cease-fire and talks on arms control. However, Nixon
warned that the introduction of more sophisticated
Soviet weapons would lead the U.S. to reconsider the
nature of its arms deliveries to Israel. Rabin appreci-
ated this hint about increased American support for
Israel and believed that it had been prompted by the
deep penetration raids and need to counteract the Soviet
role in Egypt. He therefore cabled Jerusalem: "We
have achieved a marked improvement in the United States'
position. Continuation of that improvement depends
first and foremost on keeping up our air raids in the
heart of Egypt."9 From Rabin's perspective, provoking
the Soviets served Israeli interests as the United
States would be forced to come closer to the Israeli
position. As we will soon see, Dayan disagreed with
this analysis and the possibility of a more severe superpower confrontation was averted.

Showdown

Egypt, by now impatient, was using the War of
Attrition to draw in the Soviet Union and spur greater
superpower concern with the issue of occupied territories (as had been evidenced in 1956).10 This coincided
with its preference for an international or United
Nations' solution for the Middle East struggle. Israel
did not favor the outbreak of a War of Attrition, but
then sought to globalize the situation in order to
secure increased American support. This course of
action starkly contrasted with its advocacy of a regional solution. Each state, for its own reason, encouraged the participation of a superpower. This turned an
Arab-Israeli conflict into a Soviet-American confrontation.
In March, SAM-3's and Soviet personnel began
arriving in Egypt, and three squadrons of fighter
aircraft with Soviet crews followed on April 1.11 The
Soviets did not acknowledge these developments, but
obliquely indicated that Soviet members of the military
were in Egypt by charging that Israel was recruiting
American soldiers in West Germany. This has always
been the Soviet modus operandi in such matters. At
the same time, Soviet Muslims "volunteered" their
services to the Palestinian fedayeen; none were trans-
ported to the Middle East.12 While fortifying their
position in Egypt, the Soviets tried to renew negotiations. Many peace demonstrations were staged in the
Soviet Union at the end of February and, on March 10,
Dobrynin asked Kissinger to help arrange a cease-fire.
The following day, Dobrynin urged Rogers to resume Big
Two talks. Israel agreed to a cease-fire on March 17
but then backed out the same day after SAM-3 batteries

with Soviet personnel were discovered in Egypt.13 It
appears, therefore, that the Soviets were hoping that
the lull of a cease-fire would permit them to install
the missiles and improve their military position.
Egypt, with probable Soviet approval, extended an invitation to Nahum Goldmann, President of the World
Jewish Congress, but Israel refused to authorize his
visit. The timing was inopportune, but Israel also
objected to Egypt's procedure of choosing its opponent's negotiator. The United States went along with
the Soviet cease-fire proposal, announcing on March
23 another freeze in Phantom deliveries. Sisco was
then dispatched to Egypt on April 10.

The Soviets were probably serious about peace
negotiations in March 1970, but their military involvement in Egypt worked against any Israeli movement in
that direction. Their position appeared to harden on
Israeli use of waterways and on a formal peace treaty,
but these were probably intended as trade-offs on the
crucial issue of land. The Soviets called for Israeli
withdrawal "from occupied Arab territory," but significantly did not include the word "all." Gaza was not
mentioned and the "el-Qeneitra area" replaced the usual
call for return of the entire Golan Heights. By June,
the same Soviet commentator hardened his position by
not suggesting any territorial concessions and stating
that Israel's legal boundaries were those of 1947. He
nevertheless advocated the pre-war 1967 lines as the
appropriate borders.14

In Israel, Allon wanted to strike at anti-aircraft
sites in the interior even if they were manned by
Soviet personnel, but Dayan was more cautious. He was
ready to accept the Soviet military role in Egypt as
long as it was not extended to within thirty kilometers
of the Canal and he constantly redefined the areas
which Israel should bomb so as to avoid challenging the
Soviets. He told a television audience on March 20
that Israel was not capable of an "all-out confrontation"
with the Soviets and would have "a very difficult situation" should the Soviets act more forcefully and the
United States fail to respond.15

Once aircraft flown by Soviet pilots entered the
fray, Dayan was even more reluctant to provoke the
Soviets. On April 18, Israeli planes had their first
encounter with Soviet-manned aircraft and Dayan immediately ended deep penetration raids. He was surely
concerned about the presence of Soviet pilots, but
Israel's inability to counter the SAM-3's was also an
important consideration. Interestingly, the pilots
communicated in Russian rather than attempt to conceal
their identities. This may possibly have been a signal
to the United States and Israel that the bombing missions had better be halted. Israel, which had previous-

ly pointed out the presence of Soviet military personnel at SAM-3 sites, did not want to publicize the
presence of Soviet pilots. It believed that any
clamor would only force the Soviets to continue their
involvement in order to save face.[16] However, the U.S.
pressured Israel on this point as it wanted to display
Soviet aggressive behavior at a time when it was preparing to move into Cambodia. Israel gave in and, on
April 28, it revealed the Soviet aerial role in Egypt.
The Soviets did not admit to having pilots there, but
Kosygin indirectly indicated that such was the case
when he failed to issue a denial when queried about
the subject.[17]

Speaking on May 4, Dayan said that he was reliev-
ed that there had not been a serious Soviet-Israeli
confrontation in Egypt, and he expressed hope that
members of Soviet crews were not casualties of Israeli
air attacks. He explained the cessation of deep
penetration raids by bluntly stating that Israel did
not want to engage Soviet pilots. Dayan averred that
Israel would maintain its position along the Canal,
but that challenging the Soviets further to the west
would necessitate American support.[18]

Soviet military participation in combat situations
in Egypt represented the first such action outside the
communist-ruled states since the Second World War. It
is interesting to note that Soviet threats to intervene
in Egypt in 1956 and 1967 were not carried out, while
direct involvement in 1970 was not preceded by any
threat. In this instance the Soviet military role was
induced by Egyptian weakness and inability to protect
itself against Israeli bombing missions. Furthermore,
the Soviet opportunity to play a diplomatic role in
the Middle East was enhanced by Egypt's poor performance in battle. [19] Kissinger's theory that Israeli
retention of the territories reduced Soviet influence
in the area must therefore be viewed circumspectly.

Israel always expected to benefit more from
superpower competition in the region than from
hegemony of either the U.S. or U.S.S.R., as ample
freedom of action was sought. Events in early 1970
were therefore developing favorably from this perspective but Israeli military success against Egypt
may have gone too far, precipitating direct Soviet
involvement. The strategic balance was therefore
altered unfavorably, just as it was in late 1982 when
the Soviets came to the assistance of a weakened Syria.
For Israel, military prowess can lead to Soviet encir-
clement.

Due to the expanding Soviet role in Egypt, the
United States came to view Israel as a more strategic
anti-Soviet asset. For the Americans, the Soviet
military presence had to be analyzed in the context of

Mediterranean and NATO security interests. After all,
Soviet surveillance flights over the Sixth Fleet were
conducted from Egyptian airfields.20 Nixon wrote to
Kissinger in March 1970: "We are for Israel because
Israel in our view is the only state in the Mideast
which is pro-freedom and an effective opponent to
Soviet expansion."21

The Dubious Peace

Buttressed by Soviet military power, Egypt became
more amenable to a political settlement. In his May
Day speech, Nasser implied that he would welcome a
diplomatic initiative. He obviously realized that only
the Americans could deliver the Israelis; the Soviets
could defend Egypt but were not capable of enticing
Israel into negotiations. Then on June 2, Dobrynin
told Rogers that Egypt was ready to make some concessions in order to arrange a cease-fire.22 Israel was
also moving in this direction, due to American prodding
rather than favorable objective conditions. The United
States wanted to defuse the situation in order to avoid
any serious confrontation with the Soviet Union so it
first applied the stick by refusing to deliver Phantoms.
Then it successfully switched to the carrot, promising
to release the aircraft. Israel responded as, on May
26, it finally accepted SC 242 as the basis for negotiations. It had registerd approval of this resolution
on other occasions, such as in Eban's speech to the
General Assembly on October 8, 1968, but such declara-
tions had been conditional. Now Israel announced un-
equivocal acceptance and it permitted Nahum Goldmann to
engage in personal diplomacy. In June, he met with
Tito, a close friend of Nasser, and with King Hassan of
Morocco. In return for its moderate stance, Israel expected the United States to adopt a more strongly anti-
Soviet position in regard to deployment in Egypt, but
it did not request any direct American military involvement on the Israeli side.

On June 19, a major American diplomatic effort was
launched through the release of another Rogers' plan
(known as "Rogers B" or "Rogers II"). It was less
specific than the December 1969 plan, calling only for a
cease-fire and the initiation of talks under the auspices of Jarring. It was addressed to Israel, Egypt
and Jordan but Syria was excluded as it had not accepted SC 242. Israel preferred direct negotiations to
mediation by Jarring but "Rogers B" offended her less
than "Rogers A" as it did not propose the details of a
territorial solution. Furthermore, "Rogers B" (as contrasted with "Rogers A") was not apparently cleared
with the Soviets so both Israel and Egypt were less
wary about superpower collusion at their expense.23 It
is interesting to note that Israel was able to reject
the original "Rogers Plan" because the American admin-

istration was divided over its merits and sent out contradictory signals. "Rogers B" was supported in a more
unified manner by U.S. officials, thereby permitting
Israel less leeway to turn it down.

The Soviet Union was not hostile to "Rogers B,"
but felt left out of the process. In order to get involved in the diplomatic effort, a Soviet plan was presented to a meeting of the Big 4 on June 24. It was
then released on July 9 by the Soviet embassy in
London, although it was dated July 11. A denunciation
of terrorism was deleted from the public version, possibly to make it easier for Nasser to accept a cease-
fire.[24] Otherwise, the Soviet plan was not noticeably
dissimilar from "Rogers A," proposing a withdrawal from
territories in return for a termination of the state of
war and guarantees of Israel's borders. Strangely, the
details of the plan were not published in the Soviet
Union until October, by which time "Rogers B" had been
made operative.[25] This suggests that the Soviets, as
of July, expected "Rogers B" to be adopted and did not
want to lose face by publicizing their own non-adopted
plan.

On June 3, Nixon said that the United States had
to meet the communist threat in Vietnam in order to
show allies in other parts of the world (he specifically included the Middle East) that they could rely on
American commitments. This pleased Israel and it was
even more delighted by Nixon's remarks in an interview
on July 1. He stressed the danger of the Soviet role
in Egypt, claimed that the danger of superpower conflict was greater than in Vietnam and pledged an
American effort to keep Israel militarily strong as any
weakening of its position would produce an Arab assault.
In private briefings, American officials maintained
that the Soviets had upset the Arab-Israeli military
balance and had established an aerial threat to U.S.
forces in the Eastern Mediterranean.[26]

Israel remained deeply concerned about the Soviet
military role in Egypt, but its signals during June and
July 1970 were mixed. Eban said that Israel would
maintain its position along the Egyptian front, but he
urged caution and indicated that Israel would not initiate conflict with Soviet personnel. He also believed that a direct clash with the Soviets would produce "panicked retreat" on the part of Israel. Eban
cited Israel's 1956 agreement to withdraw from the
Sinai after the Soviet Union threatened intervention.
Dayan was also circumspect. His response to queries
implied that enhanced Soviet participation in Egypt's
air defense had led to Israeli inhibitions to penetrate
certain sectors of Egypt's air space.[27]

Prime Minister Meir expressed greater bravado in
the face of the Soviet challenge. She labeled the

Soviets "imperialists," said that Israel didn't fear
their military presence in Egypt and charged that they
were encouraging Egypt to go to war. She implied that
the United States would back Israel in a confrontation
and declared that the Soviets could only go as far as
the U.S. would permit them. Chief of Staff Bar-Lev
announced that Israel would fight the Soviets if they
came closer to the Canal and threatened Israeli positions.[28]

The Soviet peace plan was rejected by all Israeli
officials. Rabin called it the "throwing of sand into
the world's eyes" and a means of avoiding a direct response to the "Rogers B" plan. Director General of the
Foreign Ministry Gideon Rafael claimed that the plan
was a cover for military involvement in Egypt and that
the Soviet Union had no right to formulate peace plans
in the first place. He stressed the principle that
only the direct participants had that role (a contradictory position as Israel was soon to accept the
American-sponsored "Rogers B" plan). Eban refused to
accept the plan and pointed to Soviet direction of
Egypt's military and political affairs.[29]

Nasser was in the Soviet Union for almost three
weeks and, shortly after returning home, he announced
on July 23 that Egypt had accepted the "Rogers B" proposal. Al-Fatah's radio broadcasts from Cairo were
terminated as that organization opposed the American
initiative.[30] The Soviet Union backed Nasser's decision,
maintaining that its military assistance had made a
political solution possible. The Soviets were pleased
that the Jarring mission would provide the forum for
negotiations, but they were distressed that a cease-
fire was to be arranged under American auspices. Soviet
commentators usually did not mention "Rogers B," mentioning only a cease-fire and resumption of Jarring's
mediation.[31]

Why did Egypt agree to the American plan for a
cease-fire? The evidence is surely mixed, but it appears that both Egypt and the Soviet Union felt that the
timing was auspicious. Egypt's military position had
improved, there would be no direct negotiations with
Israel and missiles could surreptitiously be moved
closer to the Canal while the cease-fire was in effect.
There were many hints in the Soviet media that the time
was ripe for a political settlement, and a statement by
the Supreme Soviet and the communique at the end of
Nasser's visit were in accord with this sentiment.[32]
Of course, the Soviets hoped that their peace plan
would serve as the basis, not the "Rogers B" proposal.

Nasser seems to have been caught in a bind between
sentiment and reality. The military option was preferred, but the Soviet Union was unwilling to provide the
advanced weapons needed to tip the military balance in
favor of Egypt. The Soviet Union had displayed its

willingness to defend Egypt, but not to support offensive actions against Israel. Meanwhile, the United
States was providing Israel with offensive weapons.
Thus Nasser had to give serious consideration to the
American plan. When he came to Moscow, the Soviets
were still opposed to the provision of more sophisticated arms. It seems that a trade-off then took
place in which Egypt agreed to seek a political
solution and the Soviet Union expressed willingness to
back Egypt's acceptance of an American proposal. As
described by Brezhnev, the talks with Nasser were
"frank," indicating serious disagreement. Accounts by
Sadat and Heikal point in the same direction, but they
portray Nasser as the prime initiator of the cease-fire
acceptance. Brezhnev implied the opposite when he referred to "the constructive attitude adopted on this
matter" by Egypt. The elusive truth appears to be in
between.[33]

Israel leaned against the "Rogers B" plan, but it
did not close the door to a political settlement. In
July, Rabin had a discussion with Dobrynin at a party.
He had been the Israeli ambassador in Washington since
February 1968, but this was the first conversation with
his Soviet counterpart. It is also possible that Allon
met secretly with a Soviet representative in Switzerland, although this has been denied by the Israeli
government.[34] Once Nasser announced his acceptance of
"Rogers B," Israel decided to seize the diplomatic opportunity. It may have been influenced by military
factors as a Soviet-piloted aircraft entered Sinai
airspace on July 25 in pursuit of a Skyhawk and the
Soviets began to move their missiles toward the Canal
on July 29. On July 30, as a parting shot, Israel lur-
ed Soviet aircraft into a trap and downed four MiG's,
killing their pilots. The Soviets did not protest this
action as public revelation of their incompetence in
battle was not advisable. Israel too kept the incident
under wraps until October 25, when Meir discussed the
episode in New York. On July 31, Israel declared its
acceptance of "Rogers B." This produced a serious
split in the ruling coalition, eventually leading to
the defection of Menachem Begin's GAHAL movement.
Israel and Egypt had both agreed to the cease-fire because their superpower patrons had refused to be drawn
in any deeper. The United States pressured Israel to
accept "Rogers B" because it did not want a confrontation with the Soviets in the Middle East, while the
Soviets forced Egypt into a negotiating posture by refusing to supply offensive weapons that could draw the
U. S. more directly to the side of Israel.

On August 7, a cease-fire went into effect and
Jarring undertook missions to Israel, Egypt and Jordan.
The Soviet Union was excluded from the negotiating
process (although it was supportive of Jarring) so

renewed diplomacy did not serve as an impetus to improved Soviet-Israeli relations. Meir said that Israel had nothing to propose to the Soviet Union and that no basis for a rapprochement existed. She believed that contacts should be through the U.S. as intermediary, as direct discussions could disturb Israeli-American relations.35 The Israeli attitude toward the Soviet Union was conditioned by flagrant violations of the cease-fire, as Soviet missiles were moved nearer the Canal. The Soviets denied any responsibility, claiming that they were not party to any cease-fire agreement, but it was obvious that they were abetting Egypt's violations.36 As we will later see, the emplacement of SAM-3's closer to the Canal set the stage for Egypt's successful crossing of the waterway in October 1973.

The Soviets, trying to take advantage of Egypt's improved position, pressed for a political solution but Israel was not interested and abandoned the Jarring talks on September 6. Meir told Nixon that the Soviets were more responsible for the problems of the area than were the Arabs, due to their military assistance and direct presence in Egypt.37 The U.S., which had brokered the cease-fire, was furious about the violations and agreed to provide Israel with more Phantoms. The U.S. was also concerned about Soviet plans for a submarine base in Cienfuegos, Cuba, viewing it too as a violation of a previous commitment. On September 29, Nixon visited the Sixth Fleet, an act which disturbed the Soviets, so superpower tension remained extremely high. On the Egyptian front, peace prevailed despite the violations and Kosygin warned the Egyptians when he attended Nasser's funeral at the end of September that they should continue to exercise restraint.38 However, another Middle East crisis had already erupted.

Black September

The emergence of a civil war in Jordan between loyalist and Palestinian forces further strained superpower relations in the Middle East, led to increased American and Israeli distrust of the Soviet Union, and solidified the growing alliance between the United States and Israel. From the American perspective, the introduction of Syrian troops to assist the Palestinians was viewed as another Soviet probe of U.S. resolve. Consequently, American diplomats sought contacts with their Soviet counterparts in order to ease the crisis; Syrians were left out of the process for they were deemed Soviet proxies.39

The perceived framework of superpower rivalry conditioned the American reaction to Black September, leading to support for Jordan against the Soviet-Syrian-Palestinian alliance and to the soliciting of

Israeli assistance. Israel, after strong American
urging, agreed to aid the Jordanian government by
moving troops to the northern front as a signal to
deter further Syrian involvement. Syria then failed
to provide air cover for its tanks that were already
within Jordan and the monarchist forces routed the
Palestinians and the Syrian tank units. Israel felt
that it was acting on behalf of U.S. interests, a fact
which later caused extensive soul-searching as many
analysts believed that Israel should have let Hussein
fall and a Palestinian state be established on the East
Bank. For the Americans, Israel was serving as a
regional proxy in accordance with a pattern being
established by both Iran and South Vietnam. The Soviet
Union did not directly counter the successful American
strategy in Jordan, any more than the U.S. had done
anything to counter the introduction of Soviet military
personnel into Egypt. Each superpower had indicated
where its major regional commitment lay.[40]

Did the Soviet Union really encourage Syrian intervention? Probably yes, but it acted cautiously and
called for withdrawal once an Israeli countermove was
evident. Furthermore, the Soviets had assured the
United States that their military advisers in Syria
would not cross into Jordanian territory.[41] Nevertheless, Black September represented a watershed in Soviet-
American relations. It led to stronger American
military support for Israel (through the extension of
credits) so it could act as a deterrent force to Soviet
aggressive behavior in the Middle East. In fact, the
United States offered weapons to Israel that had not
even been requested as it wanted them tested for possible use in Vietnam.[42]

Frosty Interaction

An intensive Soviet anti-Zionist campaign, which
gathered momentum in November 1969 and peaked in
March 1970 (the month that Soviet military personnel
arrived in Egypt), kept Soviet-Israeli relations
rather cool.[43] On January 13, Pravda published eleven
letters from anti-Zionist Jews and, on March 4, forty
prominent Jews held a press conference to denounce
Israel and fifty-two signed an anti-Zionist statement.
The campaign tailed off in May, but the arrest on
June 15 of Soviet Jews who were charged with plotting
an airliner hijacking produced a great outcry in
Israel. In July, a petition was presented to the
Supreme Soviet by Jews seeking to emigrate and, in
August, Tekoah brought an Israeli protest about Soviet
treatment of Jews to UN Secretary General U Thant.
Later that month, Meir released a letter from fifteen
Jews in Minsk who wanted to leave the Soviet Union.

Jewish emigration dropped from 3000 in 1969 to only 1000 in 1970. The only positive development regarding Soviet Jews was the appointment in July of the initial Jewish first secretary of Birobidjan and the selection of two Jews to represent that autonomous region in the Soviet of Nationalities. In the past, only one of the five representatives had been Jewish.44

Contact between the Soviets and Israelis was minimal in 1970. The most significant encounter was at a twin-city conference in Leningrad in July, where events did not proceed smoothly. First, the Israelis were upset that their visas did not arrive promptly. Then, the Soviets protested when Israel tried to include Jerusalem mayor Teddy Kollek in the delegation, even though Jerusalem had no twin city at the conference. Israel then substituted the deputy major of Jerusalem, but the Soviets wouldn't let him participate when he arrived. When delegations from other countries were taken on a tour of the Soviet Union, the Israelis were excluded. The behavior of Israeli delegates irritated the hosts. There were meetings with Soviet Jews, and the mayor of Netanya passed out Israeli symbols (including the star of David) in a synagogue. He also attempted to offer blessings for the Israeli president, prime minister and defense minister.45 Otherwise, there was very little interaction between citizens of the two countries. Soviet groups did not travel to Israel, but Israelis did attend Soviet conferences in September on partical physics and agriculture.46

The Vietnam issue continued to divide the Soviet Union and Israel. In January 1970, a seven-man South Vietnamese delegation came to Israel to study the technical capabilities of the armed forces. Such collaboration concerned the Soviets, although Israel did not establish diplomatic relations with the Saigon government. Vietnam also affected Israeli-American relations. Rogers told Rabin that American Jews were active in opposing the U.S. role in the war, thereby implying that Israel should do something to stop them.47 As explained earlier, such an American approach had been evident as early as the spring of 1966.

Another problematic issue was West Germany. The Soviets had consistently vilified the Israelis for their ties to the Bonn government but they had to shift course after effecting their own rapprochement with the West Germans. After a non-aggression treaty was signed on August 12, the Soviets muted their criticism of German-Israeli relations but continued to draw analogies between the Israelis and Nazis.

The Palestinian problem was deemphasized by the Soviets in 1970 as they worked toward a political solution between states. Arafat made his first public

visit to the Soviet Union in February as a guest of
the Afro-Asian People's Solidarity Committee (he was
not directly invited by the government), but he then
balanced his visit by journeying to China the next
month. He was not received by either Mao Tse-tung or
Chou En-lai as his cause was receiving little international recognition at the time. Also in March, the
pro-Soviet communist parties of Lebanon, Jordan, Syria
and Iraq organized their own Palestinian guerrilla
movement in the West Bank, al-Ansar. This indicated
an absence of strong Soviet support for the PLO. In
fact, al-Ansar was expected to join the PLO and influence it from within but it was singularly unsuccessful in this endeavor. The PLO refused to include it
in its higher councils as al-Ansar favored a political
settlement and opposed the destruction of Israel.48

. . . .

   By October 1970, the Soviet Union and Israel were
almost completely alienated, even though direct conflict between them was being avoided through the
maintenance of a cease-fire on the Egyptian front.
Soon, contacts between the two states began to increase
and secret diplomacy came to play a major role. The
next few years were to be critical as the possibility
of arranging a permanent political settlement in the
Middle East was seriously examined by both parties.

6
Unrewarded Flirtations

From a low point in late 1970, Soviet-Israeli relations began to improve over the next few years.
Bilateral contacts became more extensive and Moscow
opened the doors to a mass exodus of Soviet Jews. Most
of the initiative was on the Soviet side, as it was
hoped that better relations with Israel would further
the prospects for detente with the United States.
Israel was not particularly responsive, fearing that
detente could lead to an imposed settlement in the
Middle East or a trade-off with Vietnam. Egypt too was
wary of detente, believing that the Soviet Union was
withholding advanced weaponry in order to appease the
Americans. Egypt temporarily weakened its military
position by expelling most Soviet personnel but,
paradoxically, this eventually enhanced its prospects
for initiating another war.

In order to understand the course of Soviet-
Israeli relations during this period, we must focus on
the following questions: How did the evolution of
Soviet-American detente affect Middle Eastern diplomacy? Why did the Soviet Union decide to permit Jewish
emigration on an extensive scale? Why did the Soviets
send a secret emissary to talk to Israeli officials?
Why did the Soviet Union sign a friendship treaty with
Egypt? Why did Soviet-Egyptian relations then deteriorate, leading to Sadat's ejection of Soviet troops?

These were years of active diplomacy, but no
significant accomplishment. The Soviet Union and
Israel did not reestablish formal ties, and progress
was not made toward a political settlement of the Arab-
Israeli conflict. Nevertheless, the cease-fire on the
Egyptian front prevailed and a precarious peace was
maintained. The PLO, effectively stymied in the occupied territories, therefore resorted to spectacular
acts of terrorism overseas in order to draw attention
to its cause.

Missed Opportunities

Egyptian violations of the cease-fire had led to
Israel's refusal to cooperate with the Jarring mission.
Israel had never liked Jarring's diplomacy in the first
place since it was carried out within the framework of
the United Nations. Israel still insisted on direct
talks with the Arabs, while the Soviets hoped to revive
Jarring's efforts. The Soviets tried to induce the
Israelis by asserting that the UN was most necessary
"at the first stage of a settlement," but Israel never
embraced the Jarring process with any enthusiasm.[1]
Jarring periodically renewed his rounds of negotiation,
but to no avail. Israel was cool and the Syrians had
little interest in a political settlement.

Although Israel was not willing to withdraw from
occupied territories in the absence of a directly-
negotiated peace settlement, it did consider a partial
pullback from the Suez Canal. Dayan was the chief
proponent of this position, arguing that a more secure
defense line could be established further east at the
Gidi and Mitla passes. The possibility of conflict
with Soviet personnel would also be reduced. An Israeli
pullback would lead to the reopening of the Canal, making Egypt less likely to initiate hostilities as it
would lose extensive revenue. It is also possible that
Dayan wanted the Canal operating in order to increase
superpower interest in its southern gateway, the Red
Sea. Israeli shipping en route to Eilat was threatened
at the Bab el-Mandeb Strait and an assurance of free
passage from the major powers would have helped secure
Israel's maritime links to Asian and African states.[2]

The United States was not anxious to see the Canal
reopened since it was vital to Soviet commercial interests and could also permit warships in the Mediterranean to deploy in the Indian Ocean. Nixon did not
take a strong stance on this issue, but the U.S. Navy
and Kissinger were signaling the Israelis to retain
their positions along the Canal. Dayan was unable to
convince the Israeli government to support his plan.
Therefore, the Bar-Lev line of fortifications on the
east bank of the Canal was reinforced, creating false
security in accordance with a Maginot mentality.

The United States was pleased with the continuation of a stalemate as it forced Israel to maintain a
large army on constant alert. Israel could then serve
as an important anti-Soviet military asset in the
region. The state of no war, no peace also helped
moderate Arab governments stay in power. They were
needed both militarily and financially in the confrontation with Israel, but would possibly be undermined
by radical forces if peace with Israel was achieved.
Furthermore, as discussed previously, Kissinger

believed that Arab states would have to turn toward the
U.S. in order to seek concessions from Israel. Israel
was content to preserve the status quo. Meir, in
contrast with Dayan, wanted to freeze the situation as
time was expected to work in Israel's favor. The mood
in Jerusalem was extremely confident as it was believed
that the stalemate could not lead to a superpower confrontation. Sadat was deemed too weak to effect any
significant change in Egypt's position.

The Soviet Union did not furnish Egypt with an
offensive military capability. Chief of State Nikolai
Podgornyi took a rather militant public line during his
visit in January 1971, but he referred only to a Soviet
commitment to strengthen Egypt's defensive capability.
According to Heikal, Podgornyi was privately urging
Egyptian caution and restraint.[3] Sadat realized that
he had no military option, so he advanced his own
peace plan.

Sadat presented his plan to Jarring on January 15
and went public on February 4. He wanted an iterim
agreement to reopen the Canal, secure Israeli troop
withdrawal to the Sinai passes, and extend the cease-
fire. A peace document would be deposited at the
United Nations, but there would not be a directly-nego-
tiated peace treaty. Sadat's plan was not essentially
different from that favored by Dayan, except for a
demand that Israel must agree to an eventual complete
withdrawal from occupied territory as a precondition to
the activation of an interim settlement. Israel would
not countenance such a stipulation and categorically
rejected the plan on February 9.

The Soviet Union endorsed Sadat's plan, and
Podgornyi was probably involved in its formulation.
The Soviets pressed for a political solution, but their
efforts were doomed as both Israel and Syria were
unreceptive. Talks in Moscow with Syrian president
Hafez al-Assad were marked by their "frankness," and
Kosygin condemned "extremist politicians" and those
who want "to bargain from positions of brute strength."
He also told the visiting Syrian delegation: "It is
necessary to continue marching along the road of closing the ranks of the Arab peoples, maintaining realism
in the appraisal of the situation and vigilance toward
the enemy while relying on support from the sincere
friends of the Arabs.[4]

In May, Syrian communist party leader Khaled
Bakdash was received in Moscow by Boris Ponomarev and
chief ideologist Mikhail Suslov. Members of the Syrian
delegation took notes of the meeting and they were
later leaked by one faction of the Syrian Communist
Party during an internal squabble. This transcript il-
lustrates private Soviet perceptions at the time, and
is therefore a most important document which was never
intended for public release.[5] The Soviet spokesmen

opposed a military solution as unrealistic. They
argued that a war unleashed without adequate preparation would trigger the collapse of "progressive"
regimes and possibly precipitate a Soviet-American
confrontation. Egypt and Syria were not capable of
defeating Israel, so a political solution should be
sought. It would strengthen the "progressive" regimes,
diminish Israel's international support, and improve
the Arab world image. The Soviets told the Syrians
that they would not support the Arabs if they attempted
to destroy Israel but, they added: "Of course, after
the consequences of the aggressor have been eliminated
the struggle will have to continue and aim its bayonets
at the Zionists."6

The Soviet position was not as contradictory as it
may seem. Israel's existence as a state was clearly
endorsed, "not only tactically but also as a matter
of principle." One of the Soviets averred: "Israel
is a fact. There was not a Jewish nation or a Jewish
nationality--this is obvious. But now an Israeli
nation is arising. Israel has arisen on artificial
foundations, and I do not want to justify it historical-
ly. But let us start from existing facts."7 However,
the problem was not Israel's right to exist but its
"colonialist character." The Arabs would have to continue their struggle against Israel as a Zionist entity, not striving to eliminate it but to alter its
nature. The Arab national liberation movement against
Zionism must seek to reconcile Jews and Arabs, permit
the return of Palestinian Arab refugees, end the Jewish
state concept associated with Zionism, and permit the
people of Israel to exercise their right of national
self-determination. If they should decide to unify
with another state, this would be their right as a
separate Israeli state is not required. In other
words, the Soviets opposed the military destruction of
Israel but, in the long run, advocated demographic and
ideological changes from within that could produce its
merger into a greater Palestinian entity, perhaps in
amalgamation with the West Bank and Gaza. Zionism
would be discarded, but Jews would continue to live on
their land. The Soviet position was consistent with
communist ideology and its enunciation in a party to
party forum was not at all unusual.

In May 1971, Sadat purged Ali Sabry and other
leftists who were accused of plotting against his government. He may have believed that the Soviet Union
was supporting a conspiracy, but he was also signaling
the United States of his continued interest in a new
round of diplomacy. Sadat was frustrated by the Soviet
Union's lack of military support, and the U.S. saw an
opportunity to improve relations with Egypt and possibly secure the removal of Soviet military personnel.

Secretary of State Rogers had visited Egypt on May 4,
despite the absence of diplomatic relations, as part of
an American initiative similar to the moribund Sadat
plan. The U.S. was calling for pullbacks of both
Israeli and Egyptian forces from the Canal but, more
importantly, it linked an interim settlement to the
withdrawal of Soviet forces from Egypt. That is why
the United States pursued such a course in the spring
of 1971, whereas it previously was content to let the
Canal remain closed. If Egypt was amenable to breaking
with the Soviets and moving closer to the U.S., then
the reopening of the Canal was worth the price. In
addition, the Soviet Union was not to be a party to the
diplomatic process.

   Although the Soviet Union had backed the Sadat
plan earlier that year, it opposed the Rogers initiative due to its exclusion from the negotiations and its
probable realization that its own position in Egypt was
being undermined. It appears that Sadat was ready to
renew diplomatic relations with the United States if
there was a partial settlement and that he was prepared to expel Soviet military personnel once Israel
completed its pullback. The United States was going
to reward Sadat by pressuring Israel to return all
Egyptian territory. The plan ran into numerous difficulties and was never implemented. Sadat wanted the
interim agreement to represent the first stage of a
total Israeli withdrawal, but Israel was not willing to
proffer such assurances. It did not trust the Soviets
and feared that they would transfer troops to the east
bank of the Canal once Israel drew back to the passes.
Israel also wanted a guarantee of Soviet withdrawal
from Egypt before it pulled back from the Canal.
Kissinger even wanted the Soviets to leave Egypt before
an Israeli withdrawal was initiated, while Rogers and
Sisco were prepared to implement the interim arrangement
along the Canal prior to the Soviet departure.[8] In any
case, the Soviet Union acted quickly to head off such a
settlement; it proved successful in its efforts.

   The Soviet Union had constantly turned down
Egyptian requests for a bilateral treaty, but
Podgornyi[9] suddenly arrived in May and asked Sadat to
sign one.   The Soviets were probably trying to counter
what they perceived as a declining position in Egypt,
due to the arrest of Sabry and the negotiations with
the Americans. The friendship treaty was the first
between the Soviet Union and a non-communist state, and
it called for the Soviet provision to Egypt of arms and
military training "with a view to strengthening its
capacity to eliminate the consequences of aggression."
This meant that Egypt would be assisted in recovering
occupied territory, but not in offensive actions
against Israel proper. There was no Soviet commitment
to supply troops in case of war with Israel, only an

obligation to hold consultations.

Israel viewed the treaty as an ominous sign, with
Meir saying that the Israeli negotiating position
would be hardened in response to this more extensive
Soviet penetration of the region. American officials
appeared divided · but deeply concerned. Some viewed
the treaty in the context of Arab-Israeli relations,
while others saw it as a counterweight to NATO activities in the Mediterranean.[10] In retrospect, the treaty
was indicative of Soviet weakness rather than strength
or offensive design. It should be viewed in the context of the cautionary remarks made to the Syrian communists that month, and it is evident that the Soviets
did not follow it with any encouragement of Egyptian
militancy. In fact, the Egyptians were passing the
word privately that there was less to the treaty than
met the eye. Nevertheless, it was beyond comprehension
in Israel and the United States that only a year later
Sadat would expel almost all Soviet military personnel
from Egypt.

Strange Interlude

Two mysterious episodes took place within the
space of three weeks during the spring of 1971. First,
Prime Minister Meir traveled to Scandinavia the last
week in May and rumors abounded that she had a secret
discussion with Soviet officials. Press speculation was
spurred by the simultaneous trip to Norway and Denmark
of veteran Soviet diplomat Semyon Tsarapkin, as well as
by the disappearance of Meir and her chief political
adviser Simcha Dinitz on a supposed private visit to
the small Finnish town of Rovaniemi. Some did not believe their accounts of frolicking in a sauna and suspected that they were covering for a secret conclave
with the Soviets. Meir denied that she had met any
Soviet officials, but joked that the speculation had
made Sisco "excited" and Sadat "worried."[11] The
Soviets never referred to any meeting, but also didn't
deny its existence.

Meir probably did not rendezvous with the Soviets
because a meeting at such a high level would normally
have been preceded by some substantive agreements at a
lower level. None were evident. It is also unlikely
that Meir would have met with Soviet officials below
her station or that her obvious counterpart, Kosygin,
would have risked the revelation of a meeting with the
Israeli prime minister. Nevertheless, Meir's trip did
lead to contacts with the Soviets. Her main purpose
was to attend a conference of the Second International
in Helsinki and it just so happens that Soviet journal-
ist-diplomat Victor Louis was also present. According
to some accounts, Louis approached Dinitz and arranged
to visit Israel a few weeks later.[12] Dinitz denies
meeting with Louis in Helsinki and claims that he did

not even know he was there. He maintains that Louis'
trip to Israel was worked out after the conference
through an Israeli who formerly served as a diplomat
in Moscow.[13]
     In any case, Louis arrived in Israel on June 13
for a six-day visit. He was Jewish, had been to
Israel previously in 1963 and had often represented
the Soviet Union in delicate international negotiations.
Louis was known as a source of Kremlin-inspired leaks,
was suspected of having ties to the KGB and was an unofficial representative of the Soviet government whose
statements could always be officially denied. He (and
later the Israeli foreign ministry) maintained that his
visit was for the treatment of lumbago, and he indeed
underwent some tests at a hospital in Tel Aviv, but he
surely did not travel so far to solicit the opinion of
Israeli doctors.
     Louis had discussions with former Israeli diplo-
mats who had been stationed in Moscow, but his main
session was with Meir's adviser, Dinitz. Louis called
for an improvement in relations and an increase in
trade. He asked Israel to alter its anti-Soviet stance
so that moderate forces in the Kremlin would be
strengthened and he personally visited the Western Wall
as a symbolic gesture to the Israelis. Dinitz raised
the issue of Soviet Jews but Louis was unwilling to
discuss it, claiming that it was a domestic Soviet
concern. Dinitz also questioned whether Louis' overtures had official sanction, as Dinitz was in a position to speak for the Israeli prime minister. Louis
claimed that an official letter would be received from
the Soviet government within a few weeks, substantiat-
ing his presentation to Dinitz, but no such letter
ever arrived.[14] Louis also sought appointments with
top Israeli officials but the Cabinet decided, based on
the advice of Dinitz, that meetings with Meir, Foreign
Minister Eban and Minister of Defense Dayan would not
be scheduled.
     Louis' journey to Israel was part of a Soviet pat-
tern at the time. Dobrynin was talking to journalists
about a possible Soviet-Israeli rapprochement and
Soviet correspondents in Washington dined with the
Israeli correspondent for Haaretz. MAKI leader Moshe
Sneh claims that two party members were approached by
Soviet officials and sounded out on the reestablishment
of ties. Israel too made some gesture toward the
Soviet Union. Meir and Eban called for the resumption
of diplomatic relations, with Eban maintaining that
Soviet influence in the Middle East was "incomplete" in
the absence of "some form of relationship with Israel."
Israel also toned down its anti-Soviet rhetoric, with
Meir not using the forum of the Helsinki meeting of the
Second International to protest Soviet treatment of
Jews.[15] Perhaps Israel wanted to signal to the

Americans some warming of relations with the Soviet
Union in order to counteract the American move toward
Egypt.

Victor Louis' trip to Israel was not mentioned in
the Soviet media, and Israeli censorship was only
temporarily successful in suppressing news of his
activities. In fact, the Israeli government was condemned by that country's National Editors' Association
for trying to block publication of information.[16]
The more important issue, however, is why did Louis come
to Israel and why did the Soviet Union moderate its attitude toward the Jewish state in June 1971? Many
factors seem to be pertinent. The United States was
negotiating with Egypt so the Soviets, through their
talks with the Israelis, were signaling that two could
play the game. Perhaps they wanted Egypt to cut off
its diplomacy with the Americans, fearing that a resumption of Egyptian-American relations was in the offing. Louis, during his visit seemed particularly interested in the Israeli perception of Soviet-Egyptian
relations. Egypt was obviously confused by Soviet
overtures to Israel, but Gromyko assured Foreign
Minister Mahmoud Riad that the Soviet Union was not
trying to reestablish formal relations with Meir's
government.[17]

The Soviet Union needed some relationship with
Israel in order to participate in the negotiating process, as it had been effectively excluded by the United
States. It may also have wanted to use its improved
image in Jerusalem as a steppingstone to detente with
the United States, or to induce Israel to curtail its
international campaign over Soviet Jewry. The fact
that North Vietnam presented its first peace plan the
same month may also have been relevant, as the Soviets
may have been working toward a superpower agreement on
both crises.

The Soviets may also have hoped to neutralize
Israel's support for the West in the Eastern Mediterranean. They were concerned about Israel's possible
entry into NATO, its intelligence connections to the
United States and its capacity to support the Sixth
Fleet at a time when a plot against Makarios' Cypriot
government was anticipated. In fact, Makarios visited
the Soviet Union that very month. The Soviets additionally may have wanted to gauge public and official attitudes in Israel, as their lack of diplomatic representation since 1967 had severely limited their sources of information. Although briefed by members of RAKAH, such
interpretations were clearly not typical of Israelis as
a whole.[18]

Throughout this period, the Soviet Union maintained
that it did not seek to restore relations with Israel.
Gromyko said of such reports that "they do not even

deserve to be refuted."[19] This is basically correct as
the Soviets did not want to court Israel but only
flirt with her. Their aims were tactical, as they
would not risk jeopardizing their relationship with
the Arabs by reestablishing ties with Israel. Israel
had no reason to effect a rapprochement with the
Soviet Union, but it favored official diplomatic relations as a matter of principle.

Triangulation

Director of the CIA Richard Helms was in Israel
from June 27 to July 1 to discuss the Soviet-Egyptian
treaty and the Soviet military presence in Egypt. He
met with Meir, Dayan and Eban to strengthen Israeli-
American strategic cooperation, leading to Dayan's
announcement on July 10 that NATO powers could use
Sinai airbases in operations directed at the Soviet
Union.[20] In other developments that month, the Soviets
suffered some additional setbacks in the region.
Hussein's Jordanian government again put down a challenge from the Palestinians and Numeiry's Sudanese
government survived an attempted overthrow by communists. On the Egyptian front, the Soviet role did not
change except for two incidents in October and November. Soviet aircraft flew beyond their normal zones
of operation, penetrating Sinai airspace and conducting reconnaissance along Israel's coast near Ashkelon.[21]
The Americans and Soviets were active diplomatically in attempting to work toward a Middle East settlement. As explained by Kissinger, Nixon did not want a
crisis in the area during the 1972 election year so he
began to encourage serious negotiations during the
latter half of 1971. Nixon wrote to Brezhnev on
August 5, proposing a superpower initiative, and
Brezhnev replied affirmatively on September 7. Gromyko
then met Nixon and Kissinger at the end of September
and presented the outlines of a plan based on an interim settlement with Egypt, to be followed within a year
by a comprehensive settlement. The second phase would
have to be agreed upon before the first was implemented.
Nixon agreed to work with the Soviets in resolving the
Middle East conflict, but he linked it to Soviet cooperation on Vietnam.[22]
The Soviets, anxious to further detente with the
United States due to fear of Sino-American collusion
(as will be discussed below), were ready to make concessions in the Middle East. Brezhnev suggested to
Nixon that they would withdraw their troops from Egypt
after the second stage of a peace plan, leaving only
600 military advisers. This was repeated by Gromyko to
Kissinger and by Dobrynin to Rabin. The trade-off was
that the United States would not increase its military
advisory staff in Iran beyond the 600 already there.

The Soviets were also prepared to accept an embargo on
arms deliveries to participants in the Arab-Israeli
conflict, once a settlement was achieved, and they were
ready to incur some Arab displeasure by improving relations with Israel. The heads of Arab missions in
Moscow were informed at a joint meeting that the restoration of less than complete relations with Israel was
anticipated during the first three months of 1972.
Like the Americans, the Soviets wanted to link the
Middle East and Vietnam issues, so Victor Louis'
article claiming that a settlement in Vietnam "appears
to be in sight" had clear implications for the Middle
East. He cited common Soviet-American interests and
pointed out that there would soon be a summit conference.[23]

Israel was interested in pursuing negotiations toward an interim settlement with Egypt, but was not prepared to participate in a comprehensive settlement arranged under superpower auspices. Meir registered her
objections with Nixon on December 2 and Kissinger on
December 10, but the complete collapse of the Soviet-
American initiative was brought about by the Indo-
Pakistani war over the establishment of Bangladesh.
The Soviet Union sided with India. The U.S. "tilted"
toward Pakistan and lost its gamble. It therefore
sought to compensate strategically by entering into a
naval basing agreement with Bahrein, seeking additional
base rights in Greece and strengthening Israel through
the delivery of more Phantoms. Sadat was concerned
about this extra American support for Israel, as well
as by the Soviets' transference during the conflict in
the sub-continent of military equipment from Egypt to
India. The timing was certainly not propitious for a
political settlement in the Middle East arranged by
the superpowers. The Indo-Pakistani war obstructed
negotiations, and the American presidential election
campaign then made the possibility of settlement even
dimmer still.

In February 1972, the United States proposed proximity talks on an interim settlement between Israel and
Egypt. The motive may have been related to electoral
politics, and the initiative led nowhere. Israel accepted the American overture, but Egypt rejected it.
Sadat had given up on the peace process and was hoping
to activate the war option. He also feared that Israel
and Jordan were working toward a separate peace agreement which would limit Egypt's bargaining power. After
Hussein announced his own peace plan on March 15, Egypt
broke diplomatic relations with the Hashemite monarchy.

Sadat was unable to prepare for war because the
Soviet Union refused to supply the necessary weaponry.
Soviet Minister of Defense Grechko said on May 17 that
Egypt could regain its occupied territories through

other than political means, and two MiG-23's flew over
the Sinai while he was in Egypt.[24] Nevertheless, he
privately cautioned against military action during his
visits to Cairo in both February and May 1972. Commenting on Sadat's April talks in Moscow, a Soviet
radio commentary declared: "In the military sphere,
aid from the Soviet Union to Egypt is designed to
vigorously repel Israel's aggressive designs. It
should be noted that there is no ground here for any
secret aims which endanger peace. The importance of
the Soviet military aid to Egypt lies in strengthening
Egypt's defense capability."[25] Sadat realized his pre-
dicament and opened a secret diplomatic channel to the
United States in April 1972.[26]

The Soviet Union's stance was moderate from the
fall of 1971 into the spring of 1972 as it wanted the
Suez Canal reopened to facilitate its sea access to
Vietnam and India. Vietnam came to be viewed as a
strategic asset against China, and the Soviets may have
been willing to make concessions in the Middle East in
return for some advantages in Southeast Asia. They
were deeply concerned about Sino-American ping pong
diplomacy in 1971 and Kissinger's secret visit to
Peking. Then in February 1972, Nixon traveled to China
and the Soviets were alarmed about an anti-Soviet entente. To head off this possibility, they sought detente with the United States in order to draw the U.S.
away from China. Other motivations were also fundamental, such as the need to import grain due to serious
agricultural problems and the need to acquire technology and capital for oil and gas projects in Western
Siberia. U.S. Secretary of Commerce Maurice Stans expressed interest in joint energy ventures when he
visited Moscow in November 1971, and Gulf, Exxon and
Occidental were all considering participation. Soviet-
American relations were improving despite the
Bangladesh affair and the first Nixon-Brezhnev summit
was still scheduled for May 1972.

In the Middle East, Soviet concern about Sino-
American relations had some strange repercussions.
Whereas the Soviets had previously tried to counter
Chinese ties to the Syrian Baathists and Palestinians,
they now began to fear that China would join the United
States in supporting Israel. The Soviets certainly had
an exaggerated response, but it is true that Israel was
making overtures to China at this time.[27] China was
establishing diplomatic relations with Western allies
Iran and Turkey and improving relations with Israel's
African associate, Ethiopia. China was also disengaging from the Palestinians. Delegations to Peking were
met by lower level officials and the media devoted less
attention to the Palestinian cause. Palestine day was
celebrated for the last time in May 1971.[28]

Breaking Point

In his State of the Union address, Nixon said that
the Soviet military presence in Egypt was incompatible
with detente but he nevertheless journeyed to Moscow
for a May summit with Brezhnev. Egypt was wary of the
summit, believing that the Soviet desire to seek accommodation with the United States would lead it to accept the status quo and deny Cairo advanced armaments.
Israel feared a Soviet-American solution imposed at its
expense, so it requested that Nixon avoid discussing
the Middle East in his meetings with the Soviet General
Secretary.[29]

Kissinger relates that he and Nixon exercised a
"holding action" on the Middle East, delaying discussion
until near the end of the summit and then making sure
that the final communique was "the blandest possible"
on this issue. The U.S. held the regional advantage so
the existing situation had to be maintained until the
Arabs were prepared to approach the U.S. for a solution "based on progress through attainable stages."[30]
In other words, Kissinger did not desire a comprehensive settlement that would include a Soviet role, favoring instead the beginning of step-by-step diplomacy
under American auspices. Gromyko insisted on some
joint working principles, and many specific points were
discussed. These included freedom of navigation in the
Suez Canal and Tiran, demilitarized zones and the return of UN peacekeeping forces. More significantly,
the Soviets displayed some flexibility on border
changes and it was agreed that none would be made
without the mutual consent of the concerned parties.
Negotiations would at first be indirect, but direct
talks were possible at later stages. Soviet and
American arms commitments to Egypt and Israel would be
honored despite a settlement, but new agreements would
not be signed except those for spare parts and maintenance. Gromyko permitted Kissinger to insert the following addition to the general principles: "This does not
preclude that the implementation occurs in stages or
that some issues and disputes are resolved on a priority
basis." This was Kissinger's way of securing oblique
Soviet endorsement of step-by-step diplomacy.[31]

The summit did not lead to any progress toward a
Middle East settlement, but superpower cooperation soon
became apparent in Vietnam. Peace talks began in July,
North Vietnam tabled its own peace proposals in October
and a Paris agreement supposedly ending the war was
signed on January 27, 1973. Nevertheless, Sadat believed that some deal was probably worked out behind
his back as the Soviets inexplicably failed to provide
him with an account of the summit until July 6. He
therefore decided to take the bold step of expelling

almost all Soviet military personnel from Egypt.

Soviet ambassador Vladimir Vinogradov was informed of the Egyptian decision on July 8, and the official announcement was made on July 18. Sadat made his move after the superpower summit as he knew that taking this step earlier would have strengthened the American, and thereby the Israeli, hand. He also expelled the Soviets at this time in order to help effect an alliance with Libya, which wanted the Soviets out of Egypt. On August 2, a merger of Egypt and Libya was announced.

According to Sadat, the Soviets agreed with him in April that Egypt needed a "retaliation weapon" capable of striking the interior of Israel, but no such weapon was provided. Most of the aircraft and missiles in this category could only be operated by Soviet personnel, so Moscow's reticence must be viewed in this framework. When Minister of War Mohammed Ahmed Sadiq went to the Soviet Union in June, his hosts committed themselves only to providing weapons for Egypt's defense. When Prime Minister Sidqi was there in July (before the expulsion was announced but after Vinogradov had been informed), the joint communique indicated that "Arab states have every reason to use all the means at their disposal for the liberation of Arab territories seized by Israel in 1967."[32] This meant that the Egyptians could not count on any Soviet assistance. Even Israeli Minister of Defense Dayan had realized that the Soviets would not lend much military support to Egypt prior to the American presidential election.[33]

Sadat was furious at the Soviets. He wrote to Brezhnev that he had not wanted more Soviet troops, nor to precipitate a Soviet-American confrontation. He had only hoped to liberate some of the occupied territory in order to give Egypt a stronger bargaining position. He threatened that Soviet failure to provide the necessary weapons would force him to turn to the United States as a broker: "The American claim that the United States, and the United States alone, is capable of finding a solution has been increasingly vindicated, even after the Moscow meeting."[34] Nevertheless, Sadat made another attempt to secure advanced Soviet weapons but was turned down by Brezhnev, who cited the need to preserve detente.[35]

Sadat expected the expulsion of the Soviets to unfreeze the military situation. Egypt was not content with the continuation of no war, no peace as a computer study in the spring had indicated that the chief beneficiaries were Israel and the United States. Before Sadat made his decision, Heikal discussed the condition of no war, no peace in al-Ahram, setting forth arguments both pro and con regarding the Soviet perspective on the situation. He concluded that in the long run, the Soviets would not benefit from an extended stalemate. However, they would be reluctant to alter conditions prior to the American presidential election as they wanted Nixon returned to office.[36] The expulsion may have freed Egypt to take military action sooner, but the capability was lacking. In fact, Egypt had to wait until after the American election when the Soviet attitude toward offensive action changed.

Another factor influencing Sadat's expulsion order was the Jewish emigration issue. Sadat, in a letter to Brezhnev, first complained about Soviet policies in April 1972 as the Egyptians came to believe that the Middle East conflict was being aggravated by the influx into Israel of technically trained Jews. They also felt that the fundamental aspects of the Arab-Israeli conflict were being overshadowed by the Soviet Jewry issue.[37] Incorrectly, it appears, the Egyptians thought that this had taken place at the Nixon-Brezhnev summit.

The key to Sadat's decision was the belief that the superpowers were colluding at the expense of Egypt's interests. It is extremely important to realize that Sadat's two boldest moves (the other being his trip to Jerusalem in November 1977) were motivated by the same concern. Although most Soviet military personnel (perhaps 18,000) were expelled, some were permitted to remain. The friendship treaty was not abrogated, and the Soviets retained their port facilities. They nevertheless realized the significance of their loss of position in Egypt and moved toward closer logistic cooperation with Syria. They also encouraged Syrian-Iraqi cooperation against Israel. Overall, the Soviets downplayed their departure from Egypt, claiming that their personnel had completed their missions. Ambassador Vinogradov was recalled for two months, but Egypt was not sharply criticized. The Soviets hoped to sustain their close links to the Arab world and feared that castigation of Egypt would only drive other Arabs out of their embrace. Their commentaries at the time displayed great awareness of the immediate negative impact of the expulsion on their image in other Arab states, leading one analyst to conclude that "in the long term," the trend would be toward Arab states seeking closer relations with the Soviet Union.[38]

Israel expected the expulsion to eliminate Egypt's war option. It also anticipated greater American pressure upon it to make concessions as the Soviet position in Egypt was considerably weakened. Traditionally, U.S. support for Israeli policies was strongest when the Soviet role in the region was most extensive. Israel turned out to be wrong on both counts.

Soviet Jewry

A major flow of Soviet Jewish emigrants began in March 1971. Whereas 1000 Jews had left the Soviet

Union in 1970, more than 13,000 were permitted to exit
in 1971 and almost 32,000 in 1972. Almost all settled
in Israel as the dropout rate was less than 1 percent.
Israel expected an exodus of from 200,000 to 300,000
over a twenty to thirty year period, but it proceeded
much more rapidly. The 200,000 figure was passed in
mid-1979, after only eight years.[39] Although Jewish
emigration received extensive worldwide publicity, it
was not unique. The Soviets had allowed similar programs for Armenians, Poles, Spaniards, Koreans and
Greeks, while an upsurge in German emigration coincided
with that of Jews.

Since there were no Soviet-Israeli diplomatic relations, would-be emigrants received their visas from
the Dutch embassy in Moscow. Applicants needed invitations from relatives in Israel, as family reunification
was the ostensible purpose for the emigration. They
then had to renounce their Soviet citizenship, secure
Soviet passports and permission to leave and then
travel to Austria. Israel would have preferred direct
flights from the Soviet Union, but Kremlin authorities
insisted on the indirect route. Perhaps they did not
want to irritate the Arabs unnecessarily, or felt that
direct flights were inappropriate in the absence of
formal diplomatic ties. Engendering anti-Israeli propaganda from dropouts who did not want to proceed to
the Jewish state may have played a role in later years,
but could not have been a significant factor in the
early seventies when very few turned down the opportunity to go to Israel. It should be added that many
mixed couples with one Jewish partner were processed in
Austria, as well as non-Jewish dissidents who were permitted to leave the Soviet Union with visas for Israel.

Central authorities must surely have controlled
the overall pace of Jewish emigration, but exit permission for specific applicants was regionalized. Rates
of approval for emigration varied from republic to
republic, with Georgia being particularly lenient in
letting its Jews emigrate (perhaps Georgian Jews were
the most expendable due to their low level of education).
The Soviets were clearly concerned about Arab reaction
to their policies and assured them that the Middle East
situation would be taken into account. They claimed
that Jews with military training or security information
would not be permitted to leave and that most emigrants
were elderly, female or children. These were exaggera-
tions but the Soviets did restrict the number of adult
males who could assist Israel militarily. To counter
Arab charges, the Soviets pointed out that 800,000 Jews
had already gone to Israel from Arab states.[40]

The Soviet media continued to attack Zionism and
prominent Jews were periodically called upon to denounce
Israel. In March 1971, the month that large-scale
emigration was initiated, a conference of Soviet Jewish

leaders was convened to condemn Zionism.41 Furthermore, restrictions were placed on Jews in the military,
intelligence services, diplomatic corps, sciences and
higher educational institutions because they were considered potential emigrants and could no longer be
trusted. Domestic anti-Semitism therefore increased as
Jews were permitted to leave for the Zionist homeland.
    The media related tales of woe regarding disillu-
sioned emigrants who wanted to return to the Soviet
Union, and it was promised that they would be given
priority in housing assignments if they came back.
Activities of the militant Jewish Defense League in the
United States were denounced for their anti-Soviet content, and the judicial process continued to deal with
the case of nine Jews and two non-Jews who allegedly
planned to hijack a plane to leave the Soviet Union.
They were found guilty in December 1970 and some were
sentenced to death. Golda Meir maintained that they
were "completely innocent" and the Knesset called for
the cancellation of the death sentences. Israeli communists indicated that they had directed an appeal to
chief of state Podgornyi.42 In May 1971, the capital
sentences were changed to terms of imprisonment. Despite all of these antagonistic circumstances, the Soviet
authorites continued to let Jews leave for Israel.
    Israel pushed hard for the emigration right of
Soviet Jews. It had an obvious concern about the fate of
fellow Jews, but also was anxious to secure new immigrants. Israelis traveling to the Soviet Union were
encouraged to contact Jewish activists and to mix with
Soviet Jews in synagogues. Also, many phantom invitations to Soviet Jews were sent by non-relatives, or
were addressed to those who had not sought such invitations. As mentioned previously, Israel in May 1971 even
extended the right of citizenship to Soviet Jews who had
not been granted permission to emigrate. Tekoah sent
several letters to U Thant about Soviet Jewry, and an
international conference on the subject was convened in
Brussels in late February 1971. Israel as a state was
not in the forefront of the Soviet Jewry campaign as it
wanted the issue divorced from Soviet-Israeli rela-
tions.43 However, it maintained close contact with the
major Jewish organizations and influenced the overall
tenor of the campaign. The organizations were responsible for the details and sometimes were overenthus-
iastic as they competed for publicity and funds. From
the Israeli perspective, the campaign helped undermine
detente and therefore served as a welcome impediment to
superpower collusion in the Middle East. Paradoxically,
it was due primarily to Soviet longing for detente that
Jews were allowed to emigrate in the first place.
    The Soviet leaders timed the upsurge in emigration
to coincide with the Twenty-fourth Congress of the

communist party. It served as a good will gesture
which would be duly noted by the large number of
foreign journalists in Moscow for the occasion and
also as a deterrent to Jewish demonstrators who were
expected to attract external media attention. The
Soviets also wanted to blunt the international Soviet
Jewry campaign, which had just peaked in Brussels, as
it engendered an unfavorable world image of their
system. Perhaps the death of Nasser played a role as
well, as the Soviets were less concerned about offending Egyptian sensibilities.

Internal economic considerations were pertinent,
but surely not fundamental. Localities took over the
assets of departing Jews and emigrants had to pay substantial fees to leave the country. Renunciation of
citizenship cost 500 rubles and the passport fee was
raised in late 1970 from 40 to 400 rubles. Each emigrant
therefore had to pay more than $1000, and assistance
was often provided to individuals by international
Jewish organizations. The Soviets additionally benefited from payments for rail transport to Vienna.
Victor Louis cited the desire of transport administra-
tors to meet their quotas in filling seats, but he seems
to have grossly exaggerated this line of analysis by
asserting that most Jews were permitted to leave during
the tourist off-season when many seats remained
vacant.[44] On the other side of the ledger, the Soviets
may have hoped economically to burden Israel with the
resettlement of so many immigrants. In fact, Israel
did reduce its defense expenditure in 1972 to help
meet the cost.

Some theories of Soviet motivation appear incor-
rect. Permitting Jews to go to Israel was not used as
a tactic to influence Israel to make concessions on a
peace settlement. Perhaps the Soviets expected Israel
to be more amenable, or realized that reducing the
flow of emigration would be a useful stick later on.
However, periods of Israeli intransigency did not produce any curtailment of emigration. Actually, the major
exodus began right after Meir had rejected Sadat's peace
proposal. Additionally, it is difficult to believe that
Jews resettled in Israel were expected to retain sufficient loyalty to the Soviet Union to help push Israel
away from Washington and toward Moscow.[45]

The real key to Soviet Jewish emigration lay not in
the context of Soviet-Israeli relations, but in the
arena of superpower politics. The Soviet Union wanted
to woo the United States out of the Chinese embrace and
to gain trade and financing concessions. Permitting
Jews to leave for Israel would assist the Soviets in
these endeavors as it was believed that pro-Israeli and
Jewish members of Congress (as well as those working in
the communications media) would become less anti-Soviet.

They were deemed largely responsible for the negativistic American attitude, which was highlighted by the
Soviet Jewry campaign. It was reasoned that an Israel
grateful for its receipt of immigrants would ask its
American supporters to adopt a more favorable stance
toward the Soviet Union.

The Soviet Union was trying to apply a variation
of the Rumanian model. Rumania had maintained its
diplomatic relations with Israel, had permitted Jewish
emigration and was rewarded by the United States
through the granting of most favored nation trade
status in 1975 and other economic concessions. Nixon
visited Bucharest in 1969, Ceausescu went to Washington
in 1970 and Meir became the first Israeli prime
minister to travel to a communist-ruled state when she
journeyed to Rumania in May 1972. She had also met
Ceausescu in New York in October 1970. The linkage
between Rumanian-Israeli relations and Rumanian-
American relations was not fortuitous. In June 1969,
Israeli diplomat Gideon Rafael asked Kissinger to act
favorably toward Rumania, and Rafael received a thank-
you note from the Rumanian foreign minister. Once
Nixon's trip to Rumania was arranged, Israeli-Rumanian
diplomatic representation was raised to the embassy
level.[46]

The Soviets did not receive Israel's support as
had Rumania. Whereas Rumania had maintained cordial
ties to Israel while emigration was taking place, the
Soviet Union did not. Israel therefore did not see
any purpose in rewarding the Soviets for their greater
flexibility on emigration as Moscow was not operating
in a bilateral context. Permission for Jews to emigrate was a function of Soviet-American relations, not
Soviet-Israeli relations.

Although Jewish emigration increased substantially
in 1972, the Soviets obstructed the process through the
imposition in August of an education tax. Departing
Jews were expected to repay the Soviet government for
their years of free studies, surely an insurmountable
burden for those who had received higher education. It
is possible that this tax was imposed to curry favor
with the Arabs following the expulsion of Soviet military personnel from Egypt.[47] In practice, many Jews
were granted exemptions from paying the tax and only
1435 actually paid before its implementation was sus-
pended in March 1973.[48]

Israel felt that only the Americans could induce
the Soviets to rescind the tax. Rabin met with Sisco,
and Senator Henry Jackson, a strong supporter of Israel,
threatened to introduce legislation linking Soviet
Jewish emigration to American economic concessions to
the Soviet Union.[49] Israeli public opinion and opposition leader Menachem Begin favored this strategy. Meir,

concerned about offending Nixon, was at first reluctant
but then went along. She may have had her eye on
Israeli elections scheduled to take place in 1973. The
U.S. administration advocated quiet diplomacy and rejected Jackson's approach. The Soviet Union saw Jackson
and Israel as opponents of detente. Whether Jackson's
action brought about the Soviet reversal on the tax
must remain a matter of speculation.

Accelerated Movement

Soviet-Israeli bilateral contacts increased dramatically in 1971-72 in conjunction with Soviet peace
overtures during that period. Even when Soviet citizens
traveled to Israel, the initiative was usually on the
Soviet side. Israel was amenable to most offers of
closer interaction but it felt that the Soviets had to
take the first steps since they had terminated relations. In January 1971, a Soviet representative attended a women's conference in Israel, but the first big
breakthrough was the August extension of invitations
to six Israelis by the Committee for the Defense of
Peace. As was to be their custom, the Soviets extended
invitations to individuals, even though all of the invited individuals would be traveling together as a
group. The selection of Israelis was supervised by
RAKAH, and the invitations were received no more than
three weeks before the anticipated visit. This procedure enabled the Soviets to exercise close control over
citizen exchanges and to time them for appropriate
political impact.

The Israeli delegation included only one member of
RAKAH, although five of its members belonged to the
Israel Committee for the Improvement of Relations with
the Soviet Union. It was the first non-RAKAH group of
Israeli public figures to be invited to the Soviet Union
since the 1967 diplomatic break, and its participants
were given the impression that an Israeli commitment to
withdraw from occupied territories would produce Soviet
support for direct Arab-Israeli negotiations.[50] That
same month, the Soviets also played host to Israeli
doctors, beekeepers and a chemistry professor. Three
professors of the history of science attended a conference in Moscow, where the Israeli flag was displayed.

In December 1971, Victor Louis wrote an article for
an Israeli newspaper in which he mentioned speculation
about a direct Moscow-Tel Aviv air route for Soviet
Jewish emigrants. The issue which raised the greatest
stir, however, was his suggestion that Israel assign
consular officials to the Dutch embassy in Moscow and
the Soviet Union should do likewise in regard to the
Finnish embassy in Tel Aviv. It should be pointed out
that the United States and Egypt had no official diplo-

matic relations, but Americans operated out of the
Spanish embassy in Cairo. Louis claimed that the Dutch
embassy staff had a language problem in trying to deal
with visa applications from Georgian Jews.[51] The
Israeli government refused to respond to Louis's proposal
until such time as it was presented officially. In
any case, Israel opposed the idea of exchanging low-
level representatives with the Soviet Union and insisted
on the restoration of full diplomatic relations. Media
discussion of the matter continued through 1972, but no
action was ever taken.[52] Meir believed that complete
ties were necessary, and that the Soviets should
"change their attitude a little" to help bring them
about. She claimed that greater Jewish emigration was
not a sufficient signal of Soviet intent as it was unrelated to bilateral relations. She pointed out that
periods of closer relations had not led to an increase
in emigration.[53]

In January 1972, Israel received its first Soviet
delegation since 1967 that did not come as guests of
RAKAH. Three representatives of the Union of Soviet
Societies for Friendship and Cultural Relations with
Foreign Countries attended the first congress of the
Israel-USSR Friendship Movement. They also visited
the headquarters of the MAPAM party and talked with its
Secretary General Meir Yaari. An account in New Times
cited growing peace sentiments among Israelis and it
favorably cited Yaacov Riftin, founder of a different
Soviet-Israeli friendship movement, while mentioning
that he was a Zionist.[54] That same month, at a Rome
meeting to organize a conference on the Arab-Israeli
conflict, the Soviets backed Israel's right to participate even though the eight-member Israeli delegation
included non-RAKAH figures such as Uri Avnery and
journalist Amnon Kapeliuk.[55] In March, an Israeli
women's delegation went to the Soviet Union, but relations between the two states were temporarily marred
when Soviet police charged into a crowd outside the
Moscow synagogue at Passover, injuring several Jews.

In May, seven Israelis journeyed to the Soviet
Union as guests of the Soviet Committee for the Defense
of Peace. The delegation was leftist ideologically,
but included non-RAKAH public figures. The Israelis
were apparently told that if their country began to
implement SC 242 (probably meaning a declaration of
intent on complete withdrawal and the initiation of a
partial pullback), diplomatic relations could be renewed.[56] Also in May, Moscow's Patriarch Pimen of the
Russian Orthodox Church visited Jerusalem. He met with
the Minister of Religious Affairs, the Minister of
Justice and the Mayor of Jerusalem, but Deputy Prime
Minister Allon and Minister of the Interior Burg turned down invitations to a dinner in Pimen's honor as

they felt that their presence would have lent unwarrant-
ed political significance. Similarly, no Cabinet
members were at the airport for Pimen's arrival or
departure.[57]

In June 1972, Soviet delegates (including a member
of the communist party Central Committee) attended
RAKAH's 17th congress. Representatives from East
Germany, Poland, Hungary and Mongolia were also present
and the Soviets granted an interview to an Israeli
newspaper.[58] In August, there were Israeli participants
at an archivists' conference in Moscow and members of
a friendship movement also traveled to the Soviet
Union.

The Israeli communist party, RAKAH, continued to
provide contact between the Soviet Union and Israel.
Communist delegations traveled in both directions, but
RAKAH was also an important link between the Soviet
Union and Israeli Arabs. RAKAH had started to send
Arab students to Moscow in 1963. It was the dispenser
of Soviet scholarships and it set conditions to insure
that the recipients were RAKAH loyalists. They had to
be members of the party or its youth movement for at
least three years and at least one member of a recipients's family had to be a RAKAH activist. During the
period 1967-71, 73 Arabs went to study in the U.S.S.R.
and East European communist countries and the number
jumped to 144 during the years 1972-76. About 30 percent attended schools in the Soviet Union, and more
than half were studying medicine. The next most popular
subject was engineering. RAKAH Arabs in the Soviet
Union were organized into units that had monthly
political meetings and about 30 percent of the students
became active in party affairs upon returning to
Israel.[59]

The Israeli government did not interfere with this
flow of Arab communist students, but RAKAH members were
often harassed when they tried to organize residents of
the West Bank. To a lesser extent, impediments were
also placed in their way in the heavily Arab "Little
Triangle" area of Israel. RAKAH encountered other
difficulties as well. On one occasion in 1972, it
invited to Israel two journalists from the Soviet trade
union newspaper Trud. The Israeli government would not
permit them to come, maintaining that they would only
be welcome once the Soviet Union agreed to receive two
journalists affiliated with the Israeli trade union
movement.[60]

The Soviet relationship with the Palestinians was
of growing concern to Israel. Palestinian movements
achieved little success in the occupied territories but
they were extremely active overseas in organizing airplane hijackings and attacking Israeli citizens and
facilities. In June 1971, an Israeli tanker was

attacked near the Bab el-Mandeb Strait, and Israeli
athletes were killed by Black September commandos at
the September 1972 Olympics in Munich.

The Soviet Union was supportive of the Palestinian
cause, but it urged moderation. In November 1970, one
commentator declared: "It is very important for the
Palestinians to know how to wage the struggle for the
restoration of their rights on the Palestinian soil
without impinging on the rights of others."[61] Then
in May 1971, the Soviets told the Syrian communists
that the Palestinian problem should not be overempha-
sized and the Syrian communists were criticized for
stressing Palestinian armed struggle. In May 1972, a
Jordanian communist writing in World Marxist Review
condemned "reckless actions" and censured the Palestinian movements for not endorsing SC 242. [62]

Arafat did not receive much Soviet assistance when
he visited Moscow in October 1971, but he fared much
better in July 1972. He was in the Soviet Union when
Sadat made his expulsion announcement, so the Soviet
decision to initiate the direct arming of the PLO should
be viewed in this context. Having lost position in
Egypt, the Soviets were hoping to compensate by cementing ties to the PLO. Arms for the PLO began arriving
in Syria in September, and a communist-supported Arab
Front for Participation in the Palestinian Resistance
was created in November to assist the PLO. The ineffectual al-Ansar movement, which had been backed by
Jordanian communists, was disbanded.

The period 1971-72 featured an improvement in
Soviet-Israeli relations and a corresponding decline
in Soviet-Egyptian relations. Yet in less than a year,
the Soviet Union was heavily arming Egypt and Syria
for their attack on the Jewish state. Why did the
Soviet Union decide upon the war option? It is to
this crucial question that we must now turn our attention.

7
The Breaking Point

The year 1973 proved to be a decisive turning
point in the Middle East. Egypt and Syria broke the
lengthy stalemate by attacking Israeli positions in the
occupied territories, and the ensuing non-decisive war
then produced momentum toward a political settlement.
Detente did not prevent the outbreak of the war, but it
was instrumental in ending it and generating a Geneva
peace conference. The superpowers again moved to center
stage, while Egypt and Israel acted rapidly to forestall
any imposed settlement achieved through Soviet-American
collusion. The Arabs benefited from the new conditions
established by the war as a process for the recovery of
some of the occupied territories was begun. The Soviet
Union did not gain from the termination of the stalemate
as the United States quickly seized the diplomatic
initiative and left the Soviets in the lurch. The
Geneva forum was soon abandoned for American-sponsored,
step-by-step diplomacy. The Soviet Union tried to improve relations with Israel so it could participate in
the new round of negotiations, but it was effectively
parried by clever American tactics.

To interpret properly this course of events, we
must address the following questions: Did the Soviet
Union encourage Egypt and Syria to go to war? Did it
favor the destruction of Israel? Why did the superpowers collaborate in ending the war? Why did Israel
agree to attend a Geneva conference where the Soviet
Union served as co-chairman? Why did the Soviet Union
accept the principle of direct Arab-Israeli negotiations? Why did the Soviet Union begin to support the
establishment of a Palestinian state? The answers to
these questions will provide the necessary groundwork
for an understanding of Soviet-Israeli relations for at
least a decade thereafter.

Altering the Status Quo

Egypt and Syria were frustrated by the continuing
situation of no war, no peace and were anxious to use

117

military force to recover the occupied territories.
Their advocacy of a military option grew even stronger
after the Israeli-Syrian air battle of January 8 and
Israel's downing of a Libyan civilian airplane the following month. Both Egypt and Syria also wanted to rally
their populations behind a patriotic military effort in
order to overcome some evident domestic unrest. Sadat
was faced with rising student dissent, while Assad had
to deal with Sunni Moslem religious disturbances in the
city of Hama.

In February, Egyptian national security adviser
Mohammed Hafiz Ismail went to Moscow to press the war
option. He did not receive full Soviet backing, but a
shift toward the Egyptian position was apparent. The
Soviets expressed understanding of Egypt's opposition
to any partial settlement, which meant that they did
not really agree with the Egyptians but would not press
the point. More importantly, the joint communique
stated: "The Soviet side has reaffirmed that in view
of Israel's intransigent rejection of a just political
settlement in the Middle East, the Arab states have
the full right to use any form of struggle in liberating
their occupied territories."[1] The Soviets were therefore giving up on the political process and supporting
Egypt's intention to recover the Sinai and Gaza. However, there was no indication that the Soviet Union
would supply Egypt with more advanced weapons or that an
attack on pre-June 1967 Israel would be condoned. Later
in February, Minister of War Ahmed Ismail Ali journeyed
to Moscow to continue the discussions. Sadat would sub-
sequently claim that relations with the Soviet Union
had been "almost completely paralyzed" from July 1972
to February 1973.[2] This latter month therefore represented a most significant watershed in Soviet-Egyptian
relations. In April, Prime Minister Kosygin declared:
"We consider that Egypt is entitled to have a strong
army at the present time in order to defend itself from
the aggressor and to liberate its lands."[3]

Why did the Soviet Union decide to acquiesce in
Egypt's military plans? Part of the motivation lay in
Vietnam. A peace agreement had been signed in Paris on
January 27 and the Soviets viewed it as a defeat for
the United States. Furthermore, the U.S. was about to
begin the process of withdrawing its troops, an act
which made it appear weak in Soviet eyes. Why not take
advantage in the Middle East at a time when American
willpower was ebbing? One Soviet analyst wrote: "The
Vietnam example offers striking proof that it is pre-
cisely the support by the forces of world socialism
that can secure success in the struggle for national
rights. This is another conclusion Arab progressives
have drawn from the victory of the Vietnamese people."[4]
Also influencing the Soviets were the American negotiations to sell advanced fighter aircraft to Saudi Arabia

and Kuwait and their own talks with the Egyptians to
retain logistic facilities.[5] Perhaps the Soviets
feared that they would lose their military position in
Egypt if they did not at least permit Sadat to prepare
for war. They must also have anticipated a sharp
Egyptian swing toward the United States if they failed
to aid the war effort.

Although no longer trying to restrain the
Egyptians, the Soviets still cautioned them about the
risks of their planned endeavor. A Soviet journalist
specializing on Middle Eastern affairs told a group
of Lebanese university students that the Arab states
were not prepared to face Israel in battle. The Arabs
were divided and weak, and a war could not be waged
successfully."[6] In May, Egyptian Foreign Minister
Mohammed Hassan az-Zayyat had talks in Moscow which
Pravda described as taking place in "an atmosphere of
friendship and mutual understanding."[7] This signified
that differences of opinion were expressed but not
challenged. In June, RAKAH leader Meir Wilner expressed support for a political solution, but added that
the Arabs had the right to liberate their territories
through other means.[8]

Sadat and Assad worked out joint military plans
in April (Hussein was not included) and, at first,
hoped to attack the Israeli defense line in May. Then,
at Egypt's initiative, the date was moved backward as
more Soviet arms were expected and Israel was in a
state of alert.[9] Perhaps Sadat also didn't expect
much Soviet support prior to a planned June summit
between Brezhnev and Nixon. The United States learned
about Egypt's intentions in April, but neither
Kissinger nor the Israelis believed the reports.[10]
Israel took some military precautions, but generally
carried on as usual. In early June, the Knesset called
for an upsurge in the Soviet Jewry campaign to coincide
with the superpower summit.[11] The aim was apparently
to blunt detente and deter any Soviet-American joint
effort in the Middle East. The Soviet Union did not
begin actively to support Arab war preparations, but
the addition of three key figures to the Politburo in
late April may have been related to developments in the
Middle East. The promotions of Minister of Defense
Grechko, Foreign Minister Gromyko and KGB director
Andropov added great expertise to the ruling circle and
clearly facilitated possible strategic coordination
during wartime.

Prelude to War

At the June summit in San Clemente, Nixon did not
raise the Arab-Israeli issue. Perhaps he wanted to
assure Israel and Egypt that no action was taken behind
their backs, but his plan went awry when Brezhnev had

him awakened during his last night at the California
retreat. The Soviet leader had the Middle East on his
mind and he proposed a complete Israeli withdrawal in
return for an agreement on non-belligerency. This was
a maximalist Soviet position that could not possibly
be accepted by the Israelis. It was also an inopportune time to work toward a peace settlement as Israeli
elections were scheduled for the fall. Nixon displayed
no interest in this plan and Brezhnev then warned that
in the absence of an agreement, "we will have difficulty keeping the military situation from flaring up."[12]
This comment could be interpreted as an effort by the
Soviet leader to protect himself from accusations that
he was violating the spirit of detente by failing to
consult with Nixon on threats to peace in the Middle
East.

Brezhnev was measuring Nixon's resolve in the
Middle East and seems to have found great reticence.
Nixon was not anxious to discuss the issue, did not
table any American peace proposal and did not react
when Brezhnev hinted at the prospect of war. Brezhnev
must have concluded that the United States was weakened by its Vietnam experience and could not be expected
to act decisively in the Middle East. The Soviet
Union therefore decided to support the Arab war effort
against Israel.

Watergate may have been an important factor.
Televised hearings were putting Nixon on the defensive
and distracting him from conducting an effective
foreign policy. Weakened domestically by frequent new
revelations, Nixon could not risk any divisive diplomatic forays so the prospects for an American peace
proposal on the Middle East were virtually nil. Nixon
could be expected to maintain strong backing for
Israel as he did not want to antagonize Israel's
numerous supporters in Congress at a time when his own
position was on the line. The Soviets were cognizant
of Nixon's domestic constraints and decided that an
alteration in the Arab-Israeli status quo was imperative. They also believed that American willpower,
sapped by Watergate, was at a low point. The war
option was therefore approved.

When Mohammed Hafiz Ismail returned to Moscow in
July, the Soviets agreed to continue the provision of
"all forms of aid that will prepare those peoples to
eradicate the consequences of the aggression."[13]
Although not discussed publicly, the Soviets for the
first time began to deliver weapons to Egypt that
could strike deep within Israeli-occupied territory.
Approximately thirty Scud ground-to-ground missiles
without nuclear warheads were supplied to Egypt, but no
MiG-23's as had been requested. Syria did not receive
Scuds until after the war was over.[14] The Soviets had
clearly opted to enhance Arab war potential, but were

still restricting the degree of firepower provided.
Furthermore, the Scuds were not provided in sufficient
quantity to contribute substantially to Egypt's offensive capabilities. They were really a deterrent
against an Israeli counterattack on Egyptian territory.
Nevertheless, Soviet provision of Scuds was critical
to Egypt's decision to go to war. In fact, Egypt
did not use the Scuds either in its advance across the
Canal or in its defense against Israel's later Canal
crossing.

Egypt and Syria planned for war against Israel.
They were dependent upon Soviet weapons, but it appears
that Moscow was not party to their military preparations and did not know the date of the impending offensive. Of course, the Soviets were aware of Arab
intentions and some steps taken against Israel in
September may have been related to an anticipation of
war. Three weeks prior to its initiation, the Soviets
carged Israel with violating the UN Charter and questioned its right to remain a member of the organization.[15] Then Palestinians attacked Soviet Jews in
transit to Vienna, an act that may have been abetted
by Czechoslovak and Soviet intelligence. Earlier that
month, Cuba had announced before a non-aligned conference in Algiers that it was severing its diplomatic
relations with Israel.

Controversy surrounds the issue of just when the
Soviets were informed of the date of the Arab attack.
Some American sources cite September 22, but the
Egyptians claim it was not until later. Heikal maintains that vague notification was given on October 1
and the Soviet ambassador still didn't know the precise
date as of October 5, the day before hostilities began.
Sadat points to October 3 as the date of this general
notification.[16] No matter where the truth lies, the
Soviets surely knew that war was imminent. Some
military advisers began to leave Syria by September 23,
and a satellite was launched on October 3 in an orbit
passing over the Middle East. On October 4, a message
from Brezhnev to Sadat indicated that some civilian
advisers and their dependents would be evacuated from
Egypt. They left the next day and a similar process
took place in Syria. Also on October 5, a Soviet ship
scheduled to dock at Alexandria cut short its voyage
and remained in the open sea. Many ships already at
port in Alexandria and Port Said headed out to sea.[17]

The Soviet Union sent out numerous signals that a
war was in the offing. Brezhnev and Gromyko warned
Kissinger in May, Brezhnev alerted Nixon in June, and
Gromyko discussed the matter as late as September 28
with Nixon and Kissinger. One analyst even claims that
Dobrynin told Kissinger on October 5 that the Arab assault would begin the following day.[18] This last incident appears unlikely, but the Soviets were surely

leaving hints of events to come. Citizens were being
evacuated from Cairo and Damascus, and the launching
of satellites must have been monitored by the United
States. If the Soviets were hoping for a strong
American response that could help generate a crisis
short of war, they had indeed miscalculated. The threat
of war may have been capable of accelerating an almost
inert diplomatic process, but the United States played
possum and failed to act. Despite knowledge of
Egypt's war plans in April, Nixon did not raise the
issue at the June summit. Despite repeated Soviet
hints of an impending conflagration, he did not respond. Either the United States believed that there
was a gigantic Soviet and Egyptian bluff or it cynical-
ly expected to enhance its position in Egypt as a result of another Arab-Israeli war. Israeli intelligence
seems to have downgraded the prospects for an Arab offensive as overconfidence and wish fulfillment replaced
concrete analysis in the formulation of policy.

The Course of War

In the early stages of the war, the Egyptians and
Syrians took advantage of the element of surprise and
advanced into the Sinai and Golan Heights. Israeli
forces then regrouped, solidifying the line in the
south and beginning (on October 11) an advance in the
north. By then, the Soviets had already started to resupply the Syrians (they had failed to resupply Egypt
or Syria in 1967) and this clearly influenced the
Israelis to act decisively to counter a deep Soviet
commitment. The Soviet factor was deemed crucial by
the Israelis, and leaders such as Dayan and Allon expected a Soviet veto of any Security Council cease-
fire resolution.[19] On October 9, Israeli aircraft had
bombed a Soviet cultural center during an attack on
Damascus, killing one Soviet employee and a Syrian.
Then on October 12, a Soviet ship bringing equipment
for the Euphrates hydroelectric project was shelled by
the Israelis at the port of Tartus and sunk. No crew-
men were killed but the incident elicited a sharp Soviet
warning: "The continuation of criminal acts by Israel
will lead to dire consequences for Israel itself."[20]
Soviet targets were not singled out by the Israelis as
they were hit in the context of broader offensive operations. However, it was clear that Israel would not be
deterred by a Soviet presence.

Israeli forces crossed the Suez Canal on October
16, leading the Soviets into a heightened state of
diplomacy and strategic preparedness. Kosygin, who
arrived in Cairo that day, tried to convince Sadat to
accept a cease-fire in place but the Egyptians insisted
on Israeli withdrawal. On October 19, Brezhnev used
the hot line to impress upon Nixon the seriousness of

Israel's advance and he vaguely implied that the Soviet
Union would be forced to take action. To defuse the
situation, an October 20 invitation was extended to
Kissinger.

In the meantime, the Soviet Union was resupplying
the Egyptians and Syrians and the United States was
ferrying arms to the Israelis. At first, the U.S.
tried to delay the provision of war materials as an
instrument of pressure on Israel to support a cease-
fire. Then, in order to counter continued Soviet deliveries, the arms were forwarded. American ability to
coerce Israel was therefore limited by the necessity
of confronting Soviet moves. As Kissinger later told
Heikal: "Do not deceive yourself, the United States
could not--either today or tomorrow--allow Soviet arms
to win a big victory, even if it was not decisive,
against U.S. arms. This has nothing to do with
Israel or with you."[21]

On October 21, Kissinger met in Moscow with
Brezhnev and an agreement was worked out on a cease-
fire plan to be presented to the Security Council.
Brezhnev acceded to Kissinger's suggestion that the
two superpowers would participate in the initial stage
of peace negotiations and would then play a direct role
"only when key issues were dealt with."[22] Kissinger
briefed the Israelis about his talk with Brezhnev and
the Soviet-American plan was then passed by the Security
Council on October 22 as SC 338. It called for a cease-
fire in place, implementation of SC 242, and direct
negotiations "under appropriate auspices." This latter
provision really meant that the Soviet Union and
United States would organize a Geneva peace conference,
and that the United Nations would play little part in
the process. The Soviets preferred this arrangement as
it kept out the Chinese. Note that SC 338 contained a
major Soviet concession: acceptance of direct Arab-
Israeli negotiations. This was sure to offend the
Arabs, but the Soviets would not be left out since
negotiations would be conducted within the Geneva
framework. It also included a cease-fire in place, a
position which the Soviets had pressed privately but
one which the Arabs opposed as Israel had added territory on both the Egyptian and Syrian fronts.

Israeli troops continued to encircle the Egyptian
Third Army and the Soviets were furious. They believed
that they had an American assurance that Israel would
not violate the cease-fire, and they had used this to
convince both Sadat and Assad to agree to SC 338. As
the Soviet Union did not have the necessary lines of
communication to deal with Israel during a crisis, it
reacted to Israel's military move in the context of
superpower relations. Efforts to restrain Israel had
to be made through the American government. Three
Soviet airborne divisions had already been placed on

alert, and four more were given notice after Israel's breach of the cease-fire. On October 24, Sadat asked for joint superpower intervention to stop the Israelis and Brezhnev endorsed this proposal in a message to Nixon. He warned that the Soviet Union would act unilaterally if the United States failed to collaborate. At the same time, the Soviet Union may have signaled the severity of its intentions by placing radioactive materials, possibly nuclear warheads for missiles, on a ship bound for Egypt. Much controversy surrounds this episode, with former Secretary of Defense James Schlesinger and others maintaining that the Soviets did indeed initiate the introduction of nuclear weapons into the war.[23] In any case, no such weapons were deployed in Egypt but the threat of their entry into the conflict was used as pressure by the United States in urging a termination of the Israeli advance into Egypt.

The United States reacted to the nuclear incident and the Soviet military alert by instituting its own alert during the night of October 24-25. The Soviets were aware of this American action before they received Nixon's response to Brezhnev's message. In it, the U.S. president rejected the proposal for joint intervention and a Nixon letter to Sadat threatened American military action against Soviet troops in Egypt, should they be introduced unilaterally.[24] Nixon's strong stand must have inhibited Soviet behavior, but it is also true that Israel's advance was coming to an end. On October 25, the Soviets saved face by sending seventy military observers to Egypt (American observers came later). Israel maintained that they could not enter territory under its control as the Soviet Union lacked diplomatic relations with Israel.[25] The cease-fire began to hold and neither the United States nor Soviet Union was included in UN peacekeeping forces, although Poland was.

Aftermath

Despite detente with the United States, the Soviet Union resupplied Egypt and Syria and threatened intervention. Yet an analyst of the detente process has claimed that in the development, confrontation and resolution of the war, the Soviet Union was preoccupied with preserving detente and that this consideration took precedence over support for the Arab combatants.[26] Can this possibly be the case? Let us evaluate Soviet behavior in this light.

Superpower cooperation helped end the war. Agreement was reached on SC 338, and a Geneva negotiating structure was developed. Both states turned toward the United Nations for the establishment of a framework for peace, through the passage of SC 338 and then by

the introduction of peacekeeping forces. It may also
be argued that the Soviet Union did not view the war
as a zero sum game and had no desire to see the elimination of the American client, Israel. Scud missiles
were not furnished in sufficient number to support an
Egyptian drive into Israel, and Syria did not receive
them at all. MiG-23 aircraft were withheld, and the
Soviets did not provide the Arabs with data from their
satellites. The Egyptians were warned not to use
Soviet missiles in attacks on American aircraft that
were resupplying Israel and no Soviet military commitment to assist the Arab armies was made.[27] While the
battle was raging, Meir Wilner indicated in _Pravda_ that
a solution must include "acknowledgment of the right of
the state of Israel to sovereign existence."[28] Security
Council resolution 338 indirectly advocated the same
thing through its reaffirmation of SC 242. Of course,
Israel served as a useful focus of Arab enmity against
the West. The Soviets were watching gleefully as the
Arab oil embargo began to devastate Western economies
and turn the Western allies against each other as they
competed for the limited oil supply.

Although the Soviet Union did not take any action
to deter the Egyptians and Syrians from carrying out
their war plans, it did press for an early cease-fire.
Israeli analysts probably over-estimated Soviet backing
for a military solution as the Kremlin leaders were
content to let the war end after the initial Arab advances. Moscow distorted facts by telling Sadat that
Assad wanted a cease-fire, and also encouraged Tito to
influence Sadat's decision. When this tactic proved
unsuccessful in swaying the Egyptian president, the
Soviets lied to him about American assurances of
Israel's willingness to evacuate Egyptian territory
occupied in 1967 in return for a cease-fire. Syria was
also subjected to strong pressure. A Soviet freighter
departed without unloading its military equipment, the
airlift was reduced to the provision of small-arms
ammunition, and the Soviet ambassador threatened to pull
out military technicians.[29]

The Soviet Union was not hoping for the destruction
of Israel, but rather, to advance a political solution
through the tactic of military pressure. Leading Soviet
Middle East scholar Evgenii Primakov advanced this
interpretation, and it is consistent with the plan set
forth by Sadat in his October 1 directive to Minister
of War Ahmed Ismail Ali. Sadat did not indicate any
intention to attack Israel in its pre-June 1967 borders
and maintained that Israeli losses could lead to "an
honourable solution."[30] Even the Syrians may have had
the same approach as they failed to take advantage of
Israel's disarray following their advance through the
Golan Heights. Much of northern Israel was inadequately

defended at that stage of the conflict. Furthermore, it is necessary to consider Brezhnev's peace plan of October 26. It called for a political solution, guaranteed the existence of all states in the region (the word "all_ was reiterated, although Israel was not specifically mentioned), and used the moderate phraseology that Israel should withdraw "from territories" (without stipulating "all").[31]

What about Soviet threats to intervene? They must be viewed in the context of protecting the Egyptian and Syrian governments, not as challenges to Israel's existence or efforts to confront the United States. The Soviets did not express threats until after Israeli troops had crossed the Suez Canal and they acted carefully to avoid a clash with the Americans. Kissinger argues that the chances were 3 out of 4 that the Soviets would have intervened in Egypt had not the United States implemented a military alert. A similar prospect existed on the Syrian front once Israeli forces advanced beyond the Golan Heights. Dobrynin told Kissinger as early as October 11 that the Soviets would intervene to protect Damascus, and Syrian Minister of Defense Mustapha Tlas claimed that the Soviet Union was prepared to supply 55,000 men. Syrian communist party leader Khaled Bakdash stated that Soviet personnel moved tanks to Damascus in the later stages of the war. It is possible that some Soviet military advisers were killed on the Syrian front. In July 1974, Israeli Minister of Defense Shimon Peres said he could neither confirm nor deny a specific total of twenty but "apparently there were casualties among the Soviet experts, numbers not know." He also said that senior Soviet officers had served with the Syrians.[32]

The Soviet Union risked the continuation of detente by assisting the Arab states in their war preparations, airlifting additional military equipment while the war was in progress, and threatening to intervene. Detente was therefore not paramount in Soviet calculations, but it may have served as a constraint on Soviet behavior. Great caution was taken to prevent a confrontation with the Americans and the peace process was clearly based on superpower collaboration. Detente managed to survive. It should be pointed out, however, that the Soviet Union would probably have acted similarly had there not been any detente relationship for moderation at times of superpower crisis has been a recurrent Soviet response.

The Soviet Union and United States organized a Geneva conference with themselves as co-chairmen. Israel feared this cooperative spirit, with one journalist even considering the prospects for a joint Soviet-American peacekeeping force and another averring that Israel longed for the Cold War.[33] Opposition

leader Begin, who was engaged in an electoral campaign
that could possibly have brought him to power, maintained that the Soviet role in the Middle East presented a problem for the entire "free world" and he
expected the United States to counter any Soviet
military move. Wilner condemned the "anti-peace" forces
which favored a worsening in superpower relations.[34]
After the application of strong American pressure,
Israel agreed to attend the Geneva conference.
Washington had a position of great leverage over
Jerusalem as a consequence of its resupplying Israel
at a critical stage of the war.

The Israeli government acceded to the Geneva
framework because if afforded an opportunity for direct
talks with Arab states (Egypt and Jordan attended, but
Syria did not) in the absence of Palestinian representation. The Israelis were also assured by the Americans
that proceedings at Geneva were a mere formality and
would not last long. Israel was especially reluctant
to engage in serious negotiations less than two weeks
before its Knesset elections. The ruling Labor Alignment decided to go ahead with Geneva, and even called
for a resumption of relations with the Soviet Union.
However, it insisted that the initiative must come from
the Soviet side and that the nature of the relationship
must be more cooperative than it had been prior to the
1967 break.[35] The Soviets finally had a role in peace
negotiations and wanted to take advantage of this opening. They therefore hoped to develop more cordial
ties to Israel so that they could effectively participate in the expected round of diplomacy. In his address
to the conference on December 21, Foreign Minister
Gromyko adoped a moderate tone and pointed out that the
United Nations had established the Jewish state. He
indicated Soviet recognition of its June 4, 1967 borders
as legitimate. Gromyko's soft line toward Israel may
have been related to the state's elections. The Soviet
Union preferred the reelection of Meir's Labor Alignment to a victory for the more anti-Soviet Menachem
Begin's opposition slate, so a display of cordiality
toward Israel was deemed appropriate.[36] Labor did indeed win the December 31 balloting.

Israeli Foreign Minister Eban sought a meeting
with Gromyko to lay the foundations for an improved
relationship. Kissinger helped arrange the get-together,
which took place at the Soviet mission in Geneva on
December 21. Another track was also operative as the
Soviet delegation asked to talk with Uri Avnery, a
dovish Knesset member and editor of Haolam Hazeh.
According to Avnery, he was received at the "diplomatic"
rather than "press" level and asked for his analysis of
the forthcoming Knesset elections. He was told that
the Soviets did not want to see Begin as prime minister.

The Soviets told Avnery that Gromyko was willing to see
Eban and he passed this message to Eban's staff.
Gromyko tried to make it appear that such a meeting was
not out of the ordinary, maintaining that it was natural
for a co-chairman of a conference to receive a courtesy
call from a participant.37

Gromyko and Eban met for an hour and twenty minutes. Eban raised the issue of restoring relations
and Gromyko asserted that there must first be progress
in Arab-Israeli negotiations. An agreement was reached
that whenever the Soviet and Israeli foreign ministers
were to be in the same city on official business, they
would meet. Such was not to be the case. They also
discussed the feasibility of an exchange of visits
between Meir and Brezhnev.38

There were parallel efforts to establish peace
in the Middle East as Arab-Israeli negotiations under
American auspices were conducted even before the Geneva
conference convened. According to Kissinger, the
Soviets realized that they had little leverage in the
situation and they permitted the U.S. to organize the
conference. They also were willing to endorse the
continuation of direct Arab-Israeli talks, even though
the United States was serving as broker. The Soviets
were so anxious to display their participation at
Geneva that they did not even insist on Palestinian
representation. Kissinger portrays them as trying to
gain some of the diplomatic credit on the American coat-
tails. The U.S. went along, but planned to relegate
the Soviet Union to a secondary position once the conference ended.39 In fact, the Geneva conference did
not last longer than a day. At American insistence,
it broke up into working groups and the direct negotiations resumed. The Soviets had hoped to participate in
these groups, but the U.S. was adamant that the two
superpowers should not be represented. In fact, the
working groups did not conduct any serious business
and were purely to show the Soviets that the Geneva
process was continuing. The Americans held all the
diplomatic cards as the Soviet Union did not have
particularly good relations with Israel or Egypt. The
Soviets had to watch meekly as the United States,
through the efforts of Kissinger, played the role of
peacemaker.40

The tables had certainly turned. The war may have
been initiated due to perceived American weakness, but
it ended with a demonstration of American power. Arab
clients of the Soviet Union had broken the regional
stalemate, but the Soviets were not able to capitalize
on this opportunity. First was the failure to arrange
a cease-fire while the Arabs still held the battlefield
advantage. Then came Soviet miscalculations regarding
the peace process. A great opportunity for asserting

its legitimate role in the region was missed as the Soviet Union was pushed to the diplomatic sidelines by the United States. Egypt, which had been enabled to act by the provision of Soviet weapons, distanced itself from Moscow and moved into the American orbit. Part of the Soviet Union's problem was its failure to normalize relations with Israel. Egypt, despite its lack of formal ties with Washington, sought to include the United States in the negotiations but Israel had no reason to reward the Soviet Union in the same manner. There was therefore an absence of symmetry. In addition, the Soviet Union did not try to gain any leverage through its control over Jewish emigration. Israel was not pressured into offering any quid pro quo in return for the continuation of the exodus so Soviet liberality despite the war brought no tangible benefit.

Harmonious Interaction

Soviet-Israeli bilateral relations proceeded as usual in 1973 and were not significantly affected by the war. A delegation from the Israeli Communist Youth League traveled to the Soviet Union in January, and a Soviet group repaid the visit by attending a communist youth congress in Tel Aviv in April. A Soviet women's delegation was in Israel in March and a friendship group was there in July and August. In July, an Israeli film was shown at a Moscow festival and the Soviet Union approved a September visit by a professor and students from Tel Aviv University who were planning to study archeology in Armenia. In August, ten Israeli physicists attended a conference in Moscow.

Other events were somewhat more noteworthy. In May, a leftist International Conference for Peace and Justice in the Middle East was held in Bologna. Soviet and Palestinian delegations attended. The Israeli delegation included communists such as Tewfiq Toubi, but also non-RAKAH members such as Uri Avnery. Afterwards, an Israeli Committee for Peace and Justice in the Middle East was established. It included communists and Avnery, but also the Zionist peace activist Yaacov Riftin. In June, Victor Louis made another of his mysterious visits to Israel. He ostensibly was there to participate in a conference organized by the International Press Institute, but he extended his stay an extra week and unsuccessfully attempted to meet with Prime Minister Meir. The motivation for his visit is unknown, but it appears that he was sounding out the Israelis on their knowledge of Egypt's military intentions.

As had happened many times in the past, some obstacles and irritations arose between the Soviet Union and Israel. In June, a group of Israeli theater

directors and producers visited the Soviet Union but
Moshe Dayan then became upset when one of the producers,
Yaacov Agmon, tried to engage in personal diplomacy by
developing a broader cultural exchange. Agmon returned
to Moscow to work out arrangements and Dayan made it
clear that he did not have the backing of the Israeli
government.41 That same month, the Israeli Ministry
of Commerce and Industry turned down a request by a
company to import Soviet cement. A controversy developed over whether the cement was really offered by the
Soviets, but it was clear that Israel was not prepared
to admit Soviet products.

In August, twenty-six Israeli athletes and fifteen
staff members traveled to the World Student Games in
Moscow. The Israeli flag was flown at the airport, but
a degree of disharmony was evident. The visas of
several Israeli journalists were cancelled and Israel
complained that its competitors were jeered and that
they were restricted in their travel and access to
telephones. It was also charged that Soviet Jewish
spectators were attacked after Israel defeated Puerto
Rico in a basketball match. Even more galling to the
Israelis was the presence of Yasir Arafat at the opening ceremonies of the games.42

Also in August, the Soviets accused a Jewish
emigrant of trying to smuggle icons and forbidden
documents out of the country, and the Soviets were upset
when a member of the Jewish Defense League held a press
conference in Tel Aviv. He said that a Soviet citizen
in the West would be beaten every time a Soviet Jew
was.43 In September, Israel opposed East Germany's
admission to the United Nations and tried to separate
its consideration from that of West Germany. The two
Germanies were admitted in tandem.

Although the Soviet Union endorsed Arab war preparations, and then backed Egypt and Syria during the conflict, Soviet Jewish emigration was not negatively affected. This represented a continuation of the linkage
between emigration and Soviet-American relations and
the absence of any strong correlation with bilateral
Soviet-Israeli ties or the Arab-Israeli dispute. On
March 21, one of Victor Louis' periodic contributions
appeared in Yediot Achronot in which the Israelis were
informed that the education tax on Soviet Jewish
emigrants would no longer be applied. There had already
been rumors to that effect, and Deputy Prime Minister
Allon was sufficiently encouraged to state that the
Soviet Union should not be blamed for all problems.
Foreign Minister Eban called for a resumption of rela-
tions.44 By the time the Soviets stopped enforcing the
tax, the government had received payments of more than
eight million dollars and the percentage of college
graduates among the emigrants had dropped from forty to

eleven percent.[45] The normal pattern of emigration
then resumed and the total of 35,000 Jewish departures
in 1973 was the highest recorded up to that time. In
June, Brezhnev even received Jacob Stein, Chairman
of the Conference of Presidents of Major American
Jewish Organizations. This was the first time that
the Soviet General Secretary had met with a leading
Zionist official to discuss the emigration issue.

Despite considerable Arab criticism, the Soviet
Union did not diminish the flow of Jews to Israel and
did not cut off emigration as a result of the war, as
it had in 1967. In fact, the granting of permission to
leave actually hit a monthly record of 4200 in October.
The strongest attacks on Soviet policy came from the
Libyans, who claimed that Soviet Jewish immigrants to
Israel were more dangerous than the Phantoms supplied
by the United States. They also charged the Soviets
with contributing men and expertise to Israel in return
for American wheat.[46] The Eagles of the Palestine
Revolution, who had claimed responsiblity for the attack
on Soviet Jews en route to Vienna, threatened to
strike at Soviet embassies if emigration to Israel was
not terminated.[47]

Toward a Palestinian State

The Soviet attitude toward the Palestinian question changed dramatically in 1973. Early in the year,
a Jordanian member of al-Ansar became the first communist to be appointed to the nominal legislature of the
Palestinian movement, the Palestine National Council.
Nevertheless, Palestinian communists continued to operate independently of the PLO and that organization was
not lauded by pro-Soviet spokesmen. A Lebanese communist wrote about an overemphasis on the issue of
Palestine and a Jordanian communist boasted that his
party was the only active political organization in the
West Bank.[48] In August, the clearly ineffective al-
Ansar movement was replaced by the Palestine National
Front. Like its predecessor, it was dominated by communists and was closely tied to the Jordanian party.

After the war, a change of position became evident
as the Soviet Union began to emphasize the Palestinian
question, strengthen its contacts with the PLO, and
advocate the recognition of Palestinian national rights.
To a great extent, the Soviets were trying to compensate
the Palestinians for their exclusion from the Geneva
negotiating process. They also wanted to use their ties
to the Palestinians as a springboard to their own
participation in a Middle East settlement, at a time
when American access to Arab states was greater than
their own. Furthermore they believed that a Palestinian
state was a vital component of any peace arrangement.

Arafat had spent five days in the Soviet Union in August, and he returned for a six-day visit in November. The day after he left, a Soviet-Yugoslav joint communique recognized the "national rights" of the Palestinians and this expression again appeared in a Soviet commentary on Arafat's talks in Moscow.[49] On November 28, an Arab summit in Algiers delineated the PLO as the "sole representative" of the Palestinian people. The Soviet Union sent letters to the PLO calling for a Palestinian state in the West Bank and Gaza, and the Palestine National Front also took this position. It is possible that some leading figures in the PLO concurred. Nayef Hawatmeh, leader of the Popular Democratic Front for the Liberation of Palestine, seemed to favor this approach and the Soviets told Uri Avnery at Geneva that Arafat was willing to accept such a truncated Palestinian state.[50] However, the PLO was publicly calling for a "democratic and secular state," which was based on the elimination of Israel as a separate Jewish state and the incorporation of both Jews and Arabs into a joint Palestinian state. The Soviets disapproved of this stance, instead advocating the establishment of a Palestinian state alongside Israel. Curiously, the Soviet Union predated the PLO in its call for a West Bank-Gaza state but, in this context, the Soviet position should be viewed as one of greater moderation. The existence of Israel was not to be questioned. It should be added that, publicly, the Soviets did not press for a Palestinian state, only recognition of Palestinian "national rights."

. . . .

By the end of 1973, Soviet-Israeli relations were not as strained as one may have anticipated. Despite the war, the two states had reconciled quickly as frigidity gave way to normal coolness. The Soviet Union was anxious to participate in the negotiating process for, curiously, its decision to assist Egypt's war effort undermined Moscow's power in the region once Egypt had achieved a psychological victory. Cairo then moved closer to Washington in an effort to secure concessions from Jerusalem. Israel therefore needed some leverage against the United States so it would not become subjected to an imposed American settlement so it was amenable to improved relations with the Soviet Union.

8
Shunted Aside

The Geneva negotiating process was purely an effort to cajole the Soviet Union into believing that it was participating in Middle East diplomacy. Actually, Geneva was no more than a fig leaf throughout the period January 1974-September 1975 when important agreements were made regarding the disengagement of Arab and Israeli forces. At first, the Egyptians and Israelis negotiated directly. Then in a move even more displeasing to the Soviets, the United States assumed the role of broker as Kissinger engaged in shuttle diplomacy between Egypt, Syria and Israel. The United States claimed that its efforts were conducted under the Geneva umbrella, but it was apparent that step-by-step diplomacy was replacing the comprehensive approach envisioned by the Soviets as fundamental to the Geneva framework. More importantly, the Soviets were left out in the rain while the Americans remained dry. The indignity of having been shoved out from beneath the umbrella was then compounded even further as the United States managed to garner significant credit for holding it.

The Soviet Union hoped to reconvene the Geneva conference, but it was constantly thwarted. Neither the United States nor Israel wanted to include the Soviets in the round of diplomacy, and Egypt took the same position as it believed that only the U.S. could help recover its territory. Even the Syrians became party to the American initiative. Egyptian and Syrian relations with Washington prospered as American diplomacy and financial inducement proved successful. At the same time, Israeli-American relations remained firm as Israel saw the limited agreements as a means to avoid a more comprehensive settlement. The United States was supplying an increasing quantity of arms so Israel believed that military disengagements plus sufficient firepower would permit it to avoid a more substantial withdrawal from occupied territories.

133

The Soviet Union tried to interest Israel in returning to Geneva, but it did not offer the necessary
carrots such as escalated Jewish emigration or a resumption of diplomatic relations. It had seriously
miscalculated when it permitted Egypt and Israel to
work out a first-stage disengagement, ostensibly within
the Geneva framework, as it had in effect acceded to
its own exclusion. The negotiating process then
gathered momentum, not only keeping the Soviets on the
sidelines but augmenting the diplomatic role of the
United States. The U.S. really became more than a
broker as it tried to gear settlements to its own
strategic interests. Despite Soviet misgivings, the
Kissinger shuttle became the cornerstone of negotiations. This inevitably pushed the Soviet Union closer
to the PLO, producing Arafat's first official visit
to Moscow and an emphasis on the principle that the
Palestinians must be represented in negotiations.

The Soviet Union was trying to sustain detente
as it had a continuing need for American grain and
credits. This may help explain Moscow's hesitancy in
acting too obstructively in regard to the disengagement agreements. If this was the Soviet intention, it
did not bear fruit as detente received a rude shock
from the passage of the Jackson and Stevenson amendments
by the U.S. Congress. The Soviet Union therefore
failed to receive the economic concessions for which
it was hoping.

To analyze these issues, we must ask: How was the
Soviet Union effectively excluded from the negotiating
process? Why was there a frenzied period of Soviet-
Israeli diplomatic interaction during the first half
of 1975? Why did the Soviet Union publicly endorse
the concept of a Palestinian state? How was the
emigration of Soviet Jews affected by the course of
diplomacy? Was any progress made toward the reestablishment of official Soviet-Israeli relations?

Shuttlebug

The direct negotiations initiated by SC 338 continued after the demise of the Geneva conference.
Israeli and Egyptian representatives met frequently to
work out a military disengagement, keeping both superpowers at a distance. The United States had no plan
to offer, but Kissinger (who had been Secretary of
State since September) wanted to play an active diplomatic role. He was devoting increased attention to
the Middle East now that Vietnam, China and SALT were
demanding less of his time.[1] His approach was based on
gaining an advantage over the Soviet Union by leaving
it out of the diplomatic process. Kissinger constantly
told the Soviets that he was working within the Geneva
framework and would keep them informed. In reality,

he was trying to enhance American strategic interests at Soviet expense. Kissinger was therefore upset that the Israelis and Egyptians were negotiating autonomously, not subject to American influence. He preferred a procedure whereby the United States could present Israeli concessions to the Arabs and receive some benefit in return. He expressed his anger to Rabin and indicated that Israeli concessions could be traded for an end to the oil embargo. When Israel and Egypt quickly came to an agreement without any advantages accruing to the United States, Kissinger was furious at Israeli negotiator Aharon Yariv, even accusing him of selling out the Jews.[2]

The Soviets did not object to direct Arab-Israeli talks as they took the position that a shift in military power toward the Arabs now made such an approach feasible. Previously, they had claimed that Israel's military superiority would permit it to dictate terms. The motivation underlying Soviet behavior was most likely the desire to see the Suez Canal reopened. In order to achieve this, Israeli-Egyptian negotiations would be supported even though the Soviet Union was being overshadowed diplomatically by the United States. It is true that the first-stage disengagement agreement did lead to the reopening of the Canal in June 1975. However, the Canal was losing its significance as a supply route to Vietnam as the war was in its last throes and that is why the United States was willing to facilitate its dredging and enhancement of its tonnage capacity. The Soviets appear to have judged unwisely on this issue as the meager advantages gained in regard to the Canal were more than offset by the new strategic alignment that started to take shape in the Middle East with the Israeli-Egyptian disengagement agreement. Although the Soviets insisted that the agreement was part of the Geneva process, a step toward a comprehensive settlement and a purely military arrangement with no political overtones, they were either naive or practicing self-deception on all counts.[3]

On January 18, 1974 the Israelis and Egyptians concluded their agreement and it was signed on January 24 at Kilometer 101 in the Sinai desert. Sadat insisted on this remote location as he did not want the Soviet Union to participate. The United States did not mind if the ceremonies took place in Geneva, where American and Soviet representatives could attend, but it did not press the point. Israel favored Sadat's approach as it too was wary of a Soviet role at Geneva. However, in an effort not to offend Soviet sensibilities, Deputy Prime Minister Allon declared: "Even the agreement on the separation of forces, which was signed at Kilometer 101 in the

desert, is just a branch of the Geneva complex. It
is part and parcel of the Geneva Conference and does
not matter where it takes place, here or there."[4]

Both Israel and Egypt distrusted commitments when
both superpowers were involved. In 1970, Israel agreed
to "Rogers B" as it counted on American assurances that
the Soviet Union would restrain Egypt from moving
the missiles closer to the Canal. In 1973, Egypt relied on Soviet assurances that the United States would
not permit Israel to violate the cease-fire. Each was
sadly disappointed and aggrieved. The superpowers had
agreed in 1967 on SC 242 as the basis for a settlement,
yet nothing had been achieved. Could any better results be anticipated for SC 338? Israel and Egypt
thought not so they were prepared to play their
American cards, relying on the United States as
mediator and guarantor. Perhaps a Pax Americana could
be achieved, whereas one intertwined with Soviet-
American rivalry would have little chance of success.
Israel and Egypt were prepared to give due credit to
the United States and to disregard the Soviet Union.
Of course, they expected to benefit handsomely in the
bargain as American economic largess would be bestowed
upon them as a reward for their progress toward peace
and acceptance of U.S. regional hegemony. The
Kissinger shuttle was geared up.

Israel was willing to try this method of diplomacy
as it was a way of keeping the Soviet Union apart from
Egypt. Furthermore, as long as Egypt was negotiating
on this basis, Cairo was not going to jeopardize the
talks by seeking to resupply its armed forces with
Soviet equipment. Egypt could therefore be effectively
neutralized as a military threat.[5] From the Egyptian
perspective, only the United States could pressure
Israel to make concessions. Sadat could even use this
as leverage, requiring that concessions be extracted
from Israel in return for Egypt's tilt toward
Washington rather than Moscow.[6] Accordingly, Egyptian-
American diplomatic relations were established by the
end of April.

The Soviet Union was unable to implement a
strategy similar to that of the United States due to
its poor relationship with Israel. Soviet delegation
members at Geneva had recognized this problem, but a
division in the Politburo had obstructed any rapprochement with the Jewish state. Reportedly, some
Politburo members had recommended this course, to be
accompanied by steps toward closer ties to the pro-
Western oil producers. They realized that Arab states
bordering Israel would drift away from Moscow as their
financial and military requirements could be met by
Saudi Arabia and other wealthy monarchies. A major
shift of Soviet strategy was therefore advocated, but
not approved. When Nahum Goldmann, chairman of the

World Jewish Congress, went to the Soviet capital, he
heard the familiar line: Progress toward a comprehensive solution was a pre-condition to a renewal of
Soviet-Israeli relations.[7] The Soviets missed an opportunity and had to watch Kissinger's shuttle diplomacy for another year and a half.

Golda Meir, embarrassed by Israel's lack of military preparedness in October 1973, resigned on April
10. Yitzhak Rabin was asked to form a government and
it was approved by the Knesset on June 3. This change
of leadership in Israel had no effect on the diplomatic process as Rabin was oriented toward the United
States even more strongly than was Meir. The American
government therefore continued to serve its strategic
interests by working toward an unlikely entente with
Israel and Egypt, while maintaining close relations
with Saudi Arabia as well. The entire peace initiative
had passed to Washington. Perhaps Israel could have
tried to work out a settlement on favorable terms
during the period 1967-73, but it had not displayed
such an inclination except during the euphoric months
following its victory in the Six-Day War. Now it was
the American turn. The Soviet Union, unable to orchestrate or even propose a solution, could only react to
Kissinger's shuttle initiatives.[8]

Kissinger attempted to work out a disengagement
between Israeli and Syrian forces. Predictably, the
Soviet Union wanted such negotiations to be part of
the Geneva process but the American Secretary of State
paid only lip service to this concept while actually
holding the Soviets at arm's length. Gromyko tried to
get involved in the diplomacy, meeting with Kissinger
in Washington, Geneva and Cyprus, but Kissinger just
assured him that he would keep him informed. When
the two men almost met at the Damascus airport on
February 27, Kissinger made a special effort to avoid
the Soviet foreign minister so that they would not
negotiate jointly with the Syrians. For its part,
Syria was receptive to Kissinger's efforts as it knew
that this was the only rapid way to recover territories
occupied by Israel. Although Syria had not attended
the Geneva conference (the Israelis were there and the
Palestinians were not), it had agreed in December 1973
to the establishment of an American interests section
in Damascus. Once disengagement talks had proven
fruitful, full diplomatic ties were established in
June. The American government also began to consider
the extension of economic assistance to the Baathist
regime, and it has been reported that Syria unsuccessfully sought the provision of U.S. arms.[9]

Gromyko wanted to display Soviet diplomatic involvement so he visited Syria at least three times,
received Assad in Moscow and conferred with Arafat on
four occasions. These frantic efforts served to cover

Soviet impotency and made it easier to lend support to the Kissinger mission. The Soviet position in Syria was also shored up by the provision of arms (including Mig-23's) and the implementation of a twelve-year moratorium on the repayment of Syria's military debt.[10]

Kissinger believed that the Soviets would encourage Syrian disengagement, but that they would insist on some diplomatic participation for themselves. He therefore emphasized publicly that the Soviets were playing a helpful role and he dissociated them from Syrian shelling of Israeli positions.[11] When Assad visited Moscow in April, Brezhnev expressed concern about the American initiative. He feared that it might serve as a substitute for a comprehensive settlement and thereby sell out the Palestinians. He also pointed out that Israel was only offering to return land seized in 1973, whereas it had given Egypt some of the land occupied in 1967 as well. Brezhnev fixed a critical eye on the shuttle diplomacy, but did not object to the process. He only sought more favorable terms and a linkage between a disengagement and more comprehensive peace efforts.[12]

Eventually, a disengagement was worked out that did include the return of some territory occupied by Israel since 1967. The Syrians also declared that the Soviet Union would be included in all phases of future negotiations and that Soviet-Syrian relations would remain strong.[13] The Soviet Union then endorsed the agreement and Brezhnev congratulated Assad. It was signed in Geneva in the presence of Soviet and American representatives as both Syria and the U.S. felt it necessary to assuage Soviet feelings in this manner. Israel went along with this procedure. Both Kissinger and Soviet spokesmen maintained that detente had facilitated the agreement. The Soviets called for renewed negotiations in Geneva.[14]

The Soviets at first believed that the disengagements with Egypt and Syria were military, but they soon came to recognize their political significance in determining the context of any future settlement. Similarly, the hope that the agreements would lead toward a comprehensive settlement and total Israeli withdrawal gave way to the realization that step-by-step diplomacy was a substitute rather than a stepping-stone. This was clearly the Israeli perception and intent.

Second Wind

After mediating Israeli disengagements with Egypt and Syria, Kissinger continued his shuttle missions in an effort to work out more extensive settlements between the same states. Nixon tried to contribute to this process with his June 1974 visits to Israel, Egypt, Syria, Jordan and Saudi Arabia (the enthusiasm of Sadat and Assad to receive him was significant, considering his weakened position due to Watergate) but he was forced to resign in August and the initiative remained primarily in the hands of Kissinger. The Soviet Union had already become disenchanted with Kissinger's style of diplomacy and it insisted on a return to Geneva. It obviously wanted to play a greater role in negotiations and realized that its lack of official relations with Israel would be a disadvantage in step-by-step diplomacy. Brezhnev condemned this piecemeal approach, viewing it as a means of dividing Arab states and freezing Israel's occupation of Arab territories. He indicated that it could only be supported if clearly a component of a comprehensive settlement.[15]

American strategy was to continue step-by-step negotiations while appeasing the Soviets with vague promises to return to Geneva. At the June-July 1974 Moscow summit, the final communique called for a resumption of the Geneva conference "as soon as possible." In September, newly-inaugurated Gerald Ford and Gromyko issued a joint statement on the Middle East, which set the stage for November discussions between Ford and Brezhnev in Vladivostok. The two leaders reiterated the necessity of a Geneva conference "as soon as possible" and, in a Soviet overture to Israel, recognized the right of all Middle-Eastern states to "independent existence." In the July summit communique, a similar appeal to the Palestinians had been made by the United States as there was a reference to their "legitimate interests." In February 1975, Gromyko and Kissinger agreed that the Geneva conference would reconvene at "an early date" but the American Secretary of State would not fix such a date. Meanwhile, Syria for the first time began to consider participation at Geneva. This became evident at the Assad-Brezhnev meeting in September, and the Syrians gestured to Israel that month by releasing two Jewish leaders who had been held without trial for three years.

Despite considerable talk about Geneva, the United States was stalling on the issue. Furthermore, there were counterefforts to arrange a separate settlement between Israel and Jordan. Israel still occupied all Jordanian territories seized in 1967 and Hussein hoped to recover some of them in the manner already demonstrated by Sadat and Assad. In July, Sadat and Hussein agreed that the PLO did not represent Palestinians in Jordan, a step which enhanced Hussein's negotiating status. Israel responded three days later with a Cabinet statement endorsing negotiations with Jordan and the establishment "east of Israel" of a "Jordanian-Palestinian Arab state." Israel and Jordan expected

serious negotiations to begin shortly, but first they
awaited the reaction of the Arab summit scheduled to
convene in Rabat, Morocco in October. Both were
shocked when the PLO was recognized as "the sole legitimate representative of the Palestinian people" and
the Jordanian option became a dead letter. Hussein's
status as a negotiator had been effectively undercut as
the occupied West Bank was inhabited by Palestinians
and even Jordan's remaining East Bank had a Palestinian
majority.

Egypt was unenthusiastic about a Geneva conference.
It had never welcomed a Soviet role in negotiations and
now began to maintain that an appropriate settlement
could not be achieved while the superpowers were polar-
ized. Rivalry between them, rather than "the requirements of justice," would dictate the conditions and
Egypt believed that justice was on its side. Furthermore, it was argued that an accomodation should be
reached between Jordan and the Palestinians prior to a
Geneva conference. Egypt therefore opposed its reconvening in the near future, and wanted to broaden its
eventual composition to include Britain, France and
some non-aligned states. This would reduce the possibility that the Soviet Union and United States could
impose a settlement. Sadat, in the short term, favored
the Kissinger initiative. In January 1975, he declared:
"But until the Geneva conference convenes, if the peace
operation can advance and if an opportunity should
arise for other steps toward peace, then we should not reject these opportunities. If Israel is ready to withdraw from Arab land, we must not reject this. We must
take this land."[16] Brezhnev's cancellation of his
trip to Cairo that month may have been prompted by his
anger at Egypt's continued step-by-step discussions
with Kissinger, although the Soviet claim that he was
ill may have been legitimate as he also had to forego
visits to Syria and Iraq.

Abba Eban, who had been Meir's foreign minister,
considered Israel's return to Geneva but Rabin and his
foreign minister Allon rejected this option. When
presenting his new government to the Knesset on June 3,
1974, Rabin advocated bilateral talks between Israel
and each Arab state. He declared that there should be
no other party to the negotiations, but this was surely
an exaggerated stance adopted due to internal political
considerations. Rabin's pro-American orientation was
well-known, as were his close personal ties to Kissinger.
At a press conference two weeks later, Rabin said that
Israel needed close relations with the United States to
counter Soviet threats and to secure the emigration of
Soviet Jews. He also maintained that the U.S., not the
U.S.S.R., could effect a political settlement.[17] The
step-by-step approach thus stayed alive, but Rabin tried

to present it as part of the Geneva framework. He claimed that it was a flexible formula which included different methods of negotiating, and that its aim was
"to bring about bilateral negotiations." The disengagement agreements with Egypt and Syria were part of this
process and demonstrated the advantage of segmented
talks over the convening of a large meeting including
the superpowers. Rabin distrusted Soviet-American
guarantees and did not believe that Moscow had displayed
a significant yearning for peace. He charged that the
Soviet Union had not engaged in any "formal, serious,
or significant dialogue" with Israel since the break
in relations in 1967.[18]

The Israeli prime minister believed that Israel
could never solidify a military victory through a
political solution as one of the superpowers, or both
acting in concert, would prevent this. Military victories thus served to gain time, and Rabin applied this
perception in his negotiations with Kissinger. He
wanted to delay serious discussions until 1976, a
presidential election year in the United States when the
exertion of American pressure on Israel to make concessions would be unlikely. He also wanted to wait until
American dependence on oil imports from Arab states had
diminished.[19] Rabin basically believed in the concept
of "land for time," not having much faith in the
principle of "land for peace."

Rabin's overall strategy was to reject Geneva,
stall in step-by-step negotiations, and freeze out the
Soviet Union. Nevertheless, he hoped to use this
position as a platform from which Israel could gain
some leverage over the Soviet Union. Rabin pointed out
that Moscow needed relations with Israel to balance
Washington's ties to the Arabs, and he called for their
resumption. Seeing Israel in a strong bargaining
position, he even hinted that Israel would have to be
satisfied about the pace of emigration of Soviet Jews
before it would consent to renewed relations.[20] The
Soviets were not yet ready to discuss these issues.

In late March 1967, Kissinger ended his new round
of shuttle diplomacy in failure. Egypt was still interested, but Israel was playing a delaying game and
Syria was becoming increasingly obstructive as it moved
to improve relations with the Soviet Union. Jordan was
hamstrung by the Rabat declaration. Was another Geneva
conference the way out of the impasse? The Soviet Union
thought so and an amazing sequence of negotiations with
Israel was initiated toward that end.

Rollercoaster

The collapse of the Kissinger shuttle came at a
most inopportune time for the United States. The South

Vietnamese and Cambodian governments were falling, leftists had gained the ascendancy in Portugal, there was tension with Turkey due to its occupation of territory on Cyprus, and King Feisal of Saudi Arabia was assassinated. American diplomacy was at a low ebb, Nixon's image had been badly tarnished by Watergate, and Kissinger could not concentrate his attention on the Middle East. At this point, the Soviet Union perceived an opening and began to play a more active role in the region. It hoped to reconvene the Geneva conference and realized that overtures to Israel would have to be made to bring this about.

Israel had consistently tried to isolate the Soviet Union from Middle Eastern diplomacy, but it began to reassess it position. The United States was seriously irritating Rabin's government by its pressure tactic of delaying military deliveries and many Israelis also began to question American will as a result of the growing catastrophe in Southeast Asia. Rabin disclaimed any connection between events in Southeast Asia and U.S. support for Israel but he tellingly stated: "At this stage Israel is indeed in need of receiving aid because we are not facing the Arab states. We are facing the Arab states plus the Soviet strength supplied to them. As the leader of the free world, the United States has a commitment and Israel is justified in demanding aid from it."[21] Rabin was clearly alluding to American manipulation of the arms supply, but he also appears to have had the developing post-Vietnam American mentality in mind as well as he was encouraging the United States to continue its struggle against pro-Soviet forces. Former foreign minister Eban and some members of the Cabinet wanted Israel to return to Geneva, and the most widely read newspaper editorially declared that "listening to the voices coming from Moscow is more important now than attempting to revive the U.S. initiative, whose chances of success are very small."[22] Rabin did not want to go to Geneva but the time appeared appropriate to mend fences with the Soviet Union and use this as counter-leverage against the United States.

Allon and Dobrynin had a "chance encounter" in Washington in January after Ford's State of the Union address, but more serious discussions began in April when Ambassador to the U.S. Simcha Dinitz held the first of approximately five talks with his Soviet counterpart Anatolii Dobrynin. These conclaves extended over a two-month period and were kept secret until President Ford revealed that Soviet-Israeli meetings were taking place.

Dobrynin initiated the talks and they were convened at the Soviet embassy in Washington and at restaurants. Both participants kept Kissinger informed

about their deliberations. Dobrynin may have wanted to
convince the U.S. government that Soviet-Israeli relations were cordial. Congress had voted economic sanctions against the Soviet Union in December 1974 and had
linked them to Soviet emigration policies. Jews were
not specifically mentioned, but they were obviously
the major concern. Dobrynin was anxious to have the
sanctions lifted so the appearance of improved ties to
Israel would have served his cause. Furthermore,
Dinitz was perceived as influential with Congress and
and Kissinger. Dobrynin may also have been signaling
the Arabs that continued obstinacy could produce a
Soviet rapprochement with Israel. Dinitz may have
been using the talks to show Kissinger that Israel had
a Soviet option. Such a tactic could have served to
encourage the termination of American pressure on Israel
through the withholding of arms.

Dobrynin raised the issue of returning to Geneva
and may have implied acceptance of some minor modifications in Israel's pre-1967 border. Nevertheless, no
substantive agreements were reached and Dinitz moved to
cut off the talks. Israel had always opposed this back
door approach to improved relations, favoring the official resumption of ties, and Dinitz additionally felt
that Dobrynin was using the discussions to register
some points with Kissinger. Dinitz said that he could
only continue if there was some specific purpose, adding that flirtation can only last so long. Eventually
you have to get married. Dobrynin responded that a
love affair is more important than a loveless mar-
riage.[23]

Parallel to the Dobrynin-Dinitz talks in Washington, secret April discussions took place in Jerusalem
between a visiting Soviet delegation and Israeli
officials. At least two Soviets participated and they
may have spent as many as ten days in Israel. None
was in the Politburo, but the delegation was at a high
enough level to engage in negotiations. The mission
may have been arranged by Dinitz and Dobrynin, but
Dinitz denies this. Israel tried to keep the meetings
secret and there were allegations that members of RAKAH
leaked their existence to the media. If so, this fits
in with the idea that the Soviets were trying to show
greater friendship toward Israel in order to signal
Washington and the Arab world. The Israeli Cabinet was
not informed of the Soviet mission beforehand, nor was
the United States. Once advised, the U.S. government
sought information on the deliberations.

The Soviets engaged in discussions with the most
senior Israeli ministers, so this mission to Jerusalem
must be viewed as extremely important. Prime Minister
Rabin, Foreign Minister Allon, and Defense Minister
Peres would not have met secretly with the Soviets unless this was the case. Remember that Victor Louis was

never received by any ministers of such high rank.
Israel must therefore have been seriously affected by
its perception of flagging American commitment, and the
Soviets were obviously intent on taking advantage of
U.S. weakness and preoccupation with crises outside the
Middle East.

The Soviet delegation encouraged the Israelis to
return to Geneva by indicating that diplomatic relations
could be restored once there was progress toward a
settlement. The Soviets also said that the PLO must
participate at Geneva, but they did not insist on a
separate PLO delegation. The settlement they envisioned
included almost complete Israeli withdrawal, but acceptance of minor border changes. There would be superpower
guarantees of both Israel's security and the implementation of an arms limitation agreement pertaining to the
transfer of weapons to the Middle East.[24] While the
Soviet offer was tempting, no agreement was reached with
the Soviet visitors.

During this period, there were many channels of
contact between the Israelis and Soviets. West German
and French diplomats served as useful middlemen, and
British Prime Minister Harold Wilson sounded out the
Soviets on renewing relations with Israel. Israeli
Foreign Minister Allon also discussed this issue with
the Dutch foreign minister, a significant step as the
Netherlands represented Israeli interests in Moscow.[25]
World Jewish Congress chairman Nahum Goldmann met with
Dobrynin, and Rumanian President Ceausescu rushed to
the Middle East on two days' notice to talk with the
Syrians and Egyptians about reconvening the Geneva
Conference. The Soviet journal International Affairs
was pressing the Arabs to agree to a political settlement, arguing that conditions were appropriate. The
Arabs had achieved a political victory in the 1973 war,
had unified as a result of the Rabat declaration on the
Palestinians, and had gained power through their control
of oil.[26] Furthermore, Gromyko told the Syrian foreign
minister that "Israel may get, if she desires, the
strictest guarantees" and Allon welcomed this remark,
even though Israel had traditionally opposed such
guarantees. Meanwhile, the Soviets were encouraging
the Egyptians to return to Geneva. Foreign Minister
Ismail Fahmy indicated that Egypt would possibly be
receptive were the Soviet Union to provide weapons and
offer a grace period on loans.[27]

Despite all of this diplomatic activity, the Soviet
Union was unable to organize another Geneva conference.
Syria and Egypt could most likely have been convinced
to attend, but Israel was really the obstacle. It did
not want the Soviet Union involved in a settlement,
didn't trust Soviet guarantees, did not want to negotiate with members of the PLO, and did not want to face

several Arab delegations at once as it preferred to
deal with Arab states separately. Furthermore, Rabin
had promised a public referendum on any adjustment in
the status of the West Bank so his freedom to negotiate was somewhat circumscribed. Perhaps Israel would
have been able to reestablish relations with the Soviet
Union, but any benefit derived from this was not worth
the reversal of basic tactics regarding negotiations.
Israel's long-range strategic interest was more
important than official ties to Moscow, and Israel also
wanted to continue its basically pro-American orientation in order to receive arms and financial assistance.
It therefore reverted to its American option and again
worked to exclude the Soviet Union.

Israel had been faced with a difficult choice that
actually dealt with the very essence of the Jewish
state. It could have opted for peace through negotiations at Geneva, but such a course would have produced the establishment of some Palestinian entity, a
compromise on sovereignty over East Jerusalem, extensive territorial withdrawal, and military weakening
through the institution of arms limitations. In return
for a shaky peace, Israel would have settled for a less
potent version of itself, and it also would have become
less strategically essential to the United States. A
diminution of both American assistance and commitment
would have been anticipated. Futhermore, Israel's mood
after the 1973 war was already one of serious intro-
spection and loss of confidence. Its vitality and
exuberance were sapped, not to return again until the
dramatic Entebbe raid of July 1976. The time was not
opportune for a settlement on the terms that would
have been presented at Geneva. Israel therefore decided to enhance its role as a significant international actor by retaining much of the occupied territory,
preventing the creation of a Palestinian homeland, and
maintaining its position as an advanced military power.
Its importance to the United States would thus remain
undiminished, and it would be able to avoid solutions
to the problems of the West Bank and Jerusalem. Egypt
was apparently willing to return to step-by-step diplomacy so Israel chose to negotiate over some less
essential land in the Sinai and to delay any settlement
affecting its more strategic interest. Egypt's favorable attitude toward a separate settlement really made
such an Israeli stance possible. Had Egypt insisted on
the Geneva framework, Israel may very well have followed suit.

On June 3, Rabin stated that Israel did not want
the Soviets in negotiations and that Egypt and the
United States had the same position. He also said that
the emigration of Soviet Jews had nothing to do with
the Middle East, and implied that including the Soviet

Union in peace talks was not needed in order to secure
substantial Jewish emigration.[28] On June 5, the Suez
Canal reopened and Israel voluntarily pulled back its
artillery twenty miles and halved its troop strength a-
long the Canal. The Soviets correctly realized that this
was a signal of renewed interest in step-by-step diplomacy. Israel could no longer afford to stall into
1976 as the United States was successfully applying
arms pressure. Rabin's government therefore decided
to work with Kissinger, but to reverse the pressure at
the same time. Promises of additional American
military assistance would be needed to secure Israeli
support for another disengagement. Geneva had already
become irrelevant, as was recognized by Kissinger and
Gromyko when they met in Vienna on May 20. Their joint
statement indicated discussion about a conference, but
did not specifically call for its reconvening.
     Israel was prepared for more shuttle diplomacy,
and Egypt was receptive as well as it felt threatened
by the May 30 Soviet-Libyan atomic energy agreement.
Syria chose not to participate, even though it was the
recipient of more than $100 million of American aid
in 1975. Syria complained about the sell-out of
Palestinian interests and charged that the United
States was too pro-Israeli to serve as an honest
broker. On the other hand, Syria did agree in May to
a six-month extension of the tenure of UN troops on its
border with Israel.
     Kissinger sprang into action and worked out a
second-stage disengagement between Israel and Egypt.
It was signed in Geneva on September 4, but without
Soviet or American participation in the ceremony. The
Soviet Union was upset by its lack of a negotiating
role and had clearly signaled its opposition to the
settlement a few weeks before its conclusion by offering to sell arms to pro-Western Jordan. Once the
agreement was ratified, the Soviets objected specifically to the placement of American technicians in the
Sinai to monitor Israeli and Egytian compliance. Had
they known, they would have been even more furious
about the anti-Soviet thrust of a secret agreement
worked out by Allon and Kissinger, which was later reaffirmed by Vance and Dayan in March 1979. It states
that "threats to the security and sovereignty of Israel
by a world power" will be "seen with special severity
by the U.S. government." The U.S. promised to consult
with Israel during Middle East emergencies in order to
determine the degree of assistance that could be offered, subject to Congressional limitations.[29]
Although not an outright American defense commitment,
it was surely a step toward including Israel under the
American protective umbrella. Israel therefore gave up
land to Egypt, but received additional military aid

and a significant American security commitment.

Kissinger again treated the Soviets cavalierly, disregarding them during negotiations and then stating that their participation would be "important" in a final settlement. He was able to ostracize the Soviets from Middle East diplomacy, while at the same time stressing detente in order to facilitate the Helsinki agreement on human rights, which was completed in August. The Soviets had been cooperative in Helsinki, and may even have made overtures to Israel during the spring to further collaboration with the United States in regard to Helsinki. The Middle East was another matter. Detente had given way to an American effort to secure strategic advantage, in part to compensate for setbacks in Southeast Asia.

Routinization

Although Soviet envoys came to see Rabin, and Dobrynin and Dinitz met frequently in Washington, there was no corresponding increase in lower-level bilateral contacts. Israeli municipal workers visited the Soviet Union in April 1974, political scientist Shlomo Avineri attended a Hegel conference in the Soviet Union in August, Soviet journalists participated in a communist press festival in Israel in October, and the Russian Orthodox Metropolitan of Moscow was received by the Israeli Minister of Religious Affairs in June 1975. In July, there was another leftist conference in Italy on the Arab-Israeli conflict. It took place in Rome and Uri Avnery attended. Also during this period, a tradition began in which Soviet delegates came to Israel to celebrate the victory over Nazi Germany. The Soviets were hosted by a friendship committee and the group arriving in May 1974 for the 29th anniversary was the subject of extensive newspaper coverage. Another delegation traveled to Israel in May 1975.

There were some minor incidents marring relations. In August 1974, the Soviet Union pressured British Prime Minister Harold Wilson not to pay a call at an Israeli embassy reception in London. They pointed out that he had not attended the visiting Bolshoi ballet and charged that he had not dispersed demonstrations against its appearance. Wilson did not go to the reception, but he sent three representatives.[30] That August and September, there were also repeated incidents in the Gulf of Suez between Israeli ships and a Soviet mine-clearing unit. Soviet minesweepers and helicopters were operating on the Israeli side of the cease-fire line with Egypt in an area claimed by the Israelis as under their territorial jurisdiction.

After first-stage disengagement agreements had

been signed with Egypt and Syria in 1974, Victor Louis wrote another of his articles for an Israeli newspaper in which he seemed to be reassuring the Arabs that Soviet-Israeli relations would not be restored. He mentioned that Syrian-American ties had been reestablished during Nixon's visit to Damascus (the U.S. had already renewed relations with Egypt as well), but discussed obstacles to parallel Moscow-Jerusalem ties. Louis argued that Soviet-Arab relations would be negatively affected and that an Israeli embassy in the Soviet capital could interfere in domestic affairs by offering political asylum to Soviet Jews. He also expressed concern about Jewish emigrants returning as tourists once relations were renewed. Louis also condemned Soviet Jews who went to the United States rather than Israel and he claimed that non-Jews were entering into artificial mixed marriages solely for the purpose of gaining permission to emigrate.[31] It should be added that Louis' article was also published in many Western newspapers and that it coincided with Nixon's visit to Moscow. Hints that relations would not be reestablished with Israel, and that restrictions would be placed on Jewish emigration, were probably aimed at convincing the Arabs that the Moscow summit would not produce a superpower deal at their expense.

Since the fall of 1972, Senator Henry Jackson had been threatening to introduce legislation into the U.S. Congress which would link Soviet Jewish emigration to American economic concessions to the Soviet Union. By mid-1974, it was evident that Jackson was going to act so Moscow tried to forestall his efforts by adopting a moderate stance on both the emigration issue and the resumption of relations with Israel. The Soviets expressed their concerns about Jackson's tactics to business executive Armand Hammer, and he then said that 200,000 Jews wanted to emigrate and they could all be accomodated within five years. He also maintained that the Soviet Union was prepared to renew ties to Israel and that Jews could then apply for visas at the Israeli embassy in Moscow. In October, Polish communist party leader Edward Gierek stated while in the United States that he expected all East European states to establish relations within a year. In another development that may possibly have been related, the Moscow police for the first time blocked off traffic so that Jews could more easily celebrate Simchat Torah outside the main synagogue.[32]

Despite Soviet gestures, including an offer from Dobrynin to Ford that 55,000 Jews per year could emigrate, Jackson proceeded with his legislation.[33] The U.S. administration opposed his efforts, and a deal was worked out with the assistance of Kissinger that would have led to the emigration of 60,000 Soviet citizens yearly (mostly Jews). Jackson's proposed amendment would still be introduced, but it would include provisions for an eighteen month presidential waiver. Once Kissinger and Jackson publicly exchanged assurances, the Soviets denied that a secret agreement had been reached and the deal fell through. The Jackson-Vanik amendment to the Trade Reform Act was passed in December 1974, denying most favored nation trade status and Export-Import Bank credits to "non-market economy states" that restricted emigration. The Soviet Union was not specifically mentioned, but was clearly implied. If Soviet emigration policy changed in a favorable direction, a waiver of the amendment could be applied. In addition, the Stevenson amendment to the Export-Import Bank Act placed a ceiling of $300 million on credits to the Soviet Union over a four-year period, banned credits for energy development, and limited those for energy exploration to $40 million. Therefore, even if the Soviet Union permitted the emigration of large numbers of Jews in order to comply with terms stipulated in the Jackson-Vanik amendment, it still would be subjected to credit restrictions as a consequence of the Stevenson amendment.

The Soviets protested vociferously that the United States was interfering in its internal affairs, and superpower relations deteriorated. Israel realized that Soviet Jewish emigration could be negatively affected by such a development, so Foreign Minister Allon tried to argue that it was in the Soviet interest to permit Jews to leave as emigration helped solve the pervasive domestic "Jewish problem."34 His effort was to no avail as emigration declined from 35,000 Jews in 1973 to 21,000 in 1974 and 13,000 in 1975. The drop in 1975 was probably due to the Jackson-Vanik and Stevenson amendments, as the pace of emigration remained a function of Soviet-American relations. More confusing is the decline in emigration in 1974. If the Soviet Union had wanted to influence Congres to reject Jackson's endeavor, it would have been more logical to permit more Jews to leave. In fact, as we shall see later, this tactic was used in 1979 when it appeared that the Jackson-Vanik amendment would be repealed. Perhaps the drop in emigration in 1974 was related to pique over being left out of Middle East diplomacy by Kissinger. If so, the Soviets miscalculated as the Jackson-Vanik and Stevenson amendments led to even more severe economic sanctions that had a deleterious impact on Soviet economic development.

The Soviet Union did not manipulate the emigration of Jews effectively to prevent Congressional action, nor did it act to increase the flow of Jews to encourage Israel to participate in a Geneva conference. Furthermore, more extensive bilateral contacts with Israelis

were not promoted during the spring of 1975 when the
diplomatic initiative was peaking. Also, the Soviets
could have raised the level of their May delegation to
Israel for the celebration of victory over the Nazis,
but they failed to do so as the status of their
delegates was the same as in May 1974. One must conclude that the Soviet Union hoped for the reconvening
of a Geneva conference, but was unwilling to give much
to Israel to achieve it. A maximum effort was not in
evidence as high-level talks with Israeli officials
may have been aimed less at achieving a peace settlement than at heading off Jackson's foray into linkage
politics. In addition, exclusion from shuttle diplomacy had strengthened ties between the Soviet Union
and the rejectionist Arab camp. They may have served
as a significant constraining influence.

The Palestinian Dimension

Gromyko met with Arafat several times in early
1974 in order to counter Kissinger's shuttle diplomacy,
and a Jordanian communist leader writing in the pro-
Soviet World Marxist Review in April recognized the PLO
as the "sole lawful representative" of the
Palestinians.[35] Once a disengagement agreement between
Israel and Syria had been negotiated under American
auspices, the Soviet Union moved even closer to the
PLO in order to compensate for its own exclusion from
the peace process. In addition, the Palestinians had
been left out in the cold as the disengagements had
not dealt at all with a resolution of their problems.
From the Soviet perspective, the United States was
working to effect settlements between Israel and
neighboring Arab states, including the usually militant
Syria. To reinject some radicalism into the Arab cause,
and to force themselves back into the diplomatic process, the Soviets felt it essential to move closer to
the Palestinians.

In July, Arafat made his first official visit to
the Soviet Union. Previously, he had only been a guest
of the Afro-Asian People's Solidarity Committee. The
Soviets agreed to the establishment of a PLO mission in
Moscow. However, they then delayed permission to open
it. The PLO appointed a representative in March 1975,
but the mission was not inaugurated until June 1976.
In October 1974, Arafat was buoyed by the Rabat summit's
recognition of his organization as the "sole legitimate
representative" of the Palestinian people and he then
made a triumphant appearance at the United Nations in
November. When he visited the Soviet Union later in
November, Prime Minister Kosygin received him for the
first time.
In June 1974, the Palestine National Council had

called for "an independent national people's administration throughout the part of Palestinian territory
which will be liberated." This was apparently a step
away from the concept of a democratic and secular
state to replace Israel toward acceptance of a
Palestinian state alongside Israel. Nayef Hawatmeh, a
prominent figure in the PLO and a close ally of the
Soviet Union, had foreshadowed this change of course
with an unusual article in an Israeli newspaper. This
was the first time that a PLO leader had written for an
Israeli Hebrew-language publication, although reprints
of articles published elsewhere had appeared. Hawatmeh
endorsed a West Bank-Gaza Palestinian state. However,
less than a month later, Hawatmeh indicated in a German
newspaper, that even if such a state were to be
established, the plan to create a democratic and
secular state in all of Palestine would not be abandoned. Israel must still be destroyed.36 Obviously, the
Palestinian problem was far from being resolved. Soviet
analysts discerned a growing PLO willingness to settle
for a state on Arab land then occupied by Israel. In
effect, this meant at least temporary acceptance of
Israel and the Soviets maintained that many members of
the PLO were becoming more "realistic" and no longer
believed in the elimination of the Jewish state.37
The Soviet and Palestinian positions seemed to be coming
closer together, leading Palestinian academic Walid
Khalidi to observe: "Ironically, too, in the intra-
Palestinian and inter-Arab dialogues, the argument that
the Soviet Union would not endorse anything beyond the
pre-June 1967 frontiers has been the major consideration
in the Palestinian leadership's shift from the objective
of a Palesinian democratic state to that of a state on
the West Bank, Gaza Strip, and East Jerusalem."38

The Soviet Union had privated supported the
establishment of a separate Palestinian state since
late 1973, and an April 1974 article by a Jordanian
communist in the World Marxist Review had endorsed this
position. By the fall, the Soviets began to go public
on the issue as negotiations with Israel had already
collapsed. On September 8, chief of state Podgornyi
referred to "statehood" and, on October 11, Brezhnev
mentioned a "national home." At the end of Arafat's
November visit, Pravda cited "the creation of their
national home, up to establishment of their own
statehood."39 To prepare for the eventuality of a
Palestinian state, a Palestinian Communist Organization
was created. It operated in addition to the Palestine
National Front, which included non-communists. Interestingly, the Soviet Union was more outspoken on the
statehood issue than was the PLO. Arafat, acting
cautiously, had to contend with radicals within his
ranks who believed that the establishment of a separate

Palestinian state meant a renunciation of the struggle against Israel.40

As the Soviets became diplomatically active in early 1975 in quest of a reconvened Geneva conference, they stressed the importance of the Palestinian issue to the peace process. This was to be a recurring development as they did not believe that a workable settlement was possible without resolution of the Palestinian issue. Of course, this Soviet approach only increased Israeli reluctance to return to Geneva. To strengthen the Palestinian hand at the time, Arafat was interviewed in the February issue of the World Marxist Review and he again journeyed to Moscow in late April. He met with Gromyko, Ponomarev and, apparently, Brezhnev. At the time, no indication was given that a meeting with Brezhnev had taken place but, a week later, a PLO official averred that Brezhnev had indeed received the Palestinian delegation.41 After a month had passed, the Soviet news agency TASS released a photo of Brezhnev and Arafat and a statement that they had conferred during Arafat's April-May visit. Of course, they may have chatted only briefly and no significant discussions may have transpired. It appeared from Brezhnev's ornamentation that the photo was taken on May 1. Why the meeting was first kept secret by the Soviets remains enigmatic, but it is possible that they were hiding it from the Israelis at a time of their own overtures to Jerusalem. The release of evidence by TASS can more easily be explained. It took place when Ford was conferring with Sadat in Salzburg, Austria and may have been an oblique signal that the Soviet Union was prepared to obstruct step-by-step diplomacy.42 Soviet efforts to reconvene Geneva had already met with failure. The Israelis remained obstinate and the communique issued at the end of Arafat's visit in May showed that the Soviets were unable to pressure him into attending.43

By the fall of 1975, the second-stage Israeli-Egyptian disengagement agreement had driven an additional wedge between the Soviet Union and Israel. Surprisingly, just when it appeared that relations were approaching their nadir, there was an upsurge of significant bilateral contacts, including a meeting of foreign ministers. What accounts for this dramatic turnabout? We must now begin to unravel this mystery.

9
Some Steps Toward Reconciliation

After the second-stage disengagement agreement
between Israel and Egypt, the Soviet Union and Israel
improved their relations and bilateral contacts increased dramatically. The Soviets, still hoping for a
Geneva conference, wanted to forestall any further disengagement between Israel and Syria negotiated under
American auspices. The Israelis also opposed a deal
with Syria and were fearful that the United States
would try to pressure them in that direction. Gradually, the Soviet Union and Israel developed common interests on other issues as well. Both were concerned
about Syrian-American collusion in Lebanon and about
the impact of the Ethiopian revolution on strategic
access to the Red Sea.

While fostering more cordial ties to Israel, the
Soviet Union initially became even more supportive of
the PLO and insisted upon its participation at a Geneva
conference. It also encouraged RAKAH to strengthen its
bonds with Israeli Arabs, to cooperate with dovish
Jewish groups and to begin a dialogue with the PLO.
The Soviets wanted to make sure that if a peace settlement were to be arranged, the Palestinian issue would
be a crucial component.

The election of Jimmy Carter as President of the
United States raised the possibility of an American-
sponsored initiative to achieve a comprehensive settlement, so the Soviets wanted to ensure their own inclusion in the peace process. Despite their misgivings
about Begin's election in Israel, they continued to
press for a Geneva conference and sought diplomatic cooperation with the United States. As we shall see,
this tactic backfired as Egyptian interests were not
adequately considered.

Among the questions that must be raised are: Did
the Soviet Union seriously believe that a Geneva conference could be organized prior to the American presidential election of 1976? Was Israel prepared to
switch from step-by-step diplomacy to an effort aimed

153

at a comprehensive settlement? What accounts for the
extensive Soviet-Israeli diplomatic activity during
this period? How were Soviet tactics affected by the
decline in Soviet-Egyptian relations?

Aftermath

Through the efforts of Israeli UN delegate Chaim
Herzog, a meeting was scheduled in New York between
the Soviet and Israeli foreign ministers. Israel
wanted to blunt strong American pressure on a Syrian
shuttle. The Soviet Union hoped to drive a wedge
between Jerusalem and Washington at a time when their
relations appeared particularly strong. Moscow also
was trying to send a signal to the Syrians to reject
American efforts to work out another disengagement. It
was a common Soviet tactic to try to force an Arab
state into line by displaying greater warmth toward
Israel (remember Victor Louis' trip to Israel in June
1971 to counter Egyptian-American negotiations).

On September 24, 1975, Allon and Gromyko met for
three hours (Herzog was also present) at the Soviet
mission to the United Nations. It was the first such
meeting of foreign ministers in nearly two years. In
order to dispel any American consternation, Allon conferred with Kissinger that very morning before his
session with Gromyko. Allon told Gromyko that the
Soviet Union should renew relations with Israel if it
wanted to participate fully in the diplomatic process.
Israel was concerned about its diplomatic isolation
and believed that official ties to the Soviet Union
would lead other East European (and some African)
states to follow suit. Gromyko did not want to discuss
the resumption of relations, and he chided Israel for
its second-stage disengagement with Egypt and the
placement of American technicians in the Sinai.
Gromyko said that Israel must relinquish occupied territories and work toward a resolution of the
Palestinian problem in order to bring about improved
(but not necessarily official) relations. The Soviet
foreign minister proposed a West Bank-Gaza
Palestinian state, but he indicated that it could be
linked economically to Israel. Overall, the fact that
such a meeting took place proved much more significant
than its content. Neither side was prepared to offer
meaningful concessions, although Gromyko's reference
to economic ties between Israel and a projected
Palestine may be viewed as a moderate Soviet position.[1]

On November 9, the Soviet Union requested that
the United States help reconvene the Geneva conference.
The timing was surely not propitious as the Soviets
were then supporting a UN resolution equating Zionism
with racism. Surely Israel would not come to Geneva
while such an atmosphere prevailed. The Soviets probably did not believe that organizing a conference was

feasible, but were motivated by a desire to prevent any Syrian-American rapprochement that could produce another disengagement. Although Syria denied interest in a renewed round of shuttle diplomacy, the Soviets were not convinced and they increased arms deliveries to Damascus as a means of persuasion. The Soviets must have realized that the problem of Palestinian representation at Geneva was insurmountable during an American electoral campaign and that no conference could possibly be held until 1977. The United States was sure to maintain a strongly anti-Palestinian position in the meantime, as was soon evidenced in January 1976 when an American veto was registered in the Security Council on the issue of Palestinian statehood.

The Soviet Union had witnessed Egypt's move toward the United States, which was abetted by Israel's willingness to conclude the second-stage disengagement agreement. Furthermore, Israel had been enabled to concentrate more troops in the north, posing a threat to the Soviet Union's remaining ally, Syria. With the loss of Egypt, Syria became even more crucial to Soviet strategy and it was essential that Kissinger not succeed in bringing Assad under his wing. This perception helps explain increased Soviet insistence on a major role for the PLO, as it was maintained that the PLO must participate at Geneva from the beginning of the sessions and on an equal footing with other delegations. The Palestinians had clearly been disregarded during Kissinger's shuttle diplomacy, and emphasizing their need to be recognized was popular among Arab radicals. More importantly, stressing the Palestinian factor effectively undercut any propensity that Syria may have had to renew disengagement negotiations with Kissinger. A second-stage disengagement on the Syrian front would produce charges that Syria had sold out Palestinian interests.

Although the Soviets adopted a hard line on PLO representation at Geneva, they also encouraged the PLO to moderate its stance. They called for mutual recognition with Israel as a necessity if the Palestinians were hopeful of establishing their own state. Arafat reportedly received a Soviet message calling upon him to assume his historic responsibility, even if this were to produce his assassination. Of course, the PLO was asked to join the Geneva process, which it had not endorsed.[2]

The Angolan war seriously strained detente during the winter of 1975-76, minimizing the possibility of joint superpower pressure on Israel and heightening Soviet concern that Israel could perpetuate its occupation of Arab territory. In fact, the American proposal in February 1976 to end the state of belligerency between Israel and Arab states was viewed as an effort to consolidate Israel's territorial gains. The

December 1975 publication of the Brookings Institution study of the Arab-Israeli conflict and Jimmy
Carter's success in presidential primaries early in
1976 must have reassured the Soviets that a comprehensive framework was not out of the question. The
Brookings report called for almost complete Israeli
withdrawal, self-determination for the Palestinians
and an end to step-by-step diplomacy. Most significantly, its concepts had an impact on Carter and some
of its authors became his advisers on Middle East
policy. The Israeli reaction to the Brookings report
was mixed. There was strong criticism in the press.
However, Rabin did not rule out the Brookings recom-
mendations, with several requested revisions, as the
basis for negotiations. Rabin probably did not see
much merit in the Brookings proposals, but paying some
lip service to them was helpful in stalling a renewal
of step-by-step diplomacy regarding the Golan Heights.
Rabin surely knew that no progress would be made toward
constructing a comprehensive framework until after the
American elections, so time was on Israel's side.

Dinitz and Dobrynin met occasionally in early 1976
but the May 6 session between UN delegates Herzog and
Malik created the greatest controversy. Apparently,
Herzog did not seek permission from his government to
talk with Malik. This enraged Dinitz in Washington,
who felt that his own channel to Dobrynin was being
circumvented and that Herzog was too out of touch with
policy perspectives in Jerusalem to engage in sensitive
diplomatic talks. Dinitz also charged that Herzog had
presented Malik with his analysis of American policy
toward the Middle East, a "dangerous subject" that
should have been avoided. The Israeli Cabinet discussed Herzog's actions, leading the foreign ministry to
issue a directive that all contacts in the United
States between Israeli and Soviet representatives must
be based on prior authorization from Jerusalem. Again,
the Israeli government did not want negotiations with
the Soviet Union to proceed informally; it demanded the
resumption of official relations if the Soviet Union
wanted to play a diplomatic role in arranging a
settlement.[3]

In terms of substance, Herzog and Malik were
rather conciliatory. Herzog pointed out that Israel
was participating in the United Nations, even though
the PLO had observer status, and that Israel was willing to negotiate with the PLO if it accepted SC 242
and recognized Israel's existence. Malik said that if
Israel attended a Geneva conference alongside the PLO,
then Soviet-Israeli relations could be restored once
some progress toward a settlement was achieved. Malik
did not demand substantial or total Israeli territorial
withdrawal as a precondition. To contribute further
to the more relaxed mood engendered by this meeting, a

Soviet diplomat two days afterward made a surprise
visit to the Israeli embassy in Washington.[4] Nevertheless, it was really a fool's paradise as Herzog had not
been authorized to negotiate with Malik and his government disavowed the comments he had made.

In February 1976, Brezhnev proposed limitations on
the Middle East arms race and a guarantee of the
security of all states in the area. On April 28, the
Soviet Union issued a more detailed plan, advocating a
resumption of the Geneva conference with PLO participation. Indicating that more preparatory work was needed,
it called for a two-stage conference with a short
organizational stage and a lengthier substantive stage.
The PLO was to take part in both stages. Director
General of the Israeli Foreign Ministry Shlomo Avineri
described the Soviet proposal as one without new content, but with a more moderate tone than usual.[5]
Although the PLO was emphasized and Israel's navigational rights were not mentioned, the two-stage formula
left room for considerable diplomatic maneuvering which
could have led to PLO participation in only the second
stage. Furthermore, the PLO could have been included
in a joint Arab delegation, rather than seated separately, as the phrase "on an equal footing" was omitted.

The Israeli foreign ministry prepared three
analyses of the April 28 Soviet peace plan. Avineri's
was the least optimistic as he believed that the Soviets
were not signaling Israel, but rather the Arabs to stay
in line. The other evaluations discerned a softening
of the Soviet position. For example, the PLO was
depicted as "the legitimate representative" of the
Palestinians, but not the "sole" one and the Soviet
Union averred that it had no prejudice against Israel.
Copies of the first sympathetic assessment were sent to
Israeli diplomats overseas, and it is possible that
Herzog was influenced by this document when he met with
Malik.[6]

Since the second-stage disengagement, Egypt had
aligned with the United States. Sadat visited Ford in
October 1975, and he abrogated Cairo's friendship
treaty with Moscow on March 15, 1975. He then terminated Soviet military rights at Egyptian airfields and
ports, greatly reducing Soviet capacity to support a
Mediterranean naval squadron. Airport facilities had
been particularly crucial as there were no aircraft
carriers in the region which could help provide over-
head protection for Soviet ships.[7] Furthermore, the
United States was displaying its military might by
docking a destroyer at Haifa, Israel in April. This
was the first American warship to call at an Israeli
port in twelve years.

It was obviously the right time to strengthen ties
to Syria and to seek logistic facilities there. How-

ever, strains in the Soviet-Syrian relationship had
developed over Lebanon. The Soviets had supported
Syrian intervention in January against the Phalangists,
but were becoming increasingly concerned that Syria
would work out a deal with the United States and turn
against its PLO, Sunni Moslem and Druse allies. The
Soviet perspective may have influenced the issuance of
the April 28 peace proposal as a Syrian-Israeli separate disengagement agreement had to be headed off. To
underline their sense of urgency, the Soviets for the
first time in a peace overture, referred to Israel's
nuclear capability. Perhaps this comment was intended
to spur the Arabs into diplomatic activity toward a
peaceful settlement.8

Confusing Signals

The period from June 1976 through mid-March 1977
was one in which Soviet and Israeli policies and public
statements often appeared irrational and contradictory.
The complicated and rapidly evolving situation in
Lebanon was partly responsible, as were considerations
related to the November 1976 presidential election in
the United States and the upcoming Israeli general
election scheduled for May 1977. As both states reacted to the electoral processes, their actions frequently defied the logic dictated by the practical exigencies
of international politics.
    In June 1976, Syria again intervened in Lebanon.
This time, it was encouraged by the United States and
its armed might was directed at the PLO-Sunni-Druse
alliance. The Americans saw an opportunity to deal a
telling blow to the PLO, and may also have hoped that
the green light given to the Syrians in Lebanon would
be reciprocated by Syrian participation in another
round of step-by-step diplomacy.
    The Soviets opposed Syria's intervention and even
sent Kosygin on an unsuccessful mission to Damascus to
restrain Assad. Rabin described the Soviets as "panic-
stricken" as a loss of influence in Syria would have
meant virtual exclusion from the diplomacy of the entire
Arab-Israeli conflict.9 Brezhnev personally appealed
to Assad to withdraw his troops, and a Soviet media
campaign was conducted through August. It was to no
avail. The Soviets also discontinued the delivery of
arms to Syria.
    The Lebanon crisis was deemed so important by the
Soviets that Chief of Staff Viktor Kulikov inspected the
Mediterranean naval squadron in June. Not only was
Syria defying the Soviet Union but it was collaborating
with the United States and dividing Arab ranks by attacking the PLO. Furthermore, it appeared that Syria
would become reconciled with Egypt, thus moving it

closer to the American camp. On June 23, the Syrian
and Egyptian prime ministers and defense ministers conferred in Riyadh, Saudi Arabia, the first high-level
meeting between officials of the two states in a year.
The Soviet Union was confronted with a most difficult
situation as it did not want to sever its close ties
to Syria, but it also had to display some sign of support for the PLO. It decided not to initiate major
arms deliveries to the PLO, but small quantities were
sent periodically by sea.

Seeing their position in the Middle East in decline, the Soviets attempted to broaden their contacts
with conservative Arab states and Israel. They hoped
eventually to participate in negotiations aimed at
terminating both the Arab-Israeli and Lebanese conflicts. Hussein visited Moscow in June, but little
agreement was evident. The final communique referred
to a "spirit of frankness" and there was no call for a
Geneva conference or a Palestinian state. Hussein,
however, apparently agreed not to seek a separate
settlement with Israel.[10] Soviet overtures to Saudi
Arabia were even less successful as King Khalid was
unwilling to renew diplomatic relations, or even try to
improve ties.

The Soviet Union emphasized the importance of an
Arab-Israeli settlement, citing the threat of war
engendered by the extension of instability into
Lebanon, and some gestures were made toward Israel.[11]
Soviet diplomats in Western Europe took a moderate line
toward the Jewish state and pressed for a peace conference. In Washington, Dobrynin approached Dinitz at a
West German embassy reception and asked him to step
aside for a private conversation.[12] Despite such
entreaties, Israel was not really interested. Although
Eban continued to advocate a Geneva conference including the Soviet Union, Rabin adopted an extremely anti-
Soviet posture. He accused the Soviets of aligning
with Arab extremists and terrorists, and of obstructing
a peace settlement by insisting on PLO participation at
Geneva. He claimed that Soviet-Israeli relations had
deteriorated, while American-Israeli relations had
improved. Contrary to American cooperation with Syria
at the time, he proclaimed: "It will never be redun-
dant to underline the gratitude which the people, the
Knesset and the Government of Israel feel towards the
U.S. for standing at Israel's side."[13]

Like the Soviet Union, Israel was in an extremely
difficult situation. It feared Syrian-American cooperation as it could lead to demands to return the
Golan Heights and help improve the Syrian strategic
position through occupation of parts of Lebanon. By
weakening Soviet-Syrian bonds, this cooperation could
also make Israel less attractive to the United States

as a vital asset. On the other hand, Syria was crush-
ing the PLO and it had sent word to Israel via Hussein
that its troops in Lebanon were not directed against
it and would not be deployed beyond a specific red
line.14 Israel could only benefit from a Syrian-PLO
confrontation, and perhaps that is why it did not seek
an improvement in relations with the Soviet Union.
While such a course may have duly warned the United
States about its collusion with Syria, it would also
have contributed to a peace process which Israel hoped
to delay. Electoral politics were also relevant.
Rabin may have accentuated his anti-Soviet and pro-
American rhetoric in order to assist Gerald Ford in his
campaign against Jimmy Carter. Israel would have preferred to continue dealing with Kissinger and Ford, as
Carter was identified with the Brookings report and an
effort to achieve a comprehensive solution.

Both Israel and the Soviet Union feared that Syria
would effect a rapprochement with the United States and
that Kissinger would try to arrange another disengagement between Israel and Syria. Nothing of the sort
took place as Assad gained a sphere of influence in
much of Lebanon due to American acquiescence and then
failed to compensate the United States in any fashion.
Already somewhat isolated in the Arab world as a result
of its extension of power into Lebanon and military
confrontation with the PLO, Syria could not afford to
moderate its stance toward Israel. It therefore adopted a radical position and again moved closer to the
Soviet Union.

By the fall of 1976, the Israelis came to believe
that Carter had a chance to win the American election
so they had to prepare for a comprehensive settlement
on the best terms possible. This may explain Rabin's
support for a comprehensive approach in his New Year's
(Rosh Hashanah) address and the publication in Foreign
Affairs of Allon's peace plan. Allon discussed
solutions for all aspects of the Arab-Israeli conflict,
although he clearly expressed a preference for direct
negotiations with each Arab state separately rather
than a Geneva conference presided over by the super-
powers.15

The Soviet Union saw no merit in the Allon plan as
it did not include the establishment of a Palestinian
state, nor designate a negotiating role for the PLO.16
The Soviet plan, presented to Israel on October 1,
advocated a Geneva conference in October or November
(to deal with Lebanon as well). PLO participation was
demanded, as was the creation of a Palestinian state.
Although the Soviets called for an end to the state of
war, they did not explicitly endorse a peace treaty
and demanded Israel's withdrawal from "all" occupied
territories. Israel's right to free navigation in the

Straits of Tiran was not mentioned. This Soviet plan
really had no elements that could induce the Israelis
to go to Geneva, and must therefore be viewed as an
exercise in diplomatic posturing. The Soviets were
practicing one-upsmanship on the Americans, who
obviously would not negotiate a comprehensive settlement at election time. More importantly, they were
trying to mend fences with the PLO after failing to
render much assistance during the Lebanon crisis. The
PLO had been granted full membership in the Arab League
in September, and the Soviets knew that they must make
amends verbally to compensate for their caution
militarily.

Lending credence to the interpretation that the
Soviet plan was not expected to advance the negotiating
process was the method of its announcement. If the
Soviets were truly aiming for a diplomatic solution at
that time, Brezhnev or Gromyko may have personally
presented the Soviet proposals. Instead, the medium
was an unsigned TASS release which was delivered to
the Israeli UN mission by the number two Soviet representative. Herzog then requested a meeting with
Dobrynin, who was heading the Soviet delegation, and
he gave him on October 8 an unaddressed and unsigned
response that was a repetition of remarks made by
Allon to the UN General Assembly. In it, Israel
insisted that only the original participants in the
1973 Geneva conference should take part in negotiations. Of course, this ruled out a role for the PLO.
As had occurred previously, Herzog's diplomatic action
caused some concern in Israel. The Cabinet had not
been informed that he was planning to talk with
Dobrynin, and it seems that even Rabin and Director
General of the Foreign Ministry Shlomo Avineri may
have been in the dark on this matter.[17]

After Carter' election, it appeared that there was
movement toward Geneva. Nahum Goldmann conferred with
Rumanian President Ceausescu in December and with
Moroccan King Hassan in January and, at Herzog's
initiative, there was a February 3 meeting with Soviet
UN representative Oleg Troianovskii to discuss the
Geneva process. U.S. Secretary of State Cyrus Vance
traveled to the Middle East in February and, on March
16, Carter indicated his support for the establishment
of a Palestinian "homeland." In a memorandum to Carter
on February 23, national security adviser Zbigniew
Brzezinski indicated that the United States was prepared to go to Geneva, but it should try to secure a
Soviet concession in return.[18] The Soviet Union continued to advocate a Geneva conference and, on
January 18, Brezhnev reiterated Israel's rights to
statehood and security. Shortly afterward, a significant indirect clue was provided when the news media

of the Soviet Union's ally Hungary were asked by the communist party to moderate their remarks about Israel.[19]

A complicating factor was the Israeli electoral campaign. While Rabin (and his eventual replacement as Labor candidate Shimon Peres) may have been willing to negotiate at Geneva, his chief opponent Menachem Begin was opposed to territorial concessions, a Soviet diplomatic role, and the Geneva format. With the election scheduled for May, it was therefore necessary to await the political verdict in Israel before any meaningful progress could be achieved in preparing another international conference. In addition, the rhetoric of the ruling Labor coalition had to be considered cautiously as it had become more anti-Soviet and less compromising on territorial questions in response to the rightist challenge from Begin's LIKUD. It should be mentioned, however, that LIKUD was not viewed as a serious threat to Labor's traditional dominance of Israeli politics and that foreign policy issues did not dominate the campaign. The crucial factors were internal as petty rivalries and charges of corruption brought about a split in Labor and the creation of an offshoot electoral list of the Democratic Movement for Change (DASH).

Some solid congruence of Soviet and Israeli interests was surely developing in the Red Sea area, and this boded well for a resumption of the Geneva negotiations. The Soviet Union had started to supply arms to Ethiopia, a state which was also receiving Israeli assistance and playing host to Israeli military advisers. Both the Soviet Union and Israel opposed the Eritrean secessionist movement (the Soviets had recently flipflopped on this issue), fearing the establishment of another pro-Arab government possibly aligned with Saudi Arabia. Similarly, there was mutual apprehension that the series of Arab conferences in early 1977 aimed at turning the Red Sea into an "Arab Lake" would limit their freedom of navigation. Geopolitics were drawing the Soviet Union and Israel together, but the important choice of the Israeli electorate was not yet known.

Forward Motion

On March 21, Brezhnev presented a comprehensive peace plan for the Middle East. He called for an Israeli withdrawal in two stages, demilitarized zones and guarantees by the Security Council or Big Four. The guarantors were to be permitted to place observers within UN peacekeeping units, but it was clear that they would not contribute troops. Brezhnev specifically alluded to Israeli navigational rights in the Gulf

of Aqaba, Straits of Tiran and Suez Canal, although such
rights would only become applicable after the Israeli
withdrawal was effected. More significantly, Brezhnev
did not mention the PLO or its participation at Geneva
and he did not advocate the return of Palestinians to
their homes or their right to compensation. He did,
however, support the establishment of a Palestinian
state. In a move sure to please the Israelis, the
Soviet General Secretary said that changes must be
agreed upon by the participants in the conflict. This
amounted to Israeli veto power over the terms of settlement and reduced apprehension that the superpowers
would try to impose conditions on the states directly
concerned.20

Brezhnev was most conciliatory and seriously interested in encouraging the Israelis to participate at
Geneva. He also timed his plan with an eye toward the
Americans. Vance was coming to Moscow one week later
and Brezhnev wanted to work out a joint superpower
initiative. The Soviet leader wanted to make sure
that the United States was not going to leave his
country out of the peace process (Carter had just made
an overture to the PLO on March 16) and he probably
hoped to soften Carter's human rights campaign against
the Soviet Union. When Vance arrived in the Soviet
capital, he agreed to a Geneva conference in the fall.
Rabin was receptive to Brezhnev's proposals but he
could not appear too accomodating as that would have
increased U.S. pressure on Israel to make concessions.
Such was the American tactic whenever it appeared that
there was a chance for an agreement. Furthermore,
Israel could not accept Brezhnev's concept that Israeli
withdrawal must precede a declaration of peace. It
preferred the opposite sequence, or at least simultaneous actions.

Avineri discerned greater Soviet moderation in
Brezhnev's remarks, but he did not believe that Moscow
was willing to restore diplomatic relations. Allon,
while not impressed by the degree of flexibility
displayed by Brezhnev, nevertheless thought that Israel
should seize the opportunity to seek a renewal of
relations. He pointed out that Soviet emissaries were
sounding out Israeli diplomats in the United States
and Western Europe and he declared: "Therefore, we
have announced that we are prepared to accept even a
gradual resumption of diplomatic relations between the
Soviets and ourselves."21 This was a major step toward
Moscow as it reversed Israel's previous approach to
this subject. On the Soviet side, temperate comments
prevailed and an article in the state newspaper
Izvestiia even presented the Israeli position on each
controversial issue in the Arab-Israeli conflict.22
According to Zuhair Mohsen, a prominent PLO leader,

the Soviets told Arafat that they planned to reestablish
relations with Israel, but this source must be treated
cautiously as Mohsen was a rigid rejectionist closely
aligned with the Syrians.[23] He may have been trying to
forestall any Soviet move toward Israel by building up
negative Arab pressure in advance. On the other hand,
a Soviet spokesman did tell the Hearst newspaper chain
that relations could be restored shortly and there was
a belief in the U.S. State Department that such a
course was likely as preparations were being made for
Geneva.[24]

The Carter-Sadat talks in April led Vance to the
conclusion that Eygpt would participate at Geneva, and
Carter then met with Assad on May 9 to sound him out
on the peace process.[25] Prospects appeared favorable
but then Begin unexpectedly became the Israeli prime
minister, causing consternation in both Washington and
Moscow. The superpowers continued to advocate a
Geneva conference (witness the call from the Vance-
Gromyko meeting on May 21) and were pleasantly surprised
when Begin indicated a willingness to negotiate there.
At the same time, his harder line on territorial concessions (he vowed that the settlement of Jews in the
West Bank would continue) presented a significant
obstacle to a comprehensive settlement.[26] When Begin
visited the United States in July, he agreed to some
local autonomy in the West Bank but insisted on a continued Israeli military presence. He expressed his approval of the Geneva framework but objected to PLO
participation in any form, including the inclusion of
PLO members within the delegations of Arab states. Begin
also did not want to negotiate with a unified Arab
delegation, preferring to deal separately with each
Arab state. In August, Begin conferred with Rumanian
President Ceausescu and, in September, he submitted
his own peace proposals to the Americans. Although
Begin was more adamant than Rabin on the terms of
negotiations and settlement, he was not as obstructive
as the superpowers had anticipated as he agreed to the
general Geneva formula. One must realize that Begin's
LIKUD ruled through a coalition with the dovish DASH
party as no electoral mandate had been given to conduct
a more hawkish policy toward the Arab world. Begin's
appointment of erstwhile Laborite Moshe Dayan as foreign
minister, and the increasingly moderate Ezer Weizman as
minister of defense, provided important clues about his
intended diplomatic direction.

The Soviets rejected Begin's conditions but were
willing to modify their own proposals in order to assure
the convening of a Geneva conference. Gromyko told
Carter on September 23: "If we can just establish a
miniature state for the Palestinians as big as a pencil
eraser, this will lead to a resolution of the PLO

problem for the Geneva Conference." Dobrynin informed
Vance that the Soviet Union would drop its demand for
a Palestinian state, and one Soviet commentator re-
floated the idea of a Palestinian-Jordanian confederation.[27] The Soviets also reached out diplomatically
toward Israel. Gromyko let it be known that he was
amenable to a meeting with Foreign Minister Moshe
Dayan in New York during the UN session, but problems
of protocol prevented its realization. Each side
wanted the other to request the meeting. Also, Gromyko
wanted to confer unofficially, while Dayan demanded
official status for the talks.[28] Despite this diplomatic fiasco, there was another Herzog-Troianovskii
session that month.

Extending the Circle

Immediately after Egypt and Israel agreed to a
second-stage disengagement, the Soviet friendship committee invited a delegation of five Israelis to Moscow.
The Soviets were concerned about Israel's growing
alliance with the United States and wanted to influence
Israeli opinion in the direction of a more equidistant
attitude toward the superpowers. The members of the
delegation were chosen with an eye toward expanding
contacts with non-RAKAH, leftist Israelis. Avraham
Levenbraun, a Knesset deputy, was the only RAKAH member
included. The other were MAPAM deputy Dov Zakin (who
met prior to departure with Rabin and Allon), Soviet-
Israeli friendship activist Yaacov Riftin, and liberal
journalists Amnon Kapeliuk and David Shacham. Emphasizing protocol, the Soviet hosts arranged a session with
members of the Supreme Soviet for Zakin and Levenbraun.
The other Israeli visitors were not invited. Throughout its stay, the delegation was accompanied by an
Israeli flag. After Allon and Gromyko conferred in
New York, the Soviet and Israeli flags appeared together.[29]
Also in September, a group of Israeli weightlifters
and wrestlers visited the Soviet Union, but not without
incident. They apparently tried to use the occasion to
establish contacts with Soviet Jews, attending Yom
Kippur services at the Moscow synagogue and participating in a Succot picnic outside the Soviet capital. At
this latter event, they hoisted an Israeli flag, sang
and danced to Israeli songs. A fracas then developed
as Soviet police tried to break up the party and take
down the flag.[30]
In October, Israeli delegates took part in a Moscow
meeting at the UN Associations Federation Conference.
The PLO and Zionism were never mentioned, and the
president of the U.S.S.R. Association for Assistance
to the United Nations told an Israeli that "friendly

relations" would be established soon.[31] Other than a
purported Allon meeting with Soviet officials in
Switzerland, there were some indirect signs that the
political atmosphere was improving. The chief rabbi
of Great Britain visited the Soviet Union and a
Czechoslovak delegate and Hungarian observer, for the
first time in many years, attended a London session of
the World Jewish Congress. However, there were serious
impediments to more cordial Soviet-Israeli relations.
The Soviets had endorsed the UN equation of Zionism
and racism, and Wilner's efforts to dispel Israeli
anxiety were rather fruitless.[32] From the opposite
side, another major conference on Soviet Jewry was
being organized in Brussels for February. The Soviets
tried to counter its impact by publishing an interview
with anti-Zionist, Yiddish-language editor Aaron
Vergelis.[33]

During the spring and summer of 1976, mixed reactions continued to characterize Soviet-Israeli relations. Following "Land Day" disturbances by Israeli
Arabs on March 30, Rabin accused RAKAH of inciting
demonstrators. In May, right-wing Knesset member Geula
Cohen recommended that RAKAH be declared illegal until
Soviet policy toward Jews (especially emigration activists) was changed significantly. Her suggestion did
not get very far as it was opposed by the ruling Labor
coalition. Also in May, another Soviet delegation
visited Israel for the anniversary of the victory over
Nazism. Its members were more forthcoming than in the
past and consented to interviews with individual
Israeli reporters. Perhaps the April 28 Soviet peace
plan had some effect on their behavior. In June, a
Soviet church delegation went to Jerusalem for Pente-
cost and, setting a precedent, invited the Israeli
Minister of Religious Affairs to the Soviet Union.
That same month, in a move sure to antagonize Moscow,
Hebrew University bestowed an honorary doctorate on
Soviet dissident physicist Andrei Sakharov. This was
then balanced when the Soviets condemned Israel's
rescue of airline passengers in Entebbe, Uganda. In
August, the Soviets boycotted the World Jewish Film
and Television Festival in Jerusalem, but nine Israeli
geographers attended a conference in Moscow that began
in late July. They irritated the Soviet authorities
by handing out books on Israeli geography containing
descriptions of Santa Katerina and Mt. Hermon, sites
occupied in 1967. They also passed out geography books
at the Moscow synagogue on the Sabbath.[34]

The election of Jimmy Carter in November encouraged the Soviets to expand their contacts with different segments of the Israeli population in preparation
for a Geneva conference. In December, the delegation
sent to Haifa for RAKAH's eighteenth congress included

the influential Karen Brutents, a specialist on the
Middle East and Deputy Director of the International
Department of the Central Committee.[35] The congress
called for the creation of a broad front, including
Zionists, to contest the upcoming Knesset elections so
the Democratic Front for Peace and Equality was soon
organized. While clearly controlled by RAKAH, it
included Black Panther leader Charlie Biton. He was
an active demonstrator for the rights of Oriental Jews,
and a Zionist. RAKAH also attempted to broaden its
appeal among Arabs. A new post of deputy general
secretary was created for veteran Knesset member Tewfiq
Toubi, and Moslem Arabs were recognized as an important
target group. RAKAH had always included Christian
Arabs like Toubi and Emile Habibi in the upper ranks
of the party, but did not place a Moslem in a safe spot
on the electoral list until Tewfiq Zayyad was afforded
that honor in 1973. He became mayor of Nazareth in
December 1975 as RAKAH's popularity among the Arabs
grew. RAKAH continued to have a Jewish majority in
top positions, and in its Knesset delegation. Meir
Wilner retained his post as general secretary. RAKAH's
aim was to further alliances with leftist Jews, even
though the bulk of its electoral support came from
Arabs. Interestingly, Soviet delegations to Israel almost always included at least one Jew, while Moslems
were not represented. The catering of Jewish opinion
in Israel was deemed more important than that of the
Arab minority.

By March 1977, Israel was convinced that Carter and
the Soviets would manage to convene a Geneva conference
so it acted to antagonize superpower relations so that
a settlement could not easily be imposed. Carter was
already disturbing the Soviets by his concentration on
human rights violations so the Cabinet decided that the
cause of Soviet Jews should become an important aspect
of the Israeli campaign and that world opinion had to be
enlisted.[36] Allon strongly criticized the Soviet Union
in the Knesset on March 15, and anti-Soviet rallies were
held on March 26. Allon and chief Ashkenazi rabbi
Shlomo Goren spoke at the sacred Western wall on behalf
of Soviet Jews, and the Shazar Prize for Jewish Education was awarded collectively to Hebrew teachers in the
Soviet Union. The prize money was to be used to send
Hebrew books and materials to Soviet Jews.[37]

Israel was trying to weaken detente, but it also
had very realistic concerns as the condition of Soviet
Jews had indeed deteriorated. Anatolii Shcharanskii
had been arrested in March, and there was a Soviet media
campaign linking Jewish activists to the CIA. Furthermore, the Soviets would not permit matzoh from abroad
to enter the country for use during Passover. The
Soviet-Israeli tension over the Soviet Jewish issue

became so extreme that the trip to Israel of Jewish
poet and editor Aaron Vergelis had to be canceled. He
was scheduled to make several public appearances in
Jerusalem, and to hold a press conference, but many
Soviet emigres in Israel were incensed about his planned visit due to his anti-Zionist sentiments. Apparently, the Soviet side closed the door.[38]

The fact that controversy over Soviet Jewry took
place at a time of improved Soviet-Israeli relations is
not contradictory or unexpected. Each country was really
trying to establish an important point. The Soviets
wanted to show that a more cordial political atmosphere
would not extend to their treatment of Jewish emigration
activists or dissidents. The arrest of Shcharanskii
should certainly be viewed in that context. The
Israelis hoped to prove the exact opposite, that rapprochement would not lead to the sellout of Soviet
Jewry. The campign for the rights of Soviet Jews was
therefore stepped up.

As a consequence of the Jackson and Stevenson
amendments, the emigration of Soviet Jews did not proceed smoothly. The low total of 13,000 in 1975 failed
to increase appreciably as only 14,000 Jews departed
in 1976 and 17,000 in 1977. The Soviets constantly
complained about Jews receiving unsolicited invitations, while Rabin charged that "undesirables" were
being sent to Israel. Minister of the Interior Burg
claimed that fifteen percent of those processed in
Vienna were not Jewish. Menachem Begin, engaged in a
race for the post of prime minister, told his party's
loyalists in January 1977 that Israel would agree to
restore relations if Soviet Jewish emigration were to
rise substantially.[39] As we shall see, Begin failed
to act on this commitment once he had the opportunity
to do so.

Once the Brezhnev plan was announced on March 21,
1977, the Soviet Union and Israel interacted rather
cordially. In April, there was much confusion about
an indirect trade offer that may have been made by the
Soviet Union. The letter to the Tel Aviv-Yafo Chamber
of Commerce was in French, came from a West German firm
in Paris, but had a heading indicating that the company
headquarters were in Moscow. The offer concerned the
sale of printing equipment and paper. The Israeli
foreign ministry indicated that it had no objection to
commercial dealings with the Soviet Union, even though
such ties had been lacking for many years. Israel did
have direct trade relationships with Poland, Rumania,
Hungary, Bulgaria and Yugoslavia and indirect ones with
East Germany and Czechoslovakia.[40]

Also in April, Israel permitted three Soviet UN
observers stationed in Egypt to visit UN commander
Ensio Siilasvuo in Jerusalem. The next month, eleven
Soviet space scientists were received in Israel. Their

otherwise genial stay was marred when Jewish emigrants
demonstrated outside their Tel Aviv hotel for the release of Anatolii Shcharanskii. In August, five
Israelis including RAKAH's Knesset ally Charlie Biton
traveled to the Soviet Union and, in September, there
was an Israeli pavilion at the Moscow book fair.
Political considerations were not absent as the Israeli
foreign ministry helped choose the books put on display,
and the Israeli presence was assured only when some
American publishers made it a condition of their own
participation. Later that month, the Soviets invited
the Director General of the Ministry of the Interior
to an October UNESCO conference on environmental education. Bilateral relations were developing fairly
smoothly, despite tensions caused by the Soviet Jewry
issue, as both states awaited the reconvening of the
Geneva conference.

Palestinian Linkages

RAKAH became more active among the Arab populations
of Israel and the West Bank, and gradually developed
important ties to the PLO. In January 1976, an underground newspaper published by West Bank communists
editorially called upon the PLO to accept UN resolutions, participate at Geneva, and disclaim any intention to dismantle Israel. This editorial was reprinted
on the front page of RAKAH's Arabic journal.[41] RAKAH
encouraged and helped organize Israeli Arabs for the
"Land Day" protests against Israeli policies in the
Galilee, and applauded the election of many PLO
sympathizers in the West Bank municipal elections of
April 1976. RAKAH also tried to impress upon the
Jewish population the need for a settlement, placing an
ad signed by its Politburo members in the March 3
edition of the Hebrew newspaper Haaretz. It set forth
conditions for peace which paralleled those enunciated
by the Soviet Union. In July, the communist parties
of Israel and Jordan issued their first joint statement
ever, advocating the establishment of a Palestinian
state.
At the 25th Congress of the Communist Party of the
Soviet Union in February-March 1976, Wilner and Toubi
had talks with the PLO delegation (Arafat was not
present). In March, RAKAH members again met with PLO
representatives in Athens (neither Wilner nor Arafat was
present) and, in September, a group from RAKAH (including Tewfiq Zayyad) conferred at the United Nations with
the PLO delegate. In November, RAKAH members of the
Histadrut trade union federation met with PLO members
in Prague. Therefore, contacts with the PLO were already established before RAKAH announced at its congress
in December that it would seek closer ties to Israeli

leftists. In May 1977, RAKAH and the PLO had their
first "official" meeting in Prague but, again, Wilner
and Arafat did not participate.[42] It should also be
noted that members of the PLO had been meeting
clandestinely in Western Europe with leftist Israeli
Jews since the spring of 1976.[43]

The Soviets were unsuccessful in getting Arafat
to endorse the Geneva process or agree to recognize
Israel. Nevertheless, they consented to the opening
of a PLO mission in Moscow on June 22, 1976. Mohammed
Ibrahim al-Shaer was appointed the PLO representative,
but the Soviets did not accept him as an ambassador nor
recognize the mission as an embassy. To demonstrate
the mission's non-governmental status, an official
from the Soviet Afro-Asian Solidarity Committee presided
at its dedication. On July 14, al-Shaer staged a press
conference in Moscow as the mission became an important
center of PLO publicity and diplomacy. The Soviet
Union had agreed to the establishment of such a PLO
office in July 1974, but had not permitted it to open
until nearly two years later. The timing is therefore
a critical factor and can probably be accounted for by
a need to compensate the PLO for the Soviet Union's
relative inactivity in aiding it against the Syrians
in Lebanon. Furthermore, it was necessary to balance
King Hussein's June 17-28 visit to the Soviet Union.

After Carter's election, the Soviets anticipated
the reconvening of the Geneva conference and tried to
find some realistic solution to the Palestinian
problem. The PLO continued to be supported (al-Shaer
was interviewed in New Times in January 1977), but
some compromise with Jordan had to be considered. On
December 28, 1976, Pravda strangely noted that the fate
of the inhabitants of the West Bank was being followed
by "every citizen of Amman" and that the West Bank was
"land torn away." In addition, the Soviet media omitted a passage in an Assad-Sadat communique which referred to the PLO as "the sole, legitimate representative"
of the Palestinians.[44] In March, a Soviet analyst
suggested that a Palestine-Jordan confederation could
be agreed upon prior to a Geneva conference.[45] Apparently, the Soviets were prepared to settle for less
than an independent Palestinian state in order to
achieve a comprehensive peace agreement. As discussed
earlier, they again brought up the confederation concept in September and were very conciliatory on the
Palestinian statehood issue in private discussions with
the Americans that month. At the same time, in order
to deflect PLO resentment, they hardened their position on the rights of the Palestinians to return to
Israel or secure financial compensation.[46]

Arafat had his first official meeting with Brezhnev
on April 7, 1977 (although they had apparently met in

May 1975 as well). The PLO leader was unwilling to recognize Israel and he must have been perturbed that
the PLO was not mentioned in Brezhnev's March 21 peace
plan. Brezhnev was willing to receive Arafat in an
effort to compensate for this slight, but he was surely
concerned about Arafat's visit to China that February
and indications that he was prepared to deal with the
Americans now that Carter had advocated a Palestinian
"homeland." The Arafat-Brezhnev session seems to have
ended coolly as the Soviet media began to devote less
attention to the PLO leader. Increasing support was
displayed for the views of Nayef Hawatmeh, who journeyed to the Soviet capital in June.

Although the Palestinian issue remained as con-
voluted as ever, the perspectives from Moscow,
Jerusalem and Washington as of September 1977 all included an anticipated Geneva conference by the end of
the year. Nevertheless, negative pressures were
already building up in both Israel and Egypt. Why the
conference failed to take place must now be the subject
of our continuing investigation.

10
Separate Paths

As a result of its October 1, 1977 joint statement
with the United States on the Middle East situation,
the Soviet Union anticipated the reconvening of the
Geneva Conference, a major role in ensuing negotiations,
and movement toward a comprehensive settlement. Not
one of these expectations was realized. Israel and
Egypt reacted strongly to superpower intrusion in their
affairs and seized the diplomatic initiative. Sadat
made his dramatic visit to Jerusalem, and the step-by-
step approach again came to predominate through talks
between Israel and Egypt. No progress was made on the
Syrian and Jordanian negotiating fronts.

Israel and Egypt left the Soviet Union by the way-
side and, even more galling to Moscow, must have been
their turn to the United States as a broker. American
efforts then led to the Camp David agreement in
September 1978 and the Israeli-Egyptian peace treaty of
March 1979. The Soviet Union had little to discuss
with Israel during this period, but relations did not
become acrimonious. Normal intercourse prevailed as
the Soviet Union had to bide its time awaiting more
favorable conditions. Actually, the Soviets were even
more upset about Egypt's actions than those of Israel.

Circumvention

Jimmy Carter, influenced by the Brookings report
and convinced that the Palestinian problem had to be
addressed to achieve a permanent settlement, opted for
the comprehensive approach to Arab-Israeli peace
negotiations. Kissinger's step-by-step formula was
discarded and the Soviet Union was offered a more
significant role. Vance outlined the U.S. position to
Gromyko in the spring of 1977, and the Soviet foreign
minister was obviously amenable. The Soviets,miffed at
Kissinger's disregard for them, had always favored the
comprehensive approach as it assured them of active
participation in the negotiating process.

They also felt that the Helsinki accords of 1975 had
guaranteed them a role in the settlement of Middle East
issues as European security was defined in the context
of Mediterranean affairs as well. In September, the
Soviets gave the Americans a draft of a joint statement on policy in the Middle East and this led to discussions about its content. On October 1, the superpowers released their revised draft. A major initiative to resolve the Arab-Israeli conflict was set in
motion.

The Soviet-American statement referred to Geneva
as "the only right and effective way" to achieve a
settlement and the superpowers called for the convening
of a conference there no later than December. They,
rather than the United Nations, would provide the
diplomatic auspices and guarantee the borders of Israel
and neighboring Arab states. Although they did not
specify that there must be a peace treaty, they advocated the termination of the state of war and the
establishment of "normal peaceful relations." A particular effort was made to enlist PLO participation,
although that organization was not cited. The "legitimate rights of the Palestinian people" were recognized,
and the statement asserted that "the Palestinian
people" should be represented at Geneva. Security
Council resolutions 242 and 338 were not mentioned,
making it easier for the PLO to join the diplomatic
process.

Secretary of State Vance played an important role
in preparing the joint Soviet-American position.
National Security Adviser Brzezinski was less willing
to include the Soviets in negotiations, but he went
along with Vance and Carter.[1] The president was concerned primarily with resolving the Arab-Israeli conflict and he did not gear American tactics in the
Middle East toward gaining advantages in the superpower
competition with the Soviet Union. Carter's memoirs
devote considerable attention to the area, but the
Soviet Union is not discussed in the context of Middle
East negotiations except in regard to the October 1,
1977 statement.[2] Bringing the Soviets into the talks
was deemed essential if a comprehensive settlement was
to be reached, as the Middle East dimension of American
policy predominated over aspects of East-West rivalry.
Carter's outlook differed significantly from that of
Johnson, Nixon and Kissinger, who calculated steps in
the Middle East in terms of their impact on the Soviet-
American power relationship. Carter was more concerned
with establishing peace as an ideal. He realized that
neither Israel nor Egypt favored a solution negotiated
under the auspices of the superpowers, but he thought
that they could be persuaded to go to Geneva. After
all, they had attended the original Geneva conference

in December 1973. Syria, which had boycotted the
earlier session, was again expected to be a substantial
obstacle that had to be overcome.[3]

Israel received a draft of the Soviet-American
statement on September 29, so the October 1 announcement did not catch it by surprise. Of course, Israel
had always refused to reconcile itself to similar
superpower efforts (for example, in July 1967) and its
denunciation of this one was clearly anticipated.
Carter had started to move toward superpower sponsorship of talks prior to Begin's election, and it is
possible that Israel's response under a Rabin government may not have been as negative. Begin had no
desire to negotiate about the status of the West Bank
and his foreign minister, Moshe Dayan, had already
started secret negotiations with the Egyptians (through
the good offices of Morocco) to further a separate
dialogue at the expense of a comprehensive framework.
Israel was in a strong position to oppose the October 1
statement as there was considerable controversy in
Congress over its merits. Carter had been criticizing
the Soviet Union for its human rights violations and
it was therefore difficult to generate Congressional
or public support for joint superpower diplomacy.

Israel rejected the comprehensive approach, the
inclusion of the Soviet Union in negotiations, the
omission of references to SC 242 and 338 or a final
peace treaty, the recognition of the Palestinians'
"legitimate rights," and the intention to secure
Palestinian participation at the Geneva conference.
Overall, it appeared that the United Nations was
abandoning step-by-step diplomacy, working in collaboration with the Soviet Union, and favoring the
Palestinian option over the Jordanian one as the most
appropriate path to peace.[4] Dayan was immediately
dispatched to Washington, and a Carter-Dayan working
paper was prepared on October 5. Israel did not refuse
absolutely to go to Geneva, but its representatives
engaged in critical discussions with the Americans
that aimed at circumventing the most objectionable
stipulations in the October 1 statement. Consequently,
it was proposed that the Soviet and American roles at
Geneva be reduced through the organization of working
groups headed by representatives of the United States.
Also considered was a joint Arab delegation, which
would include non-PLO Palestinians, who would then
become part of the Jordanian sub-delegation once bilateral working groups began their sessions. The
United States agreed that if Israel attended the
Geneva conference, the Soviet-American statement would
not serve as the basis for negotiations.[5] In effect,
American agreement to satisfy some of Dayan's concerns
unilaterally undermined the bilateral Soviet-American

peace initiative.

Egypt, like Israel, was disturbed by the Soviet Union's inclusion in the negotiating process. Initially, Sadat was willing to go, albeit reluctantly, to Geneva. Once he witnessed the negative reactions to the October 1 statement in Israel and in the American media (as well as American concessions to Israel regarding the Geneva format), he decided to be more assertive. Carter, fearing that the peace effort would collapse, sent Sadat a hand-written letter calling upon him to find a way out of the diplomatic impasse.[6] At first, Sadat proposed a conference in East Jerusalem attended by the Big Five, Arab states, Israel and the PLO. Sadat was hoping to dilute the Soviet role, but it was quickly apparent that the convening of such a conference was unrealistic. Then, on November 9, Sadat made his dramatic announcement about willingness to go to Jerusalem to negotiate with the Israelis. Probably he could fare better in bilateral negotiations than in comprehensive talks including other Arab delegations. He already knew through the discussions in Morocco that Israel was prepared to return all of Sinai, but he was still jeopardizing his standing in the Arab world. It is most important to realize that two of Sadat's boldest moves were aimed at preventing the superpowers from orchestrating a settlement. In July 1972, fearing that a deal had been struck at the Nixon-Brezhnev summit, he had expelled most Soviet military personnel from Egypt.

Egypt and Israel were engaged in secret negotiations even prior to the Soviet-American statement. Once the United States moved toward the concept of a joint Arab delegation as a means of presenting a fig-leaf for Palestinian participation at Geneva, Sadat realized the futility of such an endeavor and informed the Americans. Vance then told Dayan that Egypt was prepared to negotiate with Israel prior to a Geneva conference, but it is unlikely that he expected Sadat to seize the initiative in such a striking manner.[7] On November 20, the Egyptian president addressed the Knesset in Jerusalem and a new era of diplomacy was started. Sadat still insisted on complete Israeli withdrawal from occupied territories, but it had become a policy position. In the past, it had been presented as a pre-condition to settlement.

Surprisingly, the Soviet reaction to Sadat's Jerusalem venture was not strongly negative (perhaps because the American role in peace negotiations was still minimal). Gromyko, at a luncheon for Syrian foreign minister Khaddam on November 29, went out of his way not to blame Sadat for sidetracking Geneva. He said that it was too early to make any final conclusions about the conference and that the Soviet Union would continue to consult with other states on the matter.[8] In a December 23 _Pravda_ interview, Brezhnev displayed

moderation toward Israel, emphasized its right to
security and called for a political settlement. He
recognized that bilateral Egyptian-Israeli talks made
the convening of the Geneva conference more difficult,
but he did not rule out such a meeting as long as it
did not provide a "screen" for separate deals. He
also pointed out that the Sadat-Begin discussions
undercut Arab unity and prevented "friendly states" (an
obvious reference to the Soviet Union) from supporting
the Arab cause.[9]

The Soviet Union was surely concerned that Sadat's
trip to Jerusalem would short-circuit a Geneva conference, but it continued to press for such a gathering.
It was anxious to achieve a Middle East settlement as
it realized that a no war, no peace situation had
generally favored the United States since 1967. The
time seemed appropriate as the American president was
supportive of a comprehensive approach and, for the
first time, it appeared that the Palestinian problem
would be addressed. Therefore, the Soviet Union hoped
that the Egyptian-Israeli talks would lead to Geneva
and it did not react to them by moving toward the rejectionist camp. In fact, the opportunity to create
some mischief was not used. Sadat's Jerusalem journey
had already been arranged when General Sergei Sokolov,
first deputy minister of defense, arrived in Jordan on
November 16. Rather than publicize his visit in order
to display the necessity of a Soviet role in a settlement, the Soviet media (other than the military newspaper Krasnaia Zvezda) ignored his mission. Sokolov
didn't try to counter Sadat's move by offering Soviet
arms to Jordan or joining the Jordanians in a denunciation of Egyptian-Israeli separate diplomacy.

Egypt wanted to exclude the Soviet Union from
negotiations, but it offered a backhanded invitation to
attend a conference in Cairo on December 14. The
Soviets certainly did not want Sadat's initiative to
replace Geneva, nor did they want to endorse Egypt's
bilateral talks with Israel, so no Soviet representative took part. Actually, the only participants were
Egypt, Israel and the United States as a separate peace
track was being laid. Also in December, Egypt antagonized the Soviets by closing their consulates in
Alexandria, Port Said and Aswan and cultural centers in
Cairo and Alexandria. In addition, a Soviet naval
vessel was impounded after an Egyptian canal pilot was
reported overboard and missing.[10] Perhaps as a counter
to Egypt's actions, Chief of Staff Nikolai Ogarkov
visited Libya in late December.

At first, it was unclear if separate Egyptian-
Israeli diplomacy would preclude a Geneva conference and
a role for the Soviet Union. The American administration was divided over this issue, with Brzezinski

hoping to freeze out the Soviets as a gesture toward
Egypt, and Vance urging superpower collaboration.[11]
Actually, the decision to exclude the Soviets was
really made by Sadat and was foreshadowed by his letter
to Carter delivered by Foreign Minister Ismail Fahmy
immediately after the October 1 statement. In it, the
Egyptian president called for direct negotiations with
Israel either before or after Geneva, with the United
States serving as the intermediary.[12] After his trip
to Jerusalem, Sadat saw no purpose in reconvening the
Geneva conference and he proposed his own Cairo conference as a means of graceful withdrawal from the Geneva
process. The comprehensive approach was thus stillborn,
and step-by-step diplomacy under American auspices was
again alive. The Soviet Union was therefore shunted
aside, not because of any deterioration in detente or
controversy over its conditions for peace, but as a
consequence of the negotiating method adopted by the
United States (as influenced by Egypt).[13] The Soviet
Union thus suffered a rude setback in the Middle East
just at the time of its expulsion from all military
facilities in nearby Somalia. The United States eager-
ly looked forward to the strategic advantages that
could be realized from Israeli-Egyptian negotiations.

Gradually, the Soviets realized that Geneva was at
least temporarily out of the question and that the
United States had unilaterally taken charge of the
negotiating process. Sadat's separate diplomacy came
to be viewed as American-inspired, and an Egyptian-
Israeli-American strategic entente was seen as developing more substantially than in 1975 at the time of the
second-stage disengagement agreement. What could the
Soviet Union have done to assure its participation in
a resolution of the Arab-Israeli conflict? One course
would have been to improve relations with Israel (as
the U.S. had done already with Egypt), but it was not
chosen. Israeli receptivity to such an overture would
have been questionable, but the Soviets seem to have
committed a tactical blunder in not making a serious
move in that direction. Perhaps they were afraid of
losing the good will which still existed among the
Syrians and Palestinians. This permitted the United
States to play with all the diplomatic cards, while the
Soviet Union was left with half a deck. Apparently,
Carter was not concerned about a Soviet rapprochement
with Israel as it would have furthered the peace process
(although reducing American leverage over it). He
therefore did not ask the Israelis to spurn any Soviet
advances.[14]

Pax Americana

Arafat met with Brezhnev on May 9, 1978. Two days
later, members of al-Fatah's Black September movement
carried out a major attack against Israeli civilians

along that country's coastal highway. Israeli troops
then advanced into southern Lebanon to retaliate against
PLO bases there. The Soviet Union did nothing to help
the PLO, moved its Mediterranean naval squadron further
from the Lebanese coast and acceded to the deployment
of UN peacekeeping forces north of the Israeli-Lebanese
border.[15] Caution about confronting Israel and widen-
ing the conflict to include Syrian forces was clearly
paramount, although the Soviets did carry out the token
act of docking naval vessels in Latakia, Syria in June.
Did the Soviet Union encourage Black September's
assault? This is highly unlikely as it was not siding
with anti-Israeli rejectionists despite the collapse of
plans for a Geneva conference. The Soviets had not
moved closer to the PLO, and the coastal highway attack
right after Arafat's departure from Moscow seemed to be
a PLO signal to the Soviets that militancy against
Israel would not be abandoned. Contributing to this
interpretation is the Soviet Union's downgrading of the
PLO and effort to improve relations with Jordan. In
August, an _Izvestiia_ article on Soviet-Jordanian ties
was extremely upbeat and it was pointed out that Jordan
had supported the October 1, 1977 statement and was opposed to Egyptian-Israeli talks.[16] In October, Crown
Prince Hassan ibn Talal traveled to the Soviet Union
and a delegation of Jordanian sheikhs toured the Central Asian region.

The coastal road carnage engendered a Jewish protest demonstration in Moscow the following day. The
police broke it up, but no one was arrested.[17] It also
produced independent Knesset deputy Shmuel Flatto-
Sharon's introduction of a bill banning "seditious"
political parties such as RAKAH. Apparently referring
to RAKAH's ties to the PLO, he claimed that there were
"representatives of the same enemy, sitting right here
among us in this hall." Flatto-Sharon's bill was
challenged when forty members of the Knesset, including
former foreign ministers Eban and Allon, signed a statement opposing the ouster of the RAKAH-led Democratic
Front for Peace and Equality. They pointed out that
its Knesset deputies had been democratically elected.[18]
Many Israelis did not want RAKAH declared illegal
because it would then have begun to operate underground.
They also saw it as a useful alternative to the PLO, as
far as attracting Arab political support was concerned.
Furthermore, its Jewish members had displayed their
loyalty to Israel by serving in the armed forces and
there had been no acts of sabotage (although RAKAH
members were not given high security clearances).
Flatto-Sharon's efforts were unsuccessful, and RAKAH
remained a legal party with representation in the
Knesset.

There were some very indirect signs that the

Soviet Union hoped to improve relations with Israel despite separate Egyptian-Israeli diplomacy. A group of American Jews was told in Warsaw in December 1977 that Poland would possibly seek closer ties to Israel. In April, an Israeli delegation (for the first time since 1967) participated in ceremonies marking the anniversary of the Warsaw Ghetto and the dedication of Jewish barracks at the Auschwitz death camp. Poland's gesture of inviting the Israelis became controversial as the PLO sought to balance their presence. The Poles then permitted a PLO representative to lay a wreath at the memorial for Jews who died in the Warsaw Ghetto, although this act was carried out after completion of the official ceremonies. The Israelis were deeply upset and some returned home ahead of schedule. A few weeks later, Polish communist party leader Edward Gierek told a press conference that relations with Israel could be restored once the Palestinian problem was resolved, and he called for a guarantee of Israel's existence. In September, a delegation from the Hungarian communist party, including the deputy director of the Department for Foreign Relations of the Central Committee, visited Israel for ten days as guests of RAKAH. This was the initial East European group (except from the Soviet Union or Rumania) to go to Israel since the Six-Day War for any purpose other than attending a RAKAH congress, and its members held discussions with non-communist Israeli public figures.[19] While Rumania conducted an independent foreign policy toward Israel, one must assume that Poland and Hungary sought Soviet approval before making overtures to the Jewish state.

Throughout 1978, the United States tried to serve as broker between Egypt and Israel. It also sold jet aircraft to Egypt and Saudi Arabia, hoping to further ties to moderate Arab states as a means of minimizing the Soviet role in the Middle East.[20] Israel objected to the transfer of aircraft to the Arabs, but approved of the basic negotiating concept of leaving out the Soviets. Former prime minister Rabin even went so far as to assert that the first criterion indicating the readiness of an Arab state to make peace with Israel was a change in foreign policy orientation away from Moscow and toward Washington.[21] In a sense, this is what had actually been happening in the Egyptian case. In September, the faith of Egypt and Israel in American-sponsored negotiations was rewarded as a Camp David agreement on the basis for a final peace settlement was announced.

The Soviet Union criticized the Camp David formula as it did not provide a comprehensive solution, permitted Israel to retain territories in the West Bank, East Jerusalem and the Golan Heights and did not call for the establishment of a Palestinian state. It also was disturbed by the American diplomatic success and viewed it as a step toward creating a strategic bloc composed of Israel, Egypt, Saudi Arabia and Iran. Nevertheless, the Soviets again did not turn toward the rejectionists. They surely did not want another war similar to that in 1973, when the superpowers came close to direct involvement. Consequently, friction developed with the Syrians as requested advanced weapons were not provided. As will be discussed below, a gesture was even made toward Israel as the first contact with Begin's government was established.

Israel moved closer strategically to the United States. Although the abrogation of an American defense agreement with Taiwan aroused some distrust of U.S. commitments, Begin visited Washington in early March and proposed an Israeli-American defense arrangement. His defense minister Weizman had already boasted to U.S. Secretary of Defense Harold Brown that Israel had destroyed more than a thousand Soviet planes and more than four thousand Soviet tanks. He said that Israel was in the first line of defense against the Soviet Union.[22] The United States increasingly viewed Israel as a strategic asset, especially after the downfall of the Iranian monarchy early in 1979. However, it was not prepared to formalize an alliance. American dedication to Egyptian-Israeli peace remained strong, and Carter visited both Egypt and Israel in March 1979. A formal peace treaty was then completed. Gromyko held a conclave in Damascus with Assad, Arafat and Bakdash, but had little ability to alter the situation. RAKAH, expressing the same sentiments as the Soviet media, denounced the treaty as representative of the foundation of an anti-Soviet bloc. The United States was accused of monopolizing diplomacy and of planning to increase arms deliveries to Egypt and Israel (pay-offs are always greater when only one superpower is arranging a settlement) despite the establishment of peace. RAKAH described the October 1 Soviet-American statement as the appropriate basis for a settlement and advocated the creation of a Palestinian state alongside Israel.[23]

Ups and Downs

Although Israel objected to the October 1 statement and sought alterations in the Geneva formula endorsed by the Soviet Union, bilateral relations between the two states were not affected. In October, an official Israeli governmental delegation attended a UNESCO conference in the Georgian capital of Tbilisi (Soviet approval was needed). The same month, Israelis took part in a Paris conference on Middle East peace, sponsored by the pro-Soviet World Peace Council. Representatives of Zionist parties like Labor and MAPAM

were included, although the Israelis decided not to be
formal participants but rather observers with the right
to speak.[24] In November, an Israeli friendship group
hosted a Soviet singer and three other representatives
for ceremonies marking the sixtieth anniversary of the
Bolshevik revolution. The inclusion of a performer set
an important precedent by initiating cultural contact
through a back door.

In early April, 1978, Israel voiced its concern
that the secretary of the Russian Orthodox Church
mission in Jerusalem was a KGB agent, and it was announced that he would soon be leaving permanently.[25]
Despite this incident, a Soviet church delegation
traveled to Israel three weeks later and there was also
the annual May visit commemorating the victory over the
Nazis. On this occasion, Soviet participants talked to
demonstrators from the "Peace Now" movement who were
urging moderation in Israeli policy toward the Arabs.[26]
May also witnessed the death of Yaacov Riftin, a leading proponent of Soviet-Israeli friendship.

Some episodes marred the rather standardized
political atmosphere. Students at Soviet universities
in Moscow, Leningrad and Riga demonstrated in support
of Israeli Arabs to mark "Land Day." More significant,
however, was the case of RAKAH Central Committee member Hans Lebrecht and a Cypriot communist named
Panaioyitis Paschalis. The two journalists were arrested by Israeli authorities in January and charged with
aiding the PLO. This was the first time that a member
of RAKAH's Central Committee had ever been accused of
espionage, and RAKAH claimed that Lebrecht's arrest
represented retaliation for his comments at a Begin-
Sadat press conference in Ismailia, Egypt. He had
asked how it was possible to establish peace without the
participation of the Palestinians and PLO. On July 7,
Lebrecht was acquitted but Paschalis was convicted and
sentenced to a five-year term. Although he had been
found guilty of espionage, two of the three judges
curiously ruled that the PLO was not legally an enemy
of Israel.[27]

Relations suffered a sharp setback in July due to
the Shcharanskii case. On July 7, the Soviet Union
announced that his treason trial would start on July 10.
The timing may have been fortuitous, but July 7 was
also the day that the Lebrecht-Paschalis verdict was
rendered. Could the Soviets have delayed action on
Shcharanskii until the Israeli trial was over so as not
to jeopardize further the communist defendants? Less
likely is the possibility that Shcharanskii was charged
with such high crimes in retaliation for the conviction
of Paschalis since the Soviets seemed prepared to bring
such charges in any event. Another angle to consider
is whether Israel brought charges against Lebrecht to

use as a bargaining chip on the Shcharanskii case. Reacting to the opening of the Shcharanskii trial, Begin
gave a fiery anti-Soviet speech in the Knesset and a
resolution was passed supporting Shcharanskii. That
same day, Jewish Defense League militants vandalized a
Russian Orthodox church in Jerusalem, evoking a letter
of protest from Patriarch Pimen of Moscow to Israeli
president Navon.[28] On July 14, Shcharanskii was
sentenced to a thirteen-year term. Due to the
Shcharanskii furor, Begin objected to tennis matches
between Israeli and Soviet players at a junior tourna-
ment in Britain, but the Israeli tennis federation prevailed in its insistence that the competition had to
proceed as scheduled.[29]

Shortly before the Camp David agreement was an-
nouced, MAPAM Knesset representative Naftali Feder met
the chief Soviet delegate at a parliamentary union
convention in Bonn. The Soviet delegate predicted that
the Camp David negotiations would not succeed but, even
after they did, there was no negative impact.[30] A
group of veteran members of RAKAH journeyed to the
Soviet Union in October, but the most crucial event was
the ten-day visit of an Israeli delegation in November.
Its members were Tewfiq Toubi and Uzi Burstein of RAKAH,
Naftali Feder of MAPAM, Amnon Zikhroni of the leftist
Shelli party, Avraham Melamed of the National Religious
Party and Yossi Sarid (and his wife) of Labor. All
except Burstein and Zikhroni were Knesset members, and
this was the first Israeli political delegation to the
Soviet Union since 1967 that contained a Zionist
majority. Obviously, the Soviets were reaching out and
trying to include a broad spectrum of Israeli political
opinion. It was the first time that a Laborite had
been invited to participate in such a mission and it
was the initial contact with a representative of Begin's
government, as Melamed was part of LIKUD's Knesset
coalition. The Israeli delegation received extensive
media attention and participated in a press conference
prior to departure. Its members were told that despite
Soviet rejection of the Camp David agreement, it could
serve as the starting point for new negotiations.
Furthermore, the Soviet Union was prepared to renew
diplomatic relations if Israel returned to Geneva. The
Israelis responded that renewal could produce a reversal
of their country's position, not vice-versa.[31] They,
like their predecessors in previous delegations,
endorsed Soviet inclusion in the peace process as only
those Israelis with such a point of view were invited
to join political groups coming to Moscow.

The Israelis were invited by the Soviet peace
committee as individuals, not Knesset or party representatives. They were received warmly and, like all
such groups, were provided with kosher food and a

Hebrew-language interpreter. The fact that the visit
to the Soviet Union was arranged immediately after
Camp David was not surprising as the Soviets extended
a similar invitation in September 1975 after the
second-stage disengagement agreement was announced.
Again, the principle that contacts with Israel should
be encouraged whenever Jerusalem moves closer to
Washington appeared paramount. In January 1979, an
Israeli was awarded first prize in the 16-20 year old
division of a film-makers' festival in Kishinev,
Moldavia. This was the initial prize won by an Israeli
at any Soviet film festival. Also that month, Begin
told Nahum Goldmann that direct flights of Soviet
Jewish emigrants to Israel may be possible.[32] What
constituted his source of information is unclear.

Meanwhile, Sadat's trip to Jerusalem, and the
demise of the Geneva process, had short-circuited any
PLO rapprochement with the United States. This did
not, however, lead to stronger PLO ties to the Soviet
Union. As explained earlier, Arafat's March 9, 1978
meeting with Brezhnev did not produce much agreement.
Arafat was still unprepared to accept the Security
Council resolutions on the Middle East, although he
did favorably describe SC 338.[33] Soon contributing
to the friction was the Soviet Union's failure to come
to the PLO's defense once Israeli troops entered
Lebanon later that month. The Soviets did, however,
supply arms on a large scale once the hostilities had
ended. By July, PLO-Soviet relations had improved and
Arafat returned to Moscow at the end of October.

By the spring of 1979, Israel had concluded a
separate peace settlement with Egypt and had aligned
closely with American military interests. Nevertheless,
Soviet-Israeli contacts began to grow and Jewish
emigration was substantially increased. We must now
unfathom the curious motivations underlying these
events.

11
Cool Embrace

During the period between the Egyptian-Israeli treaty of March 1979 and the Lebanon war of June 1982, strategic considerations related to superpower competition became increasingly important in the Middle East. The revolution in Iran ended that country's role as an American military proxy, thereby enhancing Israel's stature in the eyes of the Pentagon. As the United States and Israel moved toward a closer strategic relationship, the Soviet Union and Syria did likewise. The Arab-Israeli conflict thus became more strongly identified with East-West rivalry, as did events in Afghanistan and the Horn of Africa. Additionally, the China factor resurfaced and again had to be considered in any evaluation of Middle East politics. Clearly, Peking and Washington had a growing coincidence of interests. Over these years, no serious steps were taken toward a comprehensive peace settlement, and Syria and Jordan did not follow the Egyptian example by seeking step-by-step solutions. Ironically, Jimmy Carter had downplayed Soviet-American relations as the predominant variable in the Middle East equation, but the separate peace process that he successfully set in motion accentuated the regional strategic dimension of the superpower struggle.

To evaluate properly the evolution of Soviet-Israeli relations up to June 1982, it is necessary to raise the following questions: Why did Israel so demonstratively seek strategic alignment with the United States? What effect did Chinese-American relations have on those between the Soviet Union and Israel? Why did Soviet Jewish emigration peak in 1979 and then drop substantially? Why did Soviet-Israeli contacts increase in frequency even though there was no movement toward an international peace conference or a resumption of diplomatic relations?

Globalization

The Soviets displayed their opposition to the

Egyptian-Israeli treaty by publishing guest articles in
their journal <u>International Affairs</u> by an Israeli
communist and the PLO representative in Moscow. Their
inclusion in the May and June editions of 1979 was
surely not coincidental, as contributions by non-Soviet
analysts were rare.[1] In July, leading Middle East
specialist Evgenii Primakov summarized Moscow's new
position on a peace settlement, as the traditional insistence on a Geneva conference was abandoned.
Primakov called for an international conference, including the PLO, but he indicated that the Soviet Union
would no longer accept the Geneva framework if it meant
that the Egyptian-Israeli treaty would serve as the
basis for further negotiations.[2]

Carter held a June summit meeting with Brezhnev
in Vienna, and American overtures were again made to
the PLO to participate in Middle East diplomacy (UN
Ambassador Andrew Young was forced to resign over this
matter in August). Gromyko, adopting a moderate line,
said that the Palestinians must have a state "even if it
is only a small one" and Soviet pressure was applied
to Arafat to accept Israel's existence.[3] The potential
for another superpower effort aimed at a comprehensive
settlement was quickly recognized by Sadat and Begin.
Neither wanted a role for the Soviet Union or concentration on the Palestinian issue, so they acted to
deflect the diplomatic initiative just as they had in
1977. Sadat visited Haifa, Israel in early September
and suggested that there could be a delay of three
years before inclusion of the PLO in the peace process.[4] Sadat was concerned that the PLO and Arab
radicals could band together in negotiations and accuse
him of selling out their cause through his separate
treaty with Israel.

Egyptian-Israeli diplomatic relations were
established in February 1980, and the Cairo government
dissolved the Egyptian-Soviet Friendship Society that
month. In November, units of the American Rapid
Deployment Force conducted exercises in Egypt. Other
events also mitigated against a renewed superpower
peace initiative. Soviet intervention in Afghanistan
in December 1979 brought about a diplomatic confrontation with the United States and also strained Soviet
relations with Arab states. The January 1980 Islamic
foreign ministers' conference produced a denunciation
of the Soviet role in Afghanistan, leading the Soviets
to counter by championing the withdrawal of Israel
from East Jerusalem. This issue had great emotional
appeal in the Islamic world, so the Soviets tried to
use it to return to the good graces of Arab, and other
Islamic, states. When Gromyko departed from Syria in
late January, the final communique called for Israeli
evacuation of East Jerusalem.[5] After the May Islamic
summit in Pakistan condemned Israeli annexation of East

Jerusalem, the Soviets played upon the issue even more, turning it into one of the basic conditions for a peace settlement.[6] Israel retaliated for the commotion over its administration of the eastern half of the city by announcing in July that its capital extended to all of Jerusalem. Previously, East Jerusalem had been incorporated into Israel, but governmental offices were located only in West Jerusalem.

Soviet-American tension in the Middle East was extremely high in 1980, making any Arab-Israeli peace endeavor by the superpowers unlikely. In January, Carter declared that the Persian Gulf was vital to American security, and he threatened the use of force to keep the oil lanes open. This proclamation was in response to Soviet intervention in Afghanistan in December. Turmoil in Iran (including the hostage crisis) raised the possibility of a superpower confrontation in that state, and the abortive American rescue attempt in April only added more fuel to the fire. In the meantime, the U.S. was organizing a Rapid Deployment Force for potential quick strikes in the Middle East. In September, the war between Iran and Iraq broke out. It divided the Arabs (Syria and Libya sided with Iran) and deflected attention from Israel. At the same time, domestic turmoil persisted in Lebanon.

All of these factors prevented any serious Arab-Israeli diplomacy under superpower auspices, but Israel did not watch impassively. It wanted to make sure that the Soviet Union would not return to negotiations and that the United States would not effect a rapprochement with the PLO. Other considerations were to brake American movement toward closer military relations with Arab states such as Saudi Arabia, Egypt, Sudan and Oman and to compete with Egypt for American largess at a time when Sadat enjoyed great popularity in the United States. Israel therefore stressed its importance as an American strategic asset against the Soviet Union and offered its own logistic facilities as an alternative to those that could possibly have been provided by the Arabs. Although Israel's strategic asset approach had definite anti-Soviet overtones, the comments of her spokesmen were aimed more at endearing the United States than at intentionally antagonizing the Soviet Union.

Begin had already called for a defense agreement in March 1979 (he had been referring to the U.S. as an "ally" since the summer of 1977), but Israel's campaign to portray itself as a strategic asset of the United States gathered momentum after the Soviet intervention in Afghanistan. Defense Minister Weizman advocated a permanent American military base in the Middle East and he portrayed the Egyptian-Israeli treaty as "a begin-

ning of a bloc, a beginning of a basis, for anti-
Sovietism." He called upon the United States to join
Israel in an anti-Soviet alliance and proclaimed that
the United States could always use Israeli military
facilities without asking for permission in advance.[7]
Begin said that Israel had to be kept strong to serve
as an ally of the "free world" against Soviet incursions in the Middle East and, in April, he offered
Israeli facilities to the U.S. for use against the
Soviet Union.[8] Foreign Minister Dayan asked the United
States to draw a "red line" against Soviet advances in
the Middle East and to be prepared to act militarily to
defend it. He offered the use of Israeli airfields
and ports and stated that the U.S. could use aircraft
delivered to Israel.[9] The Carter administration continued close military cooperation with Israel, but opposed a formal alliance as it could have produced a
strong Arab backlash. The election of Reagan in
November was therefore greeted warmly in Jerusalem by
both the ruling LIKUD and the opposition Labor Alignment as it was expected to exacerbate East-West
tensions and enhance Israel's strategic importance to
the United States.[10]

Practical arguments were presented by opposition
Laborites, and some members of the LIKUD, that the
Soviet Union should not be alienated as it could serve
as a useful participant in the peace process. It was
pointed out that Soviet guarantees would be more reliable than those from Western Europe or the United
Nations should Israel decide to relinquish most of the
occupied territory. It was also averred that a Soviet
negotiating role could moderate the Arab position and
reduce the possibility of a Soviet-American confrontation in the area. Furthermore, it was suggested that
Israel should deal directly with the Soviet Union
rather than permit the United States to control
Moscow's degree of participation. Some advantage could
conceivably be gained by this tactic.[11]

While Israel was cementing ties to the United
States, the Soviet Union and Syria were forging a close
strategic relationship. Now that Egypt had relinquished
its war option, Syria had to be strong enough to face
Israel alone. It also had to contend with internal instability as members of the outlawed Muslim Brotherhood
were stirring up Sunni sentiments against the Alawite-
dominated Assad regime. Disturbances rocked Syria in
both April and July 1980. As a consequence, Assad freed
imprisoned communists, gave greater leeway to the
communist party and permitted it to open several
offices and publish its daily newspaper. He obviously was looking for extra support to counter the fundamentalist challenge. The Soviet Union recognized
Syria's increased importance in the Arab confrontation

with Israel and delivered large quantities of arms
to the Baathist government. In July 1980, naval
commander Sergei Gorshkov visited Damascus, and a
Soviet-Syrian friendship treaty was signed on October 8.
Previously, the Syrians had shied away from such a
formal alignment with the Soviets. By late 1980, they
had reassessed their position in the context of expanding Israeli-American military relations, and they probably were seeking tacit Soviet acceptance for their
backing of Iran against Iraq.

The United States and China renewed diplomatic relations on January 1, 1979. In January 1980, application of the Jackson amendment toward China was waived,
thus making that country eligible for most-favored
nation trade status. The Sino-American rapprochement
had some significant repercussions in the Middle East.
Already in 1978, the Soviets had begun to fear that
China would align with the U.S. and seek to establish
relations with Israel. Many signals were certainly
sent between Peking and Jerusalem, but no concrete
steps toward political accomodation were ever taken.
Early in 1979, Carter sounded out Teng Hsiao-ping on
establishing diplomatic relations with Israel and he
was told that China would possibly be interested in
pursuing such a course after the conclusion of an
Egyptian-Israeli treaty. The State Department had
encouraged Carter to raise the issue in the hope that
Chinese agreement to establish relations would induce
other states to follow suit.12 However, China failed
to make a diplomatic move toward Israel, even though it
did become a tacit American ally against the Soviet
Union in Afghanistan. Although Chinese-Israeli relations did not improve, Soviet concern about this
possibility was serious during the years 1978-80 and
may have influenced Moscow to develop extensive bilateral contacts with Jerusalem during this period.

Power Play

The inauguration of Ronald Reagan in January 1981
produced an alteration in the American perspective on
the Middle East. Settlement of the Arab-Israeli conflict, and resolution of the Palestinian problem, were
deemed less essential as the new regional focus was on
countering the Soviet Union. No new peace initiative
was attempted, but strenuous efforts were made to bring
about an anti-Soviet strategic consensus. The architect of this policy was Secretary of State Alexander
Haig, who did not believe in pressuring Israel to withdraw from occupied territories as he recognized the
Jewish state as an anti-Soviet military asset. In
April, Haig journeyed to Israel, Egypt, Syria, Jordan
and Saudi Arabia to begin organizing his envisioned

entente.

That same month, the Syrians introduced Soviet missiles into Lebanon. This increased regional tensions as there was a fear that Israel would attack the missile sites. Adding to the concern was the May evacuation of the wives and children of Soviet diplomats in Syria. By July, Israel and the PLO were engaged in battle on Lebanese territory, but a ceasefire was quickly arranged. A few weeks earlier, Soviet and Syrian troops had conducted a joint landing exercise along the Syrian coast. The fact that the Soviets played the attackers and the Syrians the defenders helped allay concern that the Soviet Union was increasing its commitment to Syria's defense, but it was apparent that Soviet-Syrian military relations were expanding.13

The staging of an international peace conference would have been highly unlikely during this period of heightened superpower antagonism. Also serving as impediments were Israel's attack on Iraq's Osirak nuclear reactor in June and the retention of power by Begin's coalition in the June 30 Israeli elections. Begin wanted to take advantage of peace with Egypt to increase Jewish settlement in the West Bank and he had no reason to seek negotiations with Jordan, Syria, or certainly the Palestinians. In August, Egypt and Israel agreed to the creation of an international peacekeeping force which would move into the Sinai prior to the completion of Israel's withdrawal in April 1982. The participation of American troops was seen by the Soviets as evidence of U.S. strategic penetration of the area. In September, Soviet-Egyptian relations reached a new low as Soviet ambassador Vladimir Poliakov was expelled. Sadat was assassinated in October, the month that the U.S. Congress approved the sale of AWAC aircraft to Saudi Arabia. In November, the U.S. conducted "Bright Star" military exercises with Egypt, Sudan, Oman and Somalia. Concern with regional power predominated, as the Reagan administration based its actions on countering a perceived Soviet challenge in the area.

Israel had been pressing for a strategic agreement with the United States for nearly two years, and it found a more attentive ear in Washington once Reagan became president. In fact, Reagan had written an article for an Israeli newspaper in 1979 in which he stressed the importance of the Israeli air force in countering the Soviet Union and praised the contributions to the U.S. of the Israeli intelligence network.14 When Begin came to Washington in early September 1981, strategic cooperation was discussed and a formal agreement was then worked out by Minister of Defense Ariel (Arik) Sharon and Secretary of Defense Caspar Weinberger

and released on November 30. The United States clearly viewed Israel as a strategic asset against the
Soviet Union. Israel expected its pro-American alignment to produce more benefits in the form of economic
and military assistance. When detente was suffering,
Israel could usually count on stronger American support because its anti-Soviet role gained in value.
Similarly, Israel could anticipate reduced American
pressure in regard to territorial concessions or a comprehensive settlement. Israel did not trust an American security guarantee as it would then be the dependent party. However, security integration through a
strategic agreement would produce mutual dependence at
a time when the U.S. needed Israeli assistance against
the Soviet Union.15 Furthermore, Israel wanted to
drive a wedge between the United States and the pro-
Western Arab states which received American military
support. Their logistical facilities were becoming
more attractive to the U.S., and their military infra-
structures were being developed with American assistance.
A strategic agreement between Israel and the United
States could therefore drive these states away from
the American embrace.16

The Israeli-American strategic agreement was aimed
at countering direct Soviet threats to the Middle East
or those by "Soviet-controlled forces introduced from
outside the region." The agreement was extremely unusual as an American document (although foreign minister
Shamir apparently did not realize this when he worked
on the phraseology) in that the Soviet Union was
designated the enemy. It was made amply clear that the
agreement was not aimed at the Arabs (otherwise, a
strong Arab backlash against the U.S. would have arisen)
as it stated that "strategic cooperation is not directed at any state or group of states within the Middle
East."17

The agreement really formalized ongoing strategic
cooperation, but it was important for Israel to secure
reaffirmation of the American commitment at the time.
In the past, the U.S. had lent strong support to Israel
because it had a democratic political structure, the
pro-Israeli lobby (AIPAC) had developed significant influence in Congress, and the U.S. felt a moral responsibility to back a state that it had helped create
through the 1947 UN partition plan. By the late
seventies, Israel was becoming skeptical that these
points would be sufficient to retain American policy
on a pro-Israeli course(witness the fate of American
commitments to Taiwan and South Vietnam). The embargo
of 1973-74 had graphically illustrated U.S. dependence
on Arab oil, and American vulnerability continued to be
evident throughout the seventies as oil prices rose
rapidly and the U.S. failed to reduce its reliance on

Arab imports. Israel viewed oil as the key factor that
would tilt American policy toward the Arabs, so it
began to stress its role as a strategic asset in order
to assure itself that the U.S. commitment to its welfare would not be abrogated.

Israel obviously benefited from American military
and economic assistance, but why was it of strategic
importance to the United States? There were no
American bases there, and Israeli troops had not assisted the U.S. in the Vietnamese or other conflicts.
There were basically five reasons: 1) the CIA and
Israel's intelligence agency the Mossad shared information on developments in the Middle East. The Mossad
had excellent knowledge of the area, and it also had
valuable contacts in Eastern Europe and the Soviet
Union.[18] 2) Israel acquired data on the battlefield
performance of Soviet weapons, which it passed on to
the United States, and it also permitted the American
military to examine captured Soviet aircraft, tanks
and other instruments of war. Rabin said that he
relayed technical information on Soviet weapons to the
Americans when he served as ambassador in Washington,
and that this proved useful to Israel as American
weapons sent to Israel were modified accordingly.[19]
3) Israel tested advanced American weapons under
battleground conditions and provided analyses of their
performance to the U.S. military. Such reports were
especially important once the end of the Vietnam war
deprived the U.S. of a practical testing ground. 4)
Israel was beginning to provide logistic facilities
for the Rapid Deployment Force. American aircraft
used the Etzion air base in the Sinai for reconnaissance and transport, and Israel was capable of providing emergency medical facilities. 5) Israel was able
to act in Third World situations where the U.S. was
reluctant to be identified as a supplier of arms or
technical assistance. American subsidies were even
provided for Israeli economic aid to other states,
particularly in sub-Saharan Africa.

As part of the new strategic agreement, it was
expected that American arms would be pre-positioned in
Israel to balance the Soviet stockpile in Libya.
Israel was probably willing to provide air cover for
the Sixth Fleet and Rapid Deployment Force, as well as
permanent bases for U.S. troops, but the United States
did not want further to antagonize the Arabs and it
rejected such suggestions.

The strategic agreement was opposed by RAKAH and
Soviet-Israeli friendship groups because of its clear
anti-Moscow content. It was also criticized by some
Laborites, who feared that it would lead to a reduction
in Soviet Jewish emigration and an escalation in
espionage charges lodged against Soviet Jews. It was

also believed that the agreement would ease Soviet
entree into the Arab world, reduce the prospects for a
West Bank political settlement, and make West European
states shy away from Israel in order to prove to the
Arabs that they were not party to U.S. strategic
designs.[20] An overwhelming majority of Israelis
backed the agreement. A representative sample polled
immediately upon its announcement showed that 70.6
percent approved, 24.3 percent disapproved, and 5.3
percent were undecided. When asked whether Israel
should actively participate militarily with the United
States against Soviet expansionism in the Middle East,
64.4 percent responded yes, 32.9 percent no, and 2.7
percent were undecided.[21] Shortly afterward, the
Jerusalem government extended Israeli law to the Golan
Heights. This step, as well as the previous one regarding East Jerusalem, was made for domestic political
purposes to balance the agreement with Egypt to withdraw from all of Sinai. In protest, the U.S. refused
officially to implement the agreement, but Israeli-
American strategic cooperation continued as it had for
many years.

     In 1981 and early 1982, there was almost no chance
of concluding a comprehensive Arab-Israeli peace settlement, but the Soviet Union continued to advocate
one. It was trying to stay on good terms with Arab
states, and was also in competition with the United
States for influence in the Arab world. At the Twenty-
sixth Congress of the communist party in February 1981,
Brezhnev again called for an international conference,
but did not offer any new suggestions or concessions.
Nevertheless, the Arabs were responsive to Soviet
overtures as the United States was not advocating peace
talks and was moving closer to Egypt. In April, the
Jordanian foreign minister said that the Soviet Union
must be included in negotiations. In May, Brezhnev
went to the airport to greet the visiting King Hussein,
and he also was there when the Jordanian monarch departed from Moscow for Kiev. Hussein agreed to an international conference with the PLO as an equal participant. Brezhnev repeated the familiar Soviet conditions for a settlement, but did say that there could
be "good relations" with Israel if it became non-
agressive and stopped occupying the territory of other
states.[22] In August, the Soviets mildly rejected
Saudi Arabia's "Fahd Plan" because it did not give them
a role, nor specifically mention the PLO, but there was
general Soviet approval of its conditions. In early
November, the Saudi foreign minister endorsed the concept of an international conference with Soviet participation, although he wanted it supervised by the UN
Security Council rather than the Big Two.[23]
     Meanwhile, the first meeting of the Soviet and

Israeli foreign ministers in six years took place in
New York on September 24. As usual, the request for
such a formal conclave came from the Israelis as they
had always advocated open and official contacts. Most
lower-level, non-official exchanges between the two
countries were initiated by the Soviets. Gromyko and
Shamir were each accompanied by three colleagues and
they discussed Soviet-Israeli relations, peace negotiations and Soviet Jewry. Shamir raised the issue of
direct emigrant flights, and Gromyko was non-commital.
Gromyko expressed anger that many Jewish emigrants
were going to the United States rather than Israel.
The Soviet foreign minister also indicated that the
time was not appropriate to renew diplomatic relations.
Apparently, Gromyko told Shamir that some Arab states
did not accept Israel. This was interpreted by the
Israelis as a conciliatory statement as it implied that
all of the blame could not be laid at their door.[24]
Pravda publicized the meeting, but made clear that it
was organized at Shamir's request. The commentary
summarized Gromyko's views, but not Shamir's, and it
called for the security of all states in the region
including Israel.

Begin claimed that Israel's strong anti-Soviet
stance, and steps toward a strategic agreement with the
United States, induced Gromyko to meet with Shamir.
This is probably an accurate assessment, but it is
also true that no significant results could have been
anticipated in such a political climate. No agreements
were reached, and Shamir asserted that he only wanted
to establish contact with Gromyko, not solve any
problems. In fact, Shamir met the Polish foreign
minister four days later and was told that the Warsaw
government was not interested in restoring relations.[25]

After the strategic agreement was announced, the
Soviet Union agreed (in January 1982) to provide SAM-8
missiles to Jordan. Simultaneously, it sought to
counter strengthened Israeli-American ties (despite U.S.
freezing of the agreement due to Israel's Golan Heights
policies) by pressing for an international peace conference. Israel was surely not amenable to such a
proposal, but the Soviets must have felt that the
territorial occupation would become permanent if no
diplomatic action was at least attempted. In December
1981, the Soviets hinted that they would soon be presenting another peace plan. Also that month, the
Israeli ambassador to Rumania was invited to a reception at the Bulgarian embassy, the first time an
Israeli official had been a guest at a communist
embassy reception in the absence of diplomatic relations.[26] In January 1982, a Rumanian envoy conveyed a
message from Ceausescu to Begin which called for an
international conference. The envoy said that Rumania

could serve as a contact with the PLO and Syrians, but Begin was not interested.27 In February, Middle East specialist Evgenii Primakov published a Soviet plan. The conference he proposed was to include Middle East, West European and North African states, the PLO, and the two superpowers. China was the only member of the Security Council's Big Five notable by its absence from the Soviet formula.28 Predictably, the Soviet initiative led nowhere as Israel was content with the existing situation, and the Reagan administration had no desire to exert any pressure on the Begin government to do otherwise.

Soviet Jewry Revisited

Soviet Jewish emigration jumped from 29,000 in 1978 to 51,300 in 1979, but then declined severely to 21,500 in 1980; 9500 in 1981; and 2700 in 1982. What accounts for the abrupt increase in 1979 to a record high? Soviet-American relations were primarily responsible as it seemed that detente would be strengthened. Carter and Brezhnev held a summit conference in Vienna, the SALT II agreement had been completed, and the United States had indicated that the Jackson amendment would be repealed, thereby making the Soviet Union eligible for most-favored nation trade status. The establishment of Sino-American diplomatic relations was also a factor, as the Soviets generally increased Jewish emigration at times of such warmth between Peking and Washington in order to discourage American playing of the so-called "China card." It was probably not accidental that the initiation of large-scale emigration in the early seventies coincided with the emergence of American diplomatic contacts with the Maoist government.29 Another consideration in 1979 may have been Soviet efforts to signal the Arabs that they should not rely upon the United States as the exclusive diplomatic mediator in the Middle East, and that the PLO in particular should not succumb to American overtures. Frequently, the Soviet Union had made gestures toward Israel to demonstrate to the Arabs that two could play the game.

Explaining the sudden decline in Jewish emigration is much more complicated. One aspect that appears beyond refute is that the desire of Soviet Jews to emigrate was not diminished. Statistics on invitations sent from abroad may not be too reliable a guide as many invitations were sent unsolicited. However, the number of applicants for emigration who were turned down ("refuseniks") is rather revealing and shows that the Soviet authorities began to clamp down on permission to emigrate. In 1979, 2984 hopeful emigrants became "refuseniks" while, in 1980, the figure increased to 4741 at a time when total Jewish emigration declined substantially.[30]

Jewish emigration does not appear to have been influenced by Middle East politics. The flow was not reduced when Egypt and Israel entered into the Camp David accords and later signed a peace treaty, so it is unlikely that Israel's movement toward a strategic agreement with the United States led to the reduction in emigration in 1980. Buttressing this interpretation is the absence of any effort by the Soviets to use the pace of emigration as a political lever to pressure Israel into avoiding closer military collaboration with the United States. Furthermore, the emigration of Germans and Armenians slowed down by 1981 so factors other than Arab-Israeli diplomacy were clearly pertinent. Increased Arab protests about the exodus of Jews to Israel were not evident in 1980. The concern of Arab states appears to have been greatest about 1973, while the PLO downplayed the entire issue on Arafat's instructions as good relations with the Soviet Union were more important.[31] It should also be pointed out that the slowdown in Jewish emigration was not accompanied by propaganda about this fact directed at the Arabs.

Did the rate of "dropouts" affect Soviet policy? After the 1973 war, the percentage of emigrants settling in countries other than Israel rose steadily. By 1980, nearly two-thirds were "dropouts," and the figure rose to 81.4 percent in 1981. In general, Jews from the Ukraine and Russia were the most likely to choose the United States. Those from peripheral areas, such as Georgia or Central Asia, usually opted to live in Israel. The "dropouts" tended to be highly assimilated and limited in their Jewish identity, while the more Zionistic emigrants placed a greater emphasis on Jewish traditions and had obvious emotional attachments to Israel. This helps explain why almost 60% of the Georgian Jews emigrated, mainly to Israel, while fewer than 5 percent of the Russian Jews departed. Of course, the willingness of Soviet authorities to permit emigration was also a major variable. Jews from Georgia and Central Asia were usually less educated than their Ukrainian or Russian counterparts, and fewer obstacles were therefore placed in the way of their emigration. These Jews from the periphery were substantially represented in the exodus of the early seventies, and they preferred Israel as their destination. The departure of "heartland" Jews gathered steam in 1976, leading to an increasing "dropout" rate.[32]

Soviet spokesmen complained about the "dropouts," and those cities whose emigrants had the highest "dropout" rates in 1979 had the most extensive decreases in their emigration rates in 1980. What concerned the

Soviets was that a program with a Jewish state ostensibly based on family reunification (hopeful emigrants
had to receive invitations from "Israeli" relatives,
even though many of these relatives actually lived
elsewhere) was turning into one of pure emigration.[33]
This set a disturbing precedent as members of other
ethnic groups in the Soviet Union could then be expected to make similar demands. On the other hand, a
high "dropout" rate embarrassed Israel and perhaps
discouraged Zionistic Soviet Jews from seeking to move
there. The burgeoning "dropout" rate does not really
explain why Moscow decided to reduce Jewish emigration.
Direct flights to Israel would have helped resolve this
issue, yet the Soviets insisted that processing of the
emigrants had to be continued in Austria. In addition,
departing Armenians usually went to the United States
(often via Lebanon) so the "dropout" issue was not
solely relevant to the Jews.

One key to an understanding of the motivation underlying the growing rigidity on emigration is domestic, and the other foreign. Surely the extremely
authoritarian, communist-ruled Soviet system was not
going to tolerate unlimited emigration. Political
inclinations had alwasy been toward restriction and suppression, while the labor shortage and special need
for technologically competent personnel mitigated
against large-scale emigration of Jews and other highly educated peoples. Armand Hammer, an American
industrialist who had been befriended by Lenin, was
told by Soviet officials in 1974 that approximately
200,000 Jews wanted to leave the Soviet Union and that
they could be accomodated within five years.[34] Although
more than 200,000 probably would have emigrated if permitted to do so, the salient point is that an upper
limit on Jewish emigration was probably contemplated
long before the decline began in 1980. In fact, the
200,000 figure turned out to be a rather accurate
estimate. It must be realized that the major emigration programs for Germans and Armenians were also
scaled down considerably, so the Jewish program must
be viewed in this broader context. Germans had been
departing since 1972 at the rate of approximately
10,000 per year, but only 3500 were permitted to leave
in 1981 and fewer than 2000 in 1982. A similar fate
befell the Armenians as the total of 2450 in 1981 dropped to only 400 the following year.[35]

At the international level, the course of Soviet-
American relations provides the most cogent explanations of Soviet behavior regarding Jewish emigration.
The Senate did not ratify the SALT II treaty, and the
expected repeal of the Jackson amendment did not take
place. Adding to Soviet consternation was the waiver
of the amendment's provisions for China in January 1980.

Soviet-American relations were also set back by the
supposed discovery in the fall of 1979 of a Soviet
combat brigade in Cuba. It had actually been there
for many years but conservatives in Congress, especially those opposed to SALT II, decided that the time was
appropriate to publicize the issue. Soviet intervention in Afghanistan greatly increased superpower tension, leading to the imposition of additional American
economic sanctions against the Soviet Union and a
boycott of the Moscow Olympics. In such an atmosphere,
a decline in Soviet Jewish emigration was to be anticipated as the vagaries of detente had always been a good
barometer of Soviet emigration patterns. In effect,
American economic sanctions applied in the wake of the
Afghanistan invasion served to diminish the outflow of
Soviet Jews. Paradoxically, the institution of the
linkage concept through passage of the Jackson amendment had been aimed at increasing it.

Israel's strongly anti-Soviet rhetoric, and development of closer strategic relations with the United
States, were directly related to the deterioration of
detente. Therefore, Israel was opting to enhance its
value as an American asset even though Soviet Jewish
emigration would be negatively affected.[36] World Jewish
Congress president Nahum Goldmann criticized the Begin
government, charging that it was harming Soviet Jews.
He said that he had conferred with Dobrynin for four
hours, but that the Israeli government was no longer
interested in hearing his summaries of such sessions.
Goldmann also alleged that organizers in the United
States were trying to mobilize Jewish youth by using
Soviet Jewish emigration as a rallying point. He preferred a concentration on the issue of Jewish rights
in the Soviet Union, rather than on emigration.[37]

Although Israel still stressed the Zionist concept
of the ingathering of the exiles, enthusiasm for the
cause of Soviet Jewish emigration was decreasing.
Official ideology was clashing with practical concerns
as the absorption of Soviet Jews had strained the
Israeli social fabric. While most citizens did not
object to the financial burden of settling so many
immigrants, the equity of disbursing social benefits
became the subject of extended debate. Many Oriental
Jews complained that they had lived in Israel for years,
but were still not offered the apartments or consumer
goods bestowed upon the Soviet newcomers. Resentment
also arose because the Soviet Jews wanted to live in
major urban centers and were reluctant to settle in
the development towns of the so-called "Second Israel"
(as had Oriental immigrants before them). Also problematic was the poor social integration of Soviet
Jews, their expectation that the state would provide
for their basic needs, and their growing rate of

emigration from Israel to the United States. Furthermore, many Soviet immigrants had been professional or
white collar workers. Israel already had a labor
surplus in many areas of employment, making it difficult to place most Soviet immigrants. The Georgians,
who were generally manual laborers, small-scale entre-
preneurs, or workers in the service sector, were more
easily placed in jobs reflective of their previous
experience. Soviet Jewish immigrants did not create a
conspicuous espionage problem, but Israeli authorities
assumed that spies had been planted. The immigrants
therefore faced restrictions in acquiring high security
clearances.

Israel was not prepared to abandon the Soviet
Jewish emigration campaign, but there was a conflict
(not necessarily perceived by the average Israeli
citizen) between espousal of this cause and Israel's
desire to work against detente. The latter consideration was based on security and it came to take precedence over the former, based on Zionist ideology and
humanitarianism.

The Beehive

Although there was no improvement in Soviet-Israeli
relations, and no progress toward a comprehensive peace
settlement, bilateral interaction reached its highest
level of intensity after the Egyptian-Israeli treaty
was signed in March 1979. The initiative was mainly
on the Soviet side as an effort was made to loosen
Israel's sturdy ties to the United States and appeal
more strongly to the growing "dovish" community in the
Jewish state.

In April, the Soviet Union released five of those
convicted in the Leningrad hijacking case. Begin then
sent a personal note of thanks to Brezhnev. In May,
the yearly Soviet delegation for the anniversary of
the defeat of Nazi Germany included its most prominent
figure ever, Aleksandr Bovin. He was a political correspondent for Izvestiia, but also a leading foreign
policy adviser to the Politburo elite. Bovin's group
did not meet with any senior officials, but did have
talks with Knesset members who had visited the Soviet
Union in November. It also received a Hasidic rabbi
who was seeking permission for his followers to visit
the tomb of Rabbi Nahman in the Soviet Union. Bovin
criticized the Egyptian-Israeli treaty, but said that
Soviet-Israeli relations could be restored once Israel
"moves toward a just peace" and recognizes the
Palestinian right to statehood. He did not say that
Israel had to withdraw from all occupied territory,
and defended Israel's continued membership in the
United Nations. Bovin advocated a Soviet-American

peace initiative, and rejected the Geneva framework as it would tacitly assume the validity of Israel's treaty with Egypt.38 Also in May, Soviet officers serving as peace observers on the Syrian front received UN medals in Tiberias, Israel and the Jerusalem government permitted a delegation of West Bank mayors to travel to the Soviet Union as guests of the Soviet Committee for Friendship and Solidarity with the Palestinian People.

In June, an extremely large Russian Orthodox delegation visited Jerusalem and its Western wall. Israel continued to give official recognition only to the "Red" church. When government representatives were sent to the Orthodox and Monophysite churches to extend Easter greetings, the "Red" church authorities were visited in an official capacity while those of the "White" church were called upon unofficially. The "Red" church accepted the Israeli administration and did not raise political issues related to the status of Jerusalem. Its leaders visited government ministries in the contested capital and frequented the annexed old city of East Jerusalem.

Israel did not interfere with contacts between the "Red" church and authorities in Moscow. It also permitted members of the Greek Orthodox clergy to attend Russian Orthodox theological seminaries in the Soviet Union. The Armenian church in Israel also maintained ties to co-religionists in the Soviet republic of Armenia. Religious delegations were frequently exchanged, and Israeli Armenians recognized that the seat of the church was in the Soviet Union. Many of them studied at the religious center of Etchmiadzin, although Soviet Armenians did not go to Jerusalem for theological training. Israeli Armenians often attended colleges in the Armenian republic, but Armenian emigrees from the Soviet Union did not opt to live in Israel.

In August 1979, a group of RAKAH activists visited the Soviet Union and thirty Israeli political scientists attended a conference in Moscow. Their invitations and visas were arranged through the International Political Science Association and they were able to meet with Middle East expert Evgenii Primakov and leading Americanist Georgii Arbatov. They were told that the Soviet Union was trying to influence the PLO toward greater moderation.39 During their stay, they tried to foster contacts with Soviet Jews, particularly "refuseniks." In September, an Israeli member of the International Council of Social Democratic Women attended a women's conference in Moscow, and independent liberal Knesset deputy Shulamit Aloni traveled to Hungary and East Germany. She was the first Knesset member to visit the latter state.

There was then little interaction until the spring

of 1980. In March, three Israelis took part in Soviet
celebrations of International Women's Day and the
traditional Soviet delegation went to Israel for the
defeat of Nazism ceremonies. In May, President Navon
commuted the sentence of convicted Cypriot communist
spy Panaioyitis Paschalis, and Israel permitted
Islamic leaders from the West Bank and Gaza to travel
to the Soviet Union as part of a Jordanian delegation.
Also, a RAKAH delegation met in Moscow with Suslov,
Ponomarev and Brutents. When Meir Wilner returned, he
said that he had received the impression that diplomatic relations could be renewed once peace negotiations
were initiated if Israel agreed to the concept of a
Palestinian state in return for PLO recognition of its
existence.[40]

The dominant issue at that time was the Moscow
Olympics. As far back as July 10, 1978, Yigal Allon
had questioned in the Knesset the wisdom of attending
due to Soviet treatment of Jews, particularly
Shcharanskii. Shcharanskii's wife Avital, who had
emigrated to Israel, declared in July 1979 that she
favored a boycott so there was clearly some consideration of one before Soviet troops invaded Afghanistan.
In January 1980, the Soviets officially invited the
Israelis, but there was then American pressure not to
attend. On February 20, Jimmy Carter announced the
American boycott and Israel followed suit. In May,
the Soviet delegation in Israel for the defeat of
Germany ceremonies requested a session with the director of the Israeli Olympic Committee in order to seek
a reversal of Israel's position. The foreign ministry
vetoed such a meeting.[41] Israel did not participate
in the games, and visas for Israeli tourists planning
to attend them were cancelled. Furthermore, Yasir
Arafat was present for the opening ceremonies. Despite
the acrimonious relations, Israeli television provided
thirty-one hours of Olympics coverage. According to an
account in RAKAH's newspaper, the Israeli government
wanted only minimal coverage but it was unsuccessful in
pressuring the television executives. However, the
latter agreed that the cameras would bypass conspicuous
symbols of the Soviet system or pictures of Lenin.[42]

Despite the Olympics controversy, Israelis attending conferences in the Soviet Union during the summer
of 1980 had no problem in acquiring visas. Also, a
Soviet diplomat in Washington invited an Israeli
journalist to lunch and told him that relations could
be restored once there was progress toward a comprehensive settlement. He said that the Soviet Union was
ready to contribute to a new peace initiative.[43] A
deterioration in relations then set in, although
Israel's extension of its capital to all of Jerusalem
did not appear to be directly responsible. Some

exchanges continued to take place. Veteran RAKAH
members went to the Soviet Union in September, leftist
trade union members traveled there in November, and a
Soviet delegation visited Israel in November as guests
of the Knesset members who had gone to Moscow a year
earlier. However, a chill predominated in the diplomatic atmosphere.

Rabbi Meir Kahane and his followers, who had
vandalized Russian Orthodox church property in July
1978, were finally put on trial in Israel. Avital
Shcharanskii testified on their behalf, claiming that
their acts were justified since the Soviet Union used
violence against Jews. The defendants were found
guilty, fined, but given no prison sentences. A few
weeks later, Kahane's militants ransacked RAKAH's Tel
Aviv office to protest Charlie Biton's meeting with
Arafat.[44] Biton was a non-communist Knesset member representing the RAKAH-led Democratic Front for Peace
and Equality.

In September, Shamir was unable to arrange a
meeting with the Soviets when he attended the UN session in New York. On the other hand, Begin turned
down an invitation from Ceausescu to discuss Middle
East peace terms in Bucharest. He said that he had
been there in 1977 and protocol demanded a return
visit by the Rumanian prime minister before he would
visit Rumania again to see the president.[45] Also that
month, Israel enhanced its broadcasting to the Soviet
Union. Radio Jerusalem was loaned amplifiers by the
Ministry of Communications, and agreements were worked
out with the British Broadcasting Corporation, Voice
of America and Radio Free Europe to coordinate broadcasts so as to counteract Soviet jamming.[46] Deposed
West Bank mayors Mohammed Milhem and Fahd Kawasmeh
held a press conference in Moscow, and Soviet invitations were sent twice to other West Bank leaders,
including the moderate Elias Freij of Bethlehem. The
invitations were sent directly, bypassing the PLO, because the Soviets were presumably mad at it for encouraging Nablus mayor Bassam Shaka to forego medical
treatment offered by the Soviets after his wounding in
a bombing incident.[47]

In October, the Soviets arrested an Israeli who
was accused of entering the country with a forged
American passport bearing a name unrelated to his own.
He admitted to the charges, but was expelled in December after intervention in his case by Wilner and
Toubi.[48] Also in October, Israel arrested an Arab
doctor from the West Bank who had studied medicine in
the Soviet Union and married a Soviet woman. He was
accused of spying for the Soviets and transmitting information to them via Amman, Jordan. In January 1981,
he was sentenced to a ten-year term. In February, a

Soviet delegation (including a Central Committee member)
attended RAKAH's nineteenth congress. The site had to
be shifted from Tel Aviv to Haifa after the owner of
the rented hall refused to honor the contract. A stir
was also created when a sister of "refusenik" Ida Nudel
gave a letter to the Soviets to pass on to Brezhnev.

The period of tense relations since the summer of
1980 may have been influenced by the Olympic boycott,
but appears to have been caused primarily by events in
Syria. Domestic disturbances in July increased the
Soviet need to be protective of the Damascus regime,
and a friendship treaty was then signed in October. An
Israeli effort to exacerbate relations with the Soviets
to help the presidential prospects of Ronald Reagan
may also have been relevant prior to the November 1980
election. Once Reagan assumed office and moved toward
an anti-Soviet strategic consensus in the Middle East,
the Soviets became more cordial toward Israel in order
to steer it away from its pro-American orientation. In
February, Iosif Mendelevich was released from prison
and permitted to emigrate to Israel. He had been arrested in 1970 as a conspirator in the Leningrad hijacking case. Later that month, Brezhnev denounced
anti-Semitism in his address to the Twenty-sixth
Congress and a meeting was later held (exact date unknown) at the Oriental Institute of the Academy of
Sciences to discuss anti-Semitic aspects of Soviet
anti-Zionist campaigns.[49] In July, a Soviet diplomat
in Washington spoke for ninety minutes with a reporter
from the Israeli newspaper Haaretz. He said that the
Soviet Union was trying to moderate the positions of
extremist Arab states, and he stressed the importance
of a Soviet role in a peace settlement. His declaration that "all those who want to hold discussions with
us can find the way" may have helped pave the way for
the Gromyko-Shamir meeting that September.[50]

In September 1981, a Soviet cardiologist attended
a medical conference in Israel and the Jewish state
was again represented at the Moscow book fair. Israeli
representatives were able to distribute Hebrew calendars and Israeli post cards. In October, it appeared
that a Soviet-Israeli tourism agreement would be
signed, but the deal fell through. It is unclear if
the initiative was Soviet or Rumanian, but the detailed itinerary was certainly worked out by representatives of those two states without any Israeli participation. The Rumanians then contacted an Israel firm
which booked tours to their country and asked whether
it would be interested in packaging joint tours to
Rumania and the Soviet Union. After receiving approval
from the East European desk at the foreign ministry,
a representative from the Israeli travel agency went to
Bucharest for further discussions. He agreed to the

tour itinerary, which featured a stay of several days
in Rumania, followed by a cruise on a Soviet vessel to
Black Sea ports in the Soviet Union. Israeli passengers would be allowed to disembark and visit relatives.
Visas for the tours were to be obtained in Bucharest,
and Soviet Jewish emigrants would be permitted to
participate. The Israeli representative waited in the
Rumanian capital while a Rumanian official traveled to
Moscow to finalize the contracts. The Rumanian was
unable to do so, and the Soviets did not provide any
explanation for the collapse of negotiations. Therefore, no Israeli tours to the Soviet Union were inaugurated, although they were successfully conducted
to Rumania and, since 1981, to Hungary. Occasionally,
individual Israeli tourists were able to secure Soviet
visas in West European capitals, particularly if they
held the passport of another state.

In December 1981, there was a repetition of the
July 1981 episode with an Israeli reporter in Washington. A Soviet diplomat initiated a ninety-minute conversation at the Soviet embassy and indicated that his
country was trying to work out a peace settlement. Indeed, the former director of the Middle East section
of the foreign ministry, Mikhail Sytenko, was on a tour
of the area and it was rumored that he met secretly
with U.S. diplomat Philip Habib in Amman. The Soviet
diplomat hoped that Soviet-American relations would
improve, thereby rendering the strategic agreement
between the U.S. and Israel superfluous. Then, he
believed that closer ties would develop between the
Soviet Union and Israel.51

Soviet overtures to Israel after completion of the
strategic agreement were almost predictable. Major
Israeli delegations were invited to the Soviet Union
subsequent to the second-stage disengagement agreement
and the Camp David agreement (also remember that Bovin
went to Israel right after the peace treaty was signed
with Egypt), and the same course was repeated in
December 1981. The day following the strategic agreement's announcement, invitations went out to five
Israelis: RAKAH Politburo member David Himim, RAKAH
party secretary in Nazareth Salim Hubran, former MAPAM
Knesset member Chaya Grossman, and Labor Knesset representatives Ora Namir and Rabbi Menachem Hacohen. The
delegation therefore had a Zionist majority, but all
of its members opposed the strategic agreement. The
Soviet Peace Committee served as host, and the arrangements were made through Tewfiq Toubi. Nothing of note
took place while the group was in the Soviet Union as
it was just another example of Soviet catering to
Israeli public opinion at an opportune moment. Also
in December, a Bulgarian delegation visited the Knesset
and called for better relations. In early January 1982,

Begin met with a Rumanian envoy and, in May, the Soviet
group sent for the victory celebration for the first
time included musicians.

Convolutions

The Soviet Union had persistent difficulties in
coming to grips with the Palestinian problem. The
option of a Jordanian-Palestinian federation was not
proposed during this period, perhaps as a result of
improved Soviet relations with Syria, but there were
fluctuations in policy between support for Arafat or
alternative members of the PLO hierarchy. Additionally, a new Palestinian communist party was established
with Soviet backing.
Following the Egyptian-Israeli treaty, the Soviets
wanted to emphasize the Palestinian cause to prevent
Israel from imposing unilaterally its own solution on
the West Bank. An interview with PLO Moscow representative Mohammed al-Shaer immediately appeared in New
Times, and efforts were made to soften the PLO stance
to ease progress toward negotiations.52 When Arafat
visited the Soviet Union in November, he complained
about the "primitive weapons" he had received, but he
also said that the PLO was no longer avoiding the
Israelis. He pointed out that members of his organization had attended the August political science conference in Moscow and had challenged the views of Israeli
delegates. Gromyko pressured Arafat to go further. He
maintained that he had no appropriate response when
American or Israeli officials asked him why Israel or
other states should negotiate with the PLO when it
refuses to recognize Israel or accept UN resolutions
(apparently SC 242 and 338). Gromyko sounded out
Arafat on whether he was prepared to make "certain
tactical concessions" in order to receive recognition
"from the hostile camp." Arafat obliquely responded
that he accepted the October 1, 1977 Soviet-American
communique (which did not mention SC 242 or 338).
Gromyko, sensing that no progress could be made at the
session, then said: "I do not wish to put pressure
on you to reply on this subject. If there is a change
in your position, I ask you to notify us, since one
cannot escape this issue."53
Once Soviet troops entered Afghanistan, Soviet relations with Arafat deteriorated as his supporters in
the PLO issued contradictory statements on the Soviet
role. They were faced with a serious dilemma as
Moslem financial backers were condemning the Soviets,
while they hoped for continued Soviet military assistance. Interestingly, the Soviet journal New Times
published interviews with PLO leaders such as Nayef
Hawatmeh, who were not members of Arafat's al-Fatah

faction.54 Arafat attended the Olympics in July 1980, but tensions persisted. In September, there was the controversy over Soviet invitations to West Bank mayors. That same month, a discussion among Arab communists in World Marxist Review was critical of the PLO for not including communists on its Executive Committee and it alluded to "the crisis of the Arab national-liberation movement." The participants commented on "the present unfavourable alignment of forces in the Arab world" and said that expecting a just settlement of the Palestinian problem was "an illusion." Terroristic Palestinians opposed to diplomacy were condemned, as were "right-capitulationists" who wanted to return the West Bank to Jordan, or enter autonomy talks with Israel.55 Clearly, the Palestinian movement was going through trying times and complications only increased with the outbreak of the Iran-Iraq war and the signing of the Soviet-Syrian friendship treaty.

Meanwhile, Israel was concerned about the activities of the PLO and RAKAH. In September, the military authorities cracked down on West Bank members of the Jordanian Communist Party because of their growing connections to these organizations. After a Toubi-Arafat meeting, RAKAH attempted to stage a conference of Israeli Arabs which would emphasize their role as part of a Palestinian nation and create an alliance with the PLO. The Israeli government banned it.56 In February 1981, the PLO Executive Committee called upon Israeli Arabs to vote for RAKAH in the upcoming Knesset elections (in a sense, the legitimacy of the elections and of the Knesset was being recognized), and Meir Wilner met with PLO official Faruq Qaddumi at the Twenty-sixth Congress of the communist party in Moscow.

By the spring of 1981, Syrian missiles had been moved into Lebanon and an Israeli confrontation with the PLO was brewing. As usual, the Soviet Union proceeded cautiously, but lent strong verbal support to the Palestinians. When Hussein went to Moscow in May, the Soviets secured his endorsement of an independent Palestinian state. After Begin's reelection, arms deliveries to the PLO increased and the Soviets indicated that the PLO mission in Moscow would be raised to embassy status in October when Arafat was expected to be in the Soviet capital. In August, the Soviets protested the exclusion of the PLO from the "Fahd Plan." They soon lived up to their July promise to Arafat, and he was received by Brezhnev. Mohammed al-Shaer was then interviewed in New Times, and he was recognized by Gromyko as envoy extraordinaire on April 30, 1982.57

In late 1981, a secret Palestinian communist party organization was established in Gaza. It did not have links to the Jordanian Communist Party or RAKAH,

nor was it approved by the Soviet Union. A
Palestine Communist Party was also set up, but not
announced. It was the official pro-Soviet party and
most of its members (including its leader Naim Ashhab)
had been activists in the Jordanian party. It went
public in February 1982, recognizing the PLO as "the
sole legal representative of the Palestinian people"
and calling for representation on the PLO Executive
Committee.58 The creation of this new party was consistent with Soviet advocacy of a separate Palestinian
state, and it implicitly rejected the possibility of a
West Bank-Jordanian federation. Even the Jordanian
communists opposed this latter solution, although it
would have prevented the splitting of their movement
into separate Jordanian and Palestinian parties. Overall, the Soviets seem to have concluded that communist-
PLO collaboration should be fostered as a necessary
step toward the establishment of a Palestinian state
alongside Israel.

By the late spring of 1982, there was no momentum
toward an Arab-Israeli peace settlement and no fundamental change in the strained Soviet-Israeli relationship. Placidity set in as the dog days of summer
approached. However, diplomatic inertia soon gave way
to energetic activity as another war broke out in the
Middle East.

12
Distant Partners

The newest phase of the Lebanon war, which began in June 1982, brought about the defeat of PLO and Syrian forces by the Israelis. At first, it seemed as if the power interests of Israel and the United States had been served, and that the Soviet position in the region had been seriously weakened. Then the assassination of Lebanese president-elect Bashir Gemayel, Soviet provision of SAM-5 missiles to Syria, and battlefield victories by Syrian-aligned Moslem and Druse militias in Lebanon enhanced Syrian strength at the expense of Israel. American interests were also set back as the "Reagan Plan" for Arab-Israeli peace was a failure, Amin Gemayel's government and army slowly disintegrated, and U.S. troops suffered heavy casualties and were unsuccessful in establishing peace in Beirut. The tables had quickly turned, but the Soviet Union did not gain any immediate advantage from Syria's resurgence. Additionally, Soviet relations with the PLO were never completely repaired after Arafat's expulsion from Beirut and his movement's dispersion and eventual bifurcation.

Strains in the relationship between Jerusalem and Washington were evident during the conflict in Lebanon and were then accentuated when Begin's government rejected the "Reagan Plan." Consequently, Israel adopted a conciliatory attitude toward the Soviet Union, but the Soviets proved unreceptive. They were focusing on internal problems related to succession, and also clinging to their only remaining asset, Syria. The death of Brezhnev, and the resignation of Begin, had no discernible effect on Soviet-Israeli relations as they remained cool. Soviet Jewish emigration was also reduced to a trickle. There was clearly no movement toward an Arab-Israeli peace settlement, which became even less likely due to growing interaction with the complex Lebanon conflict. Superpower relations remained frigid, and no joint peace initiatives were attempted.

To understand this period, we must ask: Why did the Soviet Union fail to act decisively during the Lebanon war? Why did it later deploy SAM-5 missiles in Syria? Why was it unable to restore cordial relations with the PLO? Why did Israeli officials constantly call for improved ties to the Soviet Union, and why did Moscow disregard these overtures?

Cautious Reaction

Israeli troops entered Lebanon with American acquiescence to destroy the PLO infrastructure, help establish a central Lebanese government favorably disposed toward Israeli security interests, and to reduce Syrian influence and eventually produce the withdrawal of Assad's troops from Lebanese territory.[1] The immediate trigger for Israel's intervention was provided by the attempted assassination by Palestinians of her ambassador to Britain, but a military foray into Lebanon had surely been planned anyway. All terms of the Egyptian-Israeli treaty were being carried out, so the effective neutralization of Egypt freed Israel to act along her northern frontier. In effect, the attempt to destroy the PLO was part of Israel's West Bank strategy as success would have facilitated Begin's efforts to populate the area with Jewish settlers and integrate it more completely into Israel.

The Soviet Union avoided military involvement. It initially portrayed the conflict as one between Israel and the PLO (with Washington encouraging Jerusalem), and intentionally disregarded the Syrian factor. Once that was no longer possible, the defense provisions of the friendship treaty with Damascus were not applied as Israel was engaged in combat on Lebanese soil and was not attacking Syrian territory.[2] As will be explained later, Soviet assistance to the PLO during the conflict was minimal, provoking strong criticism by that movement's leaders.

The Soviets did try to assert their interests diplomatically, especially when they realized that the war machine they had built up in Syria was being destroyed. Consistent with previous tactics, the United States was approached to restrain Israel. Brezhnev warned Reagan that further Israeli attacks on Syrian troops would have "global consequences," and the American president asked Israel to moderate its actions.[3] After delaying for a few days, Israel complied but increased Israeli-American acrimony developed over the revelation by the U.S. that Israeli troops would not try to seize Beirut. This permitted PLO forces to dig in at a time when Israel was trying to hasten their departure through the threat of attacking the Lebanese

capital. Soviet Middle East analyst Evgenii Primakov
claimed that Soviet contacts with the U.S. had "a very
effective restraining character."4 This interpretation
was somewhat exaggerated as American pressure on Israel
to desist from further military advances was the pro-
duct of self-interest more than Soviet warnings (as
will be discussed below, the U.S. hoped to open a
dialogue with the PLO). The American government, and
probably Begin as well, anticipated a much more limited
Israeli operation in Lebanon and did not realize the
scale of objectives comtemplated by Minister of Defense
Sharon and many of the military leaders.

The Soviets sought superpower cooperation, but had
less leverage than during the 1973 war due to the
enormity of the Arab defeat. Brezhnev asked Reagan
not to provide American peacekeeping forces, but his
request fell upon deaf ears. The Soviets then had to
stand by while the U.S. arranged for the safe departure
from Beirut of the PLO. Brezhnev had little choice but
to say that he did not object to the Israeli troops and
"the forces defending West Beirut" from becoming "dis-
engaged." Just as the Soviet Union was unable to
modify American behavior (its ability to initiate a
dialogue with the Reagan administration was extremely
limited), so too did it appear like a paper tiger to
the Israelis. The warning issued to Israel on June 14
stressed the region's proximity to Soviet borders, but
did not include any specific threats. Begin was surely
correct in stating that his evaluation right from the
beginning of the war was that the Soviet Union would
issue condemnations not accompanied by any concrete
actions.5

What accounts for the Soviet Union's moderate
behavior during the war in Lebanon? First of all,
Arab states were deeply divided and failed to assist
the PLO or Syria. Some of the more conservative monarchies may have been secretly pleased with the PLO's
defeat, while most Arab states were unsympathetic to
Syria due to its support for Iran against Iraq. While
the Arabs surely did not side with the Israelis, they
were unwilling to aid their brethren as they fell
before the Israeli advance. In such a situation where
the Arabs were intentionally turning their heads away,
the Soviet Union was unlikely to act decisively.

Secondly, the geriatric Soviet leadership had become rather ossified, and Brezhnev's health was deteriorating. Attention was focused on a succession
struggle, and major contestant Iurii Andropov had
already secured a lead on his rivals by gaining a
pivotal post in the party Secretariat. The time was
not appropriate for any bold steps in the Middle East.
In particular, the Soviets did not want to offend West
European states when a gas pipeline agreement was being

negotiated and strong opposition was developing to the deployment of American Cruise and Pershing missiles.

Thirdly, the Soviet Union's Syrian ally had been devastated militarily through the destruction of its missile facilities and tanks in Lebanon, and the loss of ninety-two aircraft. The battlefield advantage clearly belonged to the American client, Israel, and the Soviets did not want to risk a confrontation under these conditions. Soviet relations with the PLO were also severely strained, and the U.S. held the key to negotiations with Arafat due to Israel's application of military pressure. The Soviet Union therefore proceeded cautiously. Its naval squadron in the Mediterranean was reinforced only slightly, and it stayed away from the Lebanese coast. The comment by a Supreme Soviet member that Soviet intervention "would have probably brought on a nuclear war" was certainly an overstatement, but it reflected the genuine anxiety that the Soviet Union had found itself in a hopeless position.[6]

The Soviets did not just sit on the sidelines. Assad made two secret trips to Moscow for consultations on the military situation, and the First Deputy Commander of the Soviet Air Force was dispatched to Damascus. Soviet advisers served with Syrian units, and arms were airlifted from the Soviet Union and Libya (although on a much smaller scale than during previous wars). The Soviet Union was prepared to offer maximum assistance to Syria if it became subjected to an Israeli attack, but it was not willing to become embroiled in a war on Lebanese territory. According to one report, a Soviet intention to defend Syria was clearly indicated when two airborne divisions were placed on alert and overflight rights in Turkish airspace were requested.[7]

The Syrians did not believe that Soviet actions were sufficient. They constantly called for the upgrading of the friendship treaty to a strategic alliance, which really meant that they expected military backing in Lebanon as well as within their own borders. The Syrians also stressed American support for Israel, implying that Soviet aid was not commensurate. The Soviets claimed (and they were legalistically correct) that they were living up to the terms of the friendship treaty.[8] The Lebanese government hoped the Soviet Union would do something to counter the Israelis. When the Soviet ambassador told the president and prime minister that Lebanon would solve its problems, this implied that no major assistance could be expected. Prime Minister Shafiq al-Wazzan was later explicit in telling a Soviet television interviewer that Lebanon was on fire and would not be satisfied with tears from Moscow.[9] The PLO expressed the greatest disappointment with the level of Soviet support, but this aspect will be discussed below.

Not only did the Soviet Union act weakly, but it suffered several humiliations. Its major weapons in Syrian hands (aircraft, tanks and missiles) had proven ineffective, and the Israelis had developed the technological means to circumvent missile defenses and destroy the launchers. The Israelis also captured SAM-9 missiles with their launchers, a serious setback for the Soviets as the Americans would surely be granted access to them. There were also reports that eleven Soviet advisers had been killed in an Israeli bombing attack on a downed aircraft. The Israelis were trying to destroy their own plane so electronic equipment would not fall into Syrian and Soviet hands.[10] The Soviets additionally had to watch the United States get the credit for arranging for the PLO's evacuation from Beirut, and saving Arafat and his men.

Soviet powerlessness was most strikingly displayed when the embassy in Beirut was repeatedly shelled by the Israelis in the course of combat against the PLO. It was hit at least eight times, but Soviet protests were usually mild condemnations issued by the news agency TASS. On one occasion, the Soviets did send a message to Begin via the Finnish embassy in Tel Aviv, but its tone was moderate and no Soviet countermeasures were threatened.[11] Once, Israeli troops spent several hours within the Soviet embassy compound seeking shelter from PLO gunners, but the Soviet Union decided to downplay the incident.

The Reagan Plan and Beyond

The defeat of the Syrians and PLO led Reagan on September 1 to announce a new peace plan for the Middle East. Syria, the PLO and the Golan Heights were not mentioned in reference to a solution as the emphasis was on inducing Jordan into negotiations. In a sense, the "Reagan Plan" was not directed at a comprehensive settlement (Syria was excluded and there was no provision for a Palestinian state) but at fostering step-by-step talks between Israel and Jordan under American auspices. The Soviet Union was left out completely. It was not consulted, and the plan did not call for cooperation with Moscow or assign any role to the United Nations. In fact, Reagan began his peace proposal with a discussion of the Soviet strategic threat in the Middle East. When Secretary of State Shultz later met Gromyko, the Soviet foreign minister requested regular consultations on the Arab-Israeli conflict and the convening of an international conference presided over by the two superpowers. Shultz rejected Gromyko's suggestion and said that the American ambassador in Moscow would provide the Soviets with whatever information was needed.[12]

Reagan, by lending his name to the plan, must have expected that it would succeed. The timing was probably related to the Arab conference scheduled for Fez, Morocco later that week as the U.S. wanted to strengthen the hand of the moderates and encourage a mandate for Hussein to negotiate over the West Bank. Arafat and the PLO had been weakened by events in Lebanon, so perhaps the Arab leaders would no longer insist that the PLO was "the sole legitimate representative of the Palestinian people." Fez failed to give a mandate to Hussein, and the "Reagan Plan" quickly ran into another serious problem when President-elect Bashir Gemayel of Lebanon was assassinated on September 14. Just when the United States believed that the Lebanese conflict had been settled favorably, and that attention could be shifted to the Arab-Israeli conflict, Beirut erupted again and regained the spotlight. The "Reagan Plan" was therefore confronted with inauspicious circumstances immediately after its presentation.

The Soviets viewed the "Reagan Plan" as an extension of the Camp David process, so Brezhnev quickly proposed his own alternative. At a dinner for South Yemeni leaders on September 15, the Soviet General Secretary criticized Reagan's opposition to a Palestinian state, pointing out that the U.S. was in effect questioning Israel's existence since the 1947 UN resolution created both states in the region. He also made Israeli withdrawal from Lebanon a precondition to serious negotiations. Brezhnev's plan included familiar calls for the return of occupied territories, the establishment of a West Bank-Gaza Palestinian state, ending of the state of war, and a guarantee of the security of all states in the area. Interestingly, China was included as a possible guarantor and it was stipulated that East Jerusalem must be part of the Palestinian state. In discussing Palestinian refugees, Brezhnev discussed the "opportunity" (not "right") to return or receive compensation, thereby implying that resettlement in Israel would not be insisted upon. Brezhnev again called for an international conference, gave a positive assessment of the Arab peace plan produced at Fez, and insisted on PLO participation (although he did not say "at all stages" or "on an equal footing"). Many components of previous Soviet peace plans were absent: Israeli navigational rights, withdrawal in stages, demilitarized zones, and a peace agreement after only the first stage of withdrawal. What was noteworthy about this particular plan was its timing (an obvious counter to the "Reagan Plan") and downgrading of support for the PLO. The Palestinian factor had clearly decreased in importance once PLO guerrillas were evacuated from Beirut, and

the Soviets probably believed that Arafat was prepared
to go along with an American initiative rather than
their own. Indeed, Arafat had not closed the door
on the "Reagan Plan."

Israel opposed the "Reagan Plan" because of its
emphasis on the West Bank and call for a freeze on
settlements in occupied territories. After all, many
Israelis believed that the prime aim of the Lebanon war
had been to solidify control over the West Bank.
Israel also felt betrayed by the U.S. during the war,
first receiving American approval for its actions and
then becoming subject to pressure to desist from further military advances. In Israeli eyes, Secretary of
State Haig's removal from office rendered him a hero
for challenging the American turn away from support for
the Jewish state.

Fundamental to the Israeli-American differences
were conflicting interpretations of the appropriate
role to be played by the PLO. Israel had sought to
annihilate it so that the Jerusalem government could
resolve the West Bank problem in its own way. The
United States had wanted to weaken the PLO, but not
destroy it. That is why the Americans announced that
Israeli troops would not advance into Beirut. The aim
was to head off an ignominious defeat for the PLO
through forced departure, and then to prepare the proper psychological climate for Arafat's participation in
peace negotiations. The United States therefore arranged a more noble exodus from Beirut for Arafat and
his supporters, and the Palestinian leader was able to
claim that his men had held out heroically against the
Israelis. Military defeat was converted into a propaganda victory, making it easier for the PLO to join
the negotiating process. The situation was similar to
that in Egypt after the 1973 war, when Sadat was ready
to deal with the Israelis after preserving his honor.
The "Reagan Plan" did not stipulate a role for the PLO,
but the Israelis were probably correct in believing
that the Jordanian option would soon lead to PLO
participation (with the U.S. pressing for some con-
federal arrangement in the West Bank, not a separate
Palestinian state).

Israel was furious at the United States even before the issuance of the "Reagan Plan," and it made
overtures to the Soviet Union to tweak the eagle's
nose. Begin said that Israel would renew ties if the
Soviets took the initiative, and Shamir asked them to
reverse their anti-Israeli policies and improve relations.[13] Israel was reluctant to antagonize Moscow
at a time when Soviet fortunes in the region were so
low, fearing that the Kremlin's reaction would be to
make a show of force to cover up the humiliation. For
this reason, and also to register a protest in

Washington, Israel downplayed the strategic asset concept. The United States tried to distance itself from
Israel so that it would not become a major target of
Arab opprobrium due to its inability to prevent the
Israelis from entering West Beirut after Bashir
Gemayel's assassination. The U.S. had therefore
failed to live up to its pledge to the departed PLO,
and its stock in the Arab world fell even more after
Israeli collusion in the Sabra and Shatila murders
became known. The U.S. therefore sought intentional
confrontations with Israel in order to regain some Arab
good will, producing the well-publicized incident of
the American soldier who mounted an Israeli tank and
ordered it to halt.

After Brezhnev's death on November 10, Israel
hoped for a change in Soviet policy and signaled a
desire to repair relations. Low-level contacts were
increased, and encouraging comments were expressed by
Minister of Energy Yitzhak Moda'i and Speaker of the
Knesset Menachem Savidor. Foreign Minister Shamir declared: "To the extent possible, we want to maintain
normal relations with the Soviet Union, and we will
seize every opportunity to achieve this objective."
The Israeli foreign ministry also sought an American
evaluation of the prospect for improved Soviet-Israeli
relations.[14] Despite Israel's endeavors, there was no
positive Soviet response. As we shall see, the Soviets
were planning to solidify ties to Syria and were not
interested in a rapprochement with Israel.

While the Israelis were making overtures, the
Soviets were adopting a strongly anti-Israeli posture
in order to work their way back into the good graces
of the Arabs after their lackluster support during the
Lebanon war. They pressed for the expulsion of Israel
from the International Atomic Energy Agency and, for
the first time, supported calls (labeling them a "just
demand") for removing Israel from the UN General
Assembly.[15] In the end, the Soviets backed off by
abstaining on the crucial Finnish resolution of
October 26 which postponed a vote on the issue.

The Soviet Union wanted to maintain close ties to
Syria, as the Damascus regime was the only remaining
piece of the Arab-Israeli puzzle with which the Soviets
could play. The Syrians needed Soviet military assistance to rebuild their shattered defenses, and they
also continued to push for a reinterpretation of the
Soviet Union's commitment under the 1980 friendship
treaty. Assad met Andropov after attending Brezhnev's
funeral and, the following month, Syria appointed its
first ambassador to Moscow after a two-year hiatus.
The Soviets refused to amend or reinterpret the treaty,
and they were also somewhat irritated by Syrian com-
plaints about the quality of the weapons they had

supplied, but objective conditions served to produce closer Soviet-Syrian relations nevertheless. Consistent with the Soviet Union's move toward Syria was its attitude toward governmental changes in Lebanon. When anti-Syrian president-elect Bashir Gemayel was assassinated, Soviet diplomats did not deliver personal condolences nor address consoling remarks to the family. Only a telephone call from the embassy in Beirut to the Lebanese foreign ministry served as a Soviet sign of sympathy. When Bashir's brother Amin replaced him, Brezhnev cabled his personal congratulations to a president considered more acceptable to the Syrians.

The Soviet Union and Israel both worked against the "Reagan Plan," but this did not produce more harmonious relations between them. To prevent American sponsorship of a separate solution for the West Bank, the Soviets tried to strengthen ties to Jordan. SAM-8 missiles (their sale had been arranged almost a year earlier, but it was still doubtful if they would actually be provided) were delivered in December and Hussein was told when he headed a joint Arab delegation to Moscow that the Soviet Union would do everything possible to obstruct the "Reagan Plan." Although definitely opposed to Jordanian participation in negotiations within the framework of the "Reagan Plan," the Soviets were generally supportive of the Arab "Fez Plan" and did not rule out PLO-Jordanian talks about the status of the West Bank.16

Four-Cornered Hat

By January 1983, Soviet SAM-5 missiles and crews were arriving in Syria. They drastically altered the strategic balance by converting the defeated Syria into a formidable military force. Israel did not yet have a counter to the SAM-5's, and they were capable of hitting aircraft over most of its territory and out into the Eastern Mediterranean. They also inhibited Israeli flights over Lebanon's Bekaa Valley, where Syrian troops were stationed. Additionally, the presence of Soviet personnel risked turning any Israeli preemptive strike into a direct confrontation with the Soviet Union. The situation was somewhat analogous to that of 1970, when the Soviets responded to Israeli deep penetration bombing raids in Egypt by dispatching their own pilots and missile crews to provide Egypt with an adequate aerial defense. This time, the Soviets acted after Syrian aircraft and missile batteries had been decimated by the Israelis. In both cases, the Soviets mobilized quickly to buttress the defenses of Arab allies. The difference was that in 1970, the Soviets tried to use the new strategic edge to further

the peace process. The American "Rogers B" proposals
then provided the basis for a cease-fire. In 1983,
there was no Soviet peace initiative as there were
serious differences with the PLO, and the Reagan
administration was determined to leave the Soviet Union
out of negotiations. In a way, the movement of missiles into Syria was a display of Soviet defiance aimed at emphasizing Moscow's critical importance in
arriving at any political solution.

The Soviet Union was deploying SAM-5's to obstruct
the "Reagan Plan" by making Jordan fearful of entering
into American-sponsored negotiations. Syrian-Jordanian
tensions were high, and Hussein clearly realized that
a militarily powerful Syria posed a threat to his
aspirations in the West Bank, and to his own regime as
well. The Soviets were also trying to regain their
prestige in the Arab world after their weak performance
during the Lebanon war. It was noteworthy that only
three major Arab leaders (Assad, Qaddafi and Arafat)
attended Brezhnev's funeral, so the Soviets had to act
decisively to restore Arab confidence in their relia-
bility. The provision of SAM-8's to Jordan must be
viewed in this context, as must efforts to restore
proper relations with Egypt. In January 1983, chief
Africanist Anatolii Gromyko (the foreign minister's
son) spent ten days in Cairo. The Soviets additionally were responding to American policy in the area.
American troops were stationed in Lebanon, the U.S.
was providing military assistance to the Amin Gemayel
government, and the Rapid Deployment Force was being
restructured as the Central Command. The U.S. was also
pressing for a Lebanese-Israeli treaty, and making
diplomatic overtures to both Syria and the PLO. The
delivery of Soviet missiles to Syria was therefore, at
least in part, an effort to restore some semblance of
superpower balance in a region where the United States
had gained the upper hand.

The placement of SAM-5's in Syria soon had a
crucial impact on the regional power configuration.
Syria was militarily resurrected, the Soviet Union reestablished itself as a major force that could not be
discounted, and Lebanese politics came under the increasing influence of Damascus. Israel's temporary
victory in Lebanon yielded no immediate gains as mounting casualties fostered internal dissension and pressures to withdraw from the southern Lebanese theatre.
An apparent triumph for the United States was reversed
as the American-trained Lebanese army collapsed and
U.S. troops were later forced to leave Beirut. The
Americans had suffered heavy losses while undertaking
an ill-defined mission; at the time, Soviet soldiers
were safely manning SAM-5 sites within Syrian borders.[17]
Soviet deployment of SAM-5's in Syria coincided

with a period of strong Israeli resentment against the United States. Many Israelis believed that clumsy American military moves in Lebanon had triggered the Soviet action (the missiles were therefore an antidote to the air power based on vessels in the Sixth Fleet), and that the U.S. was trying to take advantage of Israel's military victory to gain influence in Lebanon and repair relations with Syria. The U.S. had also been constraining Israel's tactical role in Lebanon, but simultaneously beseeching it not to redeploy its exposed troops further south. The presence of Israeli forces thus served as an American bargaining chip with the Syrians, a situation which the Begin government could not countenance. Anti-American sentiments ran high as Israeli lives were being lost in support of American objectives that were not consistent with Jerusalem's interests. A poll of Israelis conducted in late December 1982 and early January 1983 showed that most respondents were prepared to accept a reduction in their standard of living in order to reduce Israel's dependence on American aid: 40.8 percent said they would accept a significant reduction, 33.3 percent a small reduction, 21.7 percent no reduction, and 4.2 percent were undecided.[18]

To register its anger at the United States, Israel adopted a more moderate posture toward the Soviet Union. The more ultranationalist wing of the ruling LIKUD coalition, represented by Foreign Minister Shamir of Herut and members of the small Tehiya party, had never wanted Israel to serve as an American client. Its members therefore called for reducing reliance on the U.S. by improving relations with the Soviet Union. These rightist political figures were surely anti-Soviet ideologically, but they believed that Israel had to play the superpower balancing game and, rather unrealistically, that more harmonious ties to Moscow would serve the cause of Soviet Jewish emigration.[19] Minister of Defense Sharon requested a Soviet-Israeli conclave, apparently to deal with the issues of Lebanon and the SAM-5's. The Jerusalem Post editorially remarked: "Coming from the man who has repeatedly claimed that Israel ought to be the bulwark of the U.S. against Soviet expansionist designs both in the Middle East and in Africa, this is certainly a new and quite inexplicable twist."[20] Actually, his motivation was very clear: to prickle the United States in order to show it that Israel was indeed a strategic ally that should not be treated so lightly. Furthermore, he was trying to demonstrate that the "Reagan Plan" was doomed as a consequence of both Soviet and Israeli opposition.[21]

Chief of Staff Rafael Eytan went out of his way to downplay any Soviet-Israeli differences, partly to deflect strong public criticism of his alleged

strategic errors during the Lebanon war which may
have contributed to Soviet deployment of the SAM-5's.
He said that Soviet troops were manning SAM-5 sites to
restrain the Syrians, not to precipitate conflict with
Israel, and he maintained that the Soviets were not
prepared to use their own pilots in a combat situation. He described Soviet policy as cautious, based
upon a recognition of an American commitment to
Israel's security. Eytan argued that the missiles
were possibly delivered to Syria to counter U.S.
troop deployment in Lebanon, and he tried not to offend the Soviets by asserting that their weapons were
"superb" but that the Syrians had failed to use them
properly. He also denied that the Soviet Union had
been "stripped bare" by events in Lebanon.22

Conciliatory Israeli remarks had no effect on
the Soviets as they were committed to reestablishing
their ties to the Arabs. Karen Brutents, Deputy
Director of the International Department of the
Central Committee, described Sharon's request for
talks as playing the "Soviet card," and he said that
relations with Israel could not improve while it remained aggressive and expansionist. He also attached
the precondition of withdrawal from Lebanon and occupied territories to the resumption of diplomatic
relations.23

Israel downplayed the deployment of SAM-5's in
Syria. There were no claims that Syria had offensive
designs, or that war was imminent. A LIKUD member of
the Knesset called for negotiations with the Syrians,
and Chief of Staff Eytan seemed to place greater
emphasis on the delivery of SAM-8's to Jordan. Trying
to cause some friction between the Soviets and Jordanians, he indicated that Jordan would possibly turn
over technical information about the missiles to the
Americans.24 As strange as it may seem, Israel
wanted Syria to be militarily strong and to retain a
sizable number of its troops in Lebanon. A powerful
Syria would be able to obstruct the "Reagan Plan,"
especially by intimidating Jordan into not becoming a
party to negotiations.25 Furthermore, Israel was not
prepared to withdraw completely from Lebanon before
appropriate security arrangements were made. This
meant a continuing accomodation with Syria over zones
of influence, as the Syrians would certainly not pull
out while the Israelis remained. Israel therefore did
not press for the removal of Syrian troops as their
presence in Lebanon tended to justify Israeli actions
there. As a prominent LIKUD Knesset deputy asserted:
"If Syria throws a spanner in the works, the U.S. will
have no possible ground for blaming us, and will have
to give us a free hand."26 Additionally, Israel was
pleased that Syria had turned toward the Soviet Union,

It had feared that American entreaties would detach
the Damascus regime from the Soviet camp, and then
produce U.S. pressure on Israel to return the Golan
Heights.

Domestic factors must also be considered.
Israel's advance into Lebanon, and destruction of
Syrian missile sites there, helped spur the delivery
of SAM-5's. Emphasizing a threat from the SAM-5's
would therefore have accentuated opposition accusations
that Israel's war aims had not been realized, and that
security had actually decreased. Charges were already
prevalent that Israeli destruction of Syrian missiles
in Lebanon had made the introduction of more advanced
missiles inevitable. The government, by reacting
mildly to the SAM-5's, was thus able to defuse the
critics of its war policies, and simultaneously attempt
to soothe a population that had become restless due to
mounting casualties in southern Lebanon. Furthermore,
Israel did not plan to attack the SAM-5 sites, so why
produce a public outcry and then act impotently?

On March 16, Soviet Ambassador to Lebanon
Aleksandr Soldatov called for Israeli withdrawal from
Lebanon, even if Syria did not act likewise, and he
stressed that the military aid given to Syria was to
defend its territory. He clearly did not imply that
the Soviet Union would assist the Syrians in Lebanese
territory, but the Christian radio station in southern
Lebanon claimed that he was pledging Soviet intervention in Lebanon to support Syria in a war with
Israel.[27] This erroneous report at first alarmed the
Israelis, but a cooler perspective soon prevailed in
Jerusalem as the actual content of Soldatov's rather
conventional remarks became known. Shamir then said
that the Soviet role in Syria was mainly a reaction to
the American one in Lebanon, while Minister of Communications Mordechai Tsipori maintained that the Soviets
were trying to forestall conflict. He exclaimed: "If
they wanted to heat things up, they would keep quiet
and let it happen."28

On March 30, the Soviet Union warned Israel not
to attack Syria. A TASS release served as the medium,
and no direct message was sent to Begin's government.
The Soviets called for a comprehensive political
solution and left their own commitment to Syria vague,
stating only that the socialist countries were on
Syria's side. The proximity of the region to Soviet
borders was not mentioned, as it had been in many previous warnings, and there was no demand that Israeli
forces withdraw from Lebanon. Veteran Israeli diplomat Yosef Tekoah described the Soviet statement as
one of the mildest ever, and he pointed out that the
issuance of such statements never preceded Soviet
military action. He said that if the Soviets wanted to

assist the Syrians in attacking Israel, they would use
the element of surprise. He advised his government to
ignore the Soviet statement as Israeli policy during
the 1956 and 1973 wars had been inhibited by a fear
of Soviet involvement after similar warnings. He
expressed support for the disregard displayed in 1967
and 1982 when Israeli forces carried out their objectives despite Soviet threats.29

Did the Soviets really believe that Israel was
going to attack Syria? Probably not, as other interpretations of Moscow's behavior seem more appropriate.
The Soviet Union wanted to head off negotiations based
on the "Reagan Plan," so the March 30 statement pointedly called for a comprehensive settlement. This
really meant that the Soviet Union and Syria could not
be excluded, and that Hussein and Arafat should not
collaborate with the United States in separate discussions about the West Bank. Any step-by-step deal over
the fate of the West Bank would be viewed as a sellout
of Syrian interests as Israel would be able to deploy
most of its troops along the northern frontier. The
Soviets, by charging Israel with aggressive intentions,
were also trying to justify the emplacement in Syria
of SAM-5's with Soviet crews. Additionally, the
Soviet warning emphasized American ties to Israel.
The accentuation of this theme was probably aimed at
discouraging Jordan and the PLO from entering into
"Reagan Plan" negotiations. A few other factors may
also have been relevant. Israel had just staged the
third major international conference on Soviet Jewry,
and it is no coincidence that the Soviet Union announced on March 31 that an anti-Zionist committee
would be established (it was on April 21). Also,
several members of RAKAH (including a journalist) had
been arrested by the Israelis prior to the annual
March 30 "Land Day" protest demonstrations by Arab
citizens.

The Syrians welcomed the Soviet statement, and
seemed to place it within the context of the SAM-5's.
They argued that a "deterrent force" was needed to
counteract Israeli aggressive designs, and implied
that more Soviet military assistance was required.
"Israel's superiority" was recognized, although Syria
was taking "steps toward a strategic balance."30
The Israelis responded to the March 30 statement by
immediately telling the Soviets that they were not
planning an attack on Syria, and Wilner soon relayed a
Soviet message that Moscow did not want Syria to
initiate a war, and that Syria would not do so.31

The Soviet statement did not signify any basic
change in policy toward Israel. An anti-Zionist committee was created but, otherwise, events proceeded
along their normal course. This helps buttress the

idea that the Soviets were not really concerned about
an assault on Syria, but were stressing their opposition to the "Reagan Plan" and to their exclusion from
the peace process. On April 2, Foreign Minister
Gromyko (who had just been appointed a first deputy
prime minister) held a rare press conference at which
he condemned Arab extremists who wanted to destroy
Israel. He said that Israel must continue to exist as
a state and that eliminating it would be "unrealistic
and unjust." He said that the Palestinians also had
the right to establish a state, "albeit small," but he
did not specifically mention the PLO. He also did not
refer to any Israeli plan to attack Syria.32

The "Reagan Plan" failed to attract Hussein or
Arafat, but the United States continued its policy of
unilateral diplomacy by helping negotiate a treaty
between Israel and Lebanon (concluded on May 17). The
Reagan administration was trying to include Amin
Gemayel's Lebanese government in its anti-Soviet
strategic consensus, so it pressured the two states to
negotiate a treaty even though each party knew that it
could never be implemented. Syria was opposed, as
were large segments of the Lebanese population, and
there was little faith in George Shultz's promises to
deliver the Syrians. In fact, the Israelis did not
even want this attempted as the Golan Heights would
surely be used by Shultz as a carrot.

Reagan was determined to keep the Soviet Union
out of the negotiating process and Begin agreed,
saying that Israel would not suggest a Soviet role as
the U.S. had not requested one. Many members of the
Israeli opposition concurred, with Rabin advocating
Syrian-American, but not Soviet-American talks. The
former prime minister maintained that Soviet participation in negotiations had never been helpful to Israel.33
Foreign Minister Shamir soon began to argue that the
Soviet Union's failure to reestablish ties to Israel
eliminated it as a legitimate party to negotiations
over Lebanon, or to a comprehensive conference on the
Middle East. He declared that full diplomatic relations
were a prerequisite to any Soviet participation.34

The stalemate between Moscow and Jerusalem continued as Israel and the United States began to overcome
their differeneces by stressing the Soviet factor.
U.S. Secretary of Defense Weinberger said that his
government was prepared to reinstate the strategic
memorandum of November 1981 whenever Israel desired.35
It was already apparent that Syria would remain aligned
with the Soviet Union, and would not withdraw from
Lebanon anytime soon. The American military and
diplomatic positions in Lebanon were also deteriorating.
The United States therefore wanted Israel to serve as
its regional ally against the Soviet-Syrian-Lebanese

opposition axis. Israel had a continuing need for
U.S. military and economic assistance. Its galloping
inflation and growing unemployment were becoming a
severe burden, and Prime Minister Begin was turning
recluse and failing to provide political or moral
leadership. Casualties were still mounting in southern
Lebanon, and the national mood was somber. The resignation of Begin in September, and the assumption of
power by Shamir, did not resolve the problems and a
dispirited Israel turned again to its major patron, the
United States. In November 1983, Shamir and Reagan
established a "joint political military group" that
Reagan said would "give priority attention to the
threat to our mutual interest posed by increased Soviet
involvement in the Middle East."36 Strategic cooperation was officially reborn as Israel again assumed its
role as a partisan in the superpower competition.

Quiet Times

The period from Israel's intervention in Lebanon
in June 1982 to the end of 1983 was marked by relative
inaction in Soviet-Israeli bilateral relations. There
were no high-level meetings of government officials,
no prospects for reestablishing official ties, and no
possibility of Soviet participation in peace negotiations. Israel was busy restructuring its relationship
with the United States, while the Soviet Union was
doing likewise with Syria. The Lebanon war had widen-
ed the diplomatic chasm between Moscow and Jerusalem,
and the breach began to narrow only gradually.
At first, interaction was limited to anti-war
activities. The Israeli organization "Peace Now"
opposed its government's policies in Lebanon, and was
therefore viewed favorably by Moscow. However, the
Soviets had to act cautiously as identification with
"Peace Now" would tarnish its appeal to the Israeli
public. They therefore avoided direct contact, and
advised RAKAH not to seek joint meetings or demonstrations with "Peace Now" members. For its part, "Peace
Now" was neither Marxist nor pro-Soviet and had no
interest in collaboration anyway. The East European
media publicized "Peace Now" activities, and efforts
were made to include its members at conferences
arranged by communist front groups in Western Europe.
Communists attempted to work for "Peace Now" through
its overseas offices, and some unofficial offices were
even set up by communists posing as regular members of
"Peace Now." When Meir Wilner went to Moscow, he met
with the only Jewish member of the Communist Party's
Central Committee Veniamin Dymshits and with Jewish
generals Dragunskii and Goldman. They inquired about
Israeli peace movements and said that their demonstra-

tions had been shown on Soviet televison.37

The diplomatic ice between the Soviets and
Israelis was broken indirectly when, in late October,
president of the World Jewish Congress Edgar Bronfman
received an official invitation from the Central
Committee. Nahum Goldmann had only been to Moscow
unofficially, so the Soviets were taking an important
step (perhaps to foster a healthier and more receptive
economic climate in the West). Bronfman was supposed
to visit the Soviet Union in December, but Brezhnev's
death led to a postponement. About the same time,
there were Soviet-Israeli discussion through East
European intermediaries on the promotion of Israeli
tourism to the Soviet Union. The emphasis was on
permitting religious groups to visit the graves of
notable rabbis, but no agreement was worked out.

Israel, upset with its treatment at the hands of
the United States and with the issuance of the "Reagan
Plan," began to call for improved relations with the
Soviet Union, Consequently, with apparent government
approval, a new friendship committee named the Israel
Association for Understanding and Relations with the
Soviet Union was established. Headed by Benjamin
Akzin, a LIKUD proponent and former secretary to
Begin's mentor Ze'ev Jabotinsky, the new organization
included former ambassador to the Soviet Union Yosef
Avidar and many figures associated with the ruling
LIKUD coalition. Akzin's group was to provide an
alternative to the existing friendship committees, one
of which was closely affiliated with RAKAH and the
other (founded by the late Yaacov Riftin) with opposition Knesset parties. The Soviets showed no interest
in Akzin's committee, and never contacted it. Also
in late 1982, a committee of Soviet emigrants living
in Israel was formed to encourage tourism and cultural
exchanges with the Soviet Union.

The Soviet Union did not at first respond to
Israeli overtures, but some bilateral contacts began
to take place in the early spring. Two Soviet
emissaries made a mysterious visit to Israel in March,
and the Jewish National Fund announced plans that month
to plant a forest for the 200,000 Jewish members of
the Red Army who died during the Second World War.38
In April, the head of the Israeli tourist office in
Rome was invited to Moscow and a delegation from the
Russian Orthodox Church was received by Interior
Minister Burg. In May, the annual Soviet delegation
was enlarged through the addition of two musicians and
two dancers. It also included Igor Beliaev, political
analyst for Literaturnaia Gazeta and deputy chairman
of the Soviet anti-Zionist committee. In June, Burg
met with another Soviet religious delegation. It would
appear that this flurry of activity helps buttress the

interpretation that the Soviet statement of March 30
was not addressed primarily to Israel, despite outward
appearances. If it had been, one would have anticipated a diminution of bilateral contacts.39
   Some obstacles to improved relations were evident
despite the more relaxed atmosphere. In March, Israel
organized the conference on Soviet Jewry (which previously met in Brussels in 1971 and 1976) which had
been scheduled for Paris the previous October. It was
postponed because anti-Israeli demonstrations were
expected in the wake of the Sabra and Shatila incident
in Lebanon, and Israel's willingness to convene it in
Jerusalem was probably a slap at the Soviet Union
generated by the dwindling rate of Soviet Jewish
emigration. In April, the Soviets responded with their
anti-Zionist committee and the Weizmann Institute conferred an honorary doctorate on Andrei Sakharov. On
May 20, the murder in En Kerem (near Jerusalem) of two
Soviet Russian Orthodox nuns further exacerbated tensions. Interior Minister Burg sent condolences to the
church headquarers in Moscow, but the Soviets claimed
that Israel was partly responsible because it generally
looked the other way while acts were committed against
the Russian Orthodox Church.40 Israel failed to ap-
prehend the perpetrator, but police sources charged
that members of the church were obstructing the investigation by failing to provide necessary information.
The murder case came immediately after the Israeli-
Lebanese treaty, so relations between the Soviet Union
and Israel had reached a rather low point.
   Soviet Jewish emigration was in steep decline.
Only 2,700 Jews departed in 1982, and the figure dropped to 1,500 in 1983. Many Israelis expected the
Jewish exodus to pick up once Andropov replaced
Brezhnev, as he had been the KGB chief during the
period of extensive emigration and must have given his
imprimatur. Disappointment then set in when the flow
became even further restricted. On April 20, 1983,
Victor Louis wrote one of his occasional pieces for the
Israeli public and asserted that Jewish emigration was
ending. He claimed that many emigrants were unhappy
in the Jewish state, and indicated that requests for
emigration had tapered off. He hinted that the termination of emigration was related to the large number
of "dropouts" who went to the United States.41 More
likely was the explanation offered by dissident
historian Roy Medvedev: Emigration was a function of
Soviet-American relations, and it was apparent that
detente had deteriorated. He also pointed out that the
U.S. administration was devoting less attention to the
issue of human rights.42 One Soviet publication maintained that emigration had to be curtailed for security
reasons. In its overblown presentation, it was argued

that the Israeli intelligence network used Soviet Jews
for the purpose of espionage and encouraged emigration
in order to obtain access to state secrets. It was
asserted that this plot was unsuccessful as emigration
had been contained.43.

By the summer of 1983, Israel had decided to seek
low-level contacts with the Soviet Union in the areas
of trade, cultural agreements and consular arrangements. This was a reversal of previous policy, as it
had always been viewed as a way to let the Soviets
through the back door while avoiding the renewal of
official relations. Most likely, Israeli authorities
believed that their policy was too closely oriented
toward the United States. More importantly, they
hoped that some modest improvement of ties to Moscow
would lead to increased Soviet Jewish emigration.
Interestingly, the Soviets had recognized the territorial stalemate that had developed in the Middle East
and had started to think about Jewish emigration as an
instrument that could be used to pry concessions from
the Israelis in regard to the occupied lands. The
Soviets were spreading rumors that an Israeli agreement
to withdraw from the West Bank could produce direct
flights to Israel for a few hundred thousand Jews, and
a spokesman in New York implied that the Soviet Union
would be more forthcoming on the emigration issue if
Israel permitted it to have a major role in negotiating
an Arab-Israeli settlement.44

In July, the Soviets invited the first Israeli
political delegation since December 1981. It included
Citizens' Rights Movement Knesset deputy Shulamit
Aloni (who had joined the Labor voting bloc), Labor
party Knesset member Aharon Harel, and former general
and prominent "dove" Mati Peled. The Israelis significantly called for the development of cultural and commercial contacts as the first step toward improved relations. They visited the Moscow synagogue and requested the assistance of the Soviet Peace Committee
in securing permission to emigrate for "refuseniks" Ida
Nudel and Iosif Begun. No official response followed,
except acknowledgment that the requests had been received. The Israelis got the impression that the
Soviets would consider humanitarian requests, but would
not renew mass emigration. Peled, who had been asked
to help by the families of Israeli prisoners in
Palestinian hands, solicited Soviet aid in arranging a
meeting with the PLO to negotiate an exchange of
prisoners. Such secret talks with the PLO began while
Peled was still in Moscow. The delegation returned
home with the assessment that diplomatic relations
could not be restored soon, and with a warning from
Evgenii Primakov that the Soviet Union would intervene
if Israel were to attack Syria or SAM-5 missile sites

there.45 The Soviet position toward Israel remained
rather rigid, and there were no hints of a new
flexibility during the delegation's visit.

Soviet-Israeli relations then continued to clank
down a bumpy diplomatic road. In September, there was
again an Israeli pavilion at the Moscow book fair, but
the Soviet, Polish and Yugoslav delegations canceled
their expected participation in an Israeli conference
on Jewish resistance during the Second World War after
Radio Moscow deemed the conference an Israeli domestic
event.46 In October, Soviet officers from the UN
observation mission in Syria received medals at a
ceremony in Tiberias, Israel.

Bitter Times

Soviet-PLO relations deteriorated as Moscow
failed to provide much military assistance during the
Lebanon war. Caution was dictated by Israel's preponderance of power on the battlefield, and by the
American strategic advantage in the area. Once Arafat
and Assad became estranged, the Soviet Union was
caught in the middle and had difficulty in strengthening ties to the PLO and Syria simultaneously.

During the height of combat in June and July 1982,
Arafat repeatedly sent messages to Brezhnev via Soviet
Ambassador to Lebanon Soldatov in which he sought more
weapons and ammunition. There were two visits to
Moscow by Faruq Qaddumi, and one each by Salah Khalaf
(Abu Iyad) and Yasir abd Rabbuh, but with no result.
The PLO had little chance against the Israelis without
a large infusion of Soviet military assistance, and
Arafat therefore had to accept a cease-fire and eventual evacuation from Beirut. PLO leaders were extremely disappointed by the degree of Soviet support.
Arafat was hesitant to criticize the Soviets, saying
only that "they could do more," while Qaddumi asked
them to adopt "a stricter tone with stronger warnings
to the United States."47 The main public spokesman
turned out to be Salah Khalaf, who referred to the
Soviet attitude as "inexplicable" and stated that he
was "pained by their stand." He said that Soviet support had only been symbolic, in the form of verbal
statements, while the United States had backed Israel
concretely. He condemned Soviet "passiveness" and
described a Brezhnev letter to Arafat as "a good message written with good words, but all this is insufficient. What is important is real action."48 Even
the usually pro-Soviet Nayef Hawatmeh joined the
bandwagon, calling Soviet behavior "incomprehensible"
and advocating the introduction of Soviet troops.49

Brezhnev accepted the PLO decision to leave
Beirut under American auspices, and again proposed an

international conference to deal with the Middle East.
The PLO then toned down its anti-Soviet remarks, as it
needed Moscow's diplomatic support in negotiations.
Arafat welcomed the anticipated conference, and
Qaddumi blamed Arab disunity for the PLO's plight:
"If there were an Arab will to fight I would not
imagine the Soviet Union would hesitate to support such
a military effort.50   Still, Brezhnev offered no substantive assurances to the PLO other than a promise to
work in the Security Council to enforce the cease-fire
and attempt to deploy UN observers.51 No international
conference was convened as the United States and Israel
were surely not interested.

After PLO guerrillas were evacuated, a Brezhnev
message to Arafat praised him for his "humane decision"
which prevented greater civilian casualties and the
destruction of the Lebanese capital. The Soviet leader
wrote that the PLO had displayed "courage" and a "sense
of political responsibility."52 A few days later,
Brezhnev presented his peace plan, which was less
supportive of the PLO than previously and which adopted
a weaker position on the issue of the rights of
Palestinian refugees. When Israeli troops were implicated in the Sabra and Shatila massacre, Arafat asked
the Soviets to do something to stop Israeli actions
around Beirut (the Israelis had just entered West
Beirut after the assassination of Bashir Gemayel).
Brezhnev's response was non-committal, indicating only
that the Soviet Union would struggle to end such
"crimes" and make "the aggressor" leave Lebanon.53
Salah Khalaf, who had criticized the Soviets for their
inaction when Israeli troops occupied West Beirut,
returned to the attack but implied that Syria had influenced the Soviet Union to avoid helping the
Palestinians.54

Soviet-PLO ties had become frayed because Moscow
again failed to provide assistance, just as it had de-
sisted in 1970 and 1976 during the PLO's hours of need.
Also, the Soviets had become concerned that PLO relations with the United States would improve once
Arafat had agreed to rely on American diplomacy and
military protection to secure his departure from Beirut.
Furthermore, Arafat had turned sharply against Assad
as the Syrians had only fought the Israelis in self
defense and had not assisted the Palestinians, either
when Israeli forces crossed into Lebanon in June or
when they entered West Beirut in September. This Arab
division created serious complications for Soviet
policy, and it became even more accentuated when
Arafat established a PLO headquarters in Tunis while
most of the non-Fatah leaders of the organization
relocated in Damascus. The Soviet Union's frequent
ally Nayef Hawatmeh sided with the pro-Syrian faction,

as the PLO was both dispersed and politically divided.
     The Soviet Union continued to give symbolic back-
ing to Arafat. To commemorate the Day of Solidarity
With the Palestinian People, the Central Committee's
message to the PLO leader labeled his organization a
"vanguard fighting force," but media support for the
PLO was really weaker than before.55 Rather than
indicating the Palestinians' right "up to and including a state," there were now references worded "up
to a state." Arafat attended Brezhnev's funeral, but
his name was last on a list of foreign dignitaries present. On January 2, _Izvestiia_ referred to Palestinian
leaders opposed to the "Reagan Plan" and embarrassed
Arafat by excluding his name.56 The PLO chairman
returned to Moscow a week later and was received by
Andropov. However, Arafat refused to rule out preliminary discussions with Hussein which could lead to
negotiations based upon the "Reagan Plan." The joint
Andropov-Arafat communique referred to Soviet "understanding" (a sign of disagreement) of his call for a
confederation of Jordan and an independent Palestinian
state. Actually, the Soviets had advanced the same
proposal in the past so what really disturbed them was
their own lack of participation in the negotiating pro-
process.
     Although Soviet-PLO relations were poor, RAKAH–PLO
ties were strengthened as Wilner appeared to serve as
a Soviet proxy in keeping open the lines of communication. Wilner and Arafat met for the first time after
attending Brezhnev's funeral in Moscow and, according
to Wilner, Arafat said repeatedly that he accepted
SC 242 as the basis for negotiations.57 If so, this
represented a significant change in the PLO's position
but the time was not ripe for a political settlement
due to dissension over the "Reagan Plan," the split
in the PLO, and Israel's desire to retain the West
Bank. In April 1983, Wilner and Arafat met again
in Prague.
     RAKAH also established a working relationship
with the Palestine Communist Party. In December 1982,
Wilner conferred in Moscow with Politburo member
Suleiman Najar and a news conference was arranged. A
joint communique was released which accepted the PLO
as the sole representative of the Palestinians and
called for a Palestinian state in the West Bank, Gaza
and East Jerusalem. It advocated mutual recognition
by this state and Israel, and an addendum attached by
RAKAH declared that this was the most important point
in the communique. The two parties endorsed the
Soviet proposal for an international conference, and
indicated that the PLO should participate on an equal
footing (though the phrase "from the beginning" was
not included). It was implicitly evident that the

two communist parties were not supportive of Arafat-Hussein talks regarding a possible Palestinian-Jordanian confederation.58

By the spring of 1983, Arafat and Assad had not become reconciled (despite a May 3 meeting), the Tunis-Damascus split in the PLO persisted, Arafat and Hussein were unable to work out a joint plan to participate in negotiations, and the PLO began to experience another debilitating division in its ranks. In June, al-Fatah itself was split when rebel officers in Lebanon broke with Arafat and aligned with the Syrians. The Soviet Union encouraged a peaceful negotiation of differences, but efforts at mediation were unsuccessful as the Soviets were unable to moderate Assad's position. Cuba proposed a conference of the Soviet Union, Syria, PLO, Lebanese National Movement, and itself but it was never convened. The Soviets were careful not to take sides, and began to discuss the PLO "leadership" rather than mention Arafat personally. Arafat tried to make it appear that he enjoyed Soviet support, but such was not really the case. In fact, he refused to travel to Moscow because he knew that he would be disappointed there. When the Syrians and rebel al-Fatah units decimated the Arafat loyalists and forced them to leave Lebanon, the Soviets did not come to their assistance.

The Palestinian issue continued to bedevil the Soviets. As it became more complicated due to internal divisions and intra-Arab contradictions, the Soviets were drawn into the quagmire and rendered incapable of emphasizing the demand for Palestinian statehood as a vital component of the Arab-Israeli peace process. Israel was therefore provided with extra time to solidify its control over the West Bank, and the prospects for serious negotiations toward a political solution grew dimmer. The influence of the superpowers had decreased due to their inability to collaborate during the war in Lebanon, and both Israel and Syria had acquired greater independence of action.

13
Alienation or Reconciliation?

In the late forties, the Soviet Union used Israel to enter the Middle East political arena; in recent years, the United States has been using Israel to help remove the Soviet Union from the region. Israel has therefore served as a lodestone, not because of its intrinsic importance, but as a result of its instrumental role in the superpower rivalry.[1] Therefore, Soviet-Israeli relations are a function of many external factors and cannot be understood primarily in terms of bilateral interaction. Recognizing this fact, we must nevertheless consider whether Soviet-Israeli diplomatic relations will be restored, and under what conditions. Our evaluation of this issue will surely be relevant to an understanding of the prospects for an Arab-Israeli peace settlement and the role that the Soviet Union may possibly play in negotiations. Which states would benefit from a political settlement, and which would prefer the perpetuation of the status quo? How will domestic political changes in the Soviet Union and Israel affect the likelihood of a settlement, and how will the issue of Soviet Jewish emigration be connected to a territorial agreement? Will the course of Soviet-American relations have an impact on the peace process? Will the Soviet Union and Israel really seek to improve relations, or will their mutual coolness be reinforced by continued turmoil in the Middle East and a prolongation of extreme superpower tensions?

Parameters

The Soviet Union and Israel may have some geopolitical common interests (which need not produce any political reconciliation) revolving around their general proclivity to develop closer relations with Ethiopia and Iran. More unusual and debatable is their mutual concern for the welfare of Qaddafi's government in Libya. The Soviet Union benefits from Qaddafi's

anti-Western posture, and from the pre-positioning of
a vast weapons supply, while Israel gains from
Qaddafi's militancy and threats to neighboring African
states. As long as he is in power and is armed by the
Soviet Union, Egypt is likely to remain an Arab moderate with ties to the United States. Egypt will also
be forced to concentrate troops on its Western
frontier, far from Israel's borders. The Sudan and
Tunisia will tend to act similarly. Furthermore,
Libya's occupation of northern Chad and meddling in
the politics of West African states have aroused fear
in many countries and have encouraged them to seek
better relations with Israel.

Obvious Soviet-Israeli differences remain. Anti-
Semitism in the Soviet Union has become more virulent,
while anti-Sovietism in Israel is on the increase.
Although many Israeli politicians advocate improved
ties, this is an aspect of the diplomatic cat and
mouse game with the United States and is not based at
all on any new-found enamorment with the Kremlin.
Israel has moved away from its East European cultural
heritage, has abandoned most attributes of Marxist
ideology, and has become clearly Western in life
style and attitude. The influx of Soviet Jews has
actually raised the level of anti-Soviet feelings.
Nevertheless, it is not out of the question that
accomodation can be reached by the two states. Soviet
anti-Semites may turn out to be forthcoming on the
issue of Jewish emigration, while the burgeoning right
wing in Israel has an advantage over the Laborites in
trying to gain public support for a rapprochement. It
was Begin who evacuated Sinai, just as it was Nixon
who opened a dialogue with China.

Soviet-Israeli differences in regard to the superpower rivalry are readily apparent. Israel is clearly
aligned with the United States, and it often presents
an obstacle to Soviet foreign policy goals by working
against Soviet-American detente. As explained by
Shlomo Avineri, Israelis are strongly anti-communist
and view detente as a sign of Western weakness.[2] In
addition, Israel wants to obstruct any superpower collusion in the Middle East which can produce an imposed
Arab-Israeli settlement. While anti-Soviet, Israel
prefers a Soviet role in the area as it enhances
Israel's own value as an American strategic asset and
thereby contributes to Congressional willingness to
extend economic and military assistance. The Soviet
Union is in a position to counteract Israel's tactical
maneuvering by adopting a more benign attitude toward
the Jewish state and offering to restore diplomatic
relations. The Soviets could thus blunt Israel's
fostering of a strategic alignment against them.

Any renewal of relations, or progress toward a

comprehensive settlement, is based on the assumption
that the Soviet Union wants Israel to exist for at
least the short run. In practical terms, the Soviets
know that the United States will resupply Israel during
a war and play a major role in mediating peace. Pro-
moting a military crisis that could lead to Israel's
destruction would therefore be illogical as Israel and
the United States would probably emerge with new
advantages.3 Furthermore, Israel is likely to use
atomic weapons if it is ever on the verge of being
overrun by Arab armies and there is also the possibility of direct American intervention. If American support for Israel is greatly reduced, then Soviet backing of an Arab invasion will become a more viable
policy option.

     Based on past experience, the Soviet Union has
displayed support for Israel's existence despite its
own arming of the Arabs. Arafat has been pressured to
recognize Israel, and Sadat asserted that the Soviets
would not permit him to attack Israel within its pre-
June 1967 borders.4 Soviet warnings, from the one
issued by Bulganin during the 1956 Suez War to that
announced by TASS in March 1983, have never led to
military action. When the Soviets did intervene
directly, as in Egypt in 1970 and Syria at the end of
1982, their intentions were purely defensive.

     It is not inconceivable that Moscow and Jerusalem
could work toward a political settlement, but serious
and probably insurmountable problems would persist.
The role to be played by the PLO is bound to be controversial, and both Hussein and Assad (who represent
minority Bedouin and Alawite communities) would have
difficulty withstanding the domestic backlash against
a peace agreement with Israel. Hussein's grandfather
Abdullah was assassinated for his overtures to Israel,
and the fate of Sadat after his conclusion of a peace
treaty is well known to all. Hussein would have an
additional fear if a Palestinian state, or Palestinian-
Jordanian confederation, was established as he could
anticipate a challenge to his government similar to
that which took place in 1970-71.

     Rarely considered is the role of monarchical oil
producers such as Saudi Arabia, Kuwait, Bahrein, Qatar
and the United Arab Emirates. They prefer the status
quo and would do little to encourage a settlement.
They now fund the PLO and frontline Arab states, and
thereby receive in return a commitment to their own
security. Once their aid is no longer needed to confront Israel, and the Jewish state ceases to be the
prime target of Arab radicalism, they can expect the
fomentation of insurgencies against their conservative
brand of rule and attacks on their oil facilities.

     The prospects for change in the Soviet-Israeli

relationship must be highly speculative due to the
fluidity of the situation. The replacement of
Chernenko by a younger Soviet leader could have major
foreign policy consequences if an effort is made to
renew detente and acquire Western credits and technology. Similarly, a clear-cut victory by the Labor
Alignment in Israel would dramatically alter that
country's perception of a peace settlement. The overthrow or death of either Assad or Hussein would also
strongly influence ties between Moscow and Jerusalem,
as would the unification of the PLO or a deterioration
in Israeli-American relations. Other possibilities
to consider are greater political assertion by Soviet
Jewish emigrees in Israel or by Soviet Moslems (who
constitute one-sixth of the population), and a rise in
Soviet Jewish dissent. Of course, events in problematic Lebanon are closely intertwined and must be taken
into account.

Tying the Knot Again

If either the Soviet Union or Israel would like
to seek the restoration of full diplomatic relations,
the first step would be to send appropriate signals.
They must be subtle, especially from the Israeli
side, as direct statements by the Jerusalem government
in the past have had no effect. The Soviets correctly
interpreted them as efforts to irritate the United
States, or as salvos in the domestic political struggle. If Israel wants to make a serious attempt to
renew relations, it could respond favorably to some
new suggestion in a Soviet peace plan, offer the Soviet
Union a role in diplomatic negotiations, tone down
official statements regarding Soviet Jews, act lenient-
ly toward RAKAH, or agree to more low-level non-official contacts. For the Soviets, some practical signals
would be to include more members of the ruling coalition in delegations invited to Moscow, issue a statement supporting Israel's right to be a member of the
United Nations, organize direct flights to Israel for
some Soviet Jewish emigrees, express backing for
Israel's right of access to (or sovereignty over) holy
places in East Jerusalem as part of a final peace
settlement, send a peace plan to the Israeli government
rather than issue it through the media, and to have
Chernenko denounce Soviet anti-Semitism. The Soviets
could also develop more official contacts with Israel
rather than work through RAKAH, Victor Louis or East
European intermediaries. For example, they can request
a meeting at the ministerial level or help arrange for
the foreign ministers of the two states to confer when
in the same city, as had been agreed upon in 1973 but
not consistently implemented.

The complete renewal of diplomatic relations is
unlikely unless related to progress in comprehensive
peace negotiations. Therefore, one would generally
anticipate a gradual resumption based on passage
through preliminary stages. There are now indications
that Israel is willing to try this approach, so a
significant step would be the assignment of Israeli
and Soviet consular officials to work within the Dutch
and Finnish embassies in Moscow and Tel Aviv. Cultural exchanges could also be worked out, and mutual
athletic competitions could take place in both countries. Presently, Soviet and Israeli athletes frequently perform in the same international meets, but
only in third countries. This pattern could have been
altered by Israeli participation in the Moscow
Olympics, but Israel boycotted the games. Soviet and
Israeli basketball teams play in the same European
league, and meet each other regularly on neutral
courts, but they do not play home games with each
other as do all the other teams. Tourism by Soviet
citizens to non-communist states is severly restricted,
but Israelis are inveterate travelers and many would
like to visit the Soviet Union. Some tours could
therefore be arranged, with the Israelis agreeing not
to use the opportunity to proselytize Soviet Jews or
pass out literature to them. Some trade ties could be
reestablished, but Israel would want some guarantee
that the Soviet Union will not attempt to void contracts, as in 1956, through the application of the
principle of "force majeure."

If official relations were to be resumed after a
gradual transition period, some serious problems would
remain. Each state would fear that the other was
using its diplomatic presence to engage in covert
activities: the Israelis to contact Jewish dissidents
and the Soviets to gather intelligence information on
American military equipment and plans of the Israeli
armed forces. An Israeli embassy in Moscow could
also serve as a de facto cultural center for Soviet
Jews, and Israeli diplomats could encourage emigration.
A Soviet embassy in Tel Aviv (or perhaps Ramat Gan
again) could serve to embarrass the Israelis if large
numbers of Soviet Jewish emigrees apply to return to
their homeland. Another issue to consider is whether
restored relations will have any permanence. The
Soviets broke relations twice in the past, so what
will prevent them from acting likewise at some time
in the future? The answer may lie in a linkage
established between Soviet-Israeli ties and steps to
be carried out by Israel in the implementation of a
comprehensive peace settlement. Soviet diplomatic
whims would then be effectively constrained.

It has been argued that the Soviet Union and

Israel have a diplomatic disadvantage vis-a-vis the United States and Arab states. The U.S. is assured of Israeli dependence upon it, so it can safely cater Arab support. Arab states know that the Soviet Union sides with them against Israel, so they can make overtures to the U.S.5 Soviet-Israeli relations would therefore tend to help both parties, but does either state really favor this course? Israel would gain by establishing more contact with Soviet Jews, reducing the degree of American political pressure, and leading the Soviet Union to adopt a less stridently anti-Israeli position in the United Nations and other international forums. Ties to Moscow would also snowball. Other communist-ruled states, and some Third World countries, would surely follow suit, thereby serving to overcome Israel's diplomatic isolation.[6] On the other hand, the Soviet Union would probably become more active in Middle East negotiations and would expand its contacts with RAKAH, the PLO, and Arabs in the occupied territories. Israel also has to be concerned about the reaction of the United States. Its own role as a strategic asset would decline, so would the U.S. continue to supply military and economic assistance at the same level? While U.S. officials may relish the expected friction between Moscow and the Arabs should Soviet-Israeli relations be renewed, they will surely have mixed feelings should Israel become a less valuable ally.

Diplomatic relations would permit the Soviet Union to have another listening post in the Middle East, and to acquire much more reliable data about Israel. They would also tend to assist the Soviet effort to be a participant in negotiations, thus undercutting the American diplomatic advantage. The Soviets certainly realize that the absence of relations with Israel since 1967 has served American interests, just as the lack of relations with South Africa permitted the U.S. to play an influential role in negotiations pertaining to Zimbabwe and Namibia. However, the Soviets would have to consider the repercussions of an Arab backlash. Logistic facilities may be lost, and Syria and the PLO may move closer to the United States.7 The Arabs would surely be chagrined that the diplomatic isolation of Israel that they had strived to achieve for decades would be undermined by their supposed champion, the Soviet Union.

Assuming that both Moscow and Jerusalem opt to work toward the establishment of relations, there is still the problem of image. Israel considers itself the aggrieved party and has always insisted that the first step be taken by the Soviet Union. The Soviet Union has maintained that it cannot move toward the renewal of ties unless Israel withdraws from occupied

Arab territories. Some room for compromise therefore
exists if Israel indeed returns some Arab land as part
of a peace settlement. The most practical procedure
would be for Israel to make the concession that trade,
cultural and consular relations could be developed in
the initial stage, and then the Soviet Union could more
easily request the resumption of full diplomatic
relations.

Toward a Political Solution

Soviet-Israeli relations are bound to be affected
by any Arab-Israeli peace settlement and by the role
that the Soviet Union plays in negotiating and
guaranteeing it. The Soviets are extremely concerned
about the process of a settlement as they have been
left out of peace talks since the Geneva conference
of December 1973. They therefore reject the step-by-
step approach, which in the past has been dominated
by the United States, and advocate a comprehensive
peace conference in which they will be assured of a
role. To a great degree, Soviet participation is
dependent upon the willingness of the United States
and Israel to include it. To help force the issue,
the Soviets have to show that while they are incapable
of producing a peace settlement on their own, they can
surely obstruct one from which they are excluded. Ties
to the PLO, arming of Arab states, and endorsement of
some radical Arab demands are therefore functional
toward this end. In fact, the Soviet Union is more
essential to a settlement when the risk of war is
greatest or when a major superpower confrontation has
just been narrowly avoided, as in 1973.8 Of course,
Israel and the United States are not anxious to accept
the Soviet Union as a participant in negotiations, and
they lean toward step-by-step diplomacy. If the
Soviets are to ensure themselves of a role, they will
probably have to be in a position to offer some substantial Arab concessions to Israel. Otherwise, a
comprehensive peace conference is unlikely. Even
Syria may be induced into joining separate talks on the
Golan Heights if they are part of broader negotiations
dealing with Lebanon as well.
Developing an appropriate initiative for peace
talks is a complicated issue. The United States and
Soviet Union usually react negatively to each other's
plans, and Israel objects to Soviet plans or those produced jointly by the superpowers. Israel also opposes
UN sponsorship, and Arab and Israeli plans will not
produce a positive response from the opposite party.
The first step could therefore be informal and indirect with Rumania, for example, serving as a broker.
Secret diplomacy between the United States and PLO, as

well as leftist Israelis and the PLO, could also precede formal negotiations as the emphasis will be on
ground rules rather than substantive issues. Once
official negotiations begin, there is really no need
for any specific plan to serve as a basis of discussions. Procedural questions are most fundamental at
this stage, and the presentation of remedies for
particular problems can be made later by the
participants.

Israel, as the strongest military power and occu-
pier of Arab land, would prefer direct talks with
individual Arab states. The latter would like to pool
their strength to confront the Israelis, and to deal
with Israel in the context of a large conference where
negotiations may be considered indirect. Arab states
would also like to include additional participants
since they may be at a disadvantage in facing Israel
alone. Some American pressure on Israel would be most
helpful to their cause. The superpowers would prefer
indirect discussions so that their own role would be
enhanced, but would probably have to accede to the
Israelis on the establishment of smaller working groups
in which Israel could negotiate directly with the
Arabs. A broad conference overcomes some obstacles in
that American officials can talk to members of the PLO
(which they are unable to do bilaterally due to a
pledge to Israel) and the Arabs can negotiate with the
Israelis. Individual Arab governments fear that
acceptance of Israel's legitimacy through diplomatic
contact will produce domestic turmoil, so a multi-
lateral approach at such a conference would better
serve their interests.9

In regard to specific terms of an Arab-Israeli
peace settlement, the differences between the Soviet
and Israeli positions are not great and may be overcome as long as the Soviet Union is included as a
participant in negotiations, receives some of the
credit for the solution, and plays a role in guaranteeing the agreement. The Soviets and Israelis could
probably concur on arms limitations, demilitarized
zones (although Israel does not want peacekeeping
forces on its side of the border), navigational rights
in the Straits of Tiran and Suez Canal, and conclusion
of a peace agreement or treaty (although the Soviets
favor only a declaration ending the state of war).
The territorial settlement should be somewhat more
problematic. The Soviets would agree to a staged
Israeli withdrawal, but would press for an evacuation
of all occupied Arab lands. One way to achieve a
compromise on the latter point would be to recognize
the pre-June 1967 borders as legitimate, but permit
Israel to establish a security zone extending beyond
its borders. Another solution would be for Israel to

annex some Arab territory, but then include it in its
demilitarized zone.

The Palestinian problem is surely the most vex-
ing. Assuming that the PLO can agree upon its own
unified delegation, that PLO participation at a conference may be arranged through a staged agenda or PLO
merger into a joint Arab or Jordanian delegation, and
that the PLO and Israel agree to some form of mutual
recognition, many other issues would still remain un-
resolved. Israel, especially under a Labor government,
may be prepared to relinquish the West Bank as it
presents serious demographic and security challenges,
but Israel is unlikely to accept an independent
Palestinian state.10 The Soviet Union constantly re-
fers to the Palestinians' "right" to statehood, but
this is not an absolute endorsement of the creation
of such a state and does not completely preclude other
options.11 A middle ground would be an autonomous
West Bank whose permanent status as an independent
state, or part of a federation with Jordan, could be
determined in a future plebiscite. Autonomy would
probably be under the aegis of the United Nations,
surely not Israel, even though former prime minister
(and current foreign minister) Shamir has claimed that
the Israeli version of West Bank autonomy is similar
to that practiced in regions of the Soviet Union.12
As far as the refugee issue is concerned, the Soviets
would probably be amenable to a solution that permitted return to the West Bank rather than Israel as
they have left it unclear whether return to Israel or
the territory of the Palestine mandate is the goal.

How will a peace settlement be guaranteed? Israel
would like to minimize the importance of guarantees
through the dilineation of secure boundaries, the
establishment of demilitarized zones, and the implementation of an agreement on the limitation of arms deliveries to the area. Israel has little faith in UN
or superpower guarantees as UN troops quickly withdrew
from the Sinai in 1967, and the United States failed
to live up to a commitment to keep the Straits of
Tiran open to Israeli navigation. The UN would probably not be given a major role as guarantor, but it
could still provide observers or peacekeeping forces
to serve on the Arab side of common boundaries. The
superpowers would have to stand squarely behind a
settlement, but Israel would not trust a Soviet
guarantee to restrain the Arabs or defend Israel's
borders. An American guarantee to Israel, accompanied
by a Soviet one to the Arabs would only heighten
superpower tension.13 Nevertheless, some superpower
recognition of the inviolability of Israel's borders
would be a necessary component of a political solution.
Soviet and American troops would not have to be

stationed in the area, but the superpowers individual-
ly would have to pledge to defend Israel's borders from
attack even though this may mean in practice that only
the United States would be counted upon to do so. The
Soviet Union and United States could also promise not
to veto the deployment of UN peacekeeping forces, nor
advocate their removal without the consent of Israel
and the relevant Arab state along a common border.
The Soviet Union could additionally endorse Israel's
right to UN membership and agree to renew diplomatic
relations without the possibility of severance for a
minimum number of years (perhaps ten).

A peace settlement between Israel and the Arab
states can serve the interests of both sides if its
terms are worked out carefully. However, countervailing external forces could work against a settlement.
The Soviet Union would no longer be able to rally the
Arabs against the United States by stressing the Arab-
Israeli and Palestinian issues, and the United States
would receive less support form Israel in the areas
of intelligence and military technology. Israel
would also decline in importance as a strategic ally
that could provide logistic facilities, or even troops.
Conservative Arab monarchies would become fearful that
a radicalized Palestinian state could spread revolution, initially to Jordan and then to other states in
the Arabian peninsula.

On the other hand, the Soviet Union could be
attracted to a political solution as some trends have
favored the Arabs since 1973: Israel has become more
isolated diplomatically, the Arabs, have developed
the oil weapon, and the United States has applied pressure to Israel on several occasions.14 The Soviets
would also like to terminate the American opportunity
to serve as Middle Eastern mediator, and to secure a
role in effecting and guaranteeing a settlement. The
United States would hope to remove an obstacle to
furthering relations with the Arabs, and to secure
access to oil supplies. It could also believe the
time ripe for a settlement favorable to Israel as the
Jewish state enjoys a strong territorial advantage
after having annexed East Jerusalem, extended its law
into the Golan Heights, encouraged settlement of the
West Bank, and having occupied a portion of southern
Lebanon. The conservative monarchies could be induced
to support a settlement if they are afforded influence
through the disbursal of aid and investment capital to
the West Bank and frontline Arab states. A peace
solution guaranteeing substantial Islamic rights in
East Jerusalem, and demilitarizing any incipient
Palestinian state, would be especially alluring.

Permutations

The future of Soviet-Israeli relations will be dependent on internal politics in the two states, the parameters of superpower interaction, and the resolution of the issue of Soviet Jewish emigration. The transition of power in the Soviet Union from Chernenko to younger Politburo associates could lead to a moderation of foreign policy and efforts to restore detente. Fostering economic development would be the main goal, but improved ties to Israel may emerge as a byproduct. Moscow is likely to make overtures to Jerusalem in order to assist its rapprochement with the United States and the renewal of detente could further the Arab-Israeli peace process. The Soviets would then tend to become more cordial to the Israelis in order to be included in negotiations. Although it is difficult to ascertain the policy positions of specific Soviet political leaders, it is interesting to note that some who appeared to be particularly anti-Israeli (Suslov, Kirilenko, Pelshe) are no longer members of the Politburo as a result of death or retirement. In addition, powerful Central Committee secretary Boris Ponomarev will soon be eighty and his post could possibly pass into the hands of a successor less hostile to Israel.15 In Israel, a Labor-controlled government would be more amenable to compromise on territorial issues and acceptance of the Soviets at the negotiating table. However, it would have more difficulty than the LIKUD in selling such positions to the Israeli public. The most dramatic change in the Israeli political arena would be the election of a majority government not dependent on coalition partners. Whichever party acquires such predominance would be able to move more boldly toward a political solution, thus improving relations with the Soviet Union in the process.

If the superpowers again seek to establish detente, they may make an effort to negotiate an Arab-Israeli peace settlement. A further improvement in Sino-American relations may accelerate Soviet movement in that direction. The United States, which is especially cautious prior to presidential elections, would be more attracted to such a course should Reagan be elected to a second term. Should Reagan lose, Mondale would be expected to act within his first two years in office so that his reelection chances would not suffer irreparably should he fail. Assuming that the Soviet Union and United States do strive for a political solution in the Middle East, an improvement in Soviet-Israeli relations and some deterioration in Israeli-American relations would be anticipated. Israel would try to gain leverage over the U.S. through its contacts

with the Soviet Union, and would try to undermine
detente to protect itself against superpower collusion.

As detente has receded in recent years, Soviet
Jewish emigration had declined dramatically. Israel's
stressing of its role as an American strategic asset
is based on a recognition of these trends but, con-
versely, Israel will have to downplay its anti-Soviet
logistic posture if it hopes to secure the renewal of
mass emigration. In the past, detente and the exodus
of Jews were closely related. Now the issue of Soviet
Jewry is possibly becoming linked to that of an Arab-
Israeli territorial settlement. The Soviets have
supplied some hints in this regard, while the Israelis
have remained silent. Some symmetry is evident as
the Soviets hold the upper hand on emigration, and the
Israelis derive negotiating strength through their
occupation of Arab territory. A trade-off is indeed
possible, and was even suggested by an anonymous
Israeli Cabinet member in 1976. He proposed that Israel
return part of the Golan Heights to Syria in exchange
for Syrian promises to desist from using force against
Israel and to extend the mandate of UN peacekeeping
units, plus a Soviet commitment to permit 40,000 Jews
to leave annually over a four-year period.16 Israel
may display increased interest in such an approach if
superpower detente does not return shortly. On the
other hand, its enthusiasm for Soviet Jewish emigration
may have been dampened by the high "dropout" rate in
recent years.

If detente is resurrected, the Soviets may open
the exit doors to more Jews in order to gain good will
in the United States. They are particularly likely
to embark on such a course if they need American
credits to help overcome a severe hard currency de-
ficit. During the period 1976-78, when the Soviet
ledger was seriously imbalanced, gold reserves were
reduced through foreign sales and Jewish emigration
was increased to influence the U.S. to offer economic
concessions. If such a policy is reinstituted, emigration will be less of an economic burden for the Soviet
Union than previously as growing discrimination has
kept Jews out of advanced technical positions. Also,
it is possible that liberal economic reforms implemented by a new Soviet regime may enhance the quality
of life and seriously weaken the incentive to emigrate.
If this should take place, the Soviet Union may be
more willing to restore diplomatic relations with
Israel as the presence of Israeli diplomats in Moscow
would be less threatening in regard to proselytization
among Jews.

The Soviet Union and Israel have been estranged
since 1967, but some contacts have always been maintained. Bitterness, disappointment and aloofness

characterize their relationship, but neither party has
sought a complete divorce. Israel is not likely to do
so in the future as it is concerned about the fate of
Soviet Jews and needs to balance its ties to the
United States to avoid domination by Washington. The
Soviet Union could be tempted if such a step was necessary to uphold Moscow's stature in the Arab world. A
continuing stalemate on a territorial settlement, or
military action taken by Israel as an American
strategic ally, could force the Soviets into such a
position and they would then cut all ties to Israel
and seek its expulsion from the United Nations and
other international organizations. Divorce, as a
condition of permanent alienation, would therefore be
unilateral from the Soviet side, rather than mutual.
It would also seriously damage Soviet relations with
the United States.

Reconciliation, signified by the resumption of
diplomatic relations, would probably not take place
unless progress was made toward a political settlement
of the Arab-Israeli conflict. The Soviet Union would
most likely agree to trade, cultural or consular
contacts somewhat earlier, but not the renewal of
official ties. The Soviets would not risk offending
the Arabs by counteracting their campaign to isolate
Israel diplomatically, especially prior to peace
talks.17 Arab bargaining power would be undermined
as the Soviet Union would be needed as an advocate
of the Arab cause, not as a somewhat neutralized
broker with an embassy in Tel Aviv. Consequently,
Moscow faces constraints in its ability to woo Israel
again, while Jerusalem can be a more ardent suitor.
Neither prefers a passionate romance, but a pragmatic
reconciliation is not out of the question if a new
Arab-Israeli peace initiative ever make some headway.

Notes

Chapter 1

1. Nahum Goldmann, Yisrael Lean (Jerusalem: Schocken, 1976), p. 45.
2. Yitzhak David in Beeretz Yisrael (November 1981) :37 and Jerusalem Post, June 13, 1983, p.8.
3. Edward Sheehan, The Arabs, Israelis and Kissinger (New York: Reader's Digest Press, 1976), p.71; Marvin Kalb and Bernard Kalb, Kissinger (Boston: Little, Brown, 1974),p.516; and Riyadh home service, September 22, 1975 (BBC, Summary of World Broadcasts, 4, no. 5015, September 24, 1975) :A1.
4. Marie Syrkin, ed., Golda Meir Speaks Out (London: Weidenfeld and Nicolson, 1973), p. 239.
5. Haaretz, November 22, 1981, p.3.
6. Bernard Reich, Quest for Peace (New Bruwnswick: Transaction, 1977), p.98.
7. Cyrus Sulzberger, An Age of Mediocrity (New York:Macmillan, 1973), p. 608.
8. See John Armstrong, "Soviet Foreign Policy and Anti-Semitism," in Academic Committee on Soviet Jewry, Perspectives on Soviet Jewry (New York:Ktav, 1971), p. 74; Aryeh Yodfat, "Hayehudim Sovetiim Kegorem Beyachase Brit Hamoatsot-Yisrael," Gesher, 24, nos. 92-93 (Spring-Summer 1978):104 and Nadav Safran, "The Soviet Union and Israel: 1947-1969," in Ivo Lederer and Wayne Vucinich, eds., The Soviet Union and the Middle East (Stanford:Hoover Institution Press, 1974), p. 157.
9. Mikhail Agursky, "Russian Neo-Nazism--A Growing Threat," Midstream, XXII, no. 2 (February 1976):37. For a discussion of Soviet media attacks on Zionism, see Zvi Gitelman, "Moscow and the Soviet Jews: A Parting of the Ways," Problems of Communism, XXIX, no.1 (January-February 1980):25-29.
10. Armstrong, op.cit., p.74.
11. Michael Brecher, The Foreign Policy System of Israel (London: Oxford University Press, 1972), pp. 38-39.

12. Yodfat, op.cit., p. 103.

13. Brecher, op.cit., p. 236.

14. See Rashid Khalidi, "Soviet-Arab Relations," Arab Perspective, 4 (November-December 1983):20-21.

15. Jerry Hough, Soviet Leadership in Transition (Washington: Brookings Institution, 1980), p.113.

16. See Dina Spechler, Internal Influences on Soviet Foreign Policy: Elite Opinion and the Middle East, Research Paper No. 18, Soviet and East European Research Centre (Jerusalem: Hebrew University, December 1976); Ilana Kass, Soviet Involvement in the Middle East: Policy Formulation, 1966-73 (Boulder: Westview, 1978); and Ilana Diamant-Kass, "The Soviet Military and Soviet Policy in the Middle East 1970-73," Soviet Studies, XXVI, no. 4 (October 1974):502-521.

17. Cairo, MENA, April 20, 1970 and Jerusalem Domestic Service, April 21, 1970 (FBIS, MEA, V, no.77, April 21, 1970):H2-3.

18. London, Reuters, June 25, 1971 (FBIS,MEA,V, no. 124, June 28, 1971).

19. Haaretz, September 23, 1973, p.2.

20. Maariv, September 1, 1968.

21. Zo Haderech, January 28, 1969, p. 9.

22. Jerusalem Domestic Service, June 30, 1971 (FBIS,MEA,V, no.75, April 17, 1971):N4.

23. Jewish Observer and Middle East Review, XVII, no. 26 (June 28, 1968):7.

24. Jerusalem Domestic Service, August 26, 1973 (FBIS,MEA,V, no. 168, August 29, 1973):H2.

Chapter 2

1. J. B. Schechtman, "The U.S.S.R., Zionism, and Israel," in Lionel Kochan, ed., The Jews in Soviet Russia Since 1917, third edition (London: Oxford University Press, 1978), pp. 121-22.

2. Ibid., pp. 121-22; Jacob Hen-Tov, "Contacts Between Soviet Ambassador Maisky and Zionist Leaders During World War II," Soviet Jewish Affairs, 8, no. 1 (1968) :51; and Yaacov Ro'i, Soviet Decision Making in Practice (New Brunswick: Transaction, 1980) p.17.

3. Boris Smolar, Soviet Jewry Today and Tomorrow (New York: Macmillan, 1971), pp. 129-30.

4. Martin Ebon, "Communist Tactics in Palestine," The Middle East Journal, 2, no.3 (July 1948): 262-63 and Arnold Krammer, The Forgotten Friendship: Israel and the Soviet Bloc, 1947-53 (Urbana: University of Illinois Press, 1974), pp. 34-39.

5. M.S. Agwani, Communism in the Arab East (London: Asia Publishing House, 1969), p. 42.

6. Mohammed Heikal, The Sphinx and the Commissar (New York: Harper and Row, 1978), p. 52. For an Arab perspective on Soviet-Israeli collaboration, see Fayez Sayegh, Communism in Israel (New York: Arab Information Center, May 1948).

7. See Yaacov Ro'i, "Soviet Policies and Attitudes Toward Israel, 1948-1978--An Overview," Soviet Jewish Affairs, 8, no. 1 (1978):36; Krammer, op.cit., p. 51; and Avigdor Dagan, Moscow and Jerusalem (London: Abelard-Schuman, 1970), pp. 20-22.

8. Nahum Goldmann, Yisrael Lean (Jerusalem: Schocken, 1976), p. 44.

9. Israeli Foreign Policy Document 447, discussed by Yaacov Ro'i in Shvut, no. 9 (1982) :108-10.

10. Smolar, op.cit., pp.137-38.

11. Communist representation in the Knesset did not fluctuate very much, numbering 5 seats in the election of 1951, 6 in 1955, 3 in 1959, and 5 in 1961.

12. Maariv, January 28, 1972.

13. Pravda, September 21, 1948.

14. Mordechai Namir, Shlichut Bemoskva (Tel Aviv: Oved, 1971), p. 109.

15. Schechtman, op.cit., p.124.

16. Ro'i, Soviet Decision Making in Practice, op. cit., p. 344.

17. Aryeh Yodfat, "Hayehudim Sovetiim Kegorem Beyachasei Brit Hamoatsot-Yisrael," Gesher, 24, nos.92-93 (Spring-Summer 1978):104.

18. See Walter Eytan, The First Ten Years (New York: Simon and Schuster, 1958), pp. 140-41.

19. Haaretz, October 2, 1981 and Michael Brecher, Decisions in Israel's Foreign Policy (London: Oxford University Press, 1974), pp. 122 and 130.

20. Chana Zemer, "Yeadim Benleumim Bazira Habenleumit," Skira Chodshit (June 1973):46.

21. See Franz Borkenau, "Was Malenkov Behind the Anti-Semitic Plot?," Commentary, 15, no. 5 (May 1953): 439-45 and Paul Lendvai, "Jews Under Communism," Commentary, 52, no. 6 (December 1971):72-73.

22. See the account of Razin in Maariv, July 22, 1983.

23. Ibid.

24. Gideon Rafael, Besod Leumim (Tel Aviv: Edanim Publishers, 1981), p. 41.

25. Ro'i, Soviet Decision Making in Practice, op. cit., p. 477 and Benjamin Pinkus, "The Emigration of National Minorities from the USSR in the Post-Stalin Era," Soviet Jewish Affairs, 13, no. 1 (February 1983): 10.

26. Arthur Jay Klinghoffer, The Soviet Union and International Oil Politics (New York: Columbia University Press, 1977), pp. 149-50.

27. Dagan, op.cit., p. 83.

28. Yaacov Ro'i, ed., From Encroachment to Involvement (New York: John Wiley, 1974), pp. 163-65.

29. Judd Teller, The Kremlin, the Jews and the Middle East (New York: Thomas Yoseloff, 1957), pp.170-71.

30. Rais Khan, "Israel and the Soviet Union: A Review of Postwar Relations," Orbis, IX, no. 4 (Winter 1966):1011.

31. Meron Medzini, ed., Israel's Foreign Relations: Selected Documents, 1947-1974, Vol. I (Jerusalem: Ministry for Foreign Affairs, 1976), p. 557.

32. Dagan, op.cit., p. 133 and Surendra Bhutani, Israeli-Soviet Cold War (Delhi: Atul Prakashan, 1975), p. 85.

33. New Outlook, I, no. 6 (January 1958): 11.

34. On this last point, see Jewish Observer and Middle East Review, XXVI, no. 39 (September 29, 1977):9.

35. Jerusalem Post, March 26, 1978, p. 7 and Smolar, op.cit., pp. 213-14.

Chapter 3

1. Zo Haderech, April 28, 1966, p. 1; Jerusalem Post, January 13, 1966, p.3; Jewish Observer and Middle East Review, XVI, no. 6 (February 10, 1967):3; and Henry Christman, ed., The State Papers of Levi Eshkol (New York: Funk and Wagnalls, 1969).

2. See New Outlook, 9, no.7 (September 1966):12 and Jewish Observer and Middle East Review, XVI, no.7 (February 17, 1967):8-9.

3. Yosef Govrin, Israel-Soviet Relations: 1964-1966, Research Paper No. 29, Soviet and East European Research Centre (Jerusalem: Hebrew University, 1978), p.41 cites Za Rubezhom, no. 46, December, 1965. See also Ze'ev Katz, "A Change in Soviet-Israel Relations?," New Outlook, 7, no.3 (March-April 1964):6-10.

4. Esther Wilenska, "A Major Issue for the Working People of Israel," World Marxist Review, 7, no. 1 (January 1964):23-28.

5. Meir Wilner, "Present Developments in Israel," World Marxist Review, 10, no. 4 (April 1967):24.

6. Katz, op.cit., p.3.

7. Pravda, May 6, 1965, and September 5, 1965.

8. See Jews in Eastern Europe, III, no.4 (June 1966):57 and Govrin, op.cit., pp.38-39.

9. Ibid., p. 43.

10. "Comments of an Israeli Journalist," New Times, no. 46 (November 15, 1965):24-25.

11. New Times, no. 11 (March 16, 1966);22-23.

12. In January 1966, the Soviet Union successfully negotiated a peace agreement between India and Pakistan in the Soviet city of Tashkent.

13. Aryeh Yodfat, "Yachasei Brit Hamoatsot-Yisrael Mimot Stalin ad Milchemet Sheshet Hayamim, "Shvut, no.1 (1973):117.

14. Avigdor Dagan, Moscow and Jerusalem (London: Abelard-Schuman, 1970),p. 163. Similarly, Director of the Middle East Department of the Foreign Ministry Aleksandr Shchiborin told the Israeli charge d'affaires: "So long as you continue your activities among the Jews

there will be no improvement in our relations. Stop it, because this question is the main obstacle to an improvement of relations." See ibid., pp. 163-64.

15. Izvestiia, March 12, 1967
16. See Benjamin Pinkus, "The Emigration of National Minorities from the U.S.S.R. in the Post-Stalin Era," Soviet Jewish Affairs, 13, no. 1 (February 1983): 27-28 and Leonard Schroeter, The Last Exodus (Jerusalem: Weidenfeld and Nicolson, 1974), p. 351.
17. Jews in Eastern Europe, III, no. 6 (May 1967):15.
18. Ibid., no. 2 (May 1965): 14-29 and no. 4 (June 1966):50-56.
19. Yaacov Ro'i, "Soviet Policies and Attitudes Toward Israel, 1948-1978--An Overview," Soviet Jewish Affairs, 8, no. 1 (1978):42.
20. Yosef Govrin, "Peilutam shel Diplomatim Yisraelim Bekerev Yahadut Brit Hamoatsot Biri Haitonut Bashanim 1964-66," Shvut, no. 8 (1980):68.
21. Mohammed Heikal, The Sphinx and the Commissar (New York: Harper and Row, 1978) p. 155.
22. See New York Times, June 2, 1965, p.5.
23. Izvestiia., September 6, 1966, p.5.
24. Ibid., February 24, 1967, p. 6.
25. Ibid., January 12, 1967, p.5.
26. Both factions were called MAKI at this time but, for the sake of clarity, the faction that eventually formed the RAKAH party will be designated as RAKAH.
27. Yehuda Lahav, The Soviet Attitude Toward the Split in the Israeli Communist Party, 1964-1967, Research Paper No. 39, Soviet and East European Research Centre (Jerusalem: Hebrew University, June 1980):16-17.
28. Arie Hauslich, "What Future for the Communists?," Jewish Observer and Middle East Review, XIV, no. 33 (August 13, 1965):7.
29. Lahav, op.cit., p. 25.
30. Moshe Gilboa, Shesh Shanim-Shisha Yamim (Tel Aviv:Am Oved, 1968), p. 55.
31. Lahav, op.cit., p. 61.
32. Ibid., pp. 59-60 and Winston Burdett, Encounter With the Middle East (London: Andre Deutsch, 1970), pp. 166-68.
33. Lahav, op.cit., pp. 62-65.
34. Gideon Rafael, Besod Leumim (Tel Aviv: Edanim Publishers, 1981), pp. 117 and 121.
35. World Marxist Review, 6, no. 6 (June 1963): 94-96.
36. See Rafael, op.cit., pp. 111-12.
37. See Pravda, April 26, 1966, pp. 1 and 5.
38. Eliezer Palmor, "Yachasei Brit Hamoatsot-Yisrael," Bechinot, no. 1 (1970):105.

39. See Eliezer Doron, In Watch and Confrontation (Jerusalem:Keter, 1978), p. 27 and Heikal, op.cit., pp. 280-81.

40. Mideast Mirror, 16, no. 21 (May 23, 1964):6.

41. Zo Haderech, April 20, 1966, p. 1.

42. Heikal, op.cit., p. 168.

43. D. Volsky, "Who is Making Trouble in the Arab World?," New Times, no. 42 (October 19, 1966):7-8.

44. Jewish Observer and Middle East Review, XV, no. 49 (December 9, 1966):3.

45. Ibid., XVI, no. 2 (January 13, 1967):3.

46. Ibid., no. 3 (January 20, 1967):4.

47. Ibid., no. 1 (January 6, 1967):4.

48. Ibid., XV, no. 20 (May 20, 1966):4.

49. See Yitzhak Shichor, The Middle East in China's Foreign Policy, 1949-1977 (Cambridge: Cambridge University Press, 1979), p. 117.

50. Lahav, op.cit., p. 45.

51. Jewish Observer and Middle East Review, XV no. 16 (April 22, 1966):5.

52. John Cooley, "China and the Palestinians," Journal of Palestine Studies, I, no. 2 (Winter 1972):26.

53. Ehud Yaari, Strike Terror (New York: Sabra Books, 1970), p. 56.

54. Avraham Ben Tsur, Gormim Sovetiim Lemilchemet Sheshet Hayamim (Tel Aviv: Tsifriyat Hapoalim, 1975), p. 98.

55. Ahmad Chagouri, "Baathist Crimes in Syria," World Marxist Review, 7 no. 5 (May 1964):89 and World Marxist Review, 7 no. 6 (June 1964):54.

56. Khaled Bakdash, "Syria's New Road," ibid., 8, no. 3 (March 1965):4-10. See also Ahmad Chagouri, ibid., 8, no. 2 (February 1965):44; Chagouri, ibid., 8, no. 7 (July 1965):50-51; and Maurice Salibi, ibid., 8, no. 11 (November 1965):54-56.

57. Jewish Observer and Middle East Review, XV, no. 23 (June 10, 1966):3-4.

58. Yaari, op.cit., p. 86.

59. Pravda, May 28, 1966, p. 5.

60. Bamachane, September 12, 1966.

61. Burdett, op.cit., pp. 162-64 and Jewish Observer and Middle East Review, XV, no. 42 (October 21 1966):5.

62. Palmor, op.cit., p. 107 and Jewish Observer and Middle East Review, XV no. 46, (November 18, 1966): 2.

63. Ibid., XVI, no. 6 (February 10, 1967):3.

64. A. Sovetov, "The Soviet Union and Present International Relations," International Affairs, no. 1 (January 1966):5.

65. V. Kudryavtsev, "The Middle East Knot," International Affairs, no. 9 (September 1967):29.

there will be no improvement in our relations. Stop
it, because this question is the main obstacle to an
improvement of relations." See ibid., pp. 163-64.

15. Izvestiia, March 12, 1967
16. See Benjamin Pinkus, "The Emigration of
National Minorities from the U.S.S.R. in the Post-
Stalin Era," Soviet Jewish Affairs, 13, no. 1 (February
1983): 27-28 and Leonard Schroeter, The Last Exodus
(Jerusalem: Weidenfeld and Nicolson, 1974), p. 351.
17. Jews in Eastern Europe, III, no. 6 (May
1967):15.
18. Ibid., no. 2 (May 1965): 14-29 and no. 4
(June 1966):50-56.
19. Yaacov Ro'i, "Soviet Policies and Attitudes
Toward Israel, 1948-1978--An Overview," Soviet Jewish
Affairs, 8, no. 1 (1978):42.
20. Yosef Govrin, "Peilutam shel Diplomatim
Yisraelim Bekerev Yahadut Brit Hamoatsot Biri Haitonut
Bashanim 1964-66," Shvut, no. 8 (1980):68.
21. Mohammed Heikal, The Sphinx and the Commissar
(New York: Harper and Row, 1978) p. 155.
22. See New York Times, June 2, 1965, p.5.
23. Izvestiia., September 6, 1966, p.5.
24. Ibid., February 24, 1967, p. 6.
25. Ibid., January 12, 1967, p.5.
26. Both factions were called MAKI at this time
but, for the sake of clarity, the faction that eventually formed the RAKAH party will be designated as RAKAH.
27. Yehuda Lahav, The Soviet Attitude Toward the
Split in the Israeli Communist Party, 1964-1967,
Research Paper No. 39, Soviet and East European Research Centre (Jerusalem: Hebrew University, June
1980):16-17.
28. Arie Hauslich, "What Future for the Communists?," Jewish Observer and Middle East Review, XIV,
no. 33 (August 13, 1965):7.
29. Lahav, op.cit., p. 25.
30. Moshe Gilboa, Shesh Shanim-Shisha Yamim
(Tel Aviv:Am Oved, 1968), p. 55.
31. Lahav, op.cit., p. 61.
32. Ibid., pp. 59-60 and Winston Burdett,
Encounter With the Middle East (London: Andre Deutsch,
1970), pp. 166-68.
33. Lahav, op.cit., pp. 62-65.
34. Gideon Rafael, Besod Leumim (Tel Aviv:
Edanim Publishers, 1981), pp. 117 and 121.
35. World Marxist Review, 6, no. 6 (June 1963):
94-96.
36. See Rafael, op.cit., pp. 111-12.
37. See Pravda, April 26, 1966, pp. 1 and 5.
38. Eliezer Palmor, "Yachasei Brit Hamoatsot-
Yisrael," Bechinot, no. 1 (1970):105.

85. Haolam Hazeh, September 22, 1976, p. 15.
86. Bar Zohar, op.cit., p. 245. Bar Zohar, Eban and
and other Israelis cite Chuvakhin's messages to Moscow
so it appears that Israel was able to obtain intercept-
ed transcripts of his communications.
87. Israeli radio in Arabic, June 6, 1967 (FBIS,
MEA, no. 109, June 6, 1967):H6.
88. Burdett, op.cit., p. 330.
89. Pravda, June 8, 1967, p. 1.
90. Brecher, Decisions in Crisis, op.cit., p.101.
91. Haolam Hazeh, October 13, 1971, p. 20;
Aronson, op.cit., p. 78; and Brecher, Decisions in
Crisis, op.cit., pp. 261 and 279.
92. Karen Dawisha, Soviet Foreign Policy Toward
Egypt (New York: St. Martins,1979), p. 42.
93. Brecher, Decisions in Crisis, op.cit., p.285
and Abba Eban, Pirkeh Chaim (Tel Aviv: Tsifriyat
Maariv, 1978), p. 418.
94. Pravda, June 11, 1967, p.1.
95. K. S. Karol, "Angry Men in the Kremlin,"
New Statesman (June 16, 1967):820.
96. New York Times, June 11, 1967, p. 32.
97. Yaacov Ro'i ed., From Encroachment to Involvement (New York; John Wiley, 1974), p. 463.
98. See Aryeh Yodfat, "Brit Hamoatsot-Yisrael v
Hasichsuch Haaravi-Yisraeli," Beayot Benleumiot, 17 no.
1 (1978):13.
99. Erwin Weit, Eyewitness (London: Andre
Deutsch, 1973), pp. 139-40.
100. Eban, op.cit., p. 419.
101. See George Heitmann, "Soviet Policy and the
Middle East Crisis," Survey, no. 69 (October 1968):
143-44 and Sal Chaim, "Hasheela Hapalastinait
Umashmauyoteha Hamedinyot," Maarchot, no. 239-8
(August-September 1974):15.
102. See Tsofeh, "Taut Leolam Chozeret," Maarchot,
no. 209 (October 1970):4.
103. "Hartaot Shelo Paalu," op.cit., p. 6.
104. Gilboa, op.cit., p. 23.
105. Haaretz, March 19, 1972 and March 29, 1972.
106. Bar Zohar, op.cit., p. 245.
107. Ben Tsur, op.cit.
108. "Hartaot Shelo Paalu," op.cit., p. 27.
109. Dmitrii Volsky, "East of Suez, "New Times,
no. 18 (April 30, 1967):21 and G. Drambyants, "The
King and the Arabs," ibid., no. 12 (March 22, 1967):22.

Chapter 4

1. See comments by the Israeli Ambassador to
Britain Aharon Remez in Jewish Observer and Middle
East Review, XVI, no. 24 (June 16, 1967): 21 and
W. Byford-Jones, The Lightening War (New York: Bobbs-
Merrill, 1968), p. 190.
2. Haolam Hazeh, September 17, 1969, p.2.
3. William Quandt, Decade of Decisions (Berkeley:
University of California Press, 1977), p. 9.
4. Gideon Rafael, Besod Leumim (Tel Aviv:
Edanim Publishers, 1981), p. 178.
5. Oded Eran, The Soviet Conception of an Arab
Israeli Settlement, Research Paper No. 8, Russian and
East European Research Center (Tel Aviv: Tel Aviv
University, Fall, 1974), p. 3 Eran maintains that
even prior to the war, the Institute of Orientology
of the U.S.S.R. Academy of Sciences prepared a report
for the Central Committee of the Communist Party which
indicated Israel's military superiority over the Arab
states. See ibid., p. 1.
6. Mohammed Heikal, The Road to Ramadan (London:
Collins, 1975), p. 165 and Oded Eran, "Soviet Middle
East Policy, 1967-1973," in Itamar Rabinovich and
Haim Shaked, eds., From June to October: The Middle
East Between 1967 and 1973 (New Brunswick: Transaction,
1978), p. 31.
7. Anwar el-Sadat, In Search of Identity (London:
Collins, 1978), p. 297; Aryeh Yodfat and Yuval Arnon-
Ohanna, PLO Strategy and Tactics (London: Croom, Helm,
1981), p. 84: Hussein of Jordan, as told to Vick
Vance and Pierre Lauer, My "War" With Israel (New
York: William Morrow, 1969), p. 115; and Mohammed
Heikal, The Sphinx and the Commissar (New York:
Harper and Row, 1978), p. 187.
8. Heikal, ibid., pp. 30 and 186.
9. MAKI leader Moshe Sneh claimed that the
Soviet Union wanted Israel to return to the demograph-
ic ratio of the Jewish zone in the 1947 partition,

when Jews only slightly outnumbered Arabs. This would
be accomplished by permitting more than a million
Arab refugees to return to Israel. Furthermore, the
borders would be shifted so that the Arabs would receive much of the Negev desert, creating a land bridge
between Egypt and Jordan. See "The Soviet-Egyptian
'Solution' to the 'Israel Problem'," International
Problems, VII, Nos. 1-2 (May 1969):24-28.

10. Pravda, January 25, 1968.

11. Blema Steinberg, "Superpower Conceptions of
Peace in the Middle East," The Jerusalem Journal of
International Relations, 2, no. 4 (Summer 1977):94.

12. See Davar, June 7, 1968 and Lamerchav,
May 31, 1968.

13. Zeev Schiff, Knafayim Meal Suez (Haifa:
Shikmona, 1970), p. 120.

14. Georges Batal, Amjad Rashad and Mohammed
Harmel, "Vital Tasks of the Arab National Liberation
Movement," World Marxist Review, 11, no. 9 (September
1968): 46.

15. Mikhail Kremnev, "Middle East Detonator,"
New Times, no. 1 (January 1, 1969): 13 and Izvestiia,
July 23, 1968, p. 3.

16. G. Mirsky, "Israeli Aggression: One Year
After," New Times, no. 22 (June 5, 1968): 12-14.

17. Amos Ben-Vered, "Will Russia Intervene?,"
Jewish Observer and Middle East Review, XVII, no. 38
(September 20, 1968):4.

18. See Mideast Mirror, 20, no. 39 (September
28, 1968):4 and 20, no. 40 (October 5, 1968):5.

19. Mirsky, op.cit., p. 14.

20. See Krasnaia Zvezda, November 12, 1968, p. 3
and Pravda, November 27, 1968.

21. Skira Chodshit, November 1968, p. 289; Zo
Haderech, November 6, 1968, p. 8; and Haolam Hazeh,
March 3, 1971, p. 5.

22. Jewish Observer and Middle East Review, XVII,
no. 46 (November 15, 1968): 3 and Zo Haderech,
November 20, 1968.

23. Yitronot Vchesronot Bechidush Hayachasim
Hadiplomatiim Ben Yisrael Ubrit Hamoatsot (Jerusalem:
Leonard Davis Institute, March 1981), p. 31.

24. The text of the Soviet plan appears in
Jewish Observer and Middle East Review, XVIII, no. 4
(January 24, 1969):4.

25. Middle East Record, 1969-70, pp. 22-23.

26. Henry Kissinger, White House Years (Boston:
Little, Brown, 1979), p. 355.

27. See Igor Belyaev, "Middle East Powder Keg,"
New Times, no. 11 (March 19, 1969):7 and Y. Primakov,
"Peace Prospects in the Middle East," International
Affairs, no. 2 (February 1969):49.

28. Heikal, The Sphinx and the Commissar, op.cit.,

p. 193 and Schiff, op.cit., pp. 21 and 43.
    29.   See Middle East Record, 1969-70, p. 421.
    30.   Heikal, The Sphinx and the Commissar, op.
cit., pp. 195-96.
    31.   Middle East Record, 1969-70, p. 20.
    32.   Knesset record, July 9, 1969, Vol. 55,
p. 3496.
    33.   Jerusalem Domestic Service, June 17, 1967
(FBIS, MEA, no. 118, June 19, 1967):H1-2 and Richard
Nixon, The Memoirs of Richard Nixon (New York:
Grosset and Dunlap, 1978), p. 478.
    34.   Kissinger, op.cit., pp. 266, 352, 354 and
371.
    35.   See Yediot Achronot, November 21, 1969.
    36.   Tad Szulc, The Illusion of Peace (New York:
Viking, 1978), p. 91; Meir Ben-Ami, "Chamesh Shanim
Shel Nisyonot Tivuch Basichsuch Haaravi-Yisraeli,"
Skira Chodshit, December 1972, p. 16; and Kissinger,
op.cit., pp. 351, 353 and 360.
    37.   Michael Shafir, Rumanian Policy in the
Middle East, 1967-72, Research Paper No. 7, Soviet and
East European Research Centre (Jerusalem: Hebrew
University, April 1974), p. 53.
    38.   "Matsavam Shel Yehudei Brit-Hamoatsot-
Sikuyehem Lemachar," Gesher, 1-2 (90-91) (October 1977)
1977):194.
    39.   See Haolam Hazeh, December 25, 1968, p. 15;
Jerusalem Radio in Arabic, December 19, 1968 (FBIS,
MEA, V, no. 248, December 20, 1968):H1; and Jerusalem
Post, December 20, 1968, p. 1.
    40.   Zo Haderech, July 24, 1968, pp. 1 and 5.
    41.   Ibid., June 18, 1969, p. 7 and Maariv,
October 10, 1969.
    42.   See Haolam Hazeh, June 18, 1969, p. 5.
    43.   Jerusalem Domestic Service, February 12,
1969 (FBIS, MEA, V. no. 31, February 14, 1969):H7;
Jerusalem Domestic Service, February 16, 1969 (ibid.,
no. 32, February 17, 1969):H7; Jerusalem International
Service in English, February 23, 1969 (ibid., no. 39,
February 27, 1969):H3-4; Zo Haderech, April 6, 1968,
p. 8; and ibid., April 24, 1968, p.9.
    44.   Knesset record, May 28, 1969, Vol. 55,
pp. 2760-61.
    45.   See Zo Haderech, June 28, 1967; July 19,
1967; August 30, 1967; September 11, 1968, October 30,
1968; and Pravda, July 28, 1967, p. 4 and August 3,
1969, p. 5.
    46.   Omer, November 1, 1968, p. 2.
    47.   See Pravda, October 17, 1967, p.5.
    48.   See Moshe Decter, "Hashinui Hanidrash
Batnua Lemaan Yehudei Brit Hamoatsot," Gesher, 1-2
(90-91):(October 1977):130.
    49.   Zo Haderech, March 4, 1970.

50. See Jewish Observer and Middle East Review, XVII, no. 13 (March 29, 1968):3.

51. See Heikal, The Road to Ramadan, op.cit., p. 82.

52. S. Astakhov, "Israeli Expansionism and the Palestinian Refugees," International Affairs, no. 7 (July 1968):45; G. Mirsky, "Israeli Illusions and Miscalculations," New Times, no. 39 (October 2, 1968): 7; and Batal et al, op.cit., pp. 28 and 46.

53. Fahmi Salfiti, "The Situation in Jordan and Communist Tactics," World Marxist Review, 11, nos. 10-11 (October-November 1968):43-46 and Ehud Yaari, Strike Terror, (New York: Sabra Books, 1970), pp. 226-27.

54. Kremnev, op.cit., pp. 12-13; V. Kudriavtsev, "Middle East: Military Situation," New Times, no. 14 (April 9, 1969):15; Robert Freedman, "Soviet Policy Toward International Terrorism," in Yonah Alexander, ed., International Terrorism (New York: Praeger, 1976), pp. 118-19; and Yaari, op.cit., p. 348.

55. Sovetskaia Rossiia, April 15, 1969; Meir Vilner, "The 16th Congress of the Communist Party of Israel," World Marxist Review, 12, no. 5 (May 1969): 17; and Aryeh Yodfat, "Moscow Reconsiders Fatah," The New Middle East, no. 15 (December 1969): 16-17.

56. M. Kruglov, "The Palestine Liberation Movement," New Times, no. 38 (September 24, 1969):13.

57. See Jews in Eastern Europe, 111, no. 9 (May 1968):31-47.

58. Jewish Observer and Middle East Review, XVI, no. 31 (August 4, 1967): 10.

59. A. Ross Johnson, "Poland: End of an Era?," Problems of Communism, XIX, no. 1 (January-February 1970):28-40 and Krasnaia Zvezda, August 17, 1968,p.5.

60. Trybuna Ludu, March 20, 1968 and July 13, 1968 as cited in Survey, no. 68 (July 1968): 116-17.

61. Uri Ra'anan, "Soviet Global Policy and the Middle East, Midstream, XV, no. 5 (May 1969):8-9.

62. See Jewish Observer and Middle East Review, XVI, no. 33 (August 18, 1967): 10-12.

63. Yaacov Ro'i, ed., From Encroachment to Involvement (New York: John Wiley, 1974), p. 490; Jewish Observer and Middle East Review, XVII, no. 34 (August 23, 1968):3-4; ibid., no. 27, July 5, 1968, p.4; ibid., no. 28, July 12, 1968, p.7; and New York Times, June 22, 1968, p. 24.

64. Jewish Observer and Middle East Review, XVII, no. 35 (August 30, 1968): 5 and ibid., no. 36, September 6, 1968, p. 5. See also Peter Pithart, "The Czechoslovak-Israel Parallel," New Outlook, 12, nos. 5-6 (June-August 1969):17-23.

65. Jewish Observer and Middle East Review, XVII, no. 35 (August 30, 1968):5.

66. <u>Al-Ahram</u>, August 30, 1968 cited in <u>Middle East Record, 1968</u>, p. 20.

67. <u>Ibid.</u>, p. 12; <u>Izvestiia</u>, September 3, 1968; and TASS International Service in English, February 18, 1971 (FBIS, SOV, III, no. 34, February 19, 1971): A6-7.

Chapter 5

1.   Henry Kissinger, White House Years (Boston:
Little Brown, 1979), p. 1279. See also M. Yizhar,
"Artsot Habrit Vhazmizrach Hatikhon," Maarchot, no.231
(July 1973):21.

2.   Ibid.

3.   Kissinger, op.cit., p. 1279.

4.   Ibid., pp. 378 and 559.

5.   Haolam Hazeh, January 28, 1970, p. 10; Dan
Margolit, A Cable From the White House (Tel Aviv:
Otpaz, 1971), pp. 51-57; Avi Shlaim and Raymond Tanter,
"Decision, Process, Choice and Consequences: Israel's
Deep-Penetration Bombing in Egypt, 1970," World
Politics, XXX, no. 4 (July 1978): 494; Shlomo Aronson,
Conflict and Bargaining in the Middle East (Baltimore:
the Johns Hopkins University Press, 1978, p. 117; and
Gideon Rafael, Besod Leumim (Tel Aviv: Edanim Publish-
ers, 1981), p. 193.

6.   Mohammed Heikal, The Road to Ramadan (London:
Collins, 1975), pp. 85 and 88.

7.   Knesset record, January 6, 1970, Vol. 56,
p. 403.

8.   Pravda, January 27, 1970, p. 4 and Victor
Laptev, "Middle East Divide," New Times, no. 6
(February 10, 1970):4-6.

9.   See Yitzhak Rabin, The Rabin Memoirs
(Jerusalem: Steimatzky, 1979), pp. 130-31 and
Washington Post, February 4, 1970.

10.   See Dan Shiftan, "Matara Achat-Drachim Rabot,"
Skira Chodshit (June 1973): 23-43.

11.   Moshe Dayan, Story of My Life (London:
Sphere Books, 1976), p. 452. Heikal claims that
SAM-3's did not arrive until April 20, but this is
very unlikely. See op.cit., p. 90.

12.   Izvestiia, March 15, 1970, p. 2 and Yaacov
Ro'i, "The Role of Islam and the Soviet Muslims in
Soviet Arab Policy," Asian and African Studies, 10,
no. 3 (1975):268.

13. Zo Haderech, February 25, 1970, p.4 and Kissinger, op.cit., pp. 568-70.

14. I. Belyaev, "Middle East Crisis and Washington's Manoeuvres," International Affairs, no.4 (April 1970):30-35 and I. Belyaev, "How the Soviet Union Visualises a Middle East Settlement," New Middle East, no. 21 (June 1970): 30-33.

15. Haolam Hazeh, April 1, 1970, p. 11 and Jerusalem Post, March 22, 1970.

16. Aronson, op.cit., p. 120.

17. T. Kolesnichenko, "The USA and the Middle East," International Affairs, no. 7 (July 1970):81.

18. New Middle East, no. 21 (June 1970):19.

19. See Peter Mangold, "The Soviet Record in the Middle East," in Gregory Treverton, ed., Crisis Management and the Super-powers in the Middle East (Westmead: Gower, 1981), p. 90.

20. See Rafael, op.cit., p. 190.

21. Richard Nixon, The Memoirs of Richard Nixon (New York: Grosset and Dunlap, 1978), p. 481.

22. Rafael, op.cit., p. 203.

23. See Shlomo Slonim, United States-Israel Relations, 1967-1973: A Study in Convergence and Divergence of Interests, Jerusalem Papers on Peace Problems, no. 8 (Jerusalem: Leonard Davis Institute, September 1974), pp. 24-25.

24. Maariv, July 10, 1970.

25. Pravda, October 15, 1970.

26. New York Times, June 4, 1970, p. 18; Haaretz, July 5, 1970; and Jewish Observer and Middle East Review, XIX, no. 28 (July 10, 1970):7-8.

27. Knesset record, July 22, 1970, Vol. 58, 2606; ibid., July 15, 1970, Vol. 58, p. 2500; and Jewish Observer and Middle East Review, XIX, no. 29 (July 17, 1970):4.

28. Ibid., p. 4; Zo Haderech, July 22, 1970, p.1; and Jerusalem International Service in English, July 8, 1970 (FBIS, MEA, V, no. 131, July 8, 1970):H2.

29. Jewish Observer and Middle East Review, no. 29, op.cit., pp. 4-5 and Jerusalem Domestic Service, July 9, 1970 (FBIS, MEA, V, no. 133, July 10, 1970):H1.

30. Ehud Yaari, Strike Terror (New York: Sabra Books, 1970), p. 316.

31. See New Middle East, no. 24 (September 1970): 12.

32. Pravda, July 16, 1970, p. 5 and David Morison, "Middle East: The Soviet-UAR Posture," Mizan, XII, no. 1 (October 1970):2-3. An article in New Times maintained that there could be some constructive elements in the "Rogers Plan" so it should not be rejected before its details are known. See S. Bychkov, "Another Political Manoeuvre?" New Times, no. 27

(July 8,1971):17.
33. New Middle East, no. 25 (October 1970):17;
Anwar el-Sadat, In Search of Identity (London:Collins,
1978), pp. 198-99; and Heikal, op.cit., pp. 93-95.
34. Middle East Record, 1969-70, p. 452 and
Haolam Hazeh, August 19, 1970, p. 15.
35. Haaretz, August 21, 1970, p. 1.
36. See Pravda, October 23, 1970, p. 4.
37. Nixon, op.cit., p. 484.
38. Heikal, op.cit., p. 113.
39. Alan Dowty, "The U.S. and the Syria-Jordan
Confrontation, 1970," Jerusalem Journal of International Relations, 3, nos. 2-3 (Winter-Spring 1978):
177-88.
40. Abraham Becker, "The Superpowers in the Arab-
Israeli Conflict, 1970-1973," in Abraham Becker, Bent
Hansen and Malcolm Kerr, The Economics and Politics of
the Middle East (New York: American Elsevier, 1975),
pp. 82-83.
41. William Quandt, "The Arab-Israeli Conflict in
American Foreign Policy," in Itamar Rabinovich and Haim
Shaked, eds., From June to October: The Middle East
Between 1967 and 1973 (New Brunswick: Transaction,
1978), p. 15; Yaacov Ro'i, ed., From Encroachment to
Involvement (New York: John Wiley, 1974), pp.538-40;
Edgar O'Ballance, Arab Guerilla Power, 1967-1972
(London: Archon, 1973), p. 157; John Cooley, "China
and the Palestinians," Journal of Palestine Studies,
I,, no. 2 (Winter 1972):29; and Aronson, op.cit., p.132.
42. Slonim, op.cit., pp. 28-29; Marvin
Feuerwerger, Congress and Israel (Westport: Greenwood,
1979), p. 35; William Quandt, Decade of Decisions
(Berkeley: University of California Press, 1977), p.5;
and Los Angeles Times, November 19, 1970. Israeli
Chief of Staff Chaim Bar-Lev said that the U.S. was
ready to supply Israel with a large quantity of arms
only after it began to confront the Soviet Union in
March 1970. See Skira Chodshit, April 1971.
43. See Jonathan Frankel, The Anti-Zionist Press
Campaigns in the USSR 1969-1971; Political Implications, Research Paper No. 2 (Jerusalem: Soviet and
East European Research Centre, May 1972) and William
Korey, "Myths, Fantasies and Show Trials: Echoes of
the Past," in Academic Committee on Soviet Jewry,
Perspectives on Soviet Jewry (New York: Ktav, 1971),
pp. 42-54.
44. Lukasz Hirszowicz, "The Soviet-Jewish
Problem: Internal and International Developments,
1972-1976," in Lionel Kochan, ed., The Jews in Soviet
Russia Since 1917, third edition (London: Oxford
University Press, 1978), p. 385.
45. Jewish Observer and Middle East Review, XIX,

264

no. 30 (July 24, 1970):12; <u>Middle East Record, 1969-70</u>,
p. 452; and <u>Haolam Hazeh</u>, July 22, 1970, p. 16.
    46. <u>Zo Haderech</u>, September 16, 1970, p. 8.
    47. <u>New York Times</u>, January 22, 1970, p. 11 and
<u>Maariv</u>, January 11, 1970.
    48. See Galia Golan, <u>The Soviet Union and the
Palestine Liberation Organization</u> (New York: Praeger,
1980), p.12.

Chapter 6

1. E. Dmitriev, "Middle East Settlement," International Affairs, no. 12 (December 1970):62.

2. Mordechai Abir, "Ptichat Tealat Suez-Hebeitim Estrategim, "Maarchot, no. 236 (May 1974):10.

3. TASS, January 14, 1971 (Current Digest of the Soviet Press, XXIII, no. 3, February 16, 1971):8.

4. Pravda, January 29, 1971, p.5; Pravda, February 2, 1971, pp. 1 and 4; Radio Moscow in Rumanian, February 5, 1971 (FBIS, SOV, III, no. 26, February 8, 1971):A8; Moscow Domestic Service, February 8, 1971 (ibid., no. 27, February 9, 1971):A14-15; Radio Moscow in Arabic, February 1, 1971 (ibid., no. 22, February 2, 1971): A1-2; Radio Moscow in Arabic, February 2, 1971 (ibid., no. 23, February 3, 1971):A11; TASS International Service in English, February 2, 1971 (ibid., no. 23, February 3, 1971:A12; and Moscow Domestic Service, February 3, 1971 (ibid., no. 23, February 3, 1971):A7.

5. "The Soviet Attitude to the Palestine Problem," Journal of Palestine Studies, II, no. 1 (Autumn 1972): 187-212.

6. Ibid., p. 192.

7. Ibid., p. 191.

8. Yediot Achronot, June 11, 1971; Chana Zemer, "Ma Merits et Artsot Habrit," Skira Chodshit (November 1971):4; Gideon Rafael, Besod Leumin (Tel Aviv: Edanim Publishers, 1981), p. 244; Haolam Hazeh, March 10, 1971, p. 11; and Haaretz, April 1, 1971.

9. Anwar el-Sadat, In Search of Identity (London: Collins, 1978), p. 283-84.

10. Yediot Achronot, June 2, 1971 and June 14, 1971.

11. New York Times, June 1, 1971, p. 3; June 2, 1971, p.9; June 3, 1971, p. 10; and Yediot Achronot, June 11, 1971.

12. Haolam Hazeh, June 30, 1971, p. 14 and Jewish Observer and Middle East Review, XX, No. 27 (July 2, 1971):4.

13. Interview with Simcha Dinitz, July 3, 1983.

14. New York Times, June 29, 1971, p.3; Jewish Observer and Middle East Review, XX, no. 27 (July 2, 1971):1, 4 and 7; and Jerusalem Domestic Service, June 28, 1971 (FBIS, MEA, V, no. 125, June 29, 1971):H1, and interview with Dinitz.

15. Jewish Observer and Middle East Review, XX, no. 27 (July 2, 1971):7; ibid., no. 30, July 23, 1971, p.5; New York Times, June 24, 1971, p.1; Jerusalem Domestic Service, June 21, 1971 (FBIS, MEA, V, no.119, June 21, 1971): H1; and Time, July 5, 1971, p.24.

16. New York Times, July 6, 1971, p.3.

17. Yediot Achronot, June 24, 1971 and New York Times, July 5, 1971, p. 4.

18. See Aryeh Yodfat, "Before October 1973 and After, "New Outlook, 17, no. 9 (November-December 1974):37 and 39.

19. New York Times, June 30, 1971, p. 17. See also ibid., June 26, 1971, p. 2.

20. See Jewish Observer and Middle East Review, XX, no. 27 (July 2, 1971):4 and Zo Haderech, July 14, 1971.

21. Jewish Observer and Middle East Review, XX, no. 42 (October 15, 1971):5; ibid., no. 46, November 12, 1971, p.3; and Knesset record, December 7, 1971, Vol. 62, p. 535.

22. Henry Kissinger, White House Years (Boston: Little, Brown, 1979), pp. 1285-88.

23. Yitzhak Rabin, The Rabin Memoirs (Jerusalem: Steimatzky, 1979), p. 160; Rafael, op.cit., p. 246; and New York Times, September 14, 1971, p.3 and October 12, 1971, p. 10.

24. See Jewish Observer and Middle East Review, XXI, no. 20 (May 19, 1972):4.

25. Radio Peace and Progress in Hebrew to Israel, April 27, 1972 (FBIS, SOV, no. 84, April 28, 1972):85. In 1979, Sadat claimed that, in 1972, the Soviets had asked him to meet with Golda Meir in Tashkent to sign a peace treaty. See Radio Peace and Progress in Arabic, August 8, 1979 (FBIS, SOV, III, no. 157, August 13, 1979):H1.

26. Kissinger, op.cit., p. 1376.

27. John Cooley, "China and the Palestinians," Journal of Palestine Studies, I, no. 2 (Winter 1972): 21.

28. See Lillian Harris, "China's Relations With the PLO," Journal of Palestine Studies, VII, no. 1 (Autumn 1977):140.

29. Haolam Hazeh, March 28, 1972, p. 4.

30. Kissinger, op.cit., pp. 1246-47.

31. Rabin, op.cit., p. 167; Rafael, op.cit., p.245; Jewish Observer and Middle East Review, XXI, no. 34 (August 25, 1972):12; and Simcha Dinitz, "Detente,

Israel and the Middle East," Jerusalem Journal of
International Relations, 5, no. 4 (1981):74-75.

32. Sadat, op.cit., p. 318; Abraham Becker, "The
Superpowers in the Arab-Israeli Conflict, 1970-1973,"
in Abraham Becker, Bent Hansen and Malcolm Kerr, eds.,
The Economics and Politics of the Middle East (New
York: American Elsevier, 1975); p. 83; Radio Moscow
in Arabic, June 15, 1972 (FBIS, SOV, no. 118, June 16,
1972):B2; and TASS in English, July 14, 1972 (FBIS,
SOV, no. 138, July 17, 1972):B3.

33. Israel Home Service, May 24, 1972 (BBC, Summary of World Broadcasts, 4, no. 3999, May 26, 1972):
A3.

34. Sadat, op.cit., pp. 318, 319 and 323.

35. Marvin Kalb and Bernard Kalb, Kissinger
(Boston: Little, Brown, 1974): 451.

36. Mohammed Heikal, The Road to Ramadan (London:
Collins, 1975), p. 164; Radio Cairo, June 30, 1972
(BBC, Summary of World Broadcasts, 4, no. 4030, July 3,
1972):A1-7; and Radio Cairo, July 28, 1972 (ibid., no.
4054, July 31, 1972):A2.

37. Heikal, op.cit., p. 169 and Cairo, Voice of
the Arabs, May 25, 1972 (BBC, Summary of World Broadcasts, 4, no. 4000, May 27, 1972):A1.

38. D. Volsky, "Our Common Possession," New Times,
no. 37 (September 1972):5.

39. See Yediot Achronot, December 13, 1971.

40. Radio Moscow in Arabic, September 8, 1972
(FBIS, SOV, III, no. 178, September 12, 1972):15.

41. Lester Eckman, Soviet Policy Towards Jews and
Israel (New York: Shengold, 1974), p. 65.

42. New York Times, December 26, 1970, p.1.

43. See Haim Darin-Drabkin, "Israel and the Soviet
Union," New Outlook, 14, no. 4 (May 1971):50. Nevertheless, Israeli institutions must have irritated the
Soviets with some of their actions. Bar Ilan University offered a post to linguist Mikhail Zand even
though he had not yet received permission to emigrate.
He was also made a member of the Israeli Journalists'
Association. See Jewish Observer and Middle East
Review, XX, no. 18 (April 30, 1971):8.

44. Yediot Achronot, December 13, 1971.

45. See Jewish Observer and Middle East Review,
XX, no. 13 (March 26, 1971): 14 and New York Times,
September 8, 1971, p. 45.

46. Rafael, op.cit., pp. 91 and 94.

47. Henry Kissinger, Years of Upheaval (Boston:
Little, Brown, 1982), p. 250.

48. Benjamin Pinkus, "The Emigration of National
Minorities from the USSR in the Post-Stalin Era,"
Soviet Jewish Affairs, 13, no. 1 (February 1983): 24.

49. See Jewish Observer and Middle East Review,
XXI, no. 35 (September 1 1972):5.

50. See Nathan Yalin-Mor, "Israelis in Russia,"
New Outlook, 14, no. 8 (October-November 1971), p. 44
and New York Times, September 8, 1971, p. 9.

51. Yediot Achronot, December 13, 1971.

52. Haaretz, December 14, 1971; Yediot Achronot,
December 14, 1971; Haaretz, March 19, 1971; and New
York Times, August 6, 1972.

53. Jewish Observer and Middle East Review, XXI,
no. 5 (February 4, 1972):13.

54. G. Kahoyan, "Round Trip to Tel Aviv," New
Times, no. 12 (March 1972): 27, 29 and 31 and Israel
radio, January 25, 1972 (BBC, Summary of World Broadcasts, B, no. 3899, January 27, 1972):A20.

55. Haolam Hazeh, January 8, 1972, p. 15.

56. Zo Haderech, May 17, 1972.

57. Jewish Observer and Middle East Review, XXI,
no. 21 (June 2, 1972):9 and Israel Home Service, May
27, 1972 (BBC, Summary of World Broadcasts, 4, no.4001,
May 30, 1972):A4.

58. Maariv, June 29, 1972, p.6.

59. Israeli Labor Party, "Shigar Studentim al
yadei RAKAH Lelimudim Beartsot Mizrach Eropa,"
December 26, 1982, pp. 1-2.

60. Zo Haderech, November 29, 1972, p. 1 and
December 13, 1972, p. 8.

61. R. Petrov, "Problems of the Arab World,"
New Times, no. 44 (November 2, 1970):7.

62. "The Soviet Attitude Toward the Palestine
Problem," op.cit., p. 190 and Naim Ashhab, "To Overcome
the Crisis of the Palestine Resistance Movement,"
World Marxist Review, 15, no. 5 (May 1972):22-24.

Chapter 7

1. Cairo Domestic Service in Arabic, February 10, 1973 (FBIS, SOV, III, no. 29, February 12, 1973):B5.

2. Cairo Home Service, July 23, 1973 (BBC, Summary of World Broadcasts, 4, no. 4355, July 25, 1973):A8.

3. New Times, no. 15 (April 1973):8.

4. D. Volsky, "Middle East: New Impetus," New Times, no. 7 (February 1973):9.

5. Chaim Herzog, Milchemet Yom Hadin (Jerusalem: Edanim Publishers, 1975), p. 33.

6. Beirut, Daily Star, March 20, 1973, pp. 1-2 (FBIS, SOV, III, no. 59, March 27, 1973):B9.

7. Pravda, May 30, 1973, p. 3.

8. "Meir Vilner on the Israeli Communists' Stand," New Times, no. 24 (June 1973):11.

9. Shimon Shamir, "Nasser and Sadat, 1967-1973: Two Approaches to a National Crisis," in Itamar Rabinovich and Haim Shaked, eds., From June to October: The Middle East Between 1967 and 1973 (New Brunswick: Transaction 1978), p. 201.

10. Tad Szulc, "Seeing and Not Believing," The New Republic, 169, no. 25 (December 22, 1973):13-14.

11. Jerusalem Domestic Service, June 13, 1973 (FBIS, MEA, V. no. 115, June 14, 1973):H1.

12. Henry Kissinger, Years of Upheaval (Boston: Little, Brown, 1982), p. 297.

13. Statement of Mohammed Hafiz Ismail on Radio Moscow in Arabic, July 14, 1973 (FBIS, SOV, III, no. 136, July 16, 1973):B5.

14. See Peter Mangold, Superpower Intervention in the Middle East (New York: St. Martin's 1978), p. 169.

15. Radio Peace and Progress in Hebrew, September 16, 1973 (FBIS, SOV, III, no. 181, September 18, 1973): F3.

16. Tad Szulc, The Illusion of Peace (New York: Viking, 1978), p. 726; Marvin Kalb and Bernard Kalb, Kissinger (Boston: Little, Brown, 1974), p. 453;

Mohammed Heikal, The Road to Ramadan (London: Collins, 1975), pp. 24 and 38; and Anwar el-Sadat, In Search of Identity (London, Collins, 1978), p. 246. It is possible that Sadat and Brezhnev met secretly in Sofia, Bulgaria between September 18-21 during Brezhnev's visit to that state. See Yaacov Ro'i,ed., From Encroachment to Involvement (New York: John Wiley, 1974), p. 580.

17. Iraqi News Agency, September 13, 1973 (BBC, Summary of World Broadcasts, 4, no. 4407, September 25, 1973):A8; Sadat, op.cit., p. 247; Heikal, op.cit., p. 34; and Kissinger, op.cit., p. 469. The launching of a satellite on October 3, which is cited by several authors, may not be a crucial development as many other satellites were launched during the same time period. The orbits of the other satellites have not been revealed but launches took place on September 21 and October 2, 6, 10,15, 16 (two), 20 and 27. See Galia Golan, Yom Kippur and After (Cambridge: Cambridge University Press, 1977), p. 259.

18. Kissinger, op.cit., p. 461; Maariv, October 8, 1982; and Szulc, "Seeing and Not Believing," op.cit., p. 14.

19. Michael Brecher, Decisions in Crisis (Berkeley: University of California Press, 1980), pp. 191 and 212.

20. TASS in English, October 12, 1973 (FBIS, SOV, III, no. 199, October 15, 1973):F1-2 and Golan, op.cit., p. 256.

21. William Quandt, "Influence Through Arms Supply: The U.S. Experience in the Middle East," in Uri Ra'anan, Robert Pfaltzgraff, Jr., and Geoffrey Kemp, eds., Arms Transfers to the Third World (Boulder: Westview, 1978), pp. 124-26; Thomas Wheelock, "Arms for Israel: The Limits of Leverage," International Security, 3, no. 2 (Fall 1978): 126; and the Kalbs, op.cit., p. 512.

22. Kissinger, op.cit., p. 554.

23. Nightline ABC television, November 25, 1983. See also the Kalbs, op.cit., p. 493.

24. Kissinger, op.cit., pp. 588 and 591.

25. Haaretz, November 29, 1973, p. 1.

26. Coral Bell, The Diplomacy of Detente (New York: St. Martin's, 1977), p. 97.

27. Sadat, op.cit., pp. 260 and 325-27 and Scott Sagan, "Lessons of the Yom Kippur Alert," Foreign Policy, no. 36 (Fall 1979):163.

28. Pravda, October 17, 1973.

29. Sadat, op.cit., pp. 252-54; William Quandt, "Soviet Policy in the October Middle East War," International Affairs, 53, no. 4 (October 1977):596 and Insight Team of the Sunday Times, The Yom Kippur War (London: Andre Deutsch, 1975), p. 400.

30. Evgenii Primakov, "The Fourth Arab-Israeli War," World Marxist Review, 16, no. 12 (December 1973): 16-18 and Sadat, op.cit., pp. 325-27.

31. Leonid Brezhnev, "For a Just, Democratic Peace, for the Security of Nations and International Cooperation," New Times, no. 44 (November 1973):6.

32. The Kalbs, op.cit., p. 499; Mangold, op.cit., p. 128; Moshe Maoz, Syria Under Hafiz al-Asad: New Domestic and Foreign Policies, Jerusalem Papers on Peace Problems (Jerusalem: Leonard Davis Institute, 1975), p. 24; Zo Haderech, January 8, 1975, p. 10; Knesset record, July 2, 1974, Vol. 70, nos. 843-44, p. 2025; and Israel Home Serive, July 2, 1974 (BBC, Summary of World Broadcasts, 4, no. 4642, July 4, 1974) :A1.

33. Davar, December 7, 1973 and Amnon Kapeliuk, Lo Mechdal (Tel Aviv: Amikam, 1975), p. 145.

34. Jewish Observer and Middle East Review, XXII, no. 52 (December 28, 1973): 9 and Meir Wilner, "Israel in the Grip of Contradictions," New Times, no. 50 (December 1973):13.

35. New York Times, December 20, 1973, p. 16 and "Reayon im (Parshan Bachir) Likra Geneva," Skira Chodshit (January 1974):10. Allon had called for a resumption of relations with the Soviet Union as early as November 11.

36. Haolam Hazeh, December 26, 1973, p. 10.

37. Ibid.; Jerusalem Domestic Service, December 24, 1973 (FBIS, MEA, V, no. 248, December 26, 1973):H7-8; and Kissinger, op.cit., p. 796.

38. See Abba Eban, Pirkeh Chaim (Tel Aviv: Tsifriyat Maariv, 1978), p. 538.

39. Kissinger, op.cit., pp. 749-50, 755 and 794.

40. See William Brown, The Last Crusade: A Negotiator's Middle East Handbook (Chicago: Nelson-Hall, 1980), pp. 256-57 and Haolam Hazeh, January 3, 1974, p. 4.

41. Zo Haderech, July 11, 1973, p. 5.

42. See Jewish Observer and Middle East Review, XXII, no. 34 (August 24, 1973):4.

43. TASS in English, August 22, 1973 (FBIS, SOV, III, no. 164, August 23, 1973):F4 and Haaretz, August 29, 1973, p. 4.

44. Jewish Observer and Middle East Review, XXII, no. 12 (March 23, 1973):6.

45. Jerusalem Domestic Service, March 23, 1973 (FBIS, MEA, V, no. 60, March 28, 1973):H8.

46. Tripoli Home Service, October 4, 1973 (BBC, Summary of World Broadcasts, 4, no. 4417, October 6, 1973):A3 and ibid., October 28 (ibid., no. 4437, October 30, 1973):A1.

47. Jewish Observer and Middle East Review, XXII,

no. 41 (October 12,1973):22.

48. Karim Mroue, "The Arab National-Liberation Movement," World Marxist Review, 16, no. 2 (February 1973):21 and Maim Ashhab, "Colonialist Policy of the Israeli Aggressors," World Marxist Review, 16, no. 8 (Ausut 1973):32.

49. Pravda, November 16, 1973, p. 1 and November 27, 1973, p. 5.

50. See Galia Golan, The Soviet Union and the Palestine Liberation Organization (New York: Praeger 1980), pp. 53-54 and Jerusalem Domestic Service, December 24, 1973 (FBIS, MEA, V, no. 248, December 26, 1973):H7-8.

Chapter 8

1. William Quandt, Decade of Decisions
Berkeley: University of California Press, 1977),p. 205.
2. Tsevet itonayim bachir, Hayoresh (Tel Aviv:
Peleg, 1975), p. 10 and Haaretz, July 20, 1983.
3. TASS in English, January 25, 1974 (FBIS, SOV,
III, no. 18, January 25, 1974): F7; Moscow Domestic
Service, January 29, 1974 (ibid., no. 20, January 29,
1974):F3; and P. Demchenko, "The Middle East: From
War to Peace," International Affairs, no. 5 (May 1974):
67.
4. Jewish Observer and Middle East Review, XXIII,
no. 4 (January 25, 1974):12.
5. See Coral Bell, The Diplomacy of Detente
(New York: St. Martin's, 1977), p. 95.
6. See Edward Sheehan, The Arabs, Israelis, and
Kissinger (New York: Readers Digest Press, 1976), p.206
p.206.
7. Yaacov Ro'i, "The Soviet Attitude to the
Existence of Israel," in Roi, ed., The Limits to Power
(London: Croom Helm, 1979), p. 243; Middle-East Intelligence Survey, 2, no. 2 (April 15, 1974):14; and
Israel Radio in English for Abroad, February 17, 1974
(BBC, Summary of World Broadcasts, 4, no. 4530,
February 19, 1974):A4.
8. See Davar, April 26 and 28, 1974.
9. Quandt, op.cit., p. 237.
10. Galia Golan, "Syria and the Soviet Union Since
the Yom Kippur War," Orbis, 21, no. 4 (Winter 1978):
782.
11. Henry Kissinger, Years of Upheaval (Boston:
Little, Brown, 1982), p. 940 and Jewish Observer and
Middle East Review, XXIII, no. 13 (March 29, 1974):8.
12. Golan, op.cit., p. 783; Barry Rubin, "Soviet
Policy in the Middle East," in Naseer Aruri, ed.,
Middle East Crucible (Wilmette: Medina University Press
International, 1975), p. 308; and TASS in English,
April 11, 1974 (FBIS, SOV, III, no. 72, April 12, 1974)

:F9.

13. Damascus Home Service,May 29, 1974 (BBC, Summary of World Broadcasts, 4, no. 4613, May 31, 1974):A4. See also FBIS, SOV, III, no. 104, May 29, 1974, p. Fl and ibid., no. 105, May 30, 1974, pp.F2-3.

14. Kissinger, op.cit., p. 944; V. Alexandrov, "Middle East: A New Step Toward Peace," International Affairs, no. 8 (August 1974):86-88; I. Beliaev, "Top Priority: Geneva Conference," paper presented at 24th Pugwash Conference, Baden, Austria, August 28-September 2, 1974 in New Outlook, 18, no. 2 (February 1975):47; and Radio Peace and Progress in English to Africa, June 5, 1974 (FBIS, SOV, III, no. 110, June 6, 1974):F2-3.

15. See V. Vladimirov, "A Peaceful Settlement for the Middle East," International Affairs, no. 11 (November 1974):113 and Jewish Observer and Middle East Review, XXIV, no. 8 (February 21, 1975):6.

16. Sadat interview for Beirut's al-Anwar, January 9, 1975 (BBC, Summary of World Broadcasts, 4, no. 4802, January 13, 1975):A1 and Cairo, Voice of the Arabs, January 3, 1975 (BBC, Summary of World Broadcasts, 4, no. 4797, January 6, 1975):A7.

17. Meron Medzini, ed., Israel's Foreign Relations: Selected Documents 1974-1977, Volume III (Jerusalem: Ministry for Foreign Affairs, 1982), pp.5 and 38-39.

18. Press conference, September 13, 1974 in ibid., p. 78; interview on Israel Radio, February 21, 1975 in ibid., p. 176; and interview on Israeli television, February 14, 1975 (BBC, Summary of World Broadcasts, 4, no. 4832, February 17, 1975):A2.

19. Israel Home Service, December 13, 1974 (BBC, Summary of World Broadcasts, 4, no. 4781, December 14, 1974):A3; Yediot Achronot, January 14, 1975; and Thomas Wheelock, "Arms for Israel: The Limits of Leverage," International Security, 3, no. 2 (Fall 1978):31.

20. Davar, September 16, 1974 and New York Times, January 28, 1975, p. 3.

21. Jerusalem Domestic Service, April 5, 1975 (FBIS, MEA, V, no. 67, April 7, 1975):N1.

22. Maariv, April 21, 1975, p. 5.

23. Interview with Dinitz, July 3, 1983.

24. Haaretz, April 13, 1975, pp. 1-2 and April 14, p. 1; Zo Haderech, April 14, 1975, p. 2; New York Times, April 12, 1975, p. 3; and Jewish Observer and Middle East Review, XXIV, no. 16 (April 18, 1975):6.

25. Maariv, April 11, 1975, pp. 1-2.

26. E. Dimitriyev, "A Major Stage in the Struggle for Peace in the Middle East," International Affairs, no. 4 (April, 1975):38.

27. Sheehan, op.cit., p. 207; Jerusalem Domestic

Service, April 27, 1975 (FBIS, MEA, V, no. 82, April
28, 1975):N5; and Cairo, Voice of the Arabs, April 19,
1975 (BBC, Summary of World Broadcasts, 4, no. 4884,
April 22, 1975):A4-5.
28. Rabin interview, Israel television, June 3,
1975 (BBC, Summary of World Broadcasts, 4, no. 4922,
June 6, 1975):Al.
29. Maariv, December 9, 1983, p. 21.
30. Gideon Rafael, Besod Leumim (Tel Aviv:
Edanim Publishers, 1981), p. 306.
31. Yediot Achronot, June 28, 1974.
32. Armand Hammer, "On Trade With Russia,"
Business Week, no. 2359 (July 13, 1974):66; New York
Times, October 11, 1974, p. 4; and Jewish Observer
and Middle East Review, XXIII, no. 41 (October 11,
1974):5.
33. Gerald Ford, A Time to Heal (New York:
Harper and Row, 1979), p. 139.
34. Israel Home Service, January 22, 1975 (BBC,
Summary of World Broadcasts, 4, no. 4812, January 24,
1975):A2.
35. Naim Ashhab, "The Palestinian Aspect of the
Middle East Crisis," World Marxist Review, 17, no. 4
(April 1974):28.
36. Yediot Achronot, March 22, 1974 and Deutsche
Zeitung, April 19, 1974 as cited in Jewish Observer
and Middle East Review, XXIII, no. 21 (May 24, 1974):
16.
37. Alexander Ignatov, "The Palestinian Tragedy,"
New Times, no. 32 (August 1974):30 and Izvestiia, July
30, 1974, pp. 2 and 4.
38. Walid Khalidi, "Critique of 'the Middle East:
Imposed Solutions or Imposed problems?'," in Milton
Leitenberg and Gabriel Sheffer, eds., Great Power
Intervention in the Middle East (Elmsford: Pergamon,
1979), p. 283.
39. Pravda, September 9, October 12 and December
1, 1974.
40. See Galia Golan, The Soviet Union and the
Palestine Liberation Organization (New York: Praeger,
1980), p. 55.
41. Statement by Abd al-Muhsin abu Mayzar,
Cairo, MENA, May 9, 1975 (FBIS, MEA, V, no. 92, May 12,
1975):A2.
42. Der Spiegel, June 9, 1975, p. 17 (FBIS, SOV,
III, no. 126, June 30, 1975):F3.
43. Radio Moscow in Arabic, May 5, 1975 (FBIS,
SOV, III, no. 88, May 6, 1975):Fl.

Chapter 9

1. Haaretz, September 29, 1975, p. 1; Davar,
September 29, 1975, p. 1; IDF Radio, September 25, 1975
(BBC, Summary of World Broadcasts, 4, no. 5018,
September 27, 1975):A2; and Jewish Observer and Middle
East Review, XXIV, no. 40 (October 3, 1975):3.
2. Kuwait, as-Siyasah, January 12, 1976, pp. 1
and 11 (FBIS, MEA, V, no. 10, January 15, 1976):A1.
3. Haaretz, May 16, 1976 and May 26, 1976.
4. Milan, Correiere Della Sera, May 16, 1976,
p. 5 (FBIS, MEA, V, no. 100, May 31, 1976):N4 and
Maariv, May 25, 1976, p. 15.
5. TASS in English, April 28, 1976 (FBIS, SOV,
III, no. 84, April 29, 1976)F1-5 and Tel Aviv, Government Printing Office, May 25, 1976 (FBIS, MEA, V, no.
103, May 26, 1976):N4.
6. Jerusalem Post, June 16, 1976, pp. 1-2.
7. Amnon Sella, "Changes in Soviet Political-
Military Policy in the Middle East After 1973," Research Paper no. 25 (Jerusalem: Soviet and East
European Research Centre, July 1977), p. 1.
8. See Middle-East Intelligence Survey, 4, no. 3
(May 1-15, 1976):11.
9. Jerusalem Post, June 11, 1976.
10. TASS in English, June 28, 1976 (FBIS, SOV,III,
no. 126, June 29, 1976): F1-2.
11. Pravda, July 26, 1976, p. 1.
12. Maariv, June 3, 1976, p. 16 and June 11, 1976,
p. 1.
13. Jerusalem Post, June 16, 1976, p. 1. See also
Rabin statement on Israel Television, August 29, 1976
in Meron Medzini, ed., Israel's Foreign Relations:
Selected Documents 1974-1977, Vol. III (Jerusalem:
Ministry for Foreign Affairs, 1982), p. 487 and
Jerusalem Domestic Service, September 20, 1976 (FBIS,
MEA, V,no.183, September 20, 1976):N7.
14. Jerusalem Post, May 6, 1983, p. 18.
15. Yigal Allon, "Israel: The Case for Defensible

Borders," Foreign Affairs, 55, no. 1 (October 1976): 38-54.

16. Radio Peace and Progress in Arabic, October 7, 1976 (FBIS, SOV, III, no. 197, October 8, 1976):F2-3.

17. TASS in English, October 1, 1976 (FBIS, SOV, III, no. 193, October 4, 1976):F1-2; Jerusalem International Service, October 11, 1976 and Jerusalem Domestic Service, October 12, 1976 (FBIS, MEA, V, no. 198, October 12, 1976):N1; and Jerusalem Post, October 3, 1976, p. 1, October 12, p. 1 and October 13, p. 1.

18. Zbigniew Brzezinski, Power and Principle (New York: Farrar, Straus, Giroux, 1983), p. 87.

19. Yediot Achronot, February 14, 1977, pp. 1 and 7.

20. New Times, no. 13 (March 1977):6-7.

21. Jerusalem Domestic Service, April 17, 1977 (FBIS, MEA, V, no. 76, April 20, 1977):N4; IDF Radio, March 27, 1977 (ibid., no. 59, March 28, 1977):N2; and Paris, Le Nouvel Observateur, April 25-May 1, 1977, p. 57 (ibid., no. 84, May 2, 1977):N2.

22. Izvestiia, April 14, 1977, p. 4.

23. Al-Hamishmar, April 27, 1977, p. 1, (FBIS, MEA, V, no. 81, April 27, 1977):N3.

24. Jerusalem Post, April 17, 1977, pp. 1-2.

25. See Cyrus Vance, Hard Choices (New York: Simon and Schuster, 1983), p. 175.

26. See Jewish Observer and Middle East Review, XXVI, no. 25 (June 23, 1977):3.

27. TASS in English, September 8, 1977 (FBIS, SOV, III, no. 174, September 8, 1977): F1; Jimmy Carter, Keeping Faith (New York: Bantam, 1982), p. 293; Brzezinski, op. cit., p. 108; and O. Alov, "For a Settlement in the Middle East," International Affairs, no.9 (September 1977):67.

28. See Jerusalem Post, October 7, 1977, p. 2.

29. Israeli Television, September 29, 1975 (BBC, Summary of World Broadcasts, 4, no. 5021, October 1, 1975):A4.

30. Jewish Observer and Middle East Review, XXIV, no. 38 (September 19, 1975):11 and no. 39 (September 26, 1975):11.

31. Maariv, October 9, 1975, p. 1.

32. See Meir Wilner, "The Struggle Against Zionism is a Class Struggle," World Marxist Review, 19, no. 1 (January 1976):21-23.

33. New Times, no. 7 (February 1976):12-14.

34. Yediot Achronot, August 5, 1976.

35. Soviet Jewish emigrants demonstrated against the RAKAH congress, producing disturbances that led to the arrest of fifteen people. An unsuccessful effort was made to burn the meeting hall. See Jerusalem Post, December 19, 1976, p.3 and Maariv, December 19, 1976.

36. Haolam Hazeh, March 16, 1977, p. 4 and Jerusalem Domestic Service, March 21, 1977 (FBIS, MEA, V, no. 55, March 22, 1977):N9.

37. Jerusalem Domestic Service, March 16, 1977 (FBIS, MEA, V, no. 51, March 16, 1977):N2; Jerusalem International Service in English, March 27, 1977 (ibid., no. 59, March 28, 1977):N1; and Jewish Observer and Middle East Review, XXVI, no. 11 (March 17, 1977):9.

38. Maariv, April 27, 1977, p. 1 and Jerusalem Domestic Service, April 30, 1977 (FBIS, MEA, V, no.84, May 2, 1977):N4.

39. Zo Haderech, January 28, 1976, p. 9; Radio Moscow in English to Britain, October 20, 1975 (FBIS, SOV, III, no. 205, October 22, 1975):F5.; Jerusalem Domestic Service, December 1, 1976 (FBIS, MEA, V, no. 233, December 2, 1976):N2; Knesset record, July 7, 1976, Vol. 77, No. 5810, p. 3449; and Jerusalem Post, January 3, 1977,p.2.

40. New York Times, April 28, 1977, p. 4; Jerusalem Domestic Service, April 27, 1977 (FBIS, MEA, V, no. 82, April 28, 1977): N3; Jerusalem Television, April 26, 1977 (ibid., no. 81, April 27, 1977): N2; IDF Radio, April 27, 1977 (ibid., no. 82, April 28, 1977):N4; and Jerusalem Domestic Service, April 26, 1977 (ibid., no. 80, April 26, 1977):N2.

41. See Haaretz, January 28, 1976, p. 8.

42. Jerusalem, al-Fajr, March 11, 1976, p. 3 (FBIS, MEA, V, no. 55, March 19, 1976): N2; FBIS, MEA, V, no. 185, September 22, 1976, p. N3; Jerusalem Domestic Service, May 7, 1977 (ibid., no. 91, May 11, 1977):N8; and Yediot Achronot, September 29, 1976, p.8 and November 17, 1976, p. 2.

43. Yediot Achronot, September 22, 1976, p. 1 and September 3, 1976, pp. 1 and 7.

44. See Soviet and East European Research Centre Bulletin, no. 22 (December 15-31, 1976):3.

45. Oleg Alov, "The Settlement Issue," New Times, no. 12 (March 1977):5.

46. See Galia Golan, The Soviet Union and the Palestine Liberation Organization (New York: Praeger, 1980), pp. 80-82.

Chapter 10

1. Brzezinski has presented conflicting interpretations of the desirability of including the Soviet
Union in negotiations. See Zbigniew Brzezinski,
Francois Duchene, and Kiichi Saeki, "Peace in an
International Framework," Foreign Policy, no. 19
(summer 1975):12-13 and New York Times,October 9, 1983,
p. E19.
2. See Jimmy Carter, Keeping Faith (New York:
Bantam, 1982).
3. Interview with Jimmy Carter, March 30, 1984.
4. See Jerusalem Domestic Service, October 2,
1977 (FBIS, MEA, V, no. 191, October 3, 1977):N1 and
Jerusalem Post, July 14, 1980, p. 8.
5. See Jerusalem Post, October 25, 1977, pp. 1-2
and Moshe Dayan, Breakthrough (New York, Knopf, 1981),
p. 68.
6. Zbigniew Brzezinski, Power and Principle (New
York: Farrar, Straus, Giroux, 1983), p. 110.
7. Dayan, op.cit., p. 65.
8. Radio Moscow in Arabic to North Africa,
November 29, 1977 (FBIS, SOV, III, no. 230, November
30, 1977):F2 and Soviet and East European Research
Centre Bulletin, II, no. 22 (November 16-30, 1977):
1-2.
9. Pravda, December 23, 1977, Also note that
Meir Wilner reacted mildly to Sadat's visit to
Jerusalem. He told the Egyptian president that he
agreed with his views on a peace settlement, but
should have mentioned the PLO. See Zo Haderech,
November 23, 1977, p. 2.
10. Cairo, MENA in Arabic, October 13, 1977 (FBIS,
SOV, III, no. 199, October 14, 1977):F4.
11. Brzezinski, Power and Principle, op.cit.,
p. 112.
12. Carter, op.cit., pp. 293-94.
13. See Simcha Dinitz, "Detente, Israel and the
Middle East," Jerusalem Journal of International

Relations, 5, no. 4 (1981):78.
14. Interview with Jimmy Carter, March 30, 1984.
15. Galia Golan, "The Soviet Union and the Palestine Liberation Organization (New York: Praeger, 1980), p. 204.
16. Izvestiia, August 22, 1978.
17. Jerusalem Post, March 13, 1978, p. 1.
18. Jerusalem Post, March 29, 1978, p. 2.
19. Middle East Intelligence Survey, 5, no. 18 (December 16-31, 1977):141; Yediot Achronot, April 19, 1978, pp.1 and 8; Jerusalem Post, May 3, 1978, p. 1; and Jerusalem Domestic Service, September 15, 1978 (FBIS, MEA, V, no. 180, September 15, 1978):N6.
20. Brzezinski, Power and Principle, op.cit., p. 249.
21. Zo Haderech, July 5, 1978, p. 3.
22. Haaretz, February 18, 1979.
23. Emile Touma, "A Correct and Principled Stand," World Marxist Review, 22, no.7 (July 1979): 87-92.
24. Maariv, October 10, 1977 and Golan, op.cit., p. 177.
25. Maariv, April 7, 1978,p. 5.
26. Zo Haderech, May 31, 1978, p. 11.
27. TASS in English, January 26, 1978 (FBIS, SOV, III, no. 19, January 27, 1978):F6; Zo Haderech, January 18, 1978, p. 1; Jerusalem Domestic Service, July 7, 1978 (FBIS, MEA, V, no. 132, July 10, 1978): N14, and Haaretz, July 9, 1978.
28. I. Troyanovsky, "Desecration in Jerusalem," New Times, no. 30 (July 1978): 16-17.
29. Zo. Haderech, July 26, 1978, p. 2.
30. Jerusalem Domestic Service, September 6, 1978 (FBIS, MEA, V, no. 174, September 7, 1978):N1.
31. Pravda, December 1, 1978, p. 4; New Times no. 51 (December 1978):15-16; and Yossi Sarid, "Interesim Nifradim Ach Nifgashim," Migvan (January 1979): 26-28.
32. Jerusalem Domestic Service, January 19, 1979 (FBIS, MEA, V, no. 8, January 11, 1979):N6.
33. New Times, no. 12, (March 1978):9.

Chapter 11

1. Zahi Karkabi, "Israel: The Fruits of a Pernicious Policy," International Affairs, no. 5 (May 1979):25-33 and Mohammed al-Shaer, "The Just Cause of the Palestinian People," International Affairs, no.6 (June 1979): 25-31.

2. Beirut, Monday Morning, July 2-8, 1979 (FBIS, SOV, III, no. 79, July 6, 1979): H8-9.

3. Yitronot Vchesronot Bechidush Hayachasim Hadiplomatiim Ben Yisrael Ubrit Hamoatsot (Jerusalem: Leonard Davis Institute, March 1981), p. 41

4. Davar, September 19,1979.

5. TASS International Service in Russian, January 29, 1980 (FBIS, SOV, III, no. 21, January 30, 1980):H2.

6. See V. Konstantinov, "The Palestinian Problem and the Middle East Settlement," International Affairs, no. 7 (July 1980):49.

7. New York Times, December 31, 1979, p. 3 and CBS Television, December 30, 1979.

8. ITIM in Hebrew, February 3, 1980 (FBIS, MEA, V, no. 24, February 4, 1980):N8.

9. Haaretz, April 13, 1980.

10. See Zo Haderech, November 12, 1980, p. 3.

11. Davar, June 18, 1980; Zo Haderech, July 18, 1979, p. 2; Jerusalem Post, July 14, 1980, p. 8; and al-Hamishmar, March 31, 1980.

12. L. Dadiani, "Peking's Middle East Policy," International Affairs, no. 5 (May 1978): 49-58; L. Andreyev, "China's Middle East Policy," International Affairs, no. 10 (October 1980): 46-54; A. Ustyugov, "A Realistic Program for a Middle East Settlement," International Affairs, no. 8 (August 1981):65-72; and Yediot Achronot, February 9, 1979, p. 4 of weekend supplement.

13. Israeli Television, July 6, 1981 (FBIS, MEA, V, no. 129, July 7, 1981): Il and Jerusalem Domestic Service, July 7, 1981 (ibid., no. 130, July 8, 1981): I4.

14. Maariv, August 19, 1979.

15. See Shai Feldman, "Peacemaking in the Middle East: The Next Step," Foreign Affairs 59, no.4 (Spring 1981):767.

16. Haaretz, September 28, 1981.

17. "Memorandum of Understanding, November 30, 1981," Department of State Bulletin, 82, no. 2058 (January 1982):45 and Davar, December 2, 1981.

18. See Newsweek, XCIV, no. 10 (September 3, 1979):23.

19. Yediot Achronot, May 21, 1981.

20. See Davar, December 3, 1981.

21. Jerusalem Post, December 3, 1981, p.2.

22. TASS in English, April 18, 1981 (FBIS, SOV, III, no. 75, April 20, 1981): H3 and The Soviet Union and the Middle East, VI, no. 5 (1981):5.

23. Radio Moscow in Arabic, November 5, 1981 (FBIS, SOV, III, no. 215, November 6, 1981):H1.

24. Pravda, September 26, 1981, p. 4; Jerusalem Domestic Service, September 25, 1981 (FBIS, MEA, V, no. 186, September 28, 1981):I1; Jerusalem Domestic Service, September 26, 1981 (ibid., no. 187, September 28, 1981):I2-3; Yitzhak David, Beeretz Yisrael (November 1981); 27; and Zo Haderech, October 1, 1981, p. 2.

25. IDF Radio, October 9, 1981 (FBIS, MEA, V, no. 197, October 13, 1981):I9; Israeli Television, September 28, 1981 (ibid., no. 189, September 30, 1981):I1; Jerusalem Domestic Service, October 4, 1981 (ibid., no. 193, October 6, 1981):I2; and Jerusalem Domestic Service, September 26, 1981 (ibid., no. 187, September 28, 1981):I2-3.

26. Jerusalem Domestic Service, December 10, 1981 (FBIS, MEA, V, no. 238, December 11, 1981):I6 and Maariv, May 30, 1983.

27. Jerusalem Domestic Service, January 5, 1982 (FBIS, MEA, V, no. 3, January 6, 1982):I1 and Jerusalem Post, January 7, 1982, pp. 1-2.

28. Pravda, February 16, 1982, p. 4.

29. See Robert Freedman, "Soviet Jewry and Soviet Foreign Policy: A Preliminary Analysis," paper presented at the annual convention of the American Association for the Advancement of Slavic Studies, Washington, D.C. October 16, 1982, p. 20.

30. Z. Alexander, "Jewish Emigration from the USSR in 1980," Soviet Jewish Affairs, 11, no. 2 (May 1981):20.

31. See Arafat interview, Teheran Home Service, January 3, 1975 (BBC, Summary of World Broadcasts, 4, no. 4797, January 7, 1975):A3.

32. Alexander, op.cit., p. 12 and Z. Alexander, "Jewish Emigration from the USSR in 1981-82," Soviet Jewish Affairs, 12, no. 3 (November 1982):16.

33. Alexander, "Jewish Emigration from the USSR in 1980," op.cit., pp. 18-19.

34. New York Times, July 13, 1974, p. 17.
35. Benjamin Pinkus, "The Emigration of National Minorities from the USSR in the Post-Stalin Era," Soviet Jewish Affairs, 13 no. 1 (February 1983):31 and Theodore Friedgut, "Soviet Anti-Zionism and Anti-Semitism: Another Cycle," Research Paper no. 54 (Jerusalem: Soviet and East European Research Centre, January 1984), pp. 25-26.
36. See Haaretz, April 25, 1980.
37. Haaretz, August 8, 1980 and Nahum Goldmann, Haparodoks Hayehudi (Ramat Gan: Matsada, 1978), 9. 143.
38. Zo Haderech, May 23, 1979, p. 6; Yediot Achronot, May 15, 1979, p. 4; al-Hamishmar, May 17, 1979, p. 1; Jerusalem Domestic Service, May 11, 1979 (FBIS, MEA, V, no. 93, May 11, 1979):N5; and Moscow Television, June 4, 1979 (FBIS, SOV, III, no. 119, June 19, 1979):H1-3.
39. Davar, September 9, 1979.
40. Jerusalem Domestic Service, May 29, 1980 (FBIS, MEA, V, no. 110, June 5, 1980):N4.
41. Al-Hamishmar, September 14, 1980.
42. Zo Haderech, August 13, 1980, p. 14.
43. Jerusalem Post, July 22, 1980, pp. 1-2.
44. Zo Haderech, September 17, 1980, p. 3 and October 8, 1980, p. 2.
45. ITIM in Hebrew, September 22, 1980 (FBIS, MEA, V, no. 185, September 22, 1980):N3.
46. Yediot Achronot, September 18, 1980, p.8.
47. Jerusalem Domestic Service, September 16, 1980 (FBIS, MEA, V, no. 181, September 16, 1980):N3.
48. Zo Haderech, January 14, 1981, p. 3.
49. Davar, March 31, 1982.
50. See Haaretz, July 24, 1981, pp. 1-2.
51. Haaretz, December 13, 1981, p. 1.
52. New Times, no. 18 (April 1979): 24-25.
53. PLO document, November 13, 1979, captured by Israel near Sidon, Lebanon in June 1982. See Raphael Israeli, ed., PLO in Lebanon: Selected Documents (London: Weidenfeld and Nicolson, 1983), pp. 43-44, 50-51 and 54.
54. New Times, no. 1 (January 1980):21-22 and no. 13 (March 1980):14-15.
55. World Marxist Review, 23, no. 9 (September 1980):40-42.
56. Haaretz, September 28, 1980 and December 4, 1980.
57. New Times, no. 47 (November 1981):12-13.
58. See "Foundation of the Palestine Communist Party," Communist Affairs, I, no. 4 (October 1982): 772-73.

Chapter 12

1. On the issue of U.S. foreknowledge and approval, see Zeev Schiff, "Green Light, Lebanon," Foreign Policy, no. 50 (Spring 1983):73-85.

2. See Galia Golan, "The Soviet Union and the Israeli Action in Lebanon," International Affairs, 59, no. 1 (Winter 1982-83)8-9.

3. New York Times, December 6, 1983, p. A31.

4. Claude Khoury, "Moscow: the Israeli Annexation of South Lebanon," Monday Morning (Beirut), December 20-26, 1982, p. 33.

5. TASS in Russian, July 8, 1982 (FBIS, SOV, III, no. 31, July 8, 1982):H1; TASS in English, June 14, 1982 (ibid., no. 115, June 15, 1982):H1; IDF Radio, July 6, 1982 (FBIS, MEA, V, no. 130, July 7, 1982):I1; and Pravda, July 21, 1982.

6. Paris, AFP in English, January 22, 1983 (FBIS, MEA, V, no. 17, January 25, 1983):G6.

7. Karen Dawisha, "The U.S.S.R. in the Middle East: Superpower in Eclipse?," Foreign Affairs, 61, no. 2 (Winter 1982-83):439. See also Haaretz, June 16, 1982, p. I18.

8. Damascus Domestic Service, June 20, 1982 (FBIS, MEA, V, no. 119, June 21, 1982):H1; ibid., July 9, 1982 (ibid., no. 132, July 9):H2; ibid., August 26, 1982 (ibid., no. 167, August 27, 1982):H2; and Damascus, Tishrin, July 2, 1982, p. 8 (ibid., no. 134, July 13):H2.

9. Voice of Lebanon in Arabic, June 12, 1982 (FBIS, MEA, V, no. 114, June 14, 1982):G3 and Beirut Domestic Service, July 27, 1982 (ibid., no. 145, July 28, 1982):G2.

10. Jerusalem Post, December 2, 1982, p. 1.

11. IDF Radio in Hebrew, June 20, 1982 (FBIS, MEA, V, no. 119, June 21, 1982): I18.

12. Yediot Achronot, October 22, 1982, p. 4 in supplement.

13. AFP, August 5, 1982 (FBIS, MEA, V. no. 152,

August 6, 1982):I5 and Jerusalem Post, August 29, 1982, p. 1.

14. Yediot Achronot, November 16, 1982, pp. 1 and 7; IDF Radio in Hebrew, November 11, 1982 (FBIS, MEA, V, no. 219, November 12, 1982):I7; Jerusalem Domestic Service, November 11, 1982 (ibid.), I7; and ibid., November 17, 1982 (ibid., no. 222, November 17, 1982): I7.

15. TASS in English, October 19, 1982 (FBIS, SOV, III, no. 202, October 19, 1982):H1.

16. See Khoury, op.cit., p. 35.

17. See Rashid Khalidi, "Soviet-Arab Relations," Arab Perspectives, 4 (November-December 1983):21-23.

18. Jerusalem Post, January 25, 1983, p. 3.

19. Jerusalem Domestic Service, January 4, 1983 (FBIS, MEA, V, no. 3, January 5, 1983):I7 and Jerusalem Post, January 26, 1983, p. 1.

20. Jerusalem Post, January 30, 1983, p. 8.

21. See Haaretz, January 16, 1983, p. 7.

22. Jerusalem Domestic Service, January 6, 1983 (FBIS, MEA, V, no. 5, January 7, 1983):I7 and Maariv, April 3, 1983, pp. 13-14.

23. International Herald Tribune, February 7, 1983, p. 2.

24. Jerusalem Domestic Service, February 2, 1983 (FBIS, MEA, V, no. 24, February 3, 1983):I5.

25. Haaretz, January 3, 1983, p. 7.

26. Ehud Olmert in Jerusalem Post, May 5, 1983, p. 5.

27. Merj Ayun, Lebanon Voice of Hope in Arabic, March 17, 1983 (FBIS, MEA, V, no. 53, March 17, 1983): G1 and Beirut, Voice in Lebanon in Arabic, March 16, 1983 (ibid):G1.

28. Al-Hamishmar, March 25, 1983, p. 2 and Jerusalem Post, March 20, 1983, p.2.

29. Jerusalem Post, April 8, 1983, p. 6. See also Maariv, March 31, 1983, pp. 1 and 15; and TASS in English, March 30, 1983 (FBIS, SOV, III, no. 63, March 31, 1983):H1.

30. Damascus Domestic Service, April 1, 1983 (FBIS, MEA, V, no. 65, April 4, 1983):H1.

31. Maariv, April 3, 1983, p. 1 and Jerusalem Post, April 27, 1983, p. 3.

32. Moscow Domestic Service, April 2, 1983 (FBIS, SOV, III, no. 65, April 4, 1983):AA16 and Jerusalem Post Magazine. April 8, 1983, p. 5.

33. Jerusalem Post, May 19, 1983, p. 1; May 24, 1983, p. 1; and May 29, 1983, p. 2.

34. Jerusalem Post August 12, 1983, p. 2; Jerusalem Domestic Service, August 15, 1983 (FBIS, MEA, V, no. 159, August 16, 1983):I2 and ibid., August 18, 1983 (ibid., no. 162, August 19, 1983):I5.

35. Jerusalem Post, June 15, 1983, p. 1.

36. See New York Times, December 4, 1983, p. E21.

37. Maariv, December 30, 1982, p. 7.

38. On the emissaries, see Yediot Achronot, April 4, 1983.

39. Also during the spring of 1983, a Hungarian economic delegation visited Israel, Israelis attended celebrations in Poland marking the fortieth anniversary of the Warsaw Ghetto, and the first Polish-Israeli tourist agreement was concluded.

40. Jerusalem Post, May 23, 1983, p. 1 and Haaretz, May 22, 1983, p. 2.

41. Yediot Achronot, April 20, 1983.

42. Insight, 8, no. 4 (June 1982):6-7.

43. Sovietskaia Rossiia, August 25, 1983, p. 3.

44. Jerusalem Post, April 29, 1983, p. 1.

45. IDF Radio, July 14, 1983 (FBIS, MEA, V, no. 136, July 14, 1983):I4; Jerusalem Domestic Service, July 26, 1983 (ibid., no. 144, July 26, 1983):I3; Yediot Achronot, July 17, 1983, pp. 1 and 6; and Maariv, July 27, 1983, p. 2.

46. Jerusalem Domestic Service, September 20, 1983 (FBIS, MEA, V, no. 184, September 21, 1983):I4.

47. Frankfurter Rundschau, June 19, 1982, p. 2 (FBIS, MEA, V, no. 120, June 22, 1982):A3 and Kuwait, al-Anba, June 30, 1982) pp. 1 and 22 (ibid., no. 127, July 1, 1982):A3.

48. Radio Monte Carlo in Arabic, June 18, 1982 (FBIS, MEA, V, no. 119, June 21, 1982):A2; Le Monde, June 23, 1982, p. 4 (ibid., no. 121, June 23, 1982): A1; and Radio Monte Carlo in Arabic, June 25, 1982 (ibid., no. 124, June 28, 1982):A4.

49. AFP in English, July 15, 1982 (FBIS, MEA, V, no. 137, July 16, 1982):A3.

50. Voice of Palestine, July 22, 1982 (FBIS, MEA, V, no. 142, July 23, 1982): A1 and London, al-Majallah, July 17-23, 1982, pp. 3-5 (ibid., no. 140, July 21, 1982):A7.

51. Voice of Palestine, August 5, 1982 (FBIS, MEA, V, no. 152, August 6, 1982):A2.

52. Pravda, September 15, 1982, p. 1.

53. San'a, Voice of Palestine, September 19, 1982 (FBIS, MEA, V, no. 182, September 20, 1982):A4; AFP in English, September 19, 1982 (ibid.):A5; and Pravda, September 21, 1982, p. 1.

54. Kuwait, Ar-Ra'y al-'Amm, September 18, 1982, p. 19 (FBIS, MEA, V, no. 183, September 21, 1982):A7 and London, Ash-Sharq al-Awsat, September 23, 1982, p.3 (ibid., no. 186, September 24, 1982):A5.

55. Baghdad, Voice of PLO, November 28, 1982 (FBIS, MEA, V, no. 231, December 1, 1982):A8.

56. See The Soviet Union and the Middle East, VIII, no. 1 (1983):4.

57. ITIM in Hebrew, November 18, 1982 (FBIS, MEA,

V, no. 224, November 19, 1982):I7.

58. ITIM in Hebrew, December 23, 1982 (FBIS, MEA,
V, no. 250, December 29, 1982):I10-11; TASS in English,
December 23, 1982 (FBIS, SOV, III, no. 249, December
28, 1982):H7; and Emile Touma, "Pernicious Consequences
of an Aggressive Course," International Affairs, no. 7
(July 1983):37.

Chapter 13

1. See Theodore Friedgut, "The Domestic Image of Soviet Involvement in the Arab-Israeli Conflict," Research Paper no. 26 (Jerusalem: Soviet and East European Research Centre, August 1977), p. 37.

2. Maariv, October 17, 1976.

3. See Oded Eran, "The Soviet Conception of an Arab-Israeli Settlement," Research Paper no. 8 (Tel Aviv: Russian and East European Research Center, Fall 1974), p. 4.

4. Haaretz, February 2, 1977.

5. David Sham, "A Visit to the U.S.S.R," New Outlook, 18, no. 7 (October-November 1975):22.

6. See Yitronot Vchesronot Bechidush Hayachasim Hadiplomatiim Ben Yisrael Ubrit Hamoatsot (Jerusalem: Leonard Davis Institute, March 1981), p. 2.

7. See Yaacov Ro'i and Rita Gottlibovich, "The Feasibility of a Soviet-Israeli Dialogue: An Analysis of the Soviet Position," Research Paper no. 12 (Tel Aviv: Center for Strategic Studies, June 1981), p. 22.

8. See Eran, op.cit., p. 12.

9. See Adeed Dawisha, "Comprehensive Peace in the Middle East and the Comprehension of Arab Politics," Middle East Journal, 37, no. 1 (Winter 1983):50.

10. Minister of Defense Shimon Peres said in 1975 that West Bank communists in the Palestine National Front carried out attacks on Israeli targets during the 1973 war. This is rarely discussed by Israel but indicates some of the security problems that could arise through continued occupation. See Israel Home Service, January 13, 1975 (BBC, Summary of World Broadcasts, 4, no. 4804, January 15, 1975):A4.

11. Aryeh Yodfat, "The USA, USSR, China and the Arab-Israeli Conflict," International Problems, XX, nos. 2-4 (Summer 1981):93.

12. Yitzhak David, Beeretz Yisrael (November 1981) :27.

13. Abraham Becker, "Arms Transfer, Great Power

Intervention, and Settlement of the Arab-Israeli
Conflict," in Milton Leitenberg and Gabriel Sheffer,
eds., Great Power Intervention in the Middle East
(Elmsford: Pergamon, 1979), p. 257.

14. See Eran, op.cit., p. 6.
15. See Mikhail Agursky in Jerusalem Post,
November 9, 1982, p. 8.
16. Haaretz, February 19, 1976, p. 1.
17. See Eran, op. cit., p. 13.

Index

Abdullah (King of Jordan), 235
Abramov, Aleksandr, 21, 24
Aden, See South Yemen
Adenauer, Konrad, 48
Afghanistan, 53, 185-87, 189, 198, 201, 205
Agmon, Yaacov, 130
Akzin, Benjamin, 225
Albania, 55
Alexandria, 121, 177
Algeria, 22, 36, 37, 61, 73
Algiers, 121, 132
Ali, Ahmed Ismail, 118, 125
Allende, Salvador, 5
Allon, Yigal, 7, 31, 50, 54, 64, 80, 84, 89, 114, 122, 130, 135, 140, 142-44, 146, 149, 154, 160, 161, 163, 165-67, 179, 201
Aloni, Shulamit, 200, 227
Amer, Abdul Hakim, 39
Amit, Meir, 53
Andropov, Iurii, 58, 119, 211, 216, 226, 230
Angola, 155
Ansar, al-, 93, 116, 131
Anti-Semitism, 4, 5, 16, 20, 29, 46, 110, 203, 234, 236
Aqaba, Gulf of, 82, 162, 163
Arab-Israeli wars
  1948-49, 12, 13, 71
  1956, 25, 36, 45, 52, 222, 235
  1967, 8, 28, 47, 53-57, 61, 70, 74, 75, 78, 80,

Arab-Israeli wars (cont'd)
  81, 137, 222
  1973, 58, 117, 122-26, 144, 145, 181, 196, 211, 222, 239
  War of Attrition, 67, 77, 78, 80, 81, 83
  See also Lebanon
Arab League, 13, 17, 161
Arafat, Yasir, 41, 43, 44, 72, 73, 93, 94, 116, 130, 132, 134, 137, 150-52, 163, 169-71, 178, 179, 181, 184, 196, 201, 202, 205, 206, 209, 212-15, 218, 222, 223, 228-31, 235. See also Palestine Liberation Organization
Arbatov, Georgii, 200
Argentina, 7
Armstrong, John, 6
Ashhab, Naim, 207
Assad, Hafez al-, 66, 97, 118, 119, 123, 125, 137-39, 155, 158, 160 170, 181, 188, 210, 212, 216, 218, 228, 229, 231, 235, 236
Aswan, 177
Australia, 32
Austria, 21, 73, 109, 152, 197
Avidar, Yosef, 225
Avineri, Shlomo, 147, 157, 161, 163, 234
Avnery, Uri, 69, 114, 127-

Avnery, Uri (cont'd)
29, 132, 147

Bab el-Mandeb Strait, 10, 36, 96, 116
Baghdad Pact, 18, 22
Bahrein, 36, 104, 235
Bakdash, Khaled, 42, 43, 67, 75, 97, 126, 181
Bangladesh, 105
Banias, 44, 46
Bar-Lev, Chaim, 88
Bar-Tov, David, 33
Beam, Jacob, 66
Begin, Menachem, 4, 52, 89, 112, 127, 153, 164, 168, 175, 177, 181-84, 186-88, 190, 194, 195, 198, 199, 202, 205, 206, 209-11, 213, 215, 219, 223, 224, 234
Begun, Iosif, 227
Beirut, 8, 209-11, 213-18, 228, 229
Bekaa Valley, 217
Beliaev, Igor, 1, 225
Ben Bella, Ahmed, 34, 37
Ben Gurion, David, 7, 8, 12, 15, 17, 20, 23, 24, 27, 28, 36, 52
Ben Tsur, Abraham, 57
Bethlehem, 202
Birobidjan, 11, 92
Biton, Charlie, 167, 169, 202
Black Sea, 13, 60, 204
Bodrov, Mikhail, 20, 24, 25
Bologna, 129
Bonn, 183
Bosphorus, 51
Bovin, Aleksandr, 199, 204
Brecher, Michael, 6
Brest-Litovsk, 61
Brezhnev, Leonid, 8, 28, 37, 43, 48, 49, 53, 56, 61, 72, 81, 89, 103, 105- 108, 119-24, 126, 128, 131, 138-40, 151, 152, 157, 158, 161, 162, 163, 168, 170, 171, 176-78, 184, 186, 193, 195, 199, 203, 206, 209-11, 214, 216, 217, 225, 226, 228-30

Britain. See Great Britain
Bronfman, Edgar, 225
Brookings, Institution, 156, 160, 173
Brown, George, 47, 51
Brown, Harold, 181
Brussels, 110, 111, 166, 226
Brutents, Karen, 167, 201, 220
Brzezinski, Zbigniew, 161, 174, 177
Bucharest, 112, 202-204
Bulgaria, 19, 20, 40, 49, 168, 194, 204
Bulganin, Nikolai, 23, 235
Burg, Yosef, 114, 168, 225, 226
Burma, 49
Burstein, Uzi, 183

Cairo, 10, 40, 41, 58, 88, 105, 114, 122, 140, 177, 178, 218
Cambodia, 85, 142
Camp David agreement, 173, 180, 183, 184, 196, 204, 214
Canada, 32, 69
Carter, Jimmy, 153, 156, 160, 161, 163, 164, 166, 167, 170, 171, 173-76, 178, 181, 185- 89, 195, 201
Castro, Fidel, 49
Ceausescu, Nicolae, 56, 112, 144, 161, 164, 194, 202
Central Treaty Organization (CENTO), 37
Chad, 234
Chernenko, Konstantin, 8, 236, 243
Chile, 5
China, 17, 18, 28, 29, 41, 42, 65, 71, 73, 93, 105, 111, 123, 134, 171, 185, 189, 195, 197, 214, 234, 243
Chou En-lai, 93
Chuvakhim, Dmitrii, 28, 30, 34, 35, 44, 45, 51-53, 55-57
Citizens' Rights Movement,

Citizens' Rights Movement
(cont'd)
227
Cohen, Eli, 43
Cohen, Geula, 166
Cuba, 48, 56, 73, 90, 121,
198
Cyprus, 10, 49, 102, 137,
142, 182
Czechoslovakia, 2, 6, 13,
19, 20, 22, 23, 36, 56,
64, 71, 73-76, 166,
168-70

Damascus, 40, 43, 60, 122,
126, 137, 148, 158,
181, 189, 212, 229
Dardanelles, 51
Dayan, Moshe, 1, 3, 27, 47,
50, 52, 54, 64, 81, 83-
85, 87, 96, 97, 101,
103, 107, 122, 130,
146, 164, 165, 175,
176, 188
Democratic Front for Peace
and Equality, 167, 179,
202
Democratic Movement for
Change (DASH), 162, 164
Denmark, 100
Dimant-Kass, Ilana, 8
Dinitz, Simcha, 8, 100, 101,
142, 143, 147, 156,
159
Djibouti, 36
Dobrynin, Anatolii, 8, 65,
66, 68, 77, 83, 86,
89, 101, 103, 121,
126, 142-44, 147, 148,
156, 159, 161, 165, 198
Dominican Republic, 46
Dubcek, Alexander, 74, 75
Dymshits, Veniamin, 224

East Bank. See Jordan
Eastern Europe, 5, 13, 14,
17, 19, 20, 34, 48,
54, 55, 69, 74, 115,
154, 180, 224, 234,
236
East Germany, 48, 56, 75,
115, 130, 168, 200
East Jerusalem, 1, 7, 15,
62, 65, 66, 69, 78,

East Jerusalem (cont'd)
145, 151, 176, 180,
186, 187, 193, 214,
230, 236, 242. See
also Jerusalem
Eban, Abba, 4, 10, 14, 28,
31, 39, 48, 51, 53, 55,
56, 68, 70, 81, 82, 86-
88, 101, 103, 127, 128,
130, 140, 142, 179
Egypt, 10, 12, 17, 21-24,
30, 38, 41, 42, 51, 58,
65, 66, 71, 72, 80, 96,
98, 118, 144, 168, 171
and Israel, 12, 22, 23,
39, 40, 50-54, 57, 60,
67, 80, 81, 83-90, 96,
99, 104, 107, 108, 117-
23, 125, 127, 133-36,
138, 140, 141, 145-48,
152, 153, 165, 173, 175-
78, 180, 184-90, 193,
196, 199, 200, 205, 210,
217
and the Soviet Union
(diplomatic relations)
34, 37-39, 55-57, 59-
61, 68, 72, 102, 116,
128-30, 136, 140, 154,
157, 176, 177, 186,
190, 218
and the Soviet Union
(military relations),
40, 50, 51, 54, 63, 67,
77, 78, 80, 81, 83-91,
95, 97-100, 103-108,
112, 117-21, 123-26,
132, 144, 176, 217
and the United States,
51-53, 55, 68, 80, 81,
84, 88, 89, 98-100, 102,
105-107, 113, 114, 117,
119, 122, 123, 129, 133,
136-41, 148, 154, 155,
157, 164, 176, 178, 180,
181, 186, 187, 189, 190,
193, 234
Ehrenburg, Ilia, 16
Eilat, 36, 51, 53, 96
Eisenhower Doctrine, 24
Eliashiv, Shmuel, 21, 22
Eliav, Arie, 31
Entebbe, 145
Eritrea, 162

Ershov, Pavel, 15, 18
Eshkol, Levi, 4, 8, 27-29,
    31, 33, 34, 38, 39,
    43-45, 49-53, 57, 65,
    66, 68, 71
Ethiopia, 7, 49, 105, 153,
    162
Eytan, Rafael, 219, 220

Fahd (King of Saudi Arabia),
    193, 206
Fahmy, Ismail, 144, 178
Fatah, al-, 41-46, 50, 58,
    72, 73, 88, 178, 205,
    229, 231. See also
    Palestine Liberation
    Organization
Feder, Naftali, 183
Fedorenko, Nikolai, 50, 54
Feisal (King of Saudi
    Arabia), 2, 3, 38, 142
Fez conference, 214, 217
Finland, 55, 67, 70, 100,
    113, 213, 216, 237
First World War, 13
Flatto-Sharon, Shmuel, 179
Ford, Gerald, 139, 142, 148,
    152, 157, 160
France, 13, 17, 22-24, 29,
    32, 36, 38, 57, 65,
    66, 69, 73, 140, 144,
    168
Freij, Elias, 202

GAHAL, 89
Galilee, Sea of, 1, 44
Gavish, David, 33
Gaza, 22, 50, 71, 78, 84,
    98, 118, 132, 151, 154,
    201, 214, 230
Gemayel, Amin, 209, 217,
    218, 223
Gemayel, Bashir, 209, 214,
    216, 217, 229
Geneva conferences, 117,
    123, 126-28, 132-46,
    149, 150, 152-57, 159-
    67, 169-71, 173-79,
    181, 183, 186, 200,
    239
Germany, 11, 61. See also
    East Germany and West
    Germany
Ghana, 37, 49

Gidi Pass, 96, 97, 99
Gierek, Edward, 148, 180
Gil, Geula, 32
Glassboro summit, 62
Golan Heights, 54, 66, 78,
    84, 122, 125, 126,
    156, 159, 180, 193,
    194, 213, 221, 223,
    239, 242, 244
Goldberg, Arthur, 62
Goldmann, Nahum, 2, 14, 84,
    86, 136, 144, 161,
    184, 198, 225
Gomulka, Wladyslaw, 56, 74
Goren, Shlomo, 167
Gorshkov, Sergei, 189
Gottwald, Klement, 20
Great Britain, 12-14, 17,
    22-25, 29, 32, 36, 42,
    46, 47, 58, 140, 144,
    166, 183
Grechko, Andrei, 58, 104,
    119
Greece, 13, 28, 48, 49, 104,
    169
Gromyko, Anatolii, 218
Gromyko, Andrei, 2, 21, 31,
    38, 43, 51, 52, 58,
    62, 64, 66, 67, 102,
    103, 106, 119, 121,
    127, 128, 137, 139,
    144, 146, 150, 152,
    154, 161, 164, 165,
    173, 176, 181, 186,
    194, 203, 205, 206,
    213, 223
Grossman, Chaya, 204

Habash, George, 73
Habib, Philip, 204
Habibi, Emile, 70, 167
Hacohen, Menachem, 204
Haifa, 55, 157, 166, 186,
    203
Haig, Alexander, 189, 215
Hama, 118
Hammer, Armand, 148, 197
Harel, Aharon, 227
Hassan (King of Morocco),
    86, 161
Hassan ibn Talal, 179
Hawatmeh, Nayef, 132, 151,
    171, 205, 228, 229
Heikal, Mohammed, 33, 39,

Heikal, Mohammed (cont'd)
    75, 89, 97, 107, 121,
    123
Helms, Richard, 103
Helsinki, 100, 101
Helsinki accords, 147, 174
Herzog, Chaim, 57, 154, 156,
    157, 161, 165
Hilmi, Yusuf, 23
Himim, David, 204
Honolulu conference, 46
Hubran, Salim, 204
Humphrey, Hubert, 53
Hungary, 20, 69, 115, 162,
    166, 168, 180, 200,
    204
Hussein (King of Jordan),
    25, 40, 63, 72, 91,
    103, 104, 139, 140,
    159, 160, 170, 193,
    206, 214, 218, 222,
    223, 230, 231, 235,
    236

India, 39, 104, 105
Indian Ocean, 58, 60, 96
Indonesia, 37
Iran, 7, 13, 37, 39, 91,
    103, 105, 181, 185,
    187, 211
Iraq, 13, 22, 25, 37, 38,
    61, 82, 93, 108, 140,
    187, 190, 211
Iraq Petroleum Company, 46,
    58
Ismail, Mohammed Hafiz, 118,
    120
Ismailia, 182
Israel
  and Egypt, 12, 22, 23,
    39, 40, 50-54, 57, 60,
    67, 80, 81, 83-90, 96,
    99, 104, 107, 108, 117-
    23, 125, 127, 133-36,
    138, 140, 141, 145-48,
    152, 153, 165, 173, 175-
    78, 180, 184-90, 193,
    196, 199, 200, 205, 210,
    217
  Soviet visitors to, 31,
    34, 70, 113-15, 129,
    143, 144, 147, 150,
    166-69, 182, 199-203,
    205, 225

Israel (cont'd)
  and Syria, 35, 38, 40, 43-
    46, 49, 50, 53-58, 118,
    119, 121, 122, 127, 137-
    39, 141, 148, 153, 155,
    195, 209, 210, 212, 219-
    23, 227, 244
  and the United States
    (diplomatic relations),
    7, 24, 64, 68, 77, 78,
    87, 92, 103, 108, 112,
    113, 120, 127, 133, 137,
    140, 141, 144, 145, 150,
    153, 154, 156, 157, 159,
    160, 163, 175, 176, 180,
    181, 199, 211, 217, 219,
    221, 223, 225, 228, 233-
    36, 238, 241
  and the United States
    (military relations),
    18, 38, 47, 53-55, 60,
    63, 65, 80, 82, 83, 85,
    86, 88-91, 96, 123, 131,
    133, 142, 143, 146, 147,
    184, 185, 187-94, 198,
    204, 210, 212, 213, 216,
    220, 224, 242-44
  See also Knesset
Israeli communists, 15, 29,
    30, 34-36, 46, 69.
    See also MAKI and
    RAKAH
Italy, 13, 32, 36, 73, 147
Ivanov, Iurii, 34

Jabotinsky, Ze'ev, 225
Jackson amendment, 134, 148,
    148, 149, 168, 189,
    195, 197, 198
Jackson, Henry, 112, 113,
    148-50
Jadid, Salah, 43, 66, 67
Japan, 10, 58
Jarring, Gunnar, 62, 65, 82,
    86, 88-90, 96, 97
Jerusalem, 20, 21, 62, 78,
    83, 92, 108, 114, 143,
    145, 156, 166, 168,
    171, 173, 176-78, 182-
    84, 200, 226. See also
    East Jerusalem
Jewish Anti-Fascist Commit-
    tee, 11, 12, 16
Jewish Defense League, 47,

Jewish Defense League (cont'd)
    110, 130, 183
Johnson, Lyndon, 46, 52, 53,
    62, 174
Jordan, 9, 13, 15, 21, 24,
    38-40, 42, 43, 45, 50,
    52, 53, 61, 63, 66-68,
    71-73, 77, 78, 86, 89-
    91, 93, 103, 104, 116,
    127, 131, 139-41, 146,
    150, 151, 165, 169,
    170, 173, 175, 177,
    179, 185, 189, 190,
    193, 194, 201, 202,
    205-207, 213, 215,
    217, 218, 220, 222,
    231, 235, 241, 242
Jordanian Communist Party,
    206, 207
Jordan River, 44

Kahane, Meir, 47, 202
Kalkilia, 52
Kapeliuk, Amnon, 114, 165
Kaspi, Mordechai, 30, 35
Katz, Katriel, 29, 30, 44,
    45, 49, 52, 55
Kawasmeh, Fahd, 202
Kenya, 49
KGB, 25, 40, 58, 101, 182
Khaddam, Abd al-Halim, 176
Khalaf, Salah, 228, 229
Khalid (King of Saudi Arabia),
    159
Khalidi, Walid, 151
Khartoum summit, 58, 62
Khrushchev, Nikita, 22-24,
    27, 28, 34, 38, 39, 41,
    43
Kirilenko, Andrei, 243
Kissinger, Henry, 4, 66, 68,
    79, 80, 82, 83, 85, 86,
    96, 99, 103-106, 112,
    121, 123, 126-28, 133-
    43, 146-49, 154, 155,
    160, 173, 174
Knesset, 7, 9, 15, 24, 35,
    64, 68-70, 110, 119,
    127, 137, 140, 165-
    67, 169, 176, 179,
    183, 199-202, 204,
    206, 220, 225, 227
Kollek, Teddy, 92
Korea, 18, 21. See also

Korea (cont'd)
    South Korea
Kosygin, Aleksei, 32, 39,
    41, 43, 47, 52-54, 61,
    62, 72, 82, 85, 90,
    97, 100, 118, 122,
    150, 158
Kulikov, Viktor, 158
Kuwait, 36, 119, 235
Kuznetsov, Vasilii, 55

Labor Alignment, 8, 127,
    162, 166, 188, 192,
    204, 234, 236, 241,
    243
Labor Party, 181, 183, 227
Latakia, 179
Latrun, 78
Lebanon, 8, 42, 43, 52, 93,
    131, 153, 158-60, 170,
    179, 184-87, 190, 197,
    206, 209-212, 214, 215,
    217-221, 223, 224, 226,
    228, 229, 231, 236,
    239, 242
Lebrecht, Hans, 182
Lenin, Vladimir, 61, 197,
    201
Leningrad, 1, 92, 182
Levavi, Aryeh, 31
Levenbraun, Avraham, 165
Levin, Yehuda Leib, 10, 70
Libya, 13, 17, 80, 107, 118,
    131, 146, 177, 187,
    192, 233, 234
LIKUD, 8, 162, 164, 183,
    188, 219, 220, 225,
    243
Lithuania, 4
London, 87, 147, 166
Louis, Victor, 9, 100-102,
    104, 111, 113, 114,
    129, 130, 143, 148,
    154, 226, 236

Maiskii, Ivan, 12
Makarios, Archbishop, 102
MAKI, 34-36, 70, 76, 101
Malenkov, Georgii, 8, 19,
    20
Malik, Iakov, 14, 49, 69,
    156, 157
Malinovskii, Rodion, 58
Mao Tse-tung, 42, 93, 195

MAPAI, 15, 17, 27
MAPAM, 15, 17, 75, 114, 165,
    181, 183, 204
Mazurov, Kiril, 72
Mediterranean Sea, 46, 48,
    49, 60, 64, 86, 87, 96,
    100, 102, 174, 179,
    212, 217
Medvedev, Roy, 226
Meir, Golda, 4, 15, 16, 19,
    25, 28, 66, 68, 87-90,
    97, 100-104, 110-12,
    114, 127- 29, 137, 140
Melamed, Avraham, 183
Mendelevich, Iosif, 203
Mersa Matruh, 63
Mexico, 10
Mikhoels, Solomon, 16
Mikoian, Anastas, 25
Mikunis, Shmuel, 4, 34, 35
Milhem, Mohammed, 202
Minsk, 1
Mitla Pass, 96, 97, 99
Mnacko, Ladislav, 74, 75
Moczar, Mieczslaw, 74
Modaï, Yitzhak, 216
Mohieddin, Zakaria, 53
Mohsen, Zuhair, 163, 164
Molotov, Vyacheslav, 20
Mondale, Walter, 243
Mongolia, 115
Morocco, 22, 79, 161, 175,
    176, 214
Moscow, 1, 2, 4, 12, 15, 16,
    19, 21, 25, 30, 33-35,
    39, 43, 50-52, 55, 66,
    67, 69, 70, 81, 89,
    104-106, 109, 111, 113-
    16, 118-20, 123, 129,
    130, 132, 134, 137-39,
    144, 148, 150, 152,
    159, 164, 165, 168-71,
    179, 182-84, 186, 193,
    200-203, 205, 206,
    213, 217, 224, 225,
    227, 228, 230, 231,
    236, 237, 244
Moscow Olympics, 198, 201,
    203, 206, 237
Munich, 116

Nablus, 202
Najar, Suleiman, 230
Namibia, 238

Namir, Mordechai, 18
Namir, Ora, 204
Nasser, Gamal abd al-, 22,
    33, 38-41, 49, 50, 52,
    53, 55, 56, 61, 67,
    72, 80, 81, 83, 86-90,
    111
Nathan, Abie, 30
National Religious Party,
    183
Navon, Yitzhak, 183, 201
Nazareth, 167, 204
Nehru, Jawaharlal, 22
Netanya, 1, 92
Netherlands, 19, 55, 74,
    109, 113, 144, 237
New York, 10, 15, 50, 66,
    69, 77, 89, 112, 154,
    165, 194, 202, 227
Nguyen Cao Ky, 46
Nissim, Yitzhak, 70
Nixon, Richard, 65, 68, 79,
    80, 82, 83, 86, 87, 90,
    96, 103-106, 108, 112,
    113, 119-22, 124, 138,
    139, 142, 148, 174,
    176, 234
Nkrumah, Kwame, 37
Norway, 100
Novotny, Antonin, 74
Nudel, Ida, 203, 227
Numeiri, Gaafar, 103

Ogarkov, Nikolai, 177
Oman, 187, 190

Pakistan, 39, 104, 186
Palestine, 2, 12-15, 17
Palestine Communist Party,
    207, 230
Palestine Liberation Organ-
    ization (PLO), 1, 41,
    42, 59, 72, 73, 93, 95,
    116, 131, 132, 134,
    139, 140, 144, 150-53,
    155-61, 163-65, 169-
    71, 174, 176, 179, 180,
    182, 184, 186, 187,
    190, 193, 195, 196,
    200-202, 205-207, 209-
    11, 213-16, 218, 222,
    223, 227-31, 235, 236,
    238-41. See also
    Yasir Arafat

298

Palestine National Council,
131, 150
Palestine National Front,
131, 132, 151
Palestinian Communist Organization, 151
Palestinians, 1, 21-23, 44,
77, 83, 90, 103, 105,
121, 127, 128, 134,
137-40, 144-46, 150,
151, 155, 156, 161,
169-71, 173-75, 177,
181, 186, 190, 200,
201, 205-207, 213,
214, 223, 230, 235,
241, 242
  refugee problem, 67, 82,
  98, 214
  and the Soviet Union, 8,
  9, 71-73, 92, 93, 117,
  131, 132, 150-55, 157,
  159-61, 164, 165, 170,
  171, 178, 179, 184,
  189, 202, 205-207, 209,
  212, 228-31, 239, 241
  and Syria, 41, 43, 45,
  50, 90, 91, 116, 158,
  160
  See also Yasir Arafat and
  Palestine Liberation
  Organization
Paris, 32, 39, 118, 168,
181
Paschalis, Panaioyitis,
182, 201
Paz, Ephraim, 33
"Peace Now," 182, 224
Peking, 41, 42, 105
Peled, Mati, 57, 227
Pelshe, Arvid, 243
Peres, Shimon, 36, 52, 126,
143, 162
Persian Gulf, 187
Philippines, 46
Pimen, Patriarch, 114, 115,
183
Podgornyi, Nikolai, 43, 53,
60, 72, 73, 97, 99,
151
Poland, 3, 4, 6, 25, 48,
56, 73, 74, 115, 124,
148, 168, 180, 194,
228
Poliakov, Vladimir, 10, 190

Ponomarev, Boris, 35, 70,
97, 152, 201, 243
Popular Democratic Front
for the Liberation of
Palestine, 132, 177
Popular Front for the
Liberation of Pales-
tine, 73
Port Said, 30, 63, 121
Portugal, 142
Pozhidaev, Dmitrii, 51, 57
Prague, 230
Primakov, Evgenii, 125,
186, 195, 200, 211
Puerto Rico, 130

Qaddafi, Muammar, 80, 218,
233, 234
Qaddumi, Faruq, 206, 228,
229
Qatar, 26, 335
Qeneitra, 54, 84

Rabat, 79, 140, 141, 144,
150
Rabbuh, Yasir abd, 228
Rabin, Yitzhak, 2, 3, 45,
46, 50, 80, 82, 83,
89, 92, 103, 112, 135,
137, 140-43, 145-47,
156, 158-66, 168, 175,
180, 223
Rafael, Gideon, 50, 88, 112
RAKAH, 34-36, 39, 69, 70,
76, 102, 113, 115,
119, 129, 143, 153,
165-67, 169, 170,
179-83, 192, 200-204,
206, 222, 224, 225,
230, 236, 238
Rapacki, Adam, 48
Razin, Ben-Tsion, 20
"Reagan Plan," 213-15, 217-
20, 222, 223, 225, 230
Reagan, Ronald, 188-90, 195,
203, 209-11, 214, 218,
223, 224, 243
Red Sea, 96, 153, 162
Riad, Mahmoud, 102
Riftin, Yaacov, 114, 129,
165, 182, 225
Riga, 182
Riyadh, 159
"Rogers' Plans," 77-80,

"Rogers' Plans," (cont'd) 86-89, 218

Rogers, William, 66, 79, 80, 82, 83, 86, 92, 99

Rome, 114, 225

Rumania, 2, 13, 54-56, 60, 69, 73, 112, 144, 164, 168, 180, 194, 202-205, 239

Rusk, Dean, 36

Russian Orthodox Church, 7, 15, 29, 69, 114, 182, 183, 200, 202, 225, 226

Sabra, 216, 226, 229

Sabry, Ali, 67, 98

Sadat, Anwar al-, 78, 89, 97-100, 104-108, 111, 116, 118, 119, 121-25, 135, 136, 139, 140, 152, 157, 164, 170, 173, 176-78, 182, 184, 186, 187, 190, 215, 235

Sadiq, Mohammed Ahmed, 107

Sakharov, Andrei, 166, 226

Samu, 45, 50, 52

Sarid, Yossi, 183

Saudi Arabia, 2, 3, 38, 39, 56, 58, 80, 118, 136, 137, 139, 142, 159, 162, 180, 181, 187, 189, 193, 235

Savidor, Menachem, 216

Second World War, 11, 12, 31, 36, 48, 85, 225, 228

Semenov, Vladimir, 38, 40, 50, 66, 69

Semichastnyi, Vladimir, 58

Shacham, David, 165

Shaer, Mohammed al-, 170, 205, 206

Shah of Iran (Mohammed Reza Pahlevi), 13, 37

Shaka, Bassam, 202

Shamir, Yitzhak, 191, 194, 202, 203, 215, 216, 219, 221, 223, 224, 241

Sharett, Moshe, 6, 17, 18, 20, 23

Sharm el-Sheikh, 50

Sharon, Ariel, 10, 190, 211, 219, 220

Shatila, 216, 226, 229

Shazar, Zalman, 18

Shcharanskii, Anatolii, 7, 167-69, 182, 183, 201

Shcharanskii, Avital, 201, 202

Shelli, 183

Shepilov, Dmitrii, 23

Shukairy, Ahmed, 41, 72

Shultz, George, 213, 223

Sidqi, Aziz, 107

Siilasvuo, Ensio, 168

Sinai, 10, 50, 56, 57, 64, 89, 97, 103, 105, 118, 122, 135, 145, 146, 154, 176, 190, 192, 193, 234, 241

Sisco, Joseph, 65, 66, 84, 99, 100, 112

Slansky, Rudolf, 19, 75

Sneh, Moshe, 4, 34, 35

Sofia, 20

Sokolov, Sergei, 177

Soldatov, Aleksandr, 212, 221, 228

Somalia, 178, 190

South Africa, 7, 238

South Korea, 46

South Vietnam. See Vietnam

South Yemen, 36, 58, 214

Soviet Jews, 11, 14, 15, 22, 25, 28-30, 59, 91, 92, 101, 102, 119, 121, 167-69, 183, 200, 201, 222, 225, 227, 234, 236-38, 244, 245

emigration of, 2, 3, 6, 7, 16, 17, 21, 25, 31-33, 50, 70, 71, 92, 95, 108-14, 129-31, 134, 140, 141, 143, 145, 146, 148, 149, 166, 168, 169, 184, 185, 192, 194-99, 203, 204, 219, 226, 227, 233, 234, 236, 243, 244

Soviet Union. See Union of Soviet Socialist Republics

Spain, 114

Spechler, Dina, 8

Stalin, Iosef, 5, 11, 14,

Stalin, Iosef (cont'd)
    16, 19, 20
Stans, Maurice, 105
Stein, Jacob, 131
Stevenson amendment, 134,
    149, 168
Strategic Arms Limitation
    Treaty (SALT), 134,
    195, 197, 198
Sudan, 103, 187, 190, 234
Suez Canal, 9, 22-24, 36,
    54, 58, 60, 65, 80-82,
    85, 88, 90, 96, 97,
    99, 105, 106, 121, 122,
    126, 135, 136, 146,
    163, 240
Suez, Gulf of, 147
Sukarno, 22, 37
Sulzberger, Cyrus, 4
Suslov, Mikhail, 35, 70, 97,
    201, 243
Sweidani, Ahmed, 42
Switzerland, 89
Syria, 12, 17, 22, 28, 35,
    38, 42, 48, 51, 58,
    66, 71, 72, 82, 86,
    96, 97, 105, 144, 173,
    187, 211, 228
  and Israel, 35, 38, 40, 43-
    46, 49, 50, 53-58, 118,
    119, 121, 122, 127,
    137-39, 141, 148, 153,
    155, 195, 209, 210, 212,
    219-23, 227, 244
  and Palestinians, 41, 43,
    45, 50, 90, 91, 116,
    158, 160
  role of communists, 42,
    43, 45, 93, 97, 98,
    126, 188
  and the Soviet Union
    (diplomatic relations),
    30, 37, 42, 43, 52, 54,
    55, 57-61, 77, 98, 108,
    116, 130, 139-41, 144,
    157, 159, 160, 176, 178,
    179, 186, 203, 205, 216,
    223, 224, 228, 229, 231
  and the Soviet Union (mil-
    itary relations), 63,
    81, 85, 117, 120-26,
    138, 155, 158, 181, 185,
    188-90, 206, 209, 210,
    212, 213, 217-21, 235,

Syria (cont'd)
    238
  and the United States,
    5, 133, 137, 139, 146,
    148, 150, 153-55, 158-
    60, 175, 189, 213, 218,
    219, 221, 223, 238
Sytenko, Mikhail, 204

Taiwan, 181, 191
Tartus, 122
Tashkent conference, 30, 39
Tbilisi, 181
Tehiya, 219
Tekoah, Yosef, 33, 38, 44,
    53, 66, 69, 71, 91,
    110, 221
Tel Aviv, 18, 20, 30, 101,
    113, 129, 168, 169,
    202, 203, 213, 237,
    245
Teng Hsiao-ping, 189
Thailand, 46
Tiberias, 1, 200, 228
Tiran, Straits of, 51-53,
    57, 82, 106, 160, 163,
    240, 241
Tito, Iosip Broz, 19, 20,
    49, 55, 86, 125
Tlas, Mustapha, 67, 126
Toubi, Tewfiq, 6, 34, 70,
    129, 167, 169, 183,
    202, 204, 206
Tripartite Declaration, 17
Troianovskii, Oleg, 161,
    165
Trotskii, Leon, 5, 73
Tsarapkin, Semyon, 12, 100
Tsipori, Mordechai, 221
Tunis, 229
Tunisia, 22, 234
Turkey, 10, 13, 16, 22, 37,
    40, 105, 142, 212

Uganda, 166
Ulbricht, Walter, 56
Union of Soviet Socialist
    Republics (Soviet
    Union)
  congresses of the commun-
    ist party, 35, 110, 169,
    193, 203, 206
  and Egypt (diplomatic
    relations), 34, 37-39,

Union of Soviet Socialist
Republics (Soviet
Union) (cont'd)
55-57, 59-61, 68, 72,
102, 116, 128-30, 136,
140, 154, 157, 176, 177,
186, 190, 218
and Egypt (military re-
lations), 40, 50, 51,
54, 63, 67, 77, 78, 80,
81, 83-91, 95, 97-100,
103-108, 112, 117-21,
123-26, 132, 144, 176,
217
Israeli visitors to, 9,
31, 32, 69, 92, 113-15,
129, 130, 147, 165, 166,
169, 181, 183, 184, 200-
204, 224, 225, 227, 237
and the Palestinians, 8,
9, 71-73, 92, 93, 117,
131, 132, 150-55, 157,
159-61, 164, 165, 170,
171, 178, 179, 184,
189, 202, 205-207, 209,
212, 228-31, 239, 241
peace plans, 4, 64, 65,
72, 82, 87, 103, 126,
157, 158, 160-63, 166,
168, 171, 195, 214,
229
and Syria (diplomatic re-
lations), 30, 37, 42,
43, 52, 54, 55, 57-61,
77, 98, 108, 116, 130,
139-41, 144, 157, 159,
160, 176, 178, 179,
186, 203, 205, 216,
223, 224, 228, 229, 231
and Syria (military re-
lations), 63, 81, 85,
117, 120-26, 138, 155,
158, 181, 185, 188-90,
206, 209, 210, 212, 213,
217-21, 235, 238
and the United States,
14, 29, 36, 38, 39, 54,
56, 57, 62, 65-68, 71,
77-79, 83, 84, 95, 102-
105, 107, 108, 111, 113,
117-20, 122-30, 134,
138, 139, 142, 145-49,
153, 154, 160, 163, 169,
173-75, 178, 187, 188,

Union of Soviet Socialist
Republics (Soviet
Union) (cont'd)
191, 195, 198, 205,
211, 213, 223, 226,
234, 236, 239, 242-45
United Arab Emirates, 235
United Arab Republic, 37
United Nations, 1, 2, 12-
14, 17, 18, 21, 22,
25, 31, 33, 40, 45,
49-51, 53, 54, 61,
62, 64, 66, 69, 71,
78, 82, 83, 86, 96,
97, 106, 121, 122,
124, 130, 146, 154-
56, 161, 162, 165,
166, 168, 169, 174,
175, 179, 181, 186,
191, 193, 195, 199,
202, 213, 214, 216,
228, 229, 236, 238,
239, 241, 242, 244,
245
Security Council Resolu-
tion 242:, 62, 63,
66, 67, 78, 86, 114,
123, 136, 156, 174,
175, 205, 230
Security Council Resolu-
tion 338:, 123, 124,
134, 136, 174, 175,
184, 205
United States, 5, 6, 13,
17, 22-24, 29, 32,
47, 73, 77, 112, 155,
189, 214, 240
and Israel (diplomatic
relations), 7, 24, 64,
68, 77, 78, 87, 92,
103, 108, 112, 113,
120, 127, 133, 137,
140, 141, 144, 145,
150, 153, 154, 156,
157, 159, 160, 163,
175, 176, 180, 181,
199, 211, 217, 219,
221, 223, 225, 228,
233-36, 238, 241
and Israel (military
relations), 18, 38, 47,
53-55, 60, 63, 65, 80,
82, 83, 85, 86, 88-91,
96, 123, 131, 133, 142,

United States (cont'd)
143, 146, 147, 184, 185,
187- 94, 198, 204, 210,
212, 213, 216, 220,
224, 242-44
  and the Soviet Union, 14,
29, 36, 38, 39, 54, 56,
57, 62, 65-68, 71, 77-
79, 83, 84, 95, 102-105,
107, 108, 111, 113, 117-
20, 122-30, 134, 138,
139, 142, 145-49, 153,
154, 160, 163, 169, 173-
75, 178, 187, 188, 191,
195, 198, 205, 211,
213, 223, 226, 234, 236,
239, 242-45
  and Syria, 55, 133, 137,
139, 146, 148, 150, 153-
55, 158-60, 175, 189,
213, 218, 219, 221, 223,
238
U Thant, 51, 62, 91, 110

Vance, Cyrus, 146, 161, 163,
164, 173, 174, 176, 178
Vanik, Charles, 149
Vergelis, Aaron, 166, 168
Vienna, 111, 121, 131, 146,
168, 186, 195
Vietnam, 4, 21, 28, 29, 36,
46, 47, 54, 56, 60,
68, 71, 87, 91, 92,
102-106, 118, 120, 134,
135, 142, 191, 192
Vinogradov, Sergei, 57, 58
Vinogradov, Vladimir, 58,
107, 108
Vladivostok, 139

Warsaw, 48, 180
Warsaw Pact, 75
Washington, 53, 68, 89, 137,
142, 143, 156, 157,
159, 164, 171, 175,
181, 201, 204
Watergate, 120, 139
Wazzan, Shafiq al-, 212
Weinberger, Caspar, 190, 223
Weizman, Ezer, 57, 164, 181,
187
Weizmann, Chaim, 12
Weizmann Institute, 226
West Bank, 15, 69-73, 78,

West Bank (cont'd)
93, 98, 115, 131, 132,
140, 145, 151, 154,
164, 169, 170, 175,
180, 190, 193, 201,
202, 205, 206, 210,
214, 215, 217, 218,
227, 228, 230, 231,
241, 242
West Germany, 24, 29, 46-
48, 83, 92, 130, 144,
159, 168, 183
West Jerusalem, 187. See
also Jerusalem
Wiesel, Eli, 31
Wilenska, Esther, 4, 29,
34
Wilner, Meir, 4, 29, 34,
70, 119, 125, 127,
166, 167, 169, 170,
201, 202, 206, 222,
224, 230
Wilson, Harold, 144, 147
World Jewish Congress, 30,
75, 84, 137, 144,
166, 198, 225
World Peace Council, 181
World Zionist Organization,
2

Yaari, Meir, 114
Yariv, Aharon, 135
Yemen, 28, 54, 57, 58
"Yost Plan," 78
Young, Andrew, 186
Yugoslavia, 13, 19, 22,
36, 132, 168, 228

Zakin, Dov, 165
Zayyad, Tewfiq, 167, 169
Zayyat, Mohammed Hassan az-,
119
Zhdanov, Andrei, 16, 19,
20
Zikhroni, Amnon, 183
Zimbabwe, 238
Zionism, 2-6, 11, 12, 14,
16, 18-20, 32-34, 75,
98, 109, 110, 154,
165-67, 183, 197-99,
204
  anti-Zionism in the
Soviet Union, 60, 61,
71, 73, 74, 76, 91,

Zionism (cont'd)
    168, 203, 222, 225, 226
Zionist Organization of
    America, 12
Zuayyin, Yusuf, 43